# Ronald Reagan;
## The Hollywood Years

"The future doesn't belong to the
fainthearted.
It belongs to the brave."

Ronald Reagan, 1986

# *Sammon* Publishing

## Published by Sammon Publishing Ltd.

ISBN 0-9540031-9-5

First edition 2005

PO Box 3841
Bracknell
Berkshire
RG42 2YJ
123456789

**copyright c mcgivern October 2004**

cover design by Pentacor

# Ronald Reagan; The Hollywood Years

## Table of Contents

**For Justin and Matt Landesman**

**Stay strong and remember, "Life is all about getting up one more time than you are knocked down…"**

Fred Landesman died unexpectedly at his home on October 15th 2004, after apparently suffering a massive heart attack. He was fifty five years old.

He didn't get to see the galley proof of ***Ronald Reagan; The Hollywood Years***. He had worked so hard and enthusiastically toward its completion for over a year. He was excited about it and believed in it, and was proud of our collaboration. He was looking forward to a big promotional push through 2005, following the successful launch of his own first publication, *The John Wayne Filmography* in 2004.

I am stunned by his death. Bereft of both my writing partner and a true friend.

Many times we had discussed working together on other dream projects in the future. He lived and worked in Los Angeles, and I am based in England, yet we conversed most days, one way or another, and it was easy for him to do the Hollywood research whilst I sifted through material held over here.

He constantly told me I would have to "Americanize" my use of language if we were to sell our book in America, but eventually he admitted, "I approve what you have done…". It was always a hard job to turn Fred, once he had set his mind, so it is priceless to me now that he uttered those words…

I was first contacted by Fred about three years ago after my book, *John Wayne; A Giant Shadow* had been released in England, but wasn't, at the time, distributed in America. Fred was a John Wayne buff and a collector and wanted to add my book to his library. I was flattered. We "clicked" instantly because we had such a strong common interest, which every other John Wayne fan will recognize.

Before I knew it I was on a plane and being met at LAX by a complete stranger, a fellow writer, a fellow Wayne enthusiast, a man I felt I had known all my life. His family made me welcome in their home and Fred took me and his sons, Justin and Matt, to see all the John Wayne shrines he could think of. He told endless stories about Hollywood, the movies, the old theatres, the memorabilia, he was a font of knowledge and a joy to be with. He was also a questioner, he dredged and syphoned my own stories from me. He was both a giver and a taker…an unusual fellow. Also unusual…he readily understood my English sense of humour. I can still hear him laughing now at something ridiculous.

He was a sympathetic man without making it obvious. If I moaned about anything, Fred always had a solution…Once, recently, when I emailed him that I felt stressed about something nonsensical, he sent me back a slide show of stills and peaceful music from China with a note that read simply, "Relax."

Fred Landesman, who died tragically on
October 15th, 2004

**All photographic stills courtesy of Fred's private collection.**

## Tributes to Ronald Reagan from The Right Honourable The Baroness Margaret Thatcher.

Sir, you strode into our midst at a time when America needed you most. This great country had been through a period of national malaise bereft of any sense of moral direction. Through it all, you were unflappable and unyielding. With that Irish twinkle and that easy homespun style, which never changed, you brought a new assurance to America.
In a time of average men, you stood taller than anyone else.

You reached beyond partisanship to principles, beyond our own selves to our very souls. You reached for and touched, as Lincoln had said so long before you, the better angels of our nature.
This political instinct of truth, conviction and patriotism began long before you were President. You always had the right words, and we honour you for it.

## Gala Birthday Tribute to Ronald Reagan, Feb 3rd, 1994

President Reagan is one of the greatest men of our time, and one of the greatest American Presidents of all time.
From the very first time I met him I felt that I had to invest. The impression is still vivid in my mind: not so vivid that I can remember exactly what he said, only the clarity with which he set forth his beliefs and the way he put large truths and complex ideas into simple language.

## The Heritage Foundation's "Leadership for America" Gala, Dec 10, 1997

As an actor in Hollywood's golden age, he helped to make the American dream live for millions all over the globe. His own life was a fulfilment of that dream. He never succumbed to the embarrassment some people feel about an honest expression of love of country.
He was able to say "God Bless America" with equal fervour in public and in private

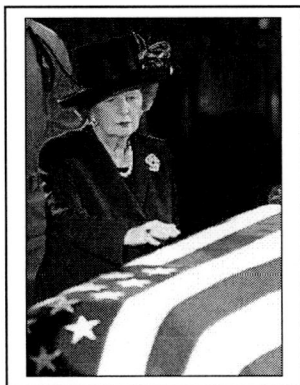

"We have lost a great president, a great American, and a great man. And I have lost a dear friend."

**Eulogy delivered by The Right Honourable The Baroness Thatcher at the funeral of President Ronald Reagan 2004**

I was driving to work at my family's candy factory in Oakland, California when I heard Ronald Reagan on the radio for the first time. It was the 1960s, and I was a young man with a young family, just beginning my lifelong work as a candy maker. Hearing Ronald Reagan's political ideas for the first time I was impressed, and thought at that moment that here was someone who could make a real difference. From that moment I became an admirer and supporter of Ronald Reagan, a man and a leader who ultimately changed the world. It was bittersweet to me that only upon his death did the world give him the tributes that were due to him for his leadership and world vision.

It is also impossible to exaggerate the impact Ronald Reagan has had on my life and our company. How Ronald Reagan came to know of our small candy company and Jelly Belly jelly beans was a series of chances and unusual connections. My good friend and mentor Russell Albers, president of a confectionery retail chain, was introduced to "Dutch" at a political reception in Los Angeles in 1966 and learned from a mutual acquaintance that Reagan was attempting to give up his pipe smoking habit by eating jelly beans. Russ was soon sending him our candy as a courtesy. This was ten years before the Jelly Belly jelly beans were born, and we were making mini gourmet jelly beans at that time. Reagan won the election becoming California's governor. Russ suggested we send the jelly beans directly to Sacramento which we continued to do thoughout his term as governor and in all the years beyond. It wasn't long before we received a very gracious letter of thanks from Governor Reagan who mentioned in his letter the jelly beans were served at meetings. That letter is on public display at our tour center and factory in California.

The first time I met Ronald Reagan in person was in 1975 at the end of his term of office as governor. He was very gracious and knew how to make you comfortable, even if you were only there for a photo. I noticed a lot of excitement and commotion around him with many, many people expressing thanks and good wishes. I had no idea he had plans to run for president, but it soon became clear why there was so much activity even though he was leaving office.

By 1976 our company had been working on many new candies to expand our business, and we introduced Jelly Belly jelly beans that summer. This was our newest candy, so we sent former Governor Reagan his usual shipment with the new style jelly beans. We had continued to send him jelly beans when he retired from office as governor and through one unsuccessful bid for the Republican Party nomination for president.

Then something remarkable and unthinkable happened. In 1980 Ronald Reagan was again on the campaign trail for the presidency and was photographed by *Time* magazine with a bowl of our Jelly Belly beans on the table in his hotel suite. The national press became aware he ate jelly beans, and then the *San Jose Mercury News* broke the story that those jelly beans were made by our California company. In January 1981 all the media wanted to know our story. We did back-to-back interviews from 8 a.m. to 7 p.m. for two straight days with reporters from around the world. One newspaper after the next, then national television and magazines, picked up the story.

When Ronald Reagan was elected President, we received a call from the Inaugural planning committee inquiring whether it would be possible to supply red, white and blue jelly beans for the Inaugural parties. Blueberry flavor had been created that summer to make up the colors of the American flag. Three and half tons of Jelly Belly jelly beans were delivered to Washington. The privilege of supplying the Inaugural Committee with candy was momentarily upstaged by the shock of receiving an invitation to attend the Washington celebrations. In a whirlwind trip, my wife and I attended the celebrations, being even more surprised to see Jelly Belly beans photographed in the official Inaugural book.

As time went on it seemed all of America wanted to taste the jelly beans President Reagan loved. We were backlogged in orders for two years. We were surprised and delighted by press reports that President Reagan gave jars of Jelly Belly beans to visiting dignitaries. One day I was watching the news reports of the space flight of the shuttle *Challenger* when the astronauts opened a surprise package sent by President Reagan. It was filled with Jelly Belly beans and those beans were floating in space.

Our story is only a small footnote to this book which carefully chronicles Ronald Reagan's career up to the point that he entered national politics. I have the greatest admiration and respect for the leadership, skill and accomplishments of Ronald Reagan. He made an enormous impact for the better on Americans and the world's citizen. His legacy will live long into the future.


Jelly Belly™jelly beans…The President's choice.

# INTRODUCTION

## *Ronald Reagan: The Hollywood Years*

by Carolyn McGivern and Fred Landesman, was a project already well in hand when the hardly unexpected headline hit the world's newswires. Still, it came as a shock to McGivern, sitting in London and Landesman, at home in the afternoon and just a fifteen-minute drive from the Simi Valley residence of the Ronald Reagan Library on June 5th. As Vice President Dick Cheney said, "Knowing that this moment would come has not made it any easier."

McGivern called Landesman and asked him if he could get to the library on June 8th to attend the laying at rest. Landesman's reply arrived the next day:

"Took the boys to see Reagan's casket. Thought this would be something historical that they would remember for the rest of their lives. We got on the 118 Freeway (Ronald Reagan Freeway) heading west. Everything was fine for the first ten minutes, then about 5 miles from the exit where we had to park all vehicles and get on buses, the entire freeway ground to a halt. It took two and a half hours to go those last five miles and then the police would only allow those cars that were already in the right lane to exit. Naturally, I was in the left lane. I was so upset, got off the next exit, got back on the highway, fought more traffic and headed home. We started out at 7:10 PM and got home at 11:15 pm. Anyway, I heard on the news that once you had parked your car, the wait to see the casket was another five to eight hours.

"As of this afternoon, the crowds are still coming. They have extended viewing until midnight, but will not allow any cars off the exit after 4 PM.

"The people swarming to see Reagan's body were a true cross section of the nation. I saw a Rolls Royce and many Volkswagens, as well as all makes of other cars. Some people were in business suits while many more wore casual clothes including shorts. One woman sported a big peace emblem, others wore cowboy hats. In Chatsworth, several people rode on horseback to a hill overlooking the freeway to bid farewell to the President while the motorcade was passing beneath. The Fire Department raised flags from their vehicles on the overpasses and saluted as the cars passed.

"On Thursday in Washington there will be a fly-by of 21 F15 Eagle jets to salute Reagan. That is a show of respect."

Respect or not, Los Angeles Times staff writer, Booth More noted, "A president was lying in repose, but the occasion could just as well have been a Saturday afternoon at Universal CityWalk...for some people these days, there is nothing they will dress up for...not even to pay their respects to a former head of state."

But even though Reagan himself never entered the Oval Office without his coat and tie, he would undoubtedly have forgiven this throng as they filed passed, some without removing their baseball caps...these were after all his fellow Americans.

**"...My fellow Americans,**

I have recently been told that I am one of the millions of Americans who will be afflicted with Alzheimer's Disease.

Upon learning this news, Nancy and I had to decide whether as private citizens we would keep this a private matter or whether we would make this news known in a public way.

In the past Nancy suffered from breast cancer and I had my cancer surgeries. We found through our open disclosures we were able to raise public awareness. We were happy that as a result many more people underwent testing.

They were treated in early stages and able to return to normal, healthy lives.

So now, we feel it is important to share it with you. In opening our hearts, we hope this might promote greater awareness of this condition. Perhaps it will encourage a clearer understanding of the individuals and families who are affected by it.

At the moment I feel just fine. I intend to live the remainder of the years God gives me on this earth doing the things I have always done. I will continue to share life's journey with my beloved Nancy and my family. I plan to enjoy the great outdoors and stay in touch with my friends and supporters.

Unfortunately, as Alzheimer's Disease progresses, the family often bears a heavy burden. I only wish there was some way I could spare Nancy from this painful experience. When the time comes I am confident that with your help she will face it with faith and courage.

In closing let me thank you, the American people, for giving me the great honor of allowing me to serve as your President. When the Lord calls me home, whenever that may be, I will leave with the greatest love for this country of ours and eternal optimism for its future.

I now begin the journey that will lead me to the sunset of my life. I know that for America there will always be a bright dawn ahead.

Thank you my friends. May God always bless you.

**Sincerely,**
**Ronald Reagan**
November 5th 1994"

When Ronald Wilson Reagan passed away at the age of ninety three at about 1:00pm Pacific Time on Saturday June 5th 2004, he had already been long gone from the public gaze, and everyone who had read that handwritten letter almost ten years before would remember him as he had been portrayed throughout his gloriously public Hollywood days; a tall, graceful man full of geniality, heroic optimism, who said what he thought- and meant, a man who turned his back on the merest hint of failure. In 1985 he had been admitted to hospital for an operation, "Cancer? Not at all. A self-contained polyp that had begun to develop a few cancer cells," had been removed. Such observances sum up Ronald Reagan beautifully. To some, his dry comment showed irresponsibility, his absolute inability to face up to the darker side of life. Others found the way he handled things then inspirational. Here was an ex-president taking cancer lightly, a man who ate jelly beans and made endless jokes rather than getting down to the serious side of his work, a man who laughed, "It's true, hard work never killed anybody, but I figure, why take the chance?" A man who insisted on taking his afternoon nap, whose favorite books were all Westerns and who found joy in menial tasks such as clearing the land on his ranch or the leaves from his pool.

How could this have possibly been the man who had lead America through such dire times when it had needed the sharpest of brains at its helm? Reagan had never allowed himself to be portrayed as an intellectual. No, here was a man who had often fallen asleep in committee meetings, who disliked arguments with colleagues, but was still a man who, somehow, got the job done.

His hopes, and his stubborn refusal to accept defeat had been infectious to a dispirited nation after the humiliations of Vietnam, the effects of financial depression and a degree of civil unrest not before witnessed in America. With his words, "We have every right to dream heroic dreams…" he had let his fellow citizens know that they had a duty to believe in themselves and their own strength and that it was safe to follow him, Dreamer in Chief.

The B movie actor helped engineer a huge surge of patriotism following those difficult Carter years of national self-doubt, he did it through the image he had successfully created long before he entered the world of big politics.

Back in 1980 it had taken the oldest ever American President to give back a sense of youth to the country. Americans may have been beaten to their knees but the old film star simply smiled and told them to get up and strut instead. He replaced Presidents who had talked of the "American Malaise" and spoken instead of American destiny and greatness, he dared to talk about the nation as the shining city on the hill. His voice may have croaked out an old fashioned tune, but the words he spoke came right from his core, and Americans wanted to believe in his confidence.

But Reagan was never quite as simple as he allowed himself to appear, rather he was a man of concise, precise conviction, who had the ability to give pleasingly adequate performances. The adept delivery of his convictions became the center point of his presidency; he could and did play to perfection the part of the national figurehead. He generated his political persona through the force of his communications. Long before he acquired political scriptwriters he had been busy polishing his style as a pitch man for General Electric, making regular TV and radio speeches, and far more often than any of his contemporaries or adversaries had. Far better than any of them, Reagan understood the medium and the value of TV, understood and knew instinctively how to talk to people in their own living rooms. He often used personal anecdotes to illustrate his points, some were true, others were not, but they got his ideas across.

He had been a movie star in Hollywood's golden days-how difficult had it been for him to look and sound exactly as a President should? He remained ramrod straight, tall, strong and handsome with his sweepingly glossy black locks (he swore he never dyed his hair) and ruddy cheeks that radiated health and clean cut values. At least he appeared to be powerful enough to lead a failing nation back to new glories. He turned out to be an effectively bold rhetorical communicator, a master of delivery in an age of television.

Long ago, in his Hollywood days, he had acquired the habit of appearing larger than life and had developed the big screen star's understanding of what worked and what didn't, how to match words and images. Some critics felt his B-Movie life must have given him an exaggerated sense of his own importance, that his masterly ability to deliver a speech sometimes disguised the fact that he didn't know what he was talking about; his lines were written on three-by-four inch cards or even on his shirt cuffs. The catch in his voice at emotional times, had to be an actor's trick. Those critics were wrong.

When America mourned the passing of its fortieth president the country witnessed the first full presidential funeral in thirty years, and Reagan was only the tenth president to lie in state under the Capitol rotunda. When Dick Cheney spoke there about Reagan, he talked about a man with the optimism of a faithful soul, an idealist, a decent man, a graceful man.

No ceremony was stinted in saying goodbye to the actor-president and the national outpouring of emotion accurately marked just how important Ronald Reagan had been and still was in the hearts and minds of Americans, especially so in today's difficult and fraught international times. A CNN spokesperson said, "No other memorial event has lasted this long and, frankly we're having trouble sorting out how we're going to do it." A producer from Fox News agreed, "We don't want to keep showing the same faces. But then again, he lived into his nineties- so we have ten decades of people to chase. The ripples keep spreading out."

He was so extraordinarily popular that at his passing all the channels sat on the back of his astonishing celebrity to connect and push their own shows to the massive audiences now tuning in, "We are living as much the Reagan worldview as any other president post-Roosevelt," commented ABC's senior vice president, Paul Slavin.

Perhaps the journalists didn't want to go wall to wall, but Ronald Reagan had been so much more than just an expired head of state. Three things had ensured he stood out from his presidential antecedents and that led to the unpresidented ceremonies in Washington. Firstly, he was one of only a handful of American presidents who were genuine outsiders, he was neither educated at an Ivy League college nor had he ever been selfishly nurtured by any of the big political machines. He had also dared to come to politics directly from the film industry. Secondly, the man who prided himself on being the straightforward mid-westerner was in fact complex and notoriously difficult to pinpoint. The out-going extravert of a personality was enormously popular, as his funeral so amply demonstrated, and yet he preferred his own company, perhaps he was even shy. He could convey warmth without inhibition. He was the champion of small-town America and yet he had fled to the brightest of city lights at the first opportunity. He was an exponent of family values, but also a man who took little notice of his own children. Even devoted Nancy once admitted that sometimes she felt she didn't really know him. Third was Reagan's obvious detachment from the decision making of his own administration, so that he frequently appeared to be a simple figurehead rather than the hands-on president that Americans had grown accustomed to. Often when he was given briefs to read for coming meetings he would be taken to task for his lack of enthusiasm, "Why haven't you read that?" His reply would usually be mumbled along the lines, "Well, *The Sound of Music* was on last night…"

Patently it all worked for Reagan, but how did he pull it off, lacking as he did the background that was a usual requirment? Some say he managed it because although he possessed a second-class brain he had a first class temperament. It might also be that he made it, not despite but *because* of his Hollywood background. He definitely radiated optimism and used humor to diffuse the Republican Party's biggest problem, the nagging pereception that it was dominated by extremists. He never really felt the need to push an agenda, and he was always fundamentally a libertarian who hated the thought of forcing his own morality down other people's throats. He possessed a marked streak of pragmatism and an unexpected toughness. He viewed the world in a simple, blinkered way, but he always saw the issues clearly. Often it was not his head that did the talking. It was the heart. Ronald Reagan was an actor who had been a contract player at Warner Brothers for most of his career; he had learned something there during those years about pouring sincerity through underplayed emotion onto the fires of civil discourse. Over-theatrical statement simply doesn't work on the big screen; nor could it on the political stage.

When, with touching solidarity each of the men who had sat behind the desk of the Oval Office turned up for the funeral of Richard Nixon at Yorba Linda, California, Reagan's own succes were amply illustrated. The slow march to their seats had been carefully orchestrated, but as each one arrived, in the order of their incumbency, there was still some vying for superiority. Reagan shuffled along with the frailty of old age, but as he staggered into view of those gathered, applause welled up and peaked as he and Nancy slumped to their seats. By the time President and Hillary Clinton appeared, an embarrassing silence had ensued. Once again, without any obvious effort, Reagan had won the Southern California vote.

Much of the emotion of that day lay in the realization that this was a dress rehearsal for Reagan's own funeral, which was rushing headlong to meet him. But the fact remained that Reagan retained such warm affection in America's heart despite the fact that he had left the movies in 1965 and politics in 1988 and had retired from public view in 1994.

His Hollywood legacy ensured that he was able to fill the ceremonial and mystical role of the presidency, even though he had never fully carried out its executive one. His film career echoed the role of the president as a romantic hero and Reagan's own Hollywood years were infused with the New Deal ideology of Roosevelt. In 1948 he campaigned for Roosevelt's successor, Harry Truman, organizing the Hollywood campaign with Lauren Bacall. In 1950 he worked for the Democratic Senate candidate Helen Douglas. But by 1952 he was backing Republican, Dwight D Eisenhower.

His political conversion was founded on many things but had two main roots; the first was the obvious fear of the power of Communism in the film industry. As president of the Screen Actor's Guild through the bitter Hollywood strikes, Reagan fought the influence of the Communists and became a confidential source for the FBI. The second was Reagan's firm belief that he actually never did change, rather, he said, it was the defining center of American politics that shifted. For him the New Deal and Roosevelt's leadership against fascist power came to embody the Americanism in which he had always believed, "America is less a place then an idea, an idea that has been deep in the souls of men ever since he started his long trail from the swamps, the inherent love of freedom."…

…So the cameras roll again as the howitzers placed across Constitution Avenue finally roar out their twenty-one-gun salute to mark the return of Ronald Reagan to the capitol. His casket is placed tenderly to rest on the rough pine boards that were first used for Abraham Lincoln's funeral, and his own words reverberate through the air until the director is satisfied, "You ain't seen nothin' yet!"

This was the start of a tearful three day send off, but the sound of the guns mark the end of an era where one ever-optimistic man reminded a whole nation what was possible…

…God speed Mr. President.

Cartoon by Patrick O'Connor reproduced by kind permsision of *The Los Angeles*

*Daily News*

# Chapter One

## 1911-1927

### The Formative Years, Tampico to Rock River

**Ronald Wilson Reagan** weighed in at a healthily impressive ten pounds when he strolled, feet first, into the world on February 6th 1911 at 4.16 am. He was born in a warm, five-roomed bakery in tiny Tampico, Illinois, right at the heartbeat of small-town-Middle-America, the second son of John Edward (Jack) and Nelle Clyde Wilson Reagan. Nothing in those quaintly humble origins suggested the remarkable journey he was embarking upon or the prominence of his destiny.

Jack, the darkly handsome patriarch, was a senior shoe salesman; ambitious, unfailingly optimistic, courageous and full of fun. He had been raised the much-loved son of a family of rural Irish immigrants and had grown up bursting with typically restless blarney, he was a lapsed Catholic and a binge drinker with a great thirst for corn whiskey. He loved alcohol and particularly enjoyed the social traditions of the Irish public house, but, like so many others of that era, he was often forced to drink alone and in secret when liquor was banned in pre-Prohibition Tampico.

He was instinctively a gentleman who always dressed immaculately. He tended to be overly buddy-buddy with everyone, including his own two sons. The eldest, Neil, never seemed to mind too much, but his overly tactile demonstrations (undoubtedly drink-driven) embarrassed the squirming and introverted young Ronald, "I can remember dimly my father coming home from the store and giving me a kiss, and he had stubble and I cried."

Jack had grown up with roots sunk deep in oppression and prejudice. It had been almost inevitable that as he blossomed into adulthood he became a committed and compassionate Democrat who hated all expressions of injustice and social, economic or political tyranny in any form. Ronald himself said that the only time his father ever showed any sign of intolerance within the family circle that he could recall was when he had refused to let him see *Birth of a Nation*, warning him darkly that it glorified the Ku Klux Klan. He had also once refused to stay in a hotel that discriminated against Jews. In spite of Jack's kind and gentle nature, Ronald admitted that he backed away from him throughout childhood... detaching himself physically and emotionally, and rejecting all shows of intimacy thereafter. Reagan's friends and relatives often complained he never would allow anyone to get too close to him and that he always found demonstrations of passion awkward and uncomfortable to deal with.

Jack was never happy sitting still; he had big ambitious dreams, he craved success and was driven toward it. He packed his young family up and moved them on a number of times, going ever closer to the bright lights of Chicago where his personal ambition of finding fame and fortune lay.

By 1913 he had scraped together enough cash to buy a Ford Model T with the admirable intention of shifting the Reagans on in a style to which they weren't yet accustomed. Unfortunately the car didn't last long enough to carry them anywhere even close to Chicago, and just one short month after its purchase, as he drove with two year old Ronald perched on the back seat, Jack crashed it into a tree. "Dutch", as his father had taken to calling him, (saying he resembled a fat Dutchman), was trapped alone in the mangled wreckage for some time and Ronald later suspected that it was this unfortunate episode that led to his lifelong claustrophobic suffering.

Meanwhile Nelle came to resent her ever restless husband's attempts to carry her away from Tampico, where she was already quite the star of the local amateur dramatic group. She was a seamstress by trade and she had no desire to head for larger towns or brighter lights, where he might have had more opportunity to find success, and she less so. In fact both husband and wife were involved with acting and the Reagans were Tampico's leading theatrical couple, starring in three plays at the Opera House in 1913 alone. Their joint appearance reportedly brought in a trainload of visitors to the town for the show *A Woman's Honor.*

Although of English-Scottish Protestant descent, Nelle, deeply in love with her devastatingly handsome charmer, had accepted a Catholic wedding and also permitted both her sons to be raised in that faith. Later, in 1910, more discontented with her lot, she rejected Catholicism and turned instead toward the Disciples of Christ for her spiritual guidance. Only Neil was baptized in the Catholic faith. Ronald would be permitted to choose his own salvation when he reached maturity.

John Neil, (Moon) had been born three years before Ronald, on September 16th 1908. He was always the more gregarious son of his father, while Ronald, quietly aloof, wistful and reserved, was typically sensible Nelle's boy.

Reagan said later that he had no recollection of family events until after they had finally moved away from Tampico to settle in Dixon in 1915. He was also apparently happily unaware of poverty, though he admitted, "Our family didn't exactly come form the wrong side of the tracks, but we were certainly always within the sound of the train whistles."

His father never had money to spare, but neither could the Reagans claim to have been poor. Young Ronald may have been reduced at times to selling popcorn at the local amusement park, but he never went hungry and his father, who was arrested for public drunkenness on a number of occasions, never had to abstain from the corn liquor he craved. His drunken binges did force the family to move on regularly perhaps, and the constant flitting from place to place must have troubled and confused even the calmest of children, but really his father's alcoholism seems to have left his young life almost untouched.

Nothing, car crashes excepted, seemed to disturb the ultra-laid back

Ronald, and throughout the early chaotic period of upheaval, he remained dreamy, mild mannered and generally contented. He was a true Mid Westerner, and Edmund Morris, one of Reagan's biographers, said there seemed to be "nothing in Reagan's eyes but this blank blue sky." This was possibly the result of him growing up in the heart of middle America, where an entirely different breed of people inhabited the land, and were nothing like those who lived in California and who Ronald would meet, move amongst and be accepted by later in his life.

When the Reagans took rented accommodation in Monmouth, Ronald could already read and was providing evidence at the age of five of his famed photographic memory. In 1917 he was registered at Willard School, where he was quickly recognized as an extraordinarily bright pupil; he regularly turned in perfect marks in spelling and arithmetic tests, and although he had severely defective eyesight he was also always involved in sport. Ronald was gifted; he reveled in his gifts and worked hard at Willard, where he had settled well and was put into third grade ahead of his classmates. He was bullied because of his high academic achievement. Still, he clearly never sought sympathy and he didn't invite anyone to place a comforting arm around his tough little shoulders. At five years old he was content in his own company and at times he could even seem to be remote, somehow standing apart from his classmates. He had shunned his father, didn't have much in common with his older brother, and in Monmouth things could have become even worse; he was almost three years younger than Neil, but was only a year behind him academically. In fact this didn't cause too much of a problem either because, whilst they didn't share many characteristics, where sport was concerned both boys were fanatical and Reagan said, "Football was a matter of life and death for us." They both enjoyed rough and tumble sports, and the tougher it came, the better. They also liked to go to more organized groups like the YMCA. Ronald played basketball for the June Bugs and was also a keen skater.

Then, in 1920, after moving house seven times in Ronald's first nine years, the family finally stopped for a while and sank some more secure roots when Jack obtained work in Dixon, a sleepy little town just twenty five miles northeast of the Tampico starting gate. This was the place the Reagan boys always considered home and Ronald returned there again and again throughout his life. Soon after arriving he succumbed to a virulent bout of pneumonia. He became so ill that doctors held out little hope for his survival. He was confined to bed for some time until he eventually began to recover some strength. Then, just as boredom began to take hold, a new neighbor brought him a set of lead soldiers to play with, "I divided 'em into formations and played with 'em while I was recuperating in bed."

Family finances were more secure by this time and Jack was employed in a local store in an Irish neighborhood, whilst Nelle took in needlework to pay for extras. She was always around the house but Ronald was perfectly happy to be left alone in his room to play with the soldiers for hours at a time, arranging them into lines, preparing them to go into battle.

Unfortunately, in the area where Jack was working, there was an abundance of bars. No matter how well he had been doing he simply couldn't resist the temptation and before long he was drinking heavily again. The money he had been putting toward raising his family soon dwindled and things took a steady turn for the worse. Nelle was unhappy, her mood increasingly scratchy. Neil stayed out playing with friends as long as he could and Ronald simply ignored everything, withdrawing deeper and deeper into his own company. He had an unusual ability not to notice things he didn't like. He backed further away from his father and remained almost untouched by the price of his alcoholism, he accepted the steadfast presence of his mother and hardly knew if his brother was around or not. Nothing interrupted his inner calm for long.

He was encouraged by Nelle to join in a recitation at the Church of Christ in Dixon. He read a piece "About Mother." From then on he went to church with her regularly, but he said this was a duty rather than a pleasure. He certainly hadn't begun his love affair with an audience yet and as often as he was able he turned his attention to boyish pursuits instead. Both he and Neil played tag in the stockyards, picked strawberries for pay, fished, went hiking and swimming in the murky canal. Ronald was a particularly strong swimmer. Both boys also started going to the local Opera House to watch screenings of Tom Mix movies and other four reelers. The life long passion for the cinema had started early.

Dixon High School was divided into two separate buildings on either side of the Rock River. Ronald attended the more affluent old red brick school, North Dixon; Neil stubbornly chose to go to South Central. In his first days at school Ronald met young Margaret Cleaver and they were soon close friends. She encouraged him to join the drama club and his coach there, BJ Frazer, recalled him as being, "head and shoulders above the rest at taking direction. He had a sense of presence on the stage, a sense of reality."

Reagan blossomed at Dixon High where he delighted in becoming chairman of a variety of committees and joined as many groups as he could get into. The kids soon noticed that he had a good sense of what they wanted and that he expressed their wishes with cool, succinct clarity and they usually voted for him to represent them; here some of his earliest and best political achievements can be noted.

In 1921 Ronald and Neil borrowed a crystal radio set from a neighbor. They were thrilled when they finally managed to tune it and could hear music coming out of the air, "Can you imagine our sense of wonder?" the isolated Midwestern Ronald Reagan asked when he was first hit by the impact of transmitted sound. Suddenly the brothers had joined a greater America; Ronald's national awareness and understanding of wider world issues grew.

Jack kept disappearing, often failing to return home for days at a time. The parents of the Reagan boys were quarreling more frequently and more violently, "My brother and I would hear some pretty fiery arguments," and Ronald once came home to find his father unconscious in the street, drunk, dead to the world, smelling of cheap whiskey. Years later he said he felt no anger toward him, only grief for him, "I wanted to pretend he wasn't there. I bent over him…I got a fistful of his overcoat and managed to drag him inside and get him to bed."

Around the same time he read *That Printer of Udell's,* by Harold Bell Wright, a book that changed his life and the way he saw it. Ronald told his mother that he wanted to be like the main character, Richard Falkner, who becomes a disciple of Christ and goes to Washington to do great deeds.

Nelle commented that her son "was thirsting for Grace" and, aged just twelve, he asked her if he could be baptized. He had made his mind up which direction he was going to take, he was making choices then that would become the cornerstones of the remainder of his life.

But above all, searching for grace or not, his only real obsession throughout the 1920's remained football. He had very weak eyes and his poor sight meant that he could never shine at baseball or any other precisely technical sport, but he was philosophical about it, and anyway football suited his dogged personality better. And Ronald was dogged. When he didn't make the cut at school, although naturally disappointed, he wasn't put off and he tried out to become captain of the school's B team instead. He refused to take "No" for an answer and worked harder to get what he wanted next time the selection was made.

Academically he was already a star pupil but, idly one day, he put on Nelle's glasses for fun and was shocked to find his vision suddenly sharpening. He could see! His own prescription pair of spectacles was made up and from that moment on he spent much of his time at Dixon's public library. He became one of its most enthusiastic visitors, averaging two withdrawals a week, and he dropped in most days after school. He called himself a voracious reader and particularly enjoyed Tom Sawyer and Huckleberry Finn.

In 1926 he started working as a laborer clearing land in the quiet township for a residential contractor. Apart from his occasional efforts as a caddy at the local golf club, this was his first paid work. He hated it so much that when the whistle blew to signify the end of day, if he was midway through his pick stroke, he would simply drop the axe and walk off site. The same building company taught him how to survey the land for development, a task that suited him much more, although he was still required to do his share of hard labor from time to time.

Whilst he enjoyed the surveying more, the heavier work helped him bulk out and by the time he was sixteen he was finally selected for the school football team, despite the fact that he was still lighter than most of the other players. His commitment paid off when he was chosen as right guard. He tackled with furious determination and people soon began to take note of his graceful and tireless running combined with enthusiasm and an increasing level of fitness and power.

He was indeed a healthy fellow and he loved the active life. The more physical the activity the better he liked it and in 1927 he became the lifeguard at Lowell Park Beach on the Rock River. He was a splendidly strong swimmer. Swimming had always appealed to him because it was one of the few sports where he hadn't needed his spectacles, where bad eyesight had been no hindrance. He liked all water sports and was a real river rat. He said he enjoyed the feeling of going somewhere purposefully and rhythmically, without there being anything to distract or divert him. Water sport really suited the massive privacy of his steadily developing personality. Edmund Morris commented, "I have marveled at Reagan's cool, unhurried progress through crises of politics and personnel and thought to myself, *he sees the world as a swimmer sees it.*"

He had taken a lifesaving course at the YMCA and was certified for competence. He was paid a salary of $15 per week, plus all the hamburgers he could eat to work at the beach. The youngster enjoyed complete authority over all who came down to the river's edge to swim or sunbathe.

Surely Ronald Reagan could not have already been planning the way his life would pan out? He was still only a schoolboy. How could he have had any sense back then of where his fate lay? And yet he was already full of obsession and drive to get exactly where he wanted to go. Was it as Morris suggests, that he saw the world as a swimmer sees it? Isolated in a detached arena, one straight lane to plough his powerful way down, no distractions to sidetrack him? Already at his first schools it seems that his fifty-meter lane was clearly marked out and he swam straight and true to reach his goal. In the coming years Ronald Reagan would rarely encounter obstacles; when he did, he simply swam on regardless, pounding relentlessly straight over the top of them.

# Chapter Two

## 1928-1932

### College to Radio Announcer

### Searching for Grace

Ronald began seeing his friend Margaret "Mugs" Cleaver on a more regular basis. She was small, dark and dour, but incredibly bright and young Ronald was always attracted by intelligence; even then it was a characteristic he rated above all others, and soon the school's model boy was going steady with its most brilliant girl. He was elected president of North Side student body, she was president of the senior class, both were members of the school dramatic society, both studied French and they hardly spent a moment of their hectic school day apart. They were reserved loners, but they reveled in each other's company and were glad to have found each other.

When he became the art director of the school magazine, Margaret wrote most of the articles. Interestingly he laid his early volumes out in the style of a silent-movie storyboard, and had sections in it such as, "Directors", "Cast", "Stage", and "Filming." He illustrated each of the sections with drawings of himself as an authority figure, sitting behind a massive desk, calling orders out to his staff through a megaphone. He drew those pictures when he was just sixteen years old; the resemblance to the man he later became was almost occult.

Even when school finished and it was time to venture out into the wider world, Ronald and Margaret remained together, both choosing to further their educations at nearby Eureka College, which was affiliated with the Disciples of Christ. Ronald majored in sociology and also studied economics. It was hardly the huge adventure he might have embarked upon perhaps, but relationships and family meant a lot to him, and he came to love Eureka and respect all that it stood for, saying that in his opinion, there was no lovelier college in the country.

Meanwhile Jack was employed close to the college for the local Works Progress Administration and his mother worked in a local dress shop. She regularly sent both her sons 50 cents a week and she always kept their rooms ready for them to come home to. Both Ronald and Neil felt the warmth and security of their family around them whilst they were away from home, although undoubtedly once they had both gone to college Nelle's home life deteriorated to an all time low as Jack continued his heavy drinking and self destructive tendencies.

The college football field became holy ground to Ronald at Eureka, although Coach Ralph McKinzie, didn't seem to appreciate his dogged talents and rarely took any notice of his efforts. He had taken the boy in dislike and was particularly irked by the way he claimed to have been the star of Dixon High; which he certainly wasn't. Ronald just about made Team 5 and was humiliated not to receive a lettered jersey. Naturally, just as when he failed to make the team at Dixon first time round, he persevered and dreamed of winning his jersey one day. He also became a sports reporter for the *Eureka Pegasus*, the school's weekly newspaper, and was assigned to cover the football matches he would have preferred to be starring in himself.

On the whole his life didn't change dramatically at college and his personality didn't undergo any radical flips either; although essentially introverted, he was just as popular at college as he had been at High School. His manner was always friendly in a mildly detached way, he was never cloying and so he was simply accepted by those around him. He was easy to be with. He required no one change their ways on his account, he accepted others as they were and he was himself personally unassuming; he offended no one- with the possible exception of Coach, and that may have been because he so badly wanted to make an impression in the one area that still meant so much to him. On the whole he considered that changing others or himself required effort and Ronald preferred an easy, relaxed lifestyle, why bother annoying people when it was so much easier to smile and keep quiet?

The only person other than Coach McKinzie that he seems to have gone out of his way for was Mugs. Margaret was one of a few girls who lived off campus. Ronald walked her to school every morning and their romance blossomed. They were used to each other, satisfied in each other's comfortable predictability. The youngsters were hard working and active around college. Whilst both his parents regularly sent small amounts of money, he did whatever he could to augment his own meager income and he had a happy knack of earning a good salary whatever he turned his hand to, even washing dishes at Lida's Wood, one of the female dormitories, "Lifeguard money paid for half my college education, and dishwashing the other half."

He and Margaret joined Alpha Epsilon Sigma, Eureka's dramatic fraternity, where the actor in Ronald was again quickly recognized. The group went to see a touring play, *Journey's End* and he so strongly identified with the hero he began to feel he *was* the hero, "Nature was trying to tell me something, namely that my heart is a ham loaf." On April 10th 1930 Ronald starred in the part of Thyrsis, a shepherd boy, in the Drama Department's Fifth Annual Theatre Tournament. He received a standing ovation and was named one of the six best actors in the tournament. He was told on that defining day he should make acting his career!

In a 1942 *Photoplay* article, entitled, *How to Make Yourself Important*, Ronald wrote, "The whole deal on how to make yourself important is…to a) love what you are doing with all your heart and soul and b) believe what you are doing is important, even if you are only grubbing for worms in the back yard. … you must love what you are doing. You must think what you are doing is important, because if it's important to you, you can bet your last ducat that other people will think so too.

"For me, the one job in the world I want to do is acting...doing what I wanted to do didn't always put me in a favorable light. For example, in college I majored in sociology and economics. Not because I liked the subjects, but because they gave me the most time for the things I really liked, namely college dramatics, football and a dive into campus politics." Here were the three things that really drove Reagan all his life.

Since joining the college drama group, a vague idea of moving out to Hollywood had been taking hold at the back of his mind, but he was also aware of the first stirrings of political aspiration at the same time. He became very actively involved in college politics quite early and in October 1930 he was elected to College Senate. When the college's new president tried to reduce the faculty, Reagan helped organize a student strike. He developed a taste for standing up in front of an audience right there, "That audience and I were together. When I came to actually presenting the motion...there was no need for parliamentary procedure. They came to their feet with a roar...it was heady wine."

In 1931 young Reagan sadly mourned the death of Knute Rockne, the legendary football coach, who died that year in a plane crash and it was back then that his fascinating association with George Gipp, the Notre Dame footballer coached by Rockne, began. Ronald found the story was so powerfully moving that he often told and re-told the story to anyone who would listen to him. Many years later, after signing his first Warner Bros contract, and well before he was cast himself as the Gipper in *Knute Rockne-All American,* he proposed it as a screenplay to the film company, offering to write it himself.

In 1932 he graduated into Depression-stricken America, scoring well above average in all studies, including an A in Public Speaking. But he admits that by then he was already crazy about acting and was determined to get to the Hollywood studios to try his hand in the movies. Thoughts of using his new qualifications in the fields of either politics or of playing football had dissolved behind what he recognized as his all consuming calling, "I did not believe you had to be standout from your fellow man in order to make your mark in the world. Average will do it." He commented wryly that he accepted he was no Flynn or Boyer, "Mr. Norm was my alias." But he said at the time of making his first choices, "For me, the one job in the world I want to do is acting. Offer me ten times the money for something else, and I wouldn't do it."

Although he obviously had a deep faith in himself to make the break, he was initially held back in his push to the top by a deep concern for his mother, who had become very insecure in her marriage, and also by his devotion to long time girlfriend, Margaret. She had let him know in no uncertain terms that she wouldn't marry an actor or move to Hollywood. To the eminently sensible Mugs this was the stuff of dreams, far-fetched and ludicrous. He enjoyed her company, he didn't want things to end. More pressingly, he also had a heavy student loan to repay and jobs were scarce out in the wide world. He was unable to embark on his life's adventure in those early months although it was now calling more insistently. He wanted to honor his loan repayments promptly, and he had regular money coming in from his lifeguard work at the river beach. Still he wrote, "I realized at the same time that dramatics was the only way I'd ever be happy." He added, as if to remind himself of his determination to get away to the film capital, that sitting on top of his lifeguard stand he often felt himself to be in the middle of a performance. He was alert and watching for danger in the water, but he was also fully aware that he was watched too. He was happily conscious of his good looks and powerful build.

And it wasn't too long before he made his move. Somehow he had persuaded Margaret to get formally engaged, but she would not marry him until he obtained real employment. He seems to have successfully hidden his desire to become a film star from her at this point, or she still firmly rejected the idea that the future of her lithe-limbed boyfriend could be with the likes of Warner Brothers. It is doubtful then that she ever witnessed the attention that the bathing beauties at Lowell Park bestowed on him, or she would not have remained so secure in the certainty. He had been doing some ad hoc work writing for the sports column of a local Iowa daily, and that was an eminently acceptable career for him in Margaret's conservative view. But that employment led directly to the birth of his interest in radio reporting, and possibly a little disinterest in his fiancé who wanted to raise their children safe in the Mid West that they had both been happy to inhabit. So when she finally ditched him, giving in to what she believed would be the inevitability of his future failure, although he was sad, commenting, "I was kinda floored," he was now free at last. Late in 1932 he set off in a borrowed Oldsmobile for Chicago, where he hoped to get some radio work before moving on to the brighter lights of Southern California.

The aspiring commentator was loaded in the gift of the gab department! But unfortunately, just like his father before him, he never made it as far as Chicago. Instead he impressed the program director of radio station WOC Davenport, Iowa, Peter MacArthur, so much that he was hired on the spot as a football sportscaster, although much of his work was reporting on baseball games. MacArthur made Reagan give a 15 minute dummy commentary on a football game, then told him, "You did great." He was paid five dollars a game and his travel expenses. Reagan said MacArthur taught him all the fundamentals of acting and was the most unforgettable character he ever met.

Whilst he lodged at the Perry Apartments, Davenport, paying a very high 18 dollars a month for the privilege, his fine voice became a massive asset in his career development. He specialized in what MacArthur told him was "visualization" of baseball games. The bare facts of a distant game were telegraphed to him, and he was required to create, on the spot, a word picture of the contest, right down to little red-haired boys making spectacular catches of foul balls in the stands. In later years one of Reagan's favorite stories has the line going dead as a ball left the pitcher's hand, leaving him to improvise many, many foul balls…completely untraceable in the next day's match reports…until normal service was resumed. Reagan's fiction did not distort the account of the game as it progressed, all the hits and runs were there, and the rest was simply entertainment. It was also good practice for the coming years.

He began to get some freelance assignments and the local Press caught on, often praising his quick tongue and crisp command of narrative.

"Success for me was where the heart is. And my heart was in dramatics. After college, I got a job as a sports announcer and eventually I worked up to broadcasting many of the biggest sports events. The job wasn't very important at first, but before long I woke up to find myself broadcasting sports events for which the sponsors paid my station hundreds of thousands of dollars a year."

Jack, Nelle, Neil and
little Dutch in 1914

Ronnie, second from left, with his school
football team

Reagan was too slow, could not
see without his glasses, and was
lighter than the rest of the Eureka
team, but he was a dedicated right
guard for the Red Devils in 1931

Young lifeguard who loved heroics
his life

The look of the matinee idol and the silky voice of the experienced radio announcer won Reagan his first contract with Warner Brothers.

Ronald Reagan displaying the physique that got him noticed in Hollywood

# Chapter Three

## 1933-1938

### WHO airwaves to Hollywood

Effective from beginning February 10th 1933 he was appointed a staff announcer at the broadcast station at $150 a month, an undreamed of salary back in Dixon, but that was not where Reagan saw things ending, he was an onwards and upwards guy. He still dreamed of getting to Hollywood, "Well, maybe radio…maybe by way of that, someday…"

In his first days at the station he spun records, served as a reporter, weatherman, network feeder, product plugger. He received no formal training, but was always around MacArthur, paying attention and learning as he went. He didn't realize he had been hired as a stopgap. In 1933 WHO Des Moines was due to switch to a new massive transmitter, with an almost national reach, which would force many of the smaller local stations to merge. Staff dismissals were bound to follow. If he had known, Reagan would have rightly assumed that he was going to be a redundant announcer.

But he seems to have been unaware of the undercurrents flowing around him, he was always the tireless eager beaver, and when he was offered a freelance assignment to cover a track event he jumped at the opportunity. He was so good that day and so impressed were the station owners, that when the axe was swung, Reagan wasn't felled, and instead was employed full time at the new, bigger WHO station as Sports Director! Then, once the new transmitter was in place and on the air, his voice began trickling out to a new audience of millions of sports listeners. He had been touched by the luck of the Irish, but he used it to great personal effect; he grabbed his chance with both hands.

Over the next 3 years he became an absolute master of the

essentials of radio announcing. He already had the natural equipment necessary for a sports presenter; lucidity, enthusiasm, eye for visual detail, and a mouth that was as fast as his brain. He had a light, sunny voice that somehow reflected the middle America in which he had grown up. He knew and understood the people he talked to through the airwaves, and they began to become familiar with him.

Back then, Des Moines, where he was now living, that stepping stone to Chicago and then distant Hollywood, was a small, dirty city with 3 theatres and 22 motion picture houses. Reagan never liked it there and did not settle even though he did enjoy leading the bachelor lifestyle at last. He began dating again. One of the girls, probably his favorite at the time, was Jeanne Tesdell. She thought he was boring and soon tired of him. Another friend was Joy Hodges, a former WHO child star, and now a regular at the station. To Reagan she seemed like a big personality who had really made the big time, (and in fact she did make it all the way to Hollywood and later success with RKO). She would also play a big part in his future career.

In the spring of 1936 Reagan accompained the Chicago Cubs to report from their training camp on Catalina Island, playground of the big Hollywood producers, which lay just off the coast of California, a quick flight or boat ride from Long Beach. He had forced WHO into the assignment by offering to count the time he spent there as his vacation. Joy Hodges was already flirting with her Hollywood career and he planned to stop off in Los Angeles to visit her and see if she could introduce him around town. He arrived in the quaint, Mediterranean style village of Avalon on the island, one of the loveliest places in the world, but never got to Hollywood that trip, he was far too busy with the Cubs.

The delay in his arrival gave him time to become even more professional in his delivery. He acquired an intimate knowledge of the personalities of the Chicago players and became lightning fast in his reactions to wire-service codes, and even though he wasn't actually at the big games, his audience preferred listening to his sport cast than the live commentaries on offer. He was becoming a celebrity in his own right in the era of popular radio. He landed the same assignment for the coming year and he could hardly be discontent with his lot. He enjoyed good health, a choice of girls, new clothes and more money than he could easily spend. He was able to help his family out, he bought a new car, had a certain amount of fame, and he was already further along his chosen path than Margaret would have thought possible. A local gossip columnist in Des Moines wrote at the time, "Watch him…he's stream lined."

"This meant folks were listening to me, lots of folks. And they listened to me, I know, not because I had any experience in broadcasting or any diction, but because I was loving doing it. You've got to work for the thing you love, you always do."

By the spring of 1937 Reagan headed back to Catalina, but this time he was determined to make the most of his summer trip and on March 12th when he arrived in Los Angeles the weather was so bad he decided not to risk the boat crossing to the island. He went over to Republic Pictures where a WHO band was playing. The bandleader introduced him to the radio-casting director and he was promptly invited to do a reading. Reagan said that it all happened so fast he was later unable to recall much of what went on but added, "In the studio the dream re-awakened."

Later that day he met up with his old singing acquaintance Joy Hodges and confessed to her that what he really wanted was a screen test. She introduced him to actor's agent Bill Meikeljohn and her own agent George Ward. Both were immediately struck by Reagan's ability and agreed to do their best to fix something up. He left Los Angeles for Catalina and carried out his training camp assignment well pleased with himself.

No sooner had he arrived back in LA on March 27 than Joy Hodges called to let him know Meikeljohn and Ward had arranged an immediate audition with casting director Max Arnow at Warner Bros. He rushed straight over. Reagan was confused when Arnow appeared to take little notice of him and even more so when he asked him curtly if his shoulders were real and then snapped, "Let me hear your voice."

His now well experienced radio-honed voice sold him on to the movies on the spot. He was offered a screen test for later that same week, but Reagan told Arnow, "I have to get back to my job in Des Moines." He was pushing his luck, but Arnow agreed to advance the test anyway. He had seen something in the attractive young man with the liquid silver delivery.

Reagan was hustled to the studio make-up department where the stylist laughed out loud at his appearance. Reagan had put in an extra effort for his test that day and thought he looked good until she spluttered, "Where did you get that haircut!" Even at twenty-six years old, he was all thick, blue-black glossy sheen, swept up high and quiffed. After she had finished sprucing him he was left to his fate and abandoned to the cameras. A brief scene was shot with Helen Valkis and Reagan says he felt an odd sense of anticlimax when it was over. He set off back to Des Moines unsure what his future might hold. It had been so exciting to be around a film studio for that short time, but once the test was over, no one said anything to give him hope of a dramatic career change.

On April 2nd 1937 he received a curt telegram from George Ward, "Warners offer contract seven years, one year's options, starting at $200 a week."

He packed his life up and set off for an uncertain world. At least his radio contract had been tight and secure. He was exchanging it for a three-month probationary period. The contract ran for seven years, but only if he made it through the first three months. When that was up he might find himself back in Dixon selling shoes in a store. But the one thing that Ronald Reagan never lacked was self-belief and he had the eternal optimist's confidence in the future and all it might hold. He told his family and friends that he would look after any one of them who followed him out to Hollywood.

He later confessed, "It was some time before I discovered that I got to Warner Brothers because my voice was considered similar to that of Ross Alexander, an actor who committed suicide when on the verge of becoming a Warner star."

Before leaving he wrote an article for the *Dispatch* and signed an agreement with the Sunday Register for a series of articles on "Life in Hollywood." Ronald Reagan was not much of a gambler and for as long as he could, he would continue covering Cubs and Sox games for the paper. He had now met every conceivable angle, and if things did go wrong in Los Angeles, he would at least have a job to go back to. He also completed his Army Extension courses and was accepted into the Cavalry Reserve Corps as a second lieutenant, an officer and a gentleman.

He arrived at Warner Bros at the back end of May 1937 and immediately fell in love with the walled and gated city with its own fire department, power plant, hospital, school, four fully equipped cinemas, thirty miles of streets, working railroad, a local radio station and the warehouses which stored the stuff of dreams, his dreams.

Max Arnow permitted him to see his screen test. Reagan felt deeply ashamed and depressed that he had ever believed he might not be going back to Des Moines and he asked, "Why did you hire me?"

Arnow smiled and said, "You'll be OK, I hope."

Reagan wanted to repay Arnow's faith in him and felt he had to make a big impression right from the start; he began showing up at the studio daily, even though he wasn't yet on payroll. He wanted to be instantly available when called to action. By May 25th he was rewarded with his first script. Unlike most new contract players he was put straight to work, and even more unusually he was given the lead in his first ever film; a 61 minute B called *Love is On the Air*, a re-write of *Hi, Nellie*. Brynie Foy, Warner's executive producer of B's had shot the same film at least six times before, but never with a radio station as its background. The arrival of

Ronald Reagan, ex-radio presenter, had given him the idea for a new angle. Foy and Reagan got on well right from the start, and Reagan claims that Foy often created B's just to keep him on salary when he might have otherwise been thrown to the scrap heap of has-beens who never had-been.

So he was cast as a radio announcer in his first life-imitating-art movie! He worked with a dialogue director, he was given new sleeker clothes, his hair was cut and styled. When the cameraman complained that his neck was too short for his shoulders, James Cagney's personal shirt maker was called in to carve a deep V collar style for him, (apparently the great Cagney's neck was also too short for his shoulders). Reagan chose to wear this pattern for the rest of his life.

He was introduced to some of the Warner actors including Ann Sheridan, Dick Powell, Leslie Howard and Olivia de Havilland. Celebrity easily impressed him and he was thrilled to find himself in the presence of such stars.

The studio press office was keen to promote his radio connection and he was photographed around the lot and appeared under headlines, "The Former Voice of WHO".

As per Hollywood custom, Arnow began searching for a fitting name for the upcoming star. No one asked Reagan for his opinion; he gave it anyway, "May I point out that I already have a lot of name recognition in a large part of the country."

Arnow scoffed, "Dutch Reagan?" and added, "You can't put that on a marquee."

Reagan replied softly, with all his characteristic charm, "How about Ronald Reagan then?"

"*Ronald Reagan*." The rhythmic syllables balanced out…ideal for display purposes, "Not bad," Arnow conceded.

Ronald Reagan, latest Warner signing recalled, "The studio publicity department had to sweat ink out of its veins to turn out a biography on me…

I like to swim, hike and sleep…I'm fairly good at every sport except tennis, which I just don't like…my favorite menu is steak smothered with onions and strawberry shortcake. I play bridge adequately, collect guns, always carry a penny as a good-luck charm and knock on wood when I make a boast or express a wish. I have a so-so convertible, which I drive myself. I'm interested in politics and governmental problems. I'm a fan of Bing Crosby…I like things colored green."

Well- he was of Irish descent.

He reported for his first day's work on June 2nd and was sent to the Warner City KDTS broadcast station where the movie was set and where he was to play ace news announcer at a small-town station, Andy McCaine.

He found the set of *Love is on the Air* was a vast improvement on his own past working environment at WHO and McCaine's studio was spacious and sleek and he had his name stenciled on the door.

The movie going public may have been misled into expecting a musical, since Dick Powell's *Varsity Show* had featured him singing "Love is on the Air Tonight" the month before the film was released. They were disappointed to discover a minor crime picture with a storyline they had heard often before and with an unfamiliar leading man. The picture did nothing in box office terms. However no one was disappointed in Reagan's casually comfortable first performance; his voice had been his strongest suit and the non-stop reporting was exciting…his "Good evening, my little friends", when he first takes over children's hour, revealed barely suppressed menace. He was acclaimed a hit in the picture which played as a second feature on Warner double-billed programs despite having difficulty carrying out simultaneous actions, like unbuttoning his pajamas whilst shouting into the phone. He could hardly have expected an easier transition into his new medium and the picture accomplished exactly what it set out to do, provide passable entertainment whilst introducing a new actor.

Whilst the film wasn't big enough to receive major reviews, a bright future was predicted for a "natural new find." As the top billing in the film he was referred to as "likeable" and "pleasing". *Variety* pointed out that Reagan was at his best when involved in fast physical action. Not a massively impressive start to his new career perhaps, but solid enough, and Reagan was quietly optimistic for the future, "Right from the start, down there amongst the "B" pictures where I began…I was sure that I was in the right business for me…I knew I'd get to the top if I kept on working and learning." At least he knew there would be no going back a failure now and every step he took from here on would be in one direction, forward.

He said he loved the "Wall of light," and the warm glow that spread through him when he was in front of the camera. He could hear people all round him but could not see anyone. He says he didn't miss them. He enjoyed the feeling of security and privacy that the "Wall" gave him. Maybe it was a bit like swimming. He was still seeing the world as a swimmer saw it and still enjoying the comfortable feel that brought.

He carried on working in B pictures for the next four years until he was referred to as the "Poor Man's Errol Flynn". He worked on hand-me-down sets and in second hand costumes (actors often wore their own clothes in Warner Bs). In fact in his second picture, the blockbusting *Hollywood Hotel* with its impressive cast, Reagan had moved from a starring role in a B movie to an A list picture, where he didn't even get a screen credit.

*Hollywood Hotel* had been an outgrowth from the popular radio series, hosted by Dick Powell, which had premiered on the CBS Radio Network in 1934. Powell was fast becoming popular in films himself and he also starred in the picture. The driving force behind the radio show was Louella Parsons. She also appeared in the film, which was not however a celluloid version of the radio show. Powell plays a saxophone player trying to break into the movie world, unsuccessful until he snares a spot on Louella's radio show. Reagan himself only appears briefly as one of Louella's staff, standing uncomfortably at her side, perhaps conscious of his position amongst the host of glittering stars clustered all around him, "I was certainly a nobody in, and to, Hollywood. I certainly hadn't learned to act by being a sports announcer. I wasn't any collar ad to look at. All I had in this world was confidence that, with the proper material, I could entertain people. And the only basis I had for this confidence was that I *wanted* to entertain people more than I wanted to do anything else."

Even so, he did not get to play the lead in his next picture, *Submarine D-1* either. In fact when he went to see it at its first screening he found he didn't appear in it at all! It starred Pat O'Brien, George Brent and Wayne Morris, and the original intention had been to have a surprise ending where none of the stars got the girl. Reagan was to be swept in as the girl's fiancé in the last reel. The sequence had been shot but for some reason was later abandoned. Still the new contract star enjoyed meeting O'Brien and Morris, who both became close friends.

At about this time Ronald Reagan began wearing his watch on the inside of his wrist in an old script reader's habit. Timing was everything in his new world and he had to learn exactly how long it took to deliver lines. He was becoming a professional movie actor very quickly, adapting to and adopting as many quirks of the trade as he thought he needed to make the big time. He loved his new life and felt that he had arrived where he was meant to be. But he wanted more. He was not content to be a bit player, who may or may not appear on screen after all the editing and cutting processes had taken place. He was prepared to do whatever it took, but was not always prepared for the details of what that dedication might involve.

Jack Warner though, had very specific ideas about what it took to be a star in glamorous Hollywood. It was not enough to practice the artifices of the actor, wearing a watch the wrong way round to look as if you were a script reader simply wouldn't cut it. To be a star in Warner's eyes involved much more dedication. He liked to see his stars exposed regularly at the beach, and even though Ronald Reagan only had walk on parts for the next few pictures, he was expected to play his role outside of the studio walls too. Reagan knew he could outshine most of the others, Errol Flynn included, at the water's edge. He was designed and built for maximum beach exposure. He was confident he looked the part, in or out of the water.

Reagan was not yet fully settled in Hollywood but he made every effort to carry out Warner's wishes. He had fully recovered from the break-up with Margaret Cleaver and could be seen around all the town hotspots and at the beach with Lana Turner and other young actesses who were also trying to get a toe hold in tinseltown. Try as he might, he was not taken as a serious threat to Flynn, no matter how good looking he might be, or how well he flexed his muscles at Jack Warner's say so. He was generally regarded by the starlets at the studio as a "porch warmer", more gab than grab and no threat to any virgin. "His skin shone with clean health, his eyes with clean thoughts," according to Joy Hodges. He took some of the girls to dinner, but they knew they were safe with him and he exuded none of the overt sexual threat that some of the other male leads did.

The girls sensed this lack of male predatory danger early on, perhaps the producers and directors did too, but Foy rated him highly as an all-action star and he cast him next in a movie where his love of horses might help his career along. After his few brief forays into the A's, Reagan was happy enough to return to Foy's fold in *Sergeant Murphy*, a picture where he had the lead again. Warners made thirty-five Bs a year and Brian (Briney) Foy was known as the "keeper of the Bs". At all times he had eight pictures in production and eight in preparation. He had twenty writers on staff, eight directors and five producers. Whenever Reagan finished a film he rushed straight to Briney and begged to be offered the next, (if he wasn't before a camera for any length of time, Warners had the right to lay him off for up to twelve weeks without pay). Foy recognized him as eager and hard working, reliable and no trouble, "He showed up in the morning…sober!"

*Sergeant Murphy* had originally been bought for James Cagney, but the shrewd star had turned it down after reading the script. But whilst it may have been a simple, mild story about horses, Reagan saw that it would allow him the chance to put to use his knowledge of the United States Cavalry, in which he was still a reserve officer. He also knew he would be seen very much to his advantage on horseback.

Foy had chosen Breezy Reeves Eason to direct the picture, a man renowned for filming horses in action; he had staged and shot the chariot race in the original *Ben Hur* in 1926 and also directed the finale of *The Charge of the Light Brigade* in 1936. *Sergeant Murphy* may not have been in the same epic league as those, but with Eason at the helm, the scenes involving the racehorse of the title were bound to be special, particularly the sequences shot at the Santa Anita Racetrack, which doubled as Aintree in England. Eason was good at action, but he had never learned how to handle dialogue, so the picture had been assigned a dialogue coach, a Warner Bros pensioner with theatrical experience, Frank Beckwith. Beckwith ran the studio acting school and he was soon hard at work with Reagan who took several giant steps forward under his tutelage. He learned to slow down his headlong rush to get his lines out and also picked up a few expressive gestures at the same time.

The story of *Sergeant Murphy* is about a cavalry horse that was trained by a private (played by Reagan) to become a top racehorse who goes on to run in the Grand National. The picture was well made and gave an interesting view of life in 1930s America.

Reagan certainly enjoyed working on the film and said, "We drove up the beautiful Monterey Peninsula, to the 11th Cavalry, where all the outdoor shooting would take place. This was a little more homelike and familiar to me than the sound stage at the studio."

Foy then placed his budding, likeable young star in a set of inconsequential B's such as *Accidents Will Happen*, in which Reagan played an insurance investigator. Up to now nothing had stretched him dramatically, but for this modest picture he did at least have to deepen his characterization. He also worked hard on all his next pictures including *Girls on Probation,* (in which he was useless, and nothing about his performance said "Lawyer" other than the sign painted on his set door), *Boy Meets Girl*, a slightly better B, where he, yet again, plays a radio announcer at a film premier, and in *Cowboy from Brooklyn* he had a minor role as Pat O'Brien's partner. He also came into contact once again with major box office presence, Dick Powell.

Powell had been increasingly unhappy making musicals at Warners and he kept asking for more dramatic material. Instead he had been given *Cowboy From Brooklyn*, which did nothing to further either his, or Reagan's, career. The mildly amusing story was a satire on singing cowboys who were in such vogue at the time.

Initially Reagan struggled for a time on the picture. He was still in awe of Powell and felt his role being drowned out by him and O'Brien. He attempted to play his character as slow and drawling, but his lines kept being cut. Finally one of the other actors took him aside and explained that his slowness was killing the scenes and forcing O'Brien to speak even faster than usual. Reagan was nothing if not a quick and keen learner and from then on he made a point of asking the other actors around how best to do things, "The very next scene called for me to make an entrance in Grand Central Station, face the Press, and, complete with straw hat and cane, do a carnival shrill act introducing our cowboy discovery. Bacon must really have been dying, working out how to rewrite the scene to get rid of slowpoke me." But he now knew how to deliver the lines, and when the director called "Action" he rushed onto the set like a real hustler and launching into his pitch. "There were no more rewrites."

# Chapter Four

## 1938-1940

### Along came Jane and the Glory Years

Studio publicists wanted to pair him off with a young Mid Western girl and decided that twenty one year old Jane Wyman fitted the bill. She was eager to play her part and apparently let out a squeal of delight when she first set eyes on Reagan. She later admitted to being unable to trust or confide in anyone until she met him, "I was drawn to him at once...he was such a sunny person...genuinely and spontaneously nice."

Although she was six years his junior, she was already way ahead of him in experience, both on and off the film set and had first arrived in Hollywood whilst he was still starring in the Dixon North High School football team. Jane already had a couple of husbands in her past to keep quiet about, and unusual memories of being given away by her parents in childhood.

Born Sarah Jane Mayfield in Saint Joseph Missouri, Jan 5th 1917, her father had left home when she was five years old and her desperate mother made what appears to be an unofficial adoption deal with some middle-aged neighbors. Jane became Miss Fulks and when the family moved to Southern California in 1928 she was taken along too. By the age of sixteen Jane was already married to salesman, Ernest Wyman, in a relationship that scarcely saw one year out.

She worked around the lots at Fox and Paramount but eventually won her first contract at Warners on May 6 1936 when she was just nineteen. Around the time of her initial introduction to Reagan, Jane suffered a nervous breakdown, as she was about to embark on a doomed second marriage. She became Mrs. Futterman just as Warners penciled her in for the steamy relationship with Reagan but neither they nor Jane were the sort to let a marriage get in the way. Within three months Mr. Futterman had been lost deep in Hollywood's secret history.

On the official record at least, Reagan and Wyman were said to have met on the set of *Brother Rat* in July 1938. In fact they had discovered their mutual attraction some time before, and if she had been overwhelmed by him, he quietly admired her beauty and apparent frailty.

Reagan had been offered the lead in A-pic *Brother Rat*, which was based on the Broadway hit about three cadets at the Virginia Military Institute. He was down to play the more serious of the group and Eddie Albert and Wayne Morris the other two. Jane Wyman was to be Reagan's love interest. In the movie, as in real life, Jane had eyes only for Reagan and the pair played their roles to touching effect. It was to be the first critical hit for Reagan after making ten pictures in just over a year.

Reagan remembered that his part should have been good enough "to be a stepping stone to stardom" but he agreed unhappily that Eddie Albert "stole all the honors, and deservedly so." Still the picture did well enough for Warners and it advanced Reagan's career and revealed his unexpected flair for light comedy. Until then Foy had determinedly placed him only in action adventure roles because of his obvious athletic ability and physical build. Reagan always remembered his straight man role as a good one, although his was really the weakest in the picture, where Reagan came out simply as "the other guy."

He was good looking, a class of LA art students voted his "the most nearly perfect male body" in Hollywood, but, as his producers had already noted, he gave off nothing of the scent of the predator. When Gable or Errol Flynn entered a room the heat waves shimmered…this was simply never the case with Reagan. The others were not only attractive to women, they were crazy *about* women…Reagan never had been. He *admired* women, but was always drawn to intellect and personality more. He was solid and dependable, and Wyman was quite right to trust him, to be confident around him. Once he made a commitment it was set in stone and he would not let her down.

She was still married and at the time he was willing to downplay his regard for her in public, and Jane is certainly remembered as the intent pursuer in the relationship all through 1938. Whatever he gave back to her in those early days, whilst safe, didn't nearly satisfy her needs. He had no desire to be seen as a marriage wrecker however, and while he waited, he talked. He had left sports behind as his favorite subject and now discussed politics and economics. Wayne Morris, his co-star in *Brother Rat*, nicknamed him "Teacher" on set. Reagan was always wholly impervious to the sarcasm, and anyway, even if neither Morris nor Wyman took much notice, Eddie Albert was a willing listener and participant in the classes.

Jane may not have paid much attention to the things he talked about at such length, but she did understand that he was bright and quick-witted and she encouraged him to enter the political arena himself by joining the Screen Actors Guild, SAG. Although he did join on her recommendation, he was not an aggressive unionist and he felt his own studio was a strict but fair employer, renewing his contract annually without question. He would do nothing to damage that relationship.

Whilst he felt that his performance in *Brother Rat* was only adequate, it was sufficiently liked by the public for Warners to reward him again with a series of up-coming pictures and also a more serious one starring Bette Davis, *Dark Victory*. At first Reagan was honored and again considered that the studio had his best interests at heart. He never complained about the parts he was handed, even those that were patently unsuitable, like the role of the heavy drinker in *Dark Victory*. He had been grateful for the chance but in his autobiography, *Where's the Rest of me?* Reagan said his role in this "Upper crust picture-making" wasn't the rewarding experience he had hoped for. He lays the blame squarely at the door of the director Edmund Goulding, "I actually believe he saw my part as a copy of his own earlier life. I was playing, he told me, the kind of young man who could dearly love Bette but at the same time the kind of fellow who could sit in the girl's dressing room dishing the dirt while they went on dressing in front of me. I had no trouble seeing him in that role, but for myself I want to think that if I stroll through where the girls are short of clothes, there will be a great scurrying about and taking to cover."

*Dark Victory* was so much a Davis picture that it is doubtful whether anyone would have even noticed what Reagan did or didn't do in it. His role would have been difficult for anyone to make important, but his problems with Goulding made the picture one he came to dislike intensely, saying, "It was a minor role and an unhappy experience of trying to fit myself to an interpretation dictated by the director and with which I was in disagreement, and, frankly, unable to really meet what it was he had in mind."

Reagan's inability robbed him of any respect in the Warner casting department and they faulted his, "Lack of what made a big star; no scandal, no color. Nice guys never quite made it."

Nevertheless his old friend Foy had recently bought some reminiscences of retired member of the Treasury Department's Secret Service, William H Moran. He drew up a series of four action adventure pictures based loosely around these and put Reagan into all four as Brass Bancroft; *Secret Service of the Air, Code of the Secret Service, Smashing the Money Ring* and *Murder in the Air.* Reagan commented dryly about his efforts in them, "I was as brave as Errol Flynn, but in a low-budget fashion."

For the first picture, *Secret Service of the Air,* Warners applied higher than usual production values, especially in Ted McCord's excellent aerial photography, and in the use of some fabulous stuntmen. Foy's brother Eddie Jr. was given the continuing role of Bancroft's sidekick, Gabby. John Litel, one of Hollywood's busiest stock actors, got the role of Saxby, Bancroft's boss. The team became a close-knit unit and all the members enjoyed each other's company.

As he shot the spy thrillers Reagan also became increasingly involved with Wyman and his political activity developed at the same time. Unlike the Writers Guild, SAG was a conservative union full of millionaire members; they began to talk about Reagan, they had noticed he stood out as a "bit of a boy scout" who eagerly attended every meeting.

Just as he was about to start shooting the spy thriller, *The Enemy Within,* Louella Parsons, the influential gossip columnist, carried both him and Jane off on a cross-country promotional tour; they were the youngsters she had picked out to promote as the stars of tomorrow. Ronald and Jane had been seeing each other for some time, but once Louella took a hand, both careers and relationships developed at a much faster pace than previously.

Years later Nancy Davis, who became the second Mrs. Reagan, claimed Jane threatened to commit suicide if Reagan didn't hurry up and agree to marry her. She said he would never have married if Jane hadn't swallowed a bottle of pills and been rushed off to hospital. Others refute Nancy's story, saying he was completely crazy about her. In his own words, "Believe it or not, love walked in…and gave me a boost."

Still Jane Wyman was reported to have suffered yet another breakdown and she was definitely hospitalized at about the time their engagement was announced. Whatever the truth, in 1939 Parsons was able to report, "Two of Hollywood's very nicest young people" had fallen in love and got engaged to be married at the end of their personal appearance tour.

It was just Reagan's luck that the most powerful movie columnist in Hollywood, happened to hail from Dixon, and Louella doted on him. She promoted herself as Ronnie and Jane's stage mother and began working with the pair and she also promised to showcase the talents of six other newcomers including Joy Hodges and Susan Hayward in the tour.

It was during this 1939 promotion that Reagan vowed he would never fly again under any circumstances after a plane they were on was caught up in a sever snowstorm, forcing them into a dangerous landing at Chicago. He did not fly again for the next twenty-five years.

Meanwhile throughout America, fans tore at his clothes, stole his socks and screamed his name. He was surprised by the adulation now surrounding him, especially as he seemed to have slid all the way back to B movies, including the useless *Naughty But Nice*. This minor musical abruptly ended Dick Powell's lengthy Warner Brothers career, whilst for Reagan, it was just another small part in his round of studio chores. Career wise he was pretty much stop-go at this time, but he simply kept his head down and did as he was told, and how he felt about it all was never leaked to the public. Still he was much saddened by the loss of his friend Powell around the studio, "I was one of thousands drawn to this very kind man, and who would think of him as a best friend...I cannot recall Dick ever saying an unkind word about anyone."

In 1939 he starred in *Hell's Kitchen*; almost literally. He later remembered the Dead End Kid's picture with shaking trepidation, "It was an experience similar to going over Niagara Falls the hard way-upstream. Counting noses and getting them all in one scene was a major chore... sometimes it was a relief when they did take off and disappear for a few hours. You never knew when a canvas chair would go up in smoke or be blown apart by the giant firecrackers they were never without. Having heard lurid tales from other actors, I approached my first picture with them in something of a sweat."

His difficulties on the picture were partly resolved by a conversation he had mid way through filming with James Cagney, who had not only worked with the kids, but had also been raised in the same New York area that spawned the unruly gang... "Just tell them you'll slap the hell out of them if they do one thing out of line."

*Hell's Kitchen* was one of Warners less successful social crusade pictures, and part of the problem undoubtedly stemmed from the fact that it had two directors, Lewis Seiler and EA Dupont...apparently Seiler found the kids too hard to handle. Still, Reagan managed to emerge from this Bryan Foy adventure fairly unscathed, and he went on to make a second movie with the kids, *Angels Wash Their Faces*.

James Cagney had himself scored a major hit in his career with *Angels With Dirty Faces,* but Reagan's performance in this one was distinctly lackluster and he felt that the picture was purely a vehicle for the Dead End Kids. He was nowhere to be seen, and glad that was the case.

In December 27th 1939 the Parsons tour pulled up in Washington. Reagan found himself in his spiritual home and being pursued by representatives and reporters of Washington's three major newspapers. He was soon deeply engaged with them in a lengthy discussion about the politics of Finland! Jane told them with a sad smile playing across her bored features that much of his general conversation went over her head. She may have felt excluded from the depths of his political dialogues but she was still quick to notice that when they went over to Mount Vernon, he stared for a long time at George Washington's desk. She secretly ordered a replica for him.

Reagan himself was suffering from boredom too…boredom with the pictures he was increasingly being used in at Warners and his next effort; part of the Brass Bancroft series, *Code of the Secret Service,* was frowned upon not only by Reagan, but also by the critics. *Variety* commented it was the kind of far-fetched stuff that Pearl White used to suffer through. Reagan was a little more tongue-in-cheek in his attitude and simply asked director Noel Smith, "When do I fight, and whom?"

After the shooting was completed Foy attempted to shape and edit it into something approaching acceptable fare, but when Reagan saw it he begged the studio not to release it. Warner Bros went ahead anyway and Reagan did his best to avoid seeing it in the theater. However he once noticed it playing in a distant city and he stood outside the theater looking at the stills displayed on the walls. The ticket taker recognized him and said, "You should be ashamed of it." And he was!

The third Secret Service movie, *Smashing the Money Ring*, dealt again with counterfeiting, but Foy ensured it was a better production this time. The title told audiences exactly what to expect, and as long as that was all they expected, the picture proved to be satisfactory. It was a typical crime story of the day, with Reagan as Bancroft once more, assigned to track down a gang of counterfeiters who had been flooding America with fake bank notes. Brass Bancroft has himself thrown into prison were he poses as a counterfeiter himself.

Reagan admitted there was much script doctoring on the set during actual filming, and the actors, director and producer did what they could with the material, but it still had such a low budget that it once again failed to make much impression.

On January 26th 1940 he and Jane were married. He moved into her house in Beverly Drive, Beverly Hills and they later rented an English-style farmhouse at Cordell Drive in the Hollywood Hills. Warner Bros were swift to use the wedding date in their publicity of their next two picture releases, *Brother Rat and a Baby*, which starred the romantic pair, and *Angel from Texas* where they were to be seen together as husband and wife for the first time.

They had married in the Wee Kirk o' Heather in Forest Lawn. Parson's husband gave Jane away. Reagan chose Will Scott, an old friend from Des Moines as his Best Man. Jane was beautiful in a pale blue dress, smocked, quilted and fur trimmed, and borrowed from the studio. The image was perfect.

*Brother Rat and a Baby*, despite the warm success of its predecessor, was only a minor Hollywood comedy and it quickly sank from sight. *An Angel from Texas,* a thin scripted effort about theatrical producers and young stars, whilst amusing, did nothing for Reagan or his new bride. By this time he had all but given up the race to make it big and Warners were only putting him in mild comedies or other lightweight material. But at least they paid his salary and he and Jane could easily afford to live the lifestyle of two glamorous Hollywood stars. But Fate hadn't finished with him, even though he could no longer see his way to the top.

Nine days before his wedding he had been electrified to hear that Warner Bros was going to produce *Knute Rockne, All American,* with Pat O'Brien in the title role. Nowhere did any promotional material indicate who had been chosen to play the doomed Notre Dame halfback, George Gipp, one of the college's greatest football players, who tragically died two weeks after playing his last game. Of course Reagan badly wanted the part and had been talking about the idea ever since first arriving in California, and long before that too. He had offered to write a script that the studio could have for free.

"Warner Brothers had thrown me to the B's. Thanks to some good advice...I played those B's as if they were A's...The boss only goes by results....It wasn't until the part of the Gipp came up that I felt, here is a job I can do.

"It was the first time, during all those four years, that I ever asked for a part. Because you've got to be sure, awful sure, that you can do something better than the guys lined up ahead of you before you ask for anything.

"Quite a few times before Knute Rockne, parts came up in pictures that I thought I'd like to play...but I realized I couldn't top the people they chose...But I knew that I could deliver the Gipp. I knew it because, when I was a kid, George Gipp was my hero, Rockne was my candidate for A Man. In addition, I knew I could play football and they wouldn't have to use a double for me."

It was inconceivable to him that anyone else should be offered the part, and when the executive producer said calmly that he thought Reagan was too skinny, he shot straight back at him, "Would it impress you to know that the Gipper weighed about 5 pounds less than I weigh right now?"

Hal Wallis, head of production, ruled that Reagan could compete with Dennis Morgan and Donald Woods in a field test on February 28th. Eventually after 3 further tests and one that lasted 6 hours, he was finally offered the part. When he had tested he fully expected to try out opposite a minor contract actor, instead, when he arrived on set he found Pat O'Brien fully made up for his part as Rockne and ready to play the few minutes that would determine whether Reagan got the job. The test scene was the one in which Gipp, ordered to carry the ball at his first practice, cocks an eyebrow and asks the coach, "How far?"

He was overwhelmed by O'Brien's generosity and breathless when he was told he would play George Gipp, a character who ran 80 yards against Notre Dame the first time he put on a football jersey and who would go on to be recognized as one of the best footballers of all time. O'Brien said the film would make Reagan a star overnight and the grateful actor himself enthusiastically responded,

"That part opened the door. A few people around the lot knew me by name…and the fans started writing in."

But before he could move onto his dream picture, he had to complete his final Secret Service film, *Murder in the Air,* released in June 1940. Reagan could have looked forward to a diminishing future in the junior leagues, making more Brass Bancroft stories, a B movie star, with occasional minor appearances in A pictures if he hadn't now suddenly, and unexpectedly found himself in the middle of an up-turn. He had pursued his coveted role with fierce determination, and the part of Gipp was one of the only times he ever asked for a specific role and kept pestering until he got what he wanted. Perhaps if he had done more of that his career might have developed faster and gone further than it did.

In preparing the screenplay for *Rockne,* Robert Buckner used the files of Notre Dame and the private papers of Rockne's widow, who would be present throughout the shooting of the movie. Many of the football sequences were shot, from April 11th 1940, at Loyola University.

Apart from his subsequent role in *King's Row*, Reagan's portrayal of Gipp, is probably his best remembered, and it was his personal favorite. Despite only playing a few scenes in the picture, he played them with such conviction that they amply highlighted his particular talents, the Gipper appearing as an extension of his own image. In one scene he was big headed, but not beyond redemption, in the next he was sentimental and in the third he was dead. His big moment came when he urged Coach Rockne to win one for the Gipper, (much of this emotional scene is missing from the movie because of a legal technicality involving the television rights to the original radio script on which the film was based.)

Reagan had been considered a competent player, now suddenly he found himself complimented and most reviewers agreed, he had been the perfect choice for the gifted footballer. He had made the part his own, just as he had known he would.

His career moved up a gear after his performance; he had been working for three years at Warners, and finally he was a name to be reckoned with, "It was the springboard that bounced me into a wider variety of parts. It's true, I got some unmerited criticism from sports writers. One of them wondered why producers never picked real football players for such parts. As I practically earned my way through college playing football, that disturbed me. However that criticism was nicely balanced by some unmerited praise from the same general source, for another sports writer said I was so accurate in my portrayal of Gipp that I even imitated his slight limp. Actually, I wasn't trying to limp. I just wasn't used to my new football shoes and my feet hurt."

He went on that the day after the film's preview, "Before I was out of bed the phone rang. It was a studio call to get into wardrobe for costume fittings right away. As a result of the preview the night before, a new door had been opened. Suddenly there were people on the lot greeting me who hadn't previously acknowledged my existence…"

He had just tasted his first sweet success when war broke out in Europe. Reagan had been well aware of the drift of world events. He was better informed than most screen actors of his day, he was also a young and childless officer in the United States Cavalry Reserve. If America entered the war, he was sure to be one of the first to be called up for service.

Warner Bros moved quickly to put Lieutenant Reagan into military uniform, and any uniform would do at that time. Within twenty-four hours of completing work on *Knute Rockne: All-American* on June 4th, he had been cast as a young General George Armstrong Custer in *Santa Fe Trail,* starring Errol Flynn as JEB Stewart. Reagan says Flynn was an interesting character who stayed away from the studio for four days when he discovered how big Raymond Massey's part in the picture, as John Brown, was going to be. He was also apparently not too keen on having Reagan, fresh from his heady triumph on the football field, as his co-star. Reagan found Flynn difficult to deal with and there were some sticky moments, mainly concerning the superstar's insecurities. Flynn worried constantly about being upstaged and jockeyed all the time to ensure he got the most prominent camera positions, particularly when he was vying with other heroic characters, "Errol was a strange person, terribly unsure of himself and needlessly so. He was a beautiful piece of machinery, likeable and with great charm, and yet convinced he lacked ability as an actor. As a result he was conscious every moment of scenes favoring other actors and their position on the screen in relation to himself. He was apparently unaware of his own striking personality."

He hated the way Flynn attempted to upstage him, he did after all take some pride in his own assets, but the picture once and for all established Reagan's viability in big-budget productions. He acquitted himself well, bringing a relaxed, likeable quality to the invented friendship between JEB Stewart and Custer. His skilled horsemanship was also of value in the making of the film, and Reagan at least enjoyed the equine side of the movie.

Before either *Knute* or *Santa Fe* opened Reagan was already hard at work on *Murder in the Air*, and *Tugboat Annie Sails Again*. It seems to have been a case of striking whilst the iron was hot. The studio was now consistently grooming him as the good-looking All-American boy. They had had a new Reagan picture in the theaters on average once every seven weeks for the last five years and Warner Bros were sure they would soon be loosing him to the war effort, they wanted their money's worth at a time when he was doing so much better for the studio. They were happy to use him for propaganda purposes and, as the hero of a kid-flick, they knew he could subvert US neutrality restraints in place at that time. Adult films could not suggest that the Axis powers were involved in terrorism, but films targeting children could easily be used to teach patriotic children the value of vigilance. Junior Secret Service Club cards were issued in cinemas, signed by "Ronald Reagan, Chief" for children willing to look out for foreign agents.

On October 8th 1940 the launch of the Eagle Squadron was announced. This was the American fighter command squadron formed to fly in combat with the RAF. The cinematic potential of the Squadron was obvious, and Reagan's name was regularly mentioned as a likely lead for any project that Warner Bros undertook. He was climbing the ranks and showed as their top feature player when the studio published its official list at the end of 1940.

The best of the rest of 1940 was a short he made with Wyman, *How to Improve Your Golf*. On the back of his effort that year, he was surprised to find himself not too far behind Cagney and Bogart, and he was being touted to join them very soon following the release of *Knute Rockne* and *Santa Fe*, even though he had not actually been the star of either picture. By early 1941 his name joined theirs on the Hollywood A list.

Reagan and Wyman became proud parents for the first time on January 4th 1941 with the arrival of Maureen Elizabeth. The birth of his daughter was an important event in the A lister's calendar that year, but before long he was preparing for his next role, Pilot Officer Jimmy Grant in *Flight Patrol,* later renamed *International Squadron.* It is impossible not to compare the picture with *A Yank in the RAF*, released two months earlier in June 1941; it is largely the same story of a daring, cocky and wisecracking American who joins the Royal Air Force and belatedly learns to respect the British flyers. But it was not so well made and the difference is largely to do with the miserly budget Warners threw at their version, as usual scrimping to cut production costs.

But this was Reagan's first top-billing in an A movie and he was determined to make the most of his chance. He had to learn to talk and gesticulate like an airman, and his character, Grant, was intriguingly complex. The script was written by Barry Trivers and told the story of a driven man, loose with money and girls. Grant takes advantage of the Hudson delivery program to escape from Los Angeles just ahead of a paternity suit. Doubtful about returning home, he is persuaded to join the RAF volunteer squadron instead.

Down in rural Kent, Grant doesn't change and makes free with other men's girls whilst his recklessness on sorties over France make him heartily disliked at Fighter Command.

Contrite after causing the death of a comrade, he is finally forced to take stock of what he has become. He doesn't like what he sees and decides to take on a dangerous mission. He executes it well but is killed on his way back across the channel. The movie was typical wartime entertainment, and every top star left in Hollywood turned out something similar.

Although it had some fairly good action scenes Reagan played Grant mechanically, his face full of deep frown lines. Perhaps he may be excused. He had been handed a poor script but he paid attention to director Lothar Mendes and was professional to a fault; he showed up on time and was prompt to depart. Mendes worked all the cast and crew hard. Reagan was devastatingly tired after his string of performances where Warner Bros had been determined to get their pound of flesh.

Working on *Flight Patrol,* Reagan must have been uncomfortably hot in his leather flying suit, but he always had the knack of looking cool and unflustered, some would say uncharitably, colorless. Over a six month period from April, he had been on set for three hundred and twenty three and a half hours, shooting up to twelve uncomfortable scenes a day. Production was slow and now taking a heavy toll. *Flight Patrol* was scheduled for release in the fall of 1941 under its new title of *International Squadron.* Reagan called this film a "shaky A", although most film critics referred to the rewrite of the Cagney-O'Brien picture *Ceiling Zero,* as another one of Foy's B's.

Warners had him lined up to play the support lead in their next major picture *Kings Row,* but shooting was postponed again and again. This was to be his twenty seventh picture in forty two months of constant work, hardly conducive to generating a happy marriage, neither was he playing the dedicated father routine with his new baby. The more success he found, the less he was at home. Since *Knute* he had shot a loan-out Western, *The Badman* for MGM, acting against Berry and Lionel Barrymore. He says that in this movie he even had to fight to protect his own close-ups; "Lionel was confined to his wheelchair at the time but he could whip that contrivance around on a dime. It's hard to smile in a scene when your foot has been run over and your shin is bleeding from a hubcap blow."

He had also played a classical pianist in Warner Bros' *Million Dollar Baby,* gone back to MGM for retakes, and then gone straight into preparation for his most demanding role to date. People in the industry had been generally uncertain about whether Reagan would make it as an actor until they saw his work in *King's Row.* Even Warners themselves had become increasingly concerned about his value and they had planned nothing special for him to follow the movie. No matter how far up the rankings he might crawl, he still seemed to lack that special something that the major stars had and he often regressed to his earlier position within the studio hierarchy.

British actor James Stephenson, who Reagan had worked with on *International Squadron*, was due to work as Dr Tower on *Kings Row*, but he died at the age of 53, just after completing *Squadron*. Claude Rains stepped into the part at the last minute.

In the movie Reagan was cast as a small-town rake who has both legs amputated unnecessarily by Charles Coburn after a rail yard accident. The choice of Reagan, Ann Sheridan and Robert Cummings as the leads raised many eyebrows within the industry. All usually played lighter roles, and were not the obvious choices to act in this dark story of sadism, incest, suicide and thwarted love in a small turn-of-the-century American town.

Reagan though, would always remain grateful for the part and says of producer, Sam Wood, that he would have done anything for him and would have said "yes" to any script he offered without even looking at it, "It was a long hard schedule and my first experience, I suppose, with an acting chore that got down inside and kind of wrung me out."

The crucial scene in the picture, where he wakes after the accident to find that both his legs have been amputated was one Reagan dreaded doing. It was intensely dramatic and he knew he had to play it just right. He lost sleep over it and talked at length to doctors, psychiatrists and amputees.

When he arrived on set to shoot the scene he was haggard after a sleepless night and he worried about how to deliver what became one of the most famous lines to come out of Hollywood, "Where's the rest of me?"

When the day arrived he climbed into the dummy bed, with holes in the mattress for his legs to go down, and stared at the empty space. Reagan later said, "Gradually the affair began to terrify me. In some weird way, I felt something horrible had happened to my body. Then gradually I became aware that the crew had assembled, the camera was in position, and the set all lighted. Sam Wood, the director, stood beside me watching me sweat.

"Want to shoot it?" he said in a low voice.

"No rehearsal?" I begged. Somehow I knew this one had to be for real.

"God rest his soul, fine director that he was, he just turned to the crew and said, "Let's make it."

"There were cries of "Lights!" and "Quiet please!" I lay back and closed my eyes, as tense as a fiddlestring. I heard Sam's low voice call, "Action!" there was a sharp *clack* which signaled the beginning of the scene. I opened my eyes dazedly, looked around, slowly let my gaze travel downward. I can't describe even now my feelings as I tried to reach for where my legs should be. "Randy!" I screamed. Ann Sheridan (bless her), burst through the door. She wasn't in the shot, and normally wouldn't have been on hand until we turned the camera around to get her entrance, but she knew it was one of those scenes where a fellow actor needed all the help he could get and at that moment in my mind, she was Randy answering my call. I asked the question-the words that had been haunting me for so many weeks- "Where's the rest of me?"

"There was no retake. It was a good scene and it came out that way in the picture. Perhaps I never did quite as well again in a single shot."

He did the line unimprovably, anguish and panic in his voice; it would have been hard to ask for anything more of him.

If Reagan had any real problems in *King's Row*, they came earlier in the film when he is called upon to appear as a careless womanizer, a man with a fortune. He is supposed to provide a clear contrast to Cummings, the earnest idealistic medical student. At this stage, Drake is not a nice person, and Reagan is visibly uncomfortable playing him, achieving it only by belabored shifting of the eyes and bowing of the head. He does not reveal an actor's relish at playing the nasty character and appears to be uncomfortable about being mistaken for one. Before he loses his legs, Drake loses his inheritance and that brings Reagan back to a plane he understood, back within his own emotional range, back to his comfort zone.

*Kings Row* turned out to be wonderful to look at, thanks to the effort of cinematographer James Wong Howe and production designer William Cameron Menzies, and was central to Reagan's Hollywood success. Above all it gave him what every actor pretending to movie stardom must obtain, a riveting scene and an unforgettable line.

If *Knute Rockne* hadn't made him a star overnight, *King's Row* undoubtedly did, and fans began tracking him for his autograph. There was little peace or tranquility in the Reagan household for sometime after the release of the film. Jane was off doing her own thing, also honing her acting skills. They saw little of each other or of little Maureen either.

On May 18th 1941, Jack Reagan prematurely died of thrombosis at the age of fifty seven. Ronald although traumatized was mainly just plain exhausted, nothing much seemed to sink in. He had been given the last three weeks of May to learn the role of Drake McHugh for *Kings Row* and those weeks turned out to be the only break he got for some time.

He went straight back to work after completing *Kings Row* as reporter in the comedy, *Nine Lives are Not Enough,* (interestingly, this is a film Reagan never mentioned in his own memoirs). He was also still hard at work on retakes for some scenes as Jimmy Grant for the Eagle Squadron picture. He was forced to work as a Pressman in the opening scenes of *Nine Lives* on Tuesdays and as Grant on Mondays.

He still had three years to run on his contract but Lew Wasserman, his agent, negotiated a new one for him. His first had called for $200 a week with increments over seven years to $1,000 a week. The new one, signed in August 1941, began at $1,650 with increments up to $5,000. No matter how tired he was, Jack Warner was determined to get the most out of him, at the price he was now costing. Reagan was rushed straight into *Juke Girl.*

The story about itinerant fruit pickers was set in steamy Florida but was shot in the winter in the California farmlands in temperatures which sometimes dipped close to freezing. Reagan recalls the filming was very uncomfortable and unsanitary. The script called for plenty of night exterior shots, forcing the actors to smoke to disguise the vaporized breath in the cold night air. Glycerin was constantly sprayed on their faces to simulate sweat. The cold and damp combined to make this the low point to date in all Reagan's years at Warners; his biggest problem being one of utter exhaustion. He recalled that this picture would have been a "Back-breaker" even if he had had any rest before embarking on it, but it came directly on top of long months of difficult work and harrowing scenes, "I discovered how nervous fatigue can creep up on you. On the night shift, going to work at 6.00pm, we shot exteriors until sunup for thirty eight nights. With all the misconceptions about pampered stars, none is so far afield as the belief that physical discomfort isn't tolerated."

The high point of the picture was his first big on-screen kiss, the first where he projected character as well as enthusiasm. He clasped Ann Sheridan's hands in his right one and pulled her powerfully toward him with his left. He kissed her forcefully.

Then he was sent straight back out to work on his next picture *Desperate Journey*, which once more starred the prickly Errol Flynn. Reagan had been offered a choice of film and he unwisely picked to co-star again with Flynn. He was once again doomed to play "the other guy." He didn't enjoy the experience and even when it was first released in August 1942, Reagan recognized that the preposterous war picture had been a poor selection, although he felt he had personally performed quietly within his range.

By this time Reagan had been enough of a star to have earned co-billing with Flynn. However that privileged top listing involved having to fight for his place on screen. Flynn didn't mind co-billing with a heroine and he hadn't been too threatened by a newcomer from the Bs, but he was loath to share an inch with another hero. And in spite of Flynn's best efforts and Walsh's fine ability as a director, the picture was impossible to take seriously. It was a big disappointment to all involved when it could have, and should have, been so good.

By the time *Kings Row* was finally released in April 1942, Reagan had been whisked off into the army and he was unable to make the most of his favorable reviews, most of which agreed that the film was a masterpiece and his performance in it, a turning point. He should have been enjoying the lavish praise and being given serious consideration for the next big parts up for grabs. He was no longer "Mr. Norm". Life was moving swiftly for him, but for the seriously hardworking and uncomplaining star, things were about to alter for ever.

When war was declared Reagan's first move had been to call his agent Lew Wasserman for advise. Lew hung up on him. Pearl Harbor couldn't have come at a worse moment for any of them. He was an officer in the US Cavalry Reserve, his time had come to serve and Lew could do nothing to help him out, even though Jack Warner was so loath to let his new star go. He was getting almost as much fan mail as Flynn himself and he was now a valuable commodity in Hollywood, but as it turned out it would be more than four years before he could resume his screen career in any meaningful way.

His poor vision, rated 7/200, made him almost legally blind and disqualified him from active duty. In 1933 he had unsuccessfully tried the first contact lenses which covered the entire eye and had to be pulled out again by suction cups. He found them too difficult to use and he was therefore not destined to be sent to any of the foreign battle fronts.

Jack Warner came up with the idea of using Reagan as a one man propaganda department to stimulate recruitment through his movies, but was disappointed when Reagan's disqualification from active duty didn't stop the United States Cavalry Reserve calling him anyway to serve as a liaison officer. His contract at the studio was immediately frozen and Reagan was the first Hollywood actor with a child to be called up. Jane Wyman was not best pleased by the financial blow that suspension of his Warner contract meant, although she assured Louella Parsons, that there was no strain on their marriage, "Don't think for a moment that Ronnie isn't still the head of his own house."

Reagan himself admitted at the time that it was difficult for him as his career had only just taken off with *Kings Row*.

Always happy to do the ground work

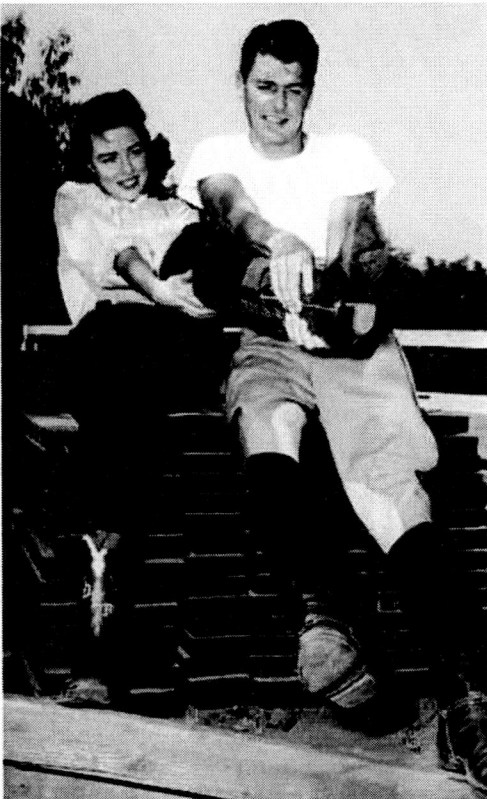

Reagan marries Jane Wyman
January 26th 1940

Happy families: Nelle checks her son's
uniform and the Reagan's at home

Reagan goes to war

# Chapter Five

## 1941-1945

### The Star goes to War

Still, his commission didn't take him away for long and after initial training in Fort De Moines, Iowa, he was back in sunny California. Lieutenant Reagan was appointed Personnel Officer and ordered to serve with the First Motion Picture Unit of the US Army Air Forces, which had its headquarters at "Fort Roach", cynical nickname given during the war to the Hal Roach studio in Culver City. And what personnel he had serving alongside him, including Clark Gable, his best friend William Holden, Alan Ladd and George Montgomery, and his pick of the best studio technicians. He became a Hollywood dormitory serviceman, but might as well have stayed at home.

Uncle Sam soon found suitable work for him and he was back making movies, a celluloid soldier resplendent in full uniform, in no time, crowding the horizon in various training projects including *Recognition of the Japanese Zero Fighter*, shot in 1943. This was a top priority project spurred by an alarming number of friendly fire downings of p-40s in the Pacific. *Zero* was recognized as a flawless picture, a pioneering example of training film as art.

After he made it, Warner Bros considered their boy to be too well known to be used in this way and he was not permitted to star in any more training films; only B actors were used thereafter. But hundreds of films were turned out from Fort Roach and on occasion the serving stars were loaned back to Warners to work on big budget productions.

February 23rd 1943 saw Reagan temporarily detached from duty to begin work on the propaganda musical, *This is The Army,* a joint patriotic venture between Warner Bros and the War Department.

Reagan played straight man stage manager and show host to a vast troupe of soldier performers. He was also the movie's only romantic interest, trying to evade Joan Leslie's advances on the ground that it was irresponsible to marry while there was a war on. *This is The Army* had already been a successful stage show written by Irving Berlin and profit from the movie was slated for the Army Emergency Relief Fund. Reagan was introduced a number of times during the making of the picture to Berlin. At one point Berlin sought Reagan out to compliment him on a sequence he had just watched him perform and he had offered him some critical advice. Berlin ended the conversation by saying, "You really should give this business some consideration when the war is over. You could have a career in showbusiness."

Reagan thanked him politely but the conversation triggered a nagging worry that refused to leave him and forced him to rethink his career to date. Was it simply that Berlin had not seen any of his previous movies, or had the war already been on long enough that people in the business were already forgetting *Knute Rockne* and *King's Row.* Could it be over so soon? Ronald who? Has-been film stars were two-a-penny in Hollywood, and the fading arc lights were just one of the many hazards that all movie actors had to contend with, no matter how brightly they shone at times. He had no time to worry about it then and the instant he was no longer required for shooting he was back in uniform.

And perhaps Reagan was changing as a man too. World War could leave no one completely untouched, and there was no man or woman in the Western world unconcerned about what their life would be like when it was all over. Some of Reagan's pre-war films had been worthy contenders and it was certainly possible to see a pattern of development in them. The beginnings of the blossoming talent which held out much hope for his future, particularly if he could learn to get "wrung out" more often in his portrayals, if he could begin to immerse himself in his characterizations, as he had done so successfully in *King's Row*.

But his conversation with Berlin, the doubts that it had raised, led to a re-evaluation of his own desires for the future. He didn't want things to simply carry on after the war in the way they had been going before. He had always taken his politics seriously and now people around him began to notice that he had become an obsessional supporter of Roosevelt and that he and the conservative actor, George Murphy, were having plenty of heated lunchtime arguments. Alan Hale complained, "If that son of a bitch doesn't stop making speeches, he'll end up in the White House." Reagan was just thirty-two. He had already been recruited into the Hollywood Democratic Committee, a radical pro-FDR activist group, organized, but not controlled by a group of Communists. They aimed to preserve a pro-Stalinist government in Washington rather than subverting movie production in California.

Reagan's personal characteristics underwent a dramatic alteration, both physically and emotionally, when he was promoted to the rank of Captain. He put on weight in both areas and the boyishly good-looking star suddenly became more manly. When attending Press showings of Army Air Forces propaganda films he now often got up before the film was screened to give the official "talk". He did it well and WH Mooring writing in *Picturegoer* said in 1947 that he did it so well, "I began to see him in the role of a politician."

As Post Adjutant, processing classified orders, he became the best-informed officer at Fort Roach, wielding an influence far above his rank. At this time he also became oddly querulous and fiercely sensitive about any form of discrimination, particularly anti-Semitism, like his father had been before him. When he resigned from Lakeside Country Club because they refused to accept Jews there, he was asked if his Father's anti-discriminatory ghost had called him into action, he replied, "It just seemed the right thing to do."

If he had been having doubts about his ability to remain in the movie business after the war he was gratified to find *This is the Army* was wildly successful, becoming the only genuine box office blockbuster of his career. Following swiftly on the heels of his success of *Kings Row*, Reagan suddenly found himself swept, on the back of it, to the top Hollywood box-office spot, rating higher for a few months in 1943 than James Cagney! That was a mighty achievement for a man who had found professional insecurity setting in just as he began to feel his way to the top. Maybe that is the film star's curse; only as they approach the top do they endure the emotional roller-coaster effect.

As it proved, Reagan had indeed already peaked as an actor. The doubts roared back into his life all too quickly, he began to suffer loss of identity as he was forced into the ordinary light of day with unscripted dialogue. Eddie Albert, a close friend of Reagan, believed it was more that he suffered from not going to war and from a sense of related humiliation. Still, he was doing his best for the war effort at home and carried out his duties efficiently, strictly observing every rule.

On March 18th, 1945 he and his wife announced that they were adopting a baby boy, Michael Edward Reagan.

In the same year the combat-camera unit of the First Motion Picture Unit entered Ohrdruf and Buchenwald just ahead of Eisenhower's advance. The raw color footage they took of the atrocities was rushed back to Fort Roach for editing before being sent on to the Pentagon. Reagan arranged a preview of it for cleared personnel. As he sat watching from the projection room, the images he witnessed carried him to Hell. He became strangely silent and withdrawn. The emotions he felt that day became the foundation of the man he was growing into, the man he would become in his not very distant future, they also reinforced his unwavering rejection of anti-Semitism.

Eventually the film was put together into a production called *Lest we Forget*. Reagan made each of his children sit through it when they reached the age of fourteen, it became a difficult rite of passage for them all.

When the war ended in 1945, Reagan returned to Warner Bros a better physical property, in superb condition and raring to do business. He was a much more mature and rounded person who had become more of a leader. This should have opened up extra avenues for him script wise. He no longer needed to be restricted to light comedy or action adventure, and he had already begun to show that perhaps he could act a bit too. He had done all his deepest thinking at Fort Roach, weighed up the pros and cons sitting at his army desk, he had deliberated at length about the way he wanted his career to develop. He believed he could combine his long-standing interest in sitting on committees with the new one of representing his fellow actors interests; he believed his political aspirations perfectly fitted his film career. He returned to the Warner studios full of hope, ever the optimist. The doubts that had assailed him during the latter war years were swept under the carpet of his own strong self-belief. He asked brightly for the next script and turned up to as many SAG meetings as he could fit in.

Jack Warner was genuinely pleased to have the easy-going, easy-to-work-with, actor back in the Hollywood fold. Neither he nor Reagan noticed any potential problem in the fact that the other megastars were also on their way home from all over the world, eager to do business, eager to resurrect their own suspended careers.

After his brief return to the studio Reagan confidently headed up to Lake Arrowhead, where Jane was shooting *The Yearling*. He had secured a generous new Warner Bros contract, guaranteeing him $150,000 annually for the next seven years. Jack Warner advised him to relax until he had found a good property for him. Despite the fact that he was one of the stars who never left America's shores Reagan felt he had earned the break and he planned to enjoy some time with his wife and children. He had no worries for the future as he awaited his next script. Later he laughed, "I was the calm vacant center of the hurricane."

And there was a hurricane boiling up in American society in those autumn months of 1945. At first a vague sense of gloom descended over the country, replacing the euphoria that winning the struggle had brought. The armed forces flooded back home in their hundreds of thousands only to find that there were few jobs available for them. The unions became increasingly agitated.

Even Reagan admitted that he gradually became bored, frustrated and equally restless. Jack Warner had told him to take things easy, but there was only so much resting it was possible to do, and he realized the studio was also beginning to promote younger talent ahead of him; even his wife was making unmistakable signs of moving ahead professionally whilst he suddenly and unexpectedly stagnated up at the lake. Warners had loaned Jane out for the major part in *The Yearling*, a Technicolor extravaganza.

When he got up to Lake Arrowhead Reagan said that she appeared tired and washed out, a woman nursing a secret grief, "Jane would come through the door, thinking about her part, and not even notice I was in the room.

"All I wanted to do was to rest up awhile, make love to my wife, and come up refreshed to a better job in an ideal world. As it came out, I was disappointed in all these postwar ambitions."

He was not alone in the disappointment.

Like so many others, he acknowledged a real lack of direction, professionally, emotionally or politically. He still considered himself to be liberal and had been expressing this through the Rooseveltian organization, the American Veterans Committee. Before leaving Fort Roach to go on his prolonged vacation, he had signed up as chairman of the AVC's Hollywood membership board. Reagan liked the fact that the group seemed not dwell on the past, but rather focused on moving forward. Gilbert A. Harrison, retired editor of The New Republic and the AVC's founder said that he was "impressed with Reagan." He had asked careful, probing questions before joining up, and after much thought, decided to give his support. Harrison said, "It was as if *he* were recruiting *me*."

As ever with Ronald Reagan, once support was given, it was total. He liked the idea of expanding the Committee into an international lobby under the aegis of the United Nations, working to contain the A-bomb. Eisenhower signed on to the idea along with film stars like Audie Murphy. Reagan himself was personally responsible for at least 200 new members joining up.

# Chapter Six

## 1945-1955

### Unions, Strikes and Political Unrest

Trouble simmered at the Warner Bros studio when the set decorators voted to go on strike. Union boss, Herbert K Sorrell, rumored to be a Communist, had called his men to act against all the major studios in defiance of wartime regulations. His own position had been strengthened after he managed to affiliate the decorators and cartoonists with his own painters' union to form the Conference of Studio Unions. He had become President of an association so strong that it posed an enormous threat to all the other craft unions in the movie business and they were in danger of being swallowed up. All sides were spoiling for a fight but the CSU decided to pick out one studio and "hammer it good." Warner Bros, the biggest motion production center in the world, was the studio chosen for destruction. Hollywood's post-war power structure was at stake and all the studio bosses looked at the escalation of events and believed that if the stage hands and decorators got away with attacking Warner Bros, the other unions would also start stirring up trouble at the smaller set ups. Hollywood's long accepted management system of practice would collapse leading to a free-for-all in the movie business.

In October 1945 mass violence erupted. Cars were overturned and used as barricades as members of CSU attempted to gain entry to Warner Bros and thousands of rival unionists faced off outside the studio gates. Production was halted and the threat of disaster hung heavy in the air, but with classic genius for avoiding the fray, Ronald Reagan remained at Lake Arrowhead throughout the 19 days of violence that followed Burbank's Black Friday.

Reagan was later defensive about his tardy reaction, "What I heard and read in the papers placed me on the side of the strikers. I was then, and continue to be, a strong believer in the rights of unions, as well as the rights of individuals…the strike is an unalienable weapon of any citizen. I knew little and cared less about the rumors about Communists."

In 1945 he thought there were more immediate threats to America's stability than the craft unions-even if Communists controlled them; Reagan was more interested in fighting those, **"The results of my weeks of freedom crystallized a determination in my mind. I would work with the tools I had: my thoughts, my speaking abilities, my reputation as an actor. I would try to bring about the regeneration of the world."**

He saw the world faced problems that the New Deal largely ignored, and he believed chief amongst these were neo-fascism and racial prejudice. In his mind screen acting paled and took on less significance. He had sat back waiting for developments but once stirred into action he began joining liberal organizations such as the Hollywood Democratic Committee. His life took a major predestined swerve immediately after the war ended, and from Black Friday on, things would never be the same again.

At first he stuck to the back room but on December 8th 1945 he appeared at the Santa Ana Municipal Bowl and made a short speech for "United America Day." He said, "The blood that has soaked into the sands of the beaches is all one color. America stands unique in the world- a country founded not on race, but on a way and an ideal. Not in spite of, but because of our polyglot background, we have had all the strength in the world. That is the American way."

Those four sentences launched his political career and forged the articulator of public hurt. He undoubtedly never surpassed them in sincerity.

He sensed the new direction but he still had a young family to raise and a mortgage to pay. He needed to work and he couldn't afford to play at politics. In January 1946 just as Jane wrapped *The Yearling*, Warner Bros informed Reagan that *Stallion Road*, the "good property" that had finally been found for him, was being downgraded to black and white and that production would be delayed until the spring. He already understood that *Stallion Road* wasn't going to be much to look forward to, being the lame story of a horse doctor dying of anthrax.

He saw clearly that he faced exactly the same problem that many returning soldiers were coping with and understood that he had to remind people who he was! What he was. In his case though it was not simply a matter of finding employment. He had to let everyone know he had been a star. The public had changed during the war, so had the movie industry. The filmgoer was more discerning and their expectations were higher. Films were no longer just being ground out. Reagan was now due only two pictures a year…that meant they had to be good ones. He had waited patiently for months for something and when he had first been offered *Stallion Road* he had liked the sound of working on location in ranching country. It had originally been planned as a vehicle for Bogart and Bacall but when they turned it down the budget was cut and all costs scaled down accordingly. It seemed he didn't rate quite as highly in Jack Warner's plans as he had assumed when he was packed off to Lake Arrowhead.

Still, he was mildly pleased when he saw the end product, which provided a good starting point for his future. It had some spectacular shots of horses racing through lush California country. Reagan had enjoyed getting back into the horsy life and he had done all his own riding and jumping in the picture and hired a former Italian cavalry officer, Nino Pepitone, as his coach. This was the start of a long friendship and partnership. Pepitone helped Reagan set up his own horse ranches, first in the Northridge section of the San Fernando Valley and later high in the rugged Malibu Hills.

Shooting the film took 109 days, an unusually long time for a motion picture of that era, but even after extensive editing, it was still not ready for release until March-April 1947. When it did eventually hit the theaters it was a very luke warm affair and it was obvious that Reagan had not been challenged sufficiently to move beyond his usual range, although what he had done, he had done well. The critics agreed, he was likeable in a second rate feature that was alright as a comeback movie.

The long delay in the film's public release gave him more time to save the world. Action seemed more pressing now than ever before as the unemployment lines lengthened across the country. Strikes paralyzed General Motors, General Electric and Big Steel and camps for the homeless were set up on the lawns of UCLA. Reagan wrote an article for AVC Bulletin saying that "native fascism" could cause the fall of democracy, "I think the AVC can be a key organization in the preservation of democracy for which 300,000 Americans died, and because I have attacked the extreme right does not mean I am ignorant of the menace of the complete left."

Reagan fully endorsed the AVC's liberal draft constitution. It called among other things for peaceful coexistence with the Soviet Union, cessation of American nuclear power to the United Nations, full employment and a minimum wage, comprehensive national health and education programs, protection of strikers from compulsory arbitration, abolition of all discriminatory legislation, minority rights to have the facility to sue for slander and federal enforcement of civil liberties.

On February he allowed his name to appear in the Communist *People's Daily World* in an article calling for the liberation of British and Dutch Indonesia. People around Hollywood began to take note of his affiliations and apparent leanings; a "file" was assembled on his activity.

But Reagan was far from turning toward Communism as a solution to the problems the world faced; he was dreaming liberal dreams and failed to see any Communist conspiracy afoot. Not until April 26th when he attended the AVC's state convention in LA did he notice with amazement a well-organized group of Communists were indeed manipulating the entire proceedings, Reagan said, "I will defend to the death the right of Communists or anyone else to belong to the AVC but…I think we will add strength to the entire liberal cause if we publicly re-affirm our belief in our present *form* of government and our belief that our present *ills* can be cured within the framework of democracy."

He confessed he did not like to be identified with the AVC's most radical chapter, but felt that he could not, responsibly, resign from the group which he still felt represented everything that was good about free speech. He was prepared to carry the consequences of his association but admitted, "I am still being called a Red in certain Hollywood circles."

He was well aware that his liberalism could be a liability as he tried to resurrect his floundering acting career, but he tried to remain loyal to the Hollywood chapter of the AVC. He was being naïve and by June 14th, when the National Convention of the AVC was held, he conceded with some disappointment that the Los Angeles area council was under Communist control. He had been urged by other members to attend the convention as a moderating influence, but perhaps fortunately, *Stallion Road's* schedule prevented him from going. Once again he successfully navigated his way through a potentially sticky situation.

The convention, without Reagan to lend his calm authority, ended in defeat for the Communists, but destroyed the AVC's solidarity. Still the whole sordid experience further stoked Reagan's smoldering political senses.

Warner's had been impressed enough with his effort in *Stallion Road* to give him the lead in their next expensive production, *The Voice of the Turtle,* a script Jack Warner had bought with him in mind. Reagan, distracted by more serious matters, almost turned the picture down because he wanted to work on *Treasure of the Sierra Madre* instead. Warner told him it was *Turtle* or nothing, and it turned out to be one of the best comedies he ever made. He gave a good account of himself, and something about the war had matured Reagan. His voice had taken on a fuller range and an ability at last to drift into the romantic. When he stood in the bathroom considering

Eleanor Parker's lingerie in the picture, he showed genuine erotic interest. He came out of the movie smiling.

On June 2nd 1946 he attended a meeting of the Hollywood Independent Citizens Committee of the Arts, Sciences and Professions, (HICCASP). He took the group seriously but even here he found there was profound argument between Communists and non-Communist members. Many of those who condemned the Communist section, including Olivia de Havilland, resigned from the group but Reagan remained a member until October 1946, in what Miss de Havilland refers to as the "role of an observer."

However, when, on July 4th 1960, Reagan angrily wrote to Hugh Hefner about his decision to allow blacklisted Dalton Trumbo to write for *Playboy,* his full disillusionment about the way he had interpreted the events of the forties could be seen clearly, "I question whether I can write in a way that will make sense to you...because so much doubt has been cast on "anti-communists", inspired by the radicalism of extremists who saw "reds" under every "cause", I feel I should reveal where I have stood and now stand.

"Following World War 2 my interest in liberalism and my fear of "neo-fascism" led to my serving on the board of directors of an organization later exposed as a "Communist Front," namely the "Hollywood Independent Citizens Comm. Of the Arts, Sciences and Professions." Incidentally, Mr Trumbo was also on that board, with John Howard Lawson and a number of others who have since attained some fame for their refusal to answer questions...

"How can I put down in less than book form the countless hours of meetings, the honest attempts at compromise, the trying to meet dishonesty, lies and cheating with conduct bound by rules of fair play? How can I make you understand that my feeling now is not prejudice born of this struggle but is realization supported by incontrovertible evidence that the American communist is in truth a member of a "Russian American Bund" owing his first allegiance to a foreign power?

"I, like you, will defend the right of any American to openly practice & preach any political philosophy from monarchy to anarchy. But this is not the case with regard to the communist. He is bound by party discipline to deny that he is a communist so that he can by subversion and stealth impose on an unwilling people the rule of the International Communist Party, which is in fact the govt. of Soviet Russia. I say to you that any man still or now a member of the "party" was a man who looked upon the death of American soldiers in Korea as a victory for his side. For proof of this I refer you to some of the ex-communists who fled the party at that time and for that reason, including some of Mr Trumbo's companions of the "Unfriendly 10".

Reagan had been personally tolerant to a fault, finding it difficult to dislike anybody (possibly because he had no deep interest in any individual) and he had been as politically lenient as one man could be. Then things took an ugly turn for the worse in Reagan's Hollywood and the labor situation broke down further.

Meanwhile, as he took to lecturing everybody and anybody about the increasingly difficult problems the nation in general and Hollywood in particular, faced, Jane Wyman commented dryly at a party, "I'm so bored with him, I'll either kill him or kill myself." The great romance was over.

He reduced everything he talked about to its simplest essence, but what Hollywood was now confronting was far from clear-cut, the ever shifting committee structures and power struggles, the dangerous undercurrents made for a highly complex melting pot. Still, he recognized that the entire movie industry was being plunged into mortal combat. His own stance firmed up and he set about persuading members of the Screen Actors Guild to cross the picket lines. At the same time he also tried to use his charm and talk the CSU out of striking.

Shortly after his attempts to smooth things over he received the threatening message that someone was going to "to fix his face". His dubious war record was suddenly picked up and viciously attacked in the *Hollywood Reporter*.

He began carrying a loaded .32 Smith and Wesson, licensed to him by the studio police, and although there had been a variety of factors coming together in those prickly and uncomfortable months of 1946 to turn the normally mild mannered Ronald Reagan into a vitriolic anti-communist, in that instant he swung radically from political left to the right.

He finally emerged from his political chrysalis, and on October 30th 1946 delivered a keynote address at an emergency mass meeting of SAG in Hollywood Legion Stadium. There were 3000 actors present, including all the major stars from Dietrich and Sinatra to Bogart and Bergman. He was talking about things he had only just begun to understand himself. Still he had carefully prepared his own speech after studying the history of Hollywood labor reform back to 1913. He intended to prove that SAG had never involved itself in craft-union disputes, and should not in the future.

When the meeting was adjourned Robert Stack commented to Reagan that he should go on and do something for the country. Reagan laughed and agreed, "When I run for President, you can vote for me." Certainly nobody present at that meeting was left in the least doubt that here was the actor who would eventually take charge of their Guild, the man who would be steering them through the most difficult times that Hollywood had ever faced. It was also the time that he began to enjoy politics more than acting.

Reagan's speech was resoundingly successful and the SAG membership voted to remain neutral through the labor disputes. He had told his fellow actors that they only had to ignore the CSU to break it. Reagan commented, careful to hide the lingering aggression he felt toward the craft union after the personal threats that had been made, "The CSU dissolved like sugar in hot water."

By December 19th 1946 he'd all-but finished with stardom as he began dedicating himself to politics. He was elected President of the Guild on March 10th 1947. In the subsequent era of the blacklist, not only did he co-operate in the purging of suspected communists but he also served as an undercover FBI informant, he later said angrily, "I discovered it first hand-the cynicism, the brutality, the complete lack of morality in their positions, and the cold-bloodedness of their attempt, at any cost, to gain control of that industry."

He felt, with some justification, that his political activity harmed his film career and after working on almost fifty pictures, he was now receiving no offers from any studio. He had plenty of other things to distract him although, before it had properly started, his new career seemed to be over when, on June 17th 1947 he once again, as in childhood, contracted a rare and acute form of viral pneumonia.

Jane Wyman rang the studio to tell them on that morning that he was running a fever and was unable to report for work on the movie, *That Hagen Girl*, which co starred Shirley Temple in her first adult movie. Her husband had already tried to turn the picture down; the script had been re-written five times, and Reagan felt it should have been six. In most of the footage he plays a man trying to convince Temple that she is not his illegitimate daughter. *That Hagen Girl* had been his first work since completing *Stallion Road* months before. It turned out to be one of his least favorite films, mostly because he couldn't identify with a man in love with a girl half his age. He was also certain it would do nothing to bolster his flagging career; any good he had done himself with *Stallion Road* would be wiped out with this ugly picture.

The movie did even less for Shirley Temple who, like Reagan, had done her best to be released from the contract. In Reagan's case he had already rejected several scripts and was not in a position to refuse another, although he did at least manage to have his most embarrassing line cut from the final release. He had objected that his character's declaration of love to the young girl was absurd, and had been proven right at a sneak preview, "Came the moment on the screen when I said to Shirley, "I love you" and the entire audience cried, en masse, "Oh No". I sat huddled in the darkness until I was certain the lobby was empty. You couldn't have got me to face that audience for a million bucks."

The Warner boss might have been forgiven for thinking, when he received the phone call from Jane Wyman, that the star was doing everything he could to get out of working on it, but in fact his life was threatened when the doctors found that no drugs or treatment aided his breathing. He became so exhausted that when he told a nurse that he couldn't breath, she had to coax him to inhale and exhale. Meanwhile, Wyman, 6 months pregnant and unwell herself, stayed by his bed, mopping his brow and doing her duty. He did not fully recover until well into 1948.

On June 26th 1947 at 11.26 am Jane gave premature birth to a baby girl who died at 8.45pm that same night. Reagan, weak with illness and seventeen pounds lighter than normal, and Wyman, devastated, inconsolable by her loss, cremated Christine Reagan 6 days later. Neither husband nor wife spoke to each other at the funeral nor for some time afterwards.

Reagan went back to work on the film he had come to despise and spent his spare time at SAG headquarters. He found solace from tragedy there in work which fascinated him. He also enjoyed the camaraderie of William Holden, Gene Kelly and others. He exulted in being head of Hollywood's major trade association at the time when improving labor relations was almost as important to national security as the country's foreign policy. He was almost perpetually absent from home. The sadness within those walls was too much for him and he simply refused to dwell there.

The relationship between Reagan and Wyman deteriorated still further and she felt he had become too grand, too political. Increasingly they began to go their separate ways. They quarreled more; it had been bad enough when he just bored her by reading the paper aloud at breakfast, now she was at her wits end. When she had been absolutely grief stricken by the loss of Christine he had done exactly as so many other men do in times of domestic crisis, staying away for long periods. When he was home she found him almost unbearable. She made the decision that set the inevitable wheels of divorce in motion when, for her own sanity she began rehearsing her next part as the deaf Mexican girl in *Johnny Belinda*. She wore earplugs, not to shut her husband's interminable droning out, but to allow her to concentrate on the sounds her own breathing made. Reagan worried about her mental state, without registering that she was simply trying to get inside her characterization, that here was an actress moving way beyond him, already lost in the role she was to play. He did notice her attraction for her co-star, Lew Ayres, although professionally at least, he was more hurt when people began mentioning his wife's name in connection with Oscar nominations and laughing at his own latest movie. When he told teenager Shirley Temple that he loved her, he had been made to look like a fool, and meanwhile his wife strode on, beginning her own recovery in spectacular and splendid style.

On October 23rd 1947 he gave evidence at a packed HUAC hearing room in Washington, "There has been a small group within the Screen Actors Guild which has consistently opposed the policy of the Guild Board and the officers of the Guild. That small clique referred has been suspected of more or less following the tactics that we associate with the Communist Party." Reagan was asked if he knew himself whether any of the clique were members of the Communist Party.

"No, sir...I do not know," but he pointed out, "As a citizen I would hesitate...to see any political party outlawed on the basis of its political ideology. We have spent a hundred and seventy years in this country on the basis that democracy is strong enough to stand up and fight against the inroads of any ideology…

"I detest, I abhor their philosophy, but I detest more than that their tactics…which are dishonest. But at the same time, I never, as a citizen, want to see our country become urged, by either fear or resentment of this group, to compromise with any of our democratic principles… I still think that democracy can do it."

He was due to star opposite his wife in the Warner movie *John Loves Mary* until the shocking headline hit the papers, "Jane Wyman, Ronald Reagan in rift." Wyman, completely disenchanted with her husband's involvement in the heavy politics of the day, had been heard commenting angrily, "If he's gonna be President, he's gonna do it without me." It was big news to the public perhaps, but no Hollywood insider was left reeling, either by the headline or Wyman's outburst.

Although Reagan later made the movie without her, and she moved up into bigger properties, he had certainly not seen the split coming in spite of all their recent problems. He was devastated at the turn of events and, ever the optimist, he thought the damage could be fixed and he began rehearsing what he was going to say to the Press, "I love Jane, and I know she loves me. I don't know what all this is about, and I don't know why Jane has done it. For my part, I hope to live with her for the rest of my life."

Unfortunately she went round town very vocally complaining that apart from everything else, he bored her in bed. Such comments were hardly going to mend a fractured marriage and they would certainly do nothing to help his ailing film career. He had been working on the high profile Warner Brothers movie, *The Voice of the Turtle,* John van Druten's play which had already been a huge Broadway hit. When Warner's bought the rights to the play they also hired Van Druten to write the screenplay and he skillfully padded out the three scene play, broadening it and adding a variety of new characters, whilst leaving the main storyline unchanged.

Hiring Van Druten had been a masterstroke by Warners and even though the hit New York play was still going strong when the film was released, those who had said the sophisticated play could not work on the screen were proved wrong. However the film did meet some sharp criticism; perhaps not on account of Reagan's performance so much as for its theme. In the film Reagan picks up a young girl of doubtful morals. She had been influenced by an easy-going gold digger who advised her, "Take what you want when you want it, if you can make it worth your while."

Ronald Reagan played the young soldier involved well, one reviewer commented, "No one could ever say he was anything but a clean-looking, straight-from-the-shoulder sort of proposition anyway, and that is all Warners needed in order to keep *The Voice of the Turtle* on the right track."

Anyone confusing his next role in *John Loves Mary* with *The Voice of the Turtle*, could be excused. Norman Krasna's play, best described as a romantic farce, had opened on Broadway, with William Prince as John and Nina Foch as Mary and it had been an immediate success. Again the show was still running when Warners began filming their version in 1948. Reagan was once more put in the uniform of a United States Army sergeant, but this time he played a returning veteran, not a soldier on furlough.

The star had questioned Warners about the film, "It was great for a couple of years on Broadway but wasn't the "returning serviceman" theme a little old hat by the time we brought it to the screen? It was."

Still Reagan was in a weak bargaining position at the studio and what he said now held little clout on the lot, after all he had had no big hits since the war ended. The producers had initially chosen the script to introduce Patricia Neal to the screen and she was selected to replace Jane Wyman in the picture that was to be directed by David Butler, a veteran of movie light comedy.

Like so many Reagan offerings before it, the movie was generally liked, but was not the huge hit Warners had been hoping for and the writer

Krasna admitted the play was based on a single joke, which had worked well in the theatre, but was far too thin as a film plot.

No longer the dedicated liberal, throughout the twelve months of 1948, Reagan became the most prominent anti-Communist in town, serving on many boards and finally considered strong enough to follow George Murphy into the Presidency of SAG. The members respected him because he bore no obvious malice toward his fellow man, whatever their race, color or creed, even though he was so morally passionate. He had a delicate business-like touch, and was seen as flexible enough to defend the union's principles. He was more than able to present a case. He was also generally good-natured and readily available to the Press. Admittedly he rarely spoke about himself, and if the newshounds did manage to get the talk round to his film career he always shuffled in acute embarrassment and soon turned the conversation to others. He no longer saw himself in the role of a screen celebrity. That may have been because he had never seen himself as an actor, rather, he had made the best of what he had, and now his enduring interest turned to public service.

Reagan worked on two more weak pictures, *Night Unto Night* and *The Girl from Jones Beach,* before setting off for England toward the end of 1948 to make the latest Warner movie *The Hasty Heart,* again with Patricia Neal. Warners had agreed to shoot *The Hasty Heart* in England to use some of the revenues from the theatres which the British Government refused to let American film makers take out of the country.

Reagan had never left American soil before and he approached the coming experience with mixed feelings and plenty of trepidation; one of his British friends had warned him soberly, "You won't mind our winter outdoors-it's indoors that's really miserable," His arrival in London was delayed because, still refusing to fly, he made the leisurely Atlantic crossing aboard the Queen Mary. He hadn't wanted to make the trip at all but he reluctantly accepted his role was a good one and might go some way to saving his almost extinguished career.

He and Neal went site-seeing round London together but to the great distress of studio publicists, who were hoping to promote them as a couple, the pair were not much seen themselves due to the dense fog swirling round the city. Visibility however was not the real problem. The tall, graceful Americans gave off absolutely no whiff of sexual chemistry. Reagan dutifully attempted to kiss Miss Neal, she gently fended him off, one more in a long line of females who found him attractive but not particularly desirable. Joy Hodges, his old friend from radio days, said he always gave her the urge to giggle when he became passionate. In Patricia Neal's case, it may simply have been that she was pining for her lover Gary Cooper. And he was also feeling lonely, "I think the thing I missed most was not having someone to love."

Jane's unsavory divorce action and harsh words apparently left him feeling remote from the female sex for several years.

She had done her worst when she stated that he bored her. She had not only walked out on a production that he thought he was directing, she left his audience yawning. This hurt not only the film star in him, but also, more importantly, the rapidly emerging politician. In finding him dull, she made the statement that the things he so passionately believed in were of little interest. She had eclipsed him professionally, she damaged his political potential more.

On December 16th 1948, he and Neal began filming in the dark jumble of hangars and sound stages that made up Elstree Studios, for the Associated British Picture Corporation, largest of the British studios. Director Vincent Sherman, was the only other American involved on *The Hasty Heart*. The stage was spread with sand and bamboo huts, erected to simulate a Burmese army hospital, one of the huts was mounted on a turntable.

Reagan spent the next three months on the freezing set in light pajamas and loose shirts playing "Yank". Richard Todd was his unknown co-star, playing a young man dying of kidney failure. At first Reagan didn't take the youngster who was working on only his second movie, seriously, but it soon became apparent that he was stealing the honors. The big American was incapable of jealousy and he went out of his way to befriend him, picking him up in his Rolls Royce in the mornings on the way to Elstree.

Todd said, "Ronnie couldn't have been nicer to a complete unknown." Reagan talked to him about his favorite subjects, politics and sport, expounding at length on what he thought should happen in the post-war world, "It was clear he did not understand the complexities of European recovery except that he noticed a number of Red threads running from East to West. He didn't like it."

In the movie at one point the young Scot, desperately trying to befriend the men he is sharing the hospital ward with, burbles on about pensions and politics until one of the other men, tired of listening, says, "If you want to talk politics, you'd better talk to "Yank"

Todd said, "When he turned the talk to home, I have never met an American who so profoundly believed in the greatness of his nation." And again, even in the picture, when the men talk about their homes, Yank says, "When I think of home I think of a little place on the Rock River; Dixon, Illinois." He must have thought about it plenty to give it such a mention in the picture.

On the first day of shooting Reagan had to perform the most demanding monologue he had ever had to learn, reciting every book of the Old Testament, and he did it nine times before the director was satisfied.

The set was unbearably cold and drafty, and Reagan was unused to and quickly became frustrated by, the haphazard workings at Elstree, which seemed to him to be designed around frustration and discomfort. He took pride in his own reliability and could not believe what he referred to as Britain's "incredible inefficiency."

Vincent Sherman, the director, had known the actor for a long time, but was surprised by this new irritable, disgruntled and conservative Reagan. They argued long into many a night about the pros and cons of Britain's Welfare State, Reagan stating that as far as he could tell, everybody in it seemed to be ill and faring badly. If this was Socialism, he wanted no part of it. Sherman said many years later that on some matters Reagan had been more correct than he, especially with regard to the Soviet Union.

Reagan later said he arrived at the third plateau of his political journey whilst working in London where he witnessed what he considered economic order turned upside down, where the Civil Servants were the masters, "I shed the last ideas I'd ever had about Government ownership of anything."

He lost his healthy glow during his months in dank Britain, Jack Warner commented, "Reagan does not look at all well." In February he had a long weekend free of retakes before going home, and he decided to head down to the south of France. He traveled with Arthur Abeles, assistant managing director of Warner Bros (UK).

Abeles soon became aware of Reagan's desolate sadness and asked the actor if he thought Jane might change her mind.

"It seems like a lost cause," Reagan confessed forlornly.

Patricia Neal said he seemed to miss Jane very much and she also felt sorry for him.

He and Jane were still making the gossip columns at home and a variety of reasons for the divorce were being thrown around, but from early in 1949 Reagan himself hardly mentioned her name again; she is conspicuously absent from his memoirs and in his autobiography he made no mention of their courtship, their life together or the divorce.

Even before *The Hasty Heart* opened in fall 1949, the long running rumors began flooding through Hollywood that Reagan's career was in decline. His new picture won some good reviews and, as usual, Reagan's performance was mildly complimented, but it had been newcomer Richard Todd who ran off with all the plaudits. Reagan's mood sank.

He had been badgering the studio to find him a good outdoor movie, preferably a Western and just before sailing for England he had been told *Ghost Mountain* had been bought for him. On his return to Hollywood he found the picture had been retitled *Rocky Mountain* and given to Errol Flynn instead. Jack Warner informed Reagan that he had not been getting the results they had been hoping for at the box-office, a common Hollywood tactic in controlling players. He wanted to show Reagan exactly who ran the business…and it wasn't the actors, but in 1946 his wife, Ann Warner, had fallen in love with Philip Wylie's novel, *Night Unto Night.* She talked husband Jack into buying the screen rights and he assigned producer Owen Crump to the job. In those days casting was handled by Jack Warner himself, but Crump had allowed Gregory Peck, exclusively a Twentieth Century-Fox contract actor, to see the script. Peck agreed with Crump that he was made to play the role of the brooding, doomed bacteriologist, John Gaylen and he wanted the part. When Crump went to Warner for the final casting permission he mentioned that he thought they could do no better than ask Peck. Warner laughed, "You've got Reagan," and added, satisfied, "He's our Gregory Peck." Mitch Tuchman wrote in *Film Comment* in 1980, "The comparison was apt. Like Peck, Reagan was tall, dark, handsome and hollow- though not quite so tall, nor quite so dark or handsome…He had the kind of talent that thrives on personality, but although he was reputed to be an intensely charismatic figure while president of the Screen Actors Guild, when he set out for the studio each morning, he left that charisma at home under the pillow with his pajamas."

There had already been times through his career when he could have leapt to the head of the pecking order. No one would have been better pleased than Jack Warner, who had persistently kept faith with the promising young actor for over thirteen years, certain that one day he would burst forth and become a valuable piece of property. But even after *King's Row*, according to casting director Sollie Biano, no one would have picked him as a romantic lead or allow a picture could be profitable on the strength of his name alone.

Still, together with his *King's Row* co-star, Ann Sheridan, he had managed to get cast for *Everybody Comes to Rick's,* a low budget film of international intrigue. But when Ingrid Bergman suddenly became available for the Sheridan role, the budget was increased and Bogart was given the Reagan role. The picture was retitled, *Casablanca*.

Reagan's contract still had another three years to run, but at a time all the big studios were being hit by the impact of television and were seeking ways to off-load many of their stars, Reagan wanted to have a little more freedom to see if he could get better work at other studios, so he and his agent, Lew Wassermann, approached Warner's with a compromise offer to revise the actor's contract. The new one, designed to win him the greatest amount of possible independence, in exchange for a 50% reduction in guaranteed salary, was soon negotiated. Reagan would make one film each year for Warners at half his former salary and would be able to work at other studios in the meantime. So he branched away from the security he had known at the Warner studio since 1937, "My face was saved and the studio wasn't hurt. One week later Lew added a five-year picture deal at Universal and I bellied up to the bar like a conquering hero ordering drinks for the house. You could hardly see my wounded ego under all those $75,000 plasters."

He was soon contracted to make a film with Ida Lupino for Universal-International, but just a few days before shooting started he broke his right thigh in a charity baseball match between comedians and leading men for Hollywood's City of Hope Hospital. He was immobilized in hospital for seven weeks and had plenty of time to brood about Jane's Best Actress Academy Award for *Johnny Belinda*.

1949 was turning out to be a bad year and when he did get out of hospital he chose not to attend the preview of *The Hasty Heart*. He was so helpless on crutches that Jane Wyman told him he could stay in her house, which was still fully staffed, whilst she was away in London filming *Stage Fright*. Once she got back, he moved home with his mother. It was a year before he could walk unaided, a year in which little was accomplished professionally.

He fretted all the time about the lack of work on the horizon. The Screen Actors Guild didn't take up more than one night of his time, and the Motion Picture Industry Council, which had elected him chairman in his absence, was not yet fully geared up to its task of helping the Hollywood Reds rehabilitate. If ever he had needed the support of the studio system, it was now, just when it was lost to him. All he was now looking at from Warner Bros was one $75,000 picture a year, and he discovered that freelance roles for a man on crutches did not flow in, "I was $160,000 down in lost work and hospital charges."

As he approached his fortieth birthday he took stock of his dire situation. He was homeless, middle-aged and loveless. Like his character, Drake, in *Kings Row*, he found himself living in a totally different world from the one he had previously inhabited. The injury had taken too long to heal up, but he knew his mind and his self esteem would take longer to recover. Over the years Reagan used Drake's cry, "Where's the rest of me?" to the point of cliché. In 1949 he felt keenly the overtones. Drake only lost both his legs, but his own divorce became absolute whilst he was in hospital, and with it, he lost his dignity. He was lonely and he missed his wife.

Then, once he could hop about again, a slow recovery started. He began dating again. He received the offer of work from Jerry Wald, who wanted him and his limp to star in *Storm Warning*, alongside Ginger Rogers and Doris Day. Wasserman had also struck a $375,000 deal with Universal for five pictures over five years. Things were looking up.

The first Universal picture he was ready to go to work on was *Louisa*, which co-starred Charles Coburn, Ruth Hussey and Spring Byington. This was a charming and unusual comedy about a grandmother and her two suitors. Reagan called it, "A good and healthy plus to any list of screen credits." And his performance as the harassed head of the family again received positive notices. He always regarded the film positively because he enjoyed working with Spring Byington and his reunion with Charles Coburn.

He then made the more serious *Storm Warning* about the Ku Klux Clan, for Warner Bros. He was kept busy filming *The Last Outpost*, a Western, for Paramount, before going on to *Bedtime for Bonzo* for Universal. It was this last picture that the political opponents of Reagan, liked to target so much, often alluding to it as if it were typical of his output, and assuming from the title that it is a mediocre comedy and that the star had been reduced to working with a chimp. In fact the film is amusing in its own right and Reagan's quiet manner in it offers a fine counterpoint to the animal's natural charm. However the chimp does manage to steal the film and Reagan admitted, "On the set he learned our business so well that going to work was a fascinating experience. Naturally his trainer was on the set, and the normal procedure called for the director, Fred de Cordova, to tell the trainer what he wanted from Bonzo. But time after time Freddie, like the rest of us, was so captivated that he'd forget and start to direct Bonzo as he did the human cast members. He'd say, "No, Bonzo, in this scene you should…" Then he'd hit his head and cry, "What the Hell am I doing?"

*The Last Outpost* fulfilled a long held wish for Reagan, and after fourteen years as a Hollywood star, he made his first starring Western. He played opposite Rhonda Fleming. One of the highlights for him was that the producers allowed him to use his own horse, Tarbaby in the picture. As a boy he had always enjoyed Westerns and Tom Mix and William S Hart were amongst his earliest heroes.

For *Hong Kong* he went straight back to Paramount where he was allowed more scope than usual as a hard, selfish ex-soldier who comes across a lost little boy. *The Hollywood Reporter* said, "Reagan's persuasive playing of the hero contributes much toward making *Hong Kong* convincing."

According to Reagan the child actor Danny Chang was the most natural scene-stealer he had met during his career, even better than the chimp, and his quiet manner and innocent face made him the natural focus of the film. A quick run of movies followed, including *She's Working Her Way Through College, The Winning Team, Tropic Zone* and *Law and Order*. *The Winning Team* starred Reagan as pitcher Grover Cleveland Alexander and for baseball buffs it remains one of the best. It gave Reagan a good opportunity as an actor and was one in which he successfully conveyed both his own enthusiasm for the game and the glorious ups and painful downs of Alexander. Although he was getting plenty of work from other studios, this was Reagan's final movie for Warner Bros, rounding off a fifteen-year stint.

Finally free of Warner Bros and out on his own as a freelance, Reagan was suddenly once more faced with the prospect of looking for his own jobs and finding decent pictures that would maintain his position as a star. He soon discovered the going was tough without studio security, and *Tropic Zone* was not a good omen for his future in the movies. It was based on the greed and corruption in the banana growing areas of South America. The picture was generally panned. *Law and Order* was stale, a very modest Western.

Increasingly he turned down offers, saying they simply didn't interest him enough, but when he was offered a part in MGM's *Prisoner of War* he jumped immediately.

It was set in the Korean War and was a story about the mistreatment of US captives. The writer, Rivkin, wove his script around the stories of ex-prisoners. Rivkin heard about men who had defied their Korean captors, others who pretended to be impressed by Communism in order to get better treatment and those who cracked under torture and co-operated fully.

MGM were so impressed by Rivkin that they rushed headlong into production as quickly as possible to get the film into 1954 theatres while the news of returning prisoners was still breaking. Still the film made only a moderate impact on a public quickly saturated with news about the Korean War camps. Reagan said, "The picture should have done better. Every torture scene and incident was based on actual happenings documented in official army records. Unfortunately, production and release were both rushed, with the idea that the picture should come out while the headlines were hot." He fully believed the story deserved a more comprehensive treatment.

In 1955 he went to work at RKO for the first time, making *Cattle Queen of Montana* with Barbara Stanwyck followed by *Tennessee's Partner* with John Payne. He had been pleased to accept the lead in another Western and delighted that it would be shot in Technicolor in Glacier National Park, Montana; part of America that was new to him and the idea of going there excited him. The location setting was a wise choice, as the spectacular scenery was perhaps the best thing about the conventional saga. Reagan took the chance to do some sight seeing at company expense, "Somehow working outdoors amid beautiful scenery and much of the time on horseback never has seemed like work to me. It's like getting paid for playing cowboy and Indian."

Cozy Reagans before the storm

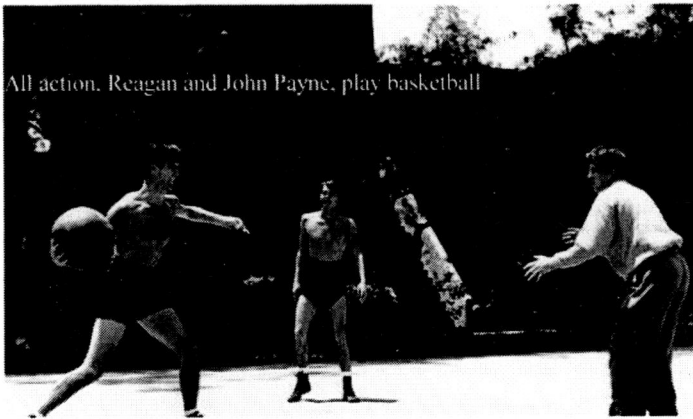
All action, Reagan and John Payne, play basketball

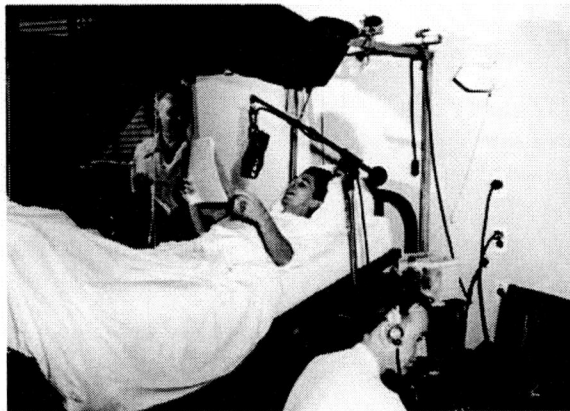

After breaking his thigh during a charity baseball match, Reagan spent weeks hospitalized and it was a year before he was able to discard his crutches.

# Chapter Seven
## 1950-1952
### Along Came Nancy

Then, as Ronald Reagan is quoted as saying, "Along came Nancy Davis and saved my soul." The political activism that had lost Reagan his first wife was about to land him his second.

The Hollywood Reporter had named Mrs. Nancy Davis as a Communist sympathizer on a list of two hundred and eight co-signers. There was, however, quite another Nancy Davis, a "tough little broad" who worked for MGM. She had been born in New York, raised in Chicago and had attended Smith College. Throughout her college years she worked in summer-stock theater productions and even appeared on Broadway in *Lute Song* along with Mary Martin and Yul Brynner before hitting Hollywood and the problems of the lists. Nancy said, "Summer stock was very good training. You didn't act right away; first you did a little bit of everything. That way, when you finally got on stage, you had an idea of what went on offstage to get you there…it was all good experience."

Rumor and gossip states that she was hired by MGM on a seven year contract by Dore Schary as a favor to her doctor father, who had been treating him for a minor ailment. She made eight motion pictures at the studio but was hardly recognized as a major star; it is doubtful whether her name would have registered with any fans, but being incorrectly identified as a Communist sympathizer could have halted any future career in its tracks before it left the station. Before Miss Davis became one with Mrs. Davis in the eyes of the public at large and the movie business in particular, Nancy had to do something.

She decided the person who could best help was Ronald Reagan, head of her union. She stands absolutely firm that it was the problem with the *list* that first brought them together, but others noted that she and Reagan were separate guests at a dinner party at Schary's mother-in-law's home weeks before the list was published. She certainly knew who he was, and what he could do for her, and seems to have gone out of her way to arrange a second meeting with him. Still Nancy was right to be so concerned about SAG confusing her with the more liberal Mrs. Davis, and right to persuade her director and friend Mervyn LeRoy to call Reagan to hint at her distress over any imagined Communist associations and to see if he could do anything to fix it. He in fact rang Reagan and said, "You're single. She's kind of cute." He hastily engineered a dinner date for the pair in 1950, presumably so they could iron the problem out, but also so Nancy could get together with a man she had already said she liked the look of.

Ronald Reagan later said he couldn't understand why LeRoy was making so much fuss about him meeting Miss Davis, but agreed to go on the blind date anyway. He booked a table at LaRue's a glamorous place on Sunset Strip, but warned Nancy that he wouldn't be out late as he had an early morning call. Twenty eight year old Nancy was nothing if not stylish, and she dressed perfectly for the occasion in a stunning black and white dress. Reagan, almost blind anyway, and certainly with no eye for fashion, focused only on the wide, intelligent eyes before him.

In spite of saying he couldn't stay out, when dinner was finished he took Nancy on to Ciro's to catch a Sophie Tucker performance. He was instantly mesmerized by Nancy, but definitely in no mood to rush anything. Errol Flynn had advised him after his divorce from Jane, "Be happy…think of the parties…think of the girls. Do what I do." And Reagan had followed that counsel to the letter for the next two years. Even after first meeting Nancy he was seen out with at least sixteen young actresses of note including Doris Day and Rhonda Fleming.

Reagan was always reticent in mentioning those dating days but once admitted that he slept with so many girls he woke up once and didn't know who he was with. Many of the girls he could hardly recall, remembered him though and often commented on his wounded air, which they felt verged on the masochistic. Nothing they did or said then seemed to erase his longing for Jane. He even visited sets where he knew she would be working, just to watch her act. She ignored him.

The other thing they all remembered vividly was his talkativeness. He never did get to grips with the fact that this failing, more than anything else, had been the root cause leading to his divorce. Doris Day laughed that talk flowed out of him in an un-ending stream, "it really wasn't conversation, it was rather talking at you. "I remember telling him that he should be touring the country making speeches."

Nancy Davis, a born receiver, was built to withstand the outpouring, "Ronnie had a great sense of humor... he didn't talk about himself. He didn't talk about his movies. He talked about lots of things, but not about "my next picture, my last picture..." He was a Civil War buff, loved horses and knew a lot about wine. In fact he had a broad knowledge about a lot of different things. I loved to listen to him talk." She never needed to do the talking herself; she was happily free of any sign of narcissism. Her main charm was an ability to laugh, she didn't force issues and was never condescending.

She became his steady, but not exclusive date, and for some time things progressed slowly. Nancy said that because he was away on location busily making movies, traveling the country on TV jobs (even though at the time he described television as a "Siberia of thespians") and was heavily involved with his work for SAG, it took them a long while to develop any serious relationship even though, on her part, she already knew he was the man for her and that there would be no other. He later asked her why she had moved in on him so determinedly. She confessed that she didn't really know but tried to explain, "When the real thing comes along, you just know it. At least I did."

She had fallen in love with him instantly, "I can't define what it was about Ronnie that made him seem so very perfect to me. I think we were just right for each other." She wanted to be with him, "My life really began when I met Ronald Reagan." During the early days of their courtship she laughed and listened and began cultivating his political nature. She loved him to the exclusion of everything else.

When Reagan first invited her out to his Northridge ranch she accepted with delight, "It wasn't a fancy place, but it was very special to Ronnie. He'd built a ring there to ride in, and put some hurdles to practice jumping, and that's what he did out there; rode and practiced jumping and bred horses with his partner." The fact the ranch was special to Reagan made it more so for Nancy, although she admitted ruefully, "You don't have many ranches in Chicago, where I was raised."

Things moved along nicely when she was introduced to Reagan's children, Michael and Maureen, "I was so nervous about meeting them, so afraid that they wouldn't like me...But as it turned out, we got along just fine." Next came his mother, Nelle. Nancy wrote, "She was an incredible woman. She visited men in jail and in the veteran's hospitals and talked to them, usually about religion. She screened films that Ronnie bought for her for the tuberculosis patients in Olive View Hospital. Ronnie and she had been very close, and now that she was getting older and living alone, he stopped by and had breakfast with her every morning." Nancy was taken along to have breakfast one morning, "It was clear that Nelle adored Ronnie and wanted him to be happy."

Nancy says her own career was just taking off when she first met Reagan, and she was delighted when he handed her a golden key on the day she was assigned her own dressing room at MGM. He sent instructions to take it to a jeweler to have it cut to fit the lock.

Throughout 1951 they dated and were seen at all the Hollywood nightclubs, although Nancy says neither of them particularly enjoyed the nightlife. Their regular spot was at Chasen's and the booth where they regularly sat is now on display in the Reagan Library. Nancy never cooked, and they always either ate out or had someone come in to make dinner at home. It became comfortable and it was not too long before Reagan settled to the quieter rhythm of life that Nancy preferred.

He and Nancy made only one picture together, *Hellcats of the Navy*. The movie was based on a book by Admirals Charles A Lockwood and Hans Christian Adamson that dealt with an actual naval operation against the Japanese in 1944. It was an odd choice of material for a 1957 Columbia release, the kind of film Warner Bros had been making during wartime, only much better. It did little business and most filmgoers lost interest in both of them as actors on the back of it. Having found each other, they also lost a little interest in Hollywood themselves. Neither needed the sentiment of the movies as their own flesh and blood romance flourished.

Reagan had gone down to San Diego to start filming the part of Commander Casey Abbott ahead of Nancy who was to play a navy nurse. When she arrived at the hotel she found a note waiting for her, "Darling, us old salts always say, "Welcome Aboard"-and My Goodness Are You Welcome!?!...I love you, Commander Abbott."

As it grew increasingly difficult for the Reagans in the film world they decided to move out of town to the stud farm where he became a full-time racehorse breeder for a short duration. Still he did continue his efforts for SAG and the Motion Picture Industry Council (MPIC), where he still considered himself to be a liberal Democrat, standing well to the left of center on the boards of both organizations. However his political development was somewhat confused; he campaigned for Helen Gahagan Douglas for Senate in 1950, against her opponent Richard Nixon, but in 1947 and 1948, as informer T-10, he had informed against his professional colleagues to the FBI investigations following the acid attack threat. Together with Jane Wyman, he had named at least six of his own SAG members suspected of being Communists. He also said though that he believed it was the business of Congress and not the industry groups to prosecute Communism.

Many movie stars affect interest in politics while they are between parts, but Reagan's drive to orate, to change, to administer was deeply serious, and by the 1950's he was much respected in union circles as he began his rise above mediocrity, working hard for the cause of his fellow actors. In Hollywood it was always fashionable to appear angst ridden, to fret about the spread of television, the world spread of Communist power; paranoia and concealment were ever the American norm. But Ronald Reagan began to reveal his real value in an age of fear and distrust. He stood out head and shoulders above the rest with his genial and attractive optimism, natural calm assurance radiated from him, soothing the nerves of those around him.

Increasingly, the people of California listened to him and took notice of what he was saying. Some hardening took place in his drive for political progress as he began his move to the right and toward Republicanism. He had been president of SAG for four years, he headed every negotiation with the producer groups. The language he used became less verbose, more to the point; in writing about the confusion over who was Red and who not, he said, "Suppose we quit using the words Communist and Communism... Substitute "pro-Russian"...watch the confusion disappear...call them pro-Russian and take away the screen. If we must fight, make the enemy be properly uniformed."

Commentators have often tried to blame Nancy for his political shift, but he had already begun that drift before he met her and certainly before he started seeing her exclusively. Their life together had begun to settle into a steady pattern by 1951 and having moved out of Hollywood they began collecting his two children to drive them out to the ranch every weekend, "Ronnie had a game where he'd pretend he was a little dog and could listen in on conversations from the telephone wires, and he'd make up all these stories of conversations he'd supposedly heard." All of them loved the weekends away from the bright lights, and they enjoyed spending time together as a family, singing and telling stories, playing games and riding. Reagan's own favorite time was when the mares at the ranch foaled. Nancy confessed at the time however, "It is difficult to get ready to marry a man who has children…"

Still on March 4th 1952 Ronald Reagan and Nancy Davis were married at the Little Brown Church in the Studio City section of the San Fernando Valley, Mr. and Mrs. William Holden were best man and matron of honor. The church was small and in a quiet area; they didn't want reporters around and wanted to keep everything simple. Nancy felt the marriage had been inevitable from the first time she had met Reagan, but said it had not been easy to get him to the alter. There had often been whispers heard that he wanted to get back with Jane and he even named his Malibu ranch Yearling Row. Still in 1952 everyone who knew them seemed genuinely happy for the couple and never doubted that this marriage was built to last.

After the ceremony they went back to the Holden's home where the wedding pictures were taken. They spent their honeymoon night at the Old Mission Inn. Seven and a half months later their first child, Patricia Ann Reagan was born. Nancy wrote, "I had of course no idea what the future would hold for us. I only knew that I loved Ronald Reagan, and being his wife was then…the most important thing in the world for me."

The first years of the marriage proved to be quite tough. Reagan's own film career was in decline and Nancy gave up working when Patti was born. They had purchased a house on a winding canyon road in Pacific Palisades, but they didn't have much money in their pockets. In November 1952 Reagan stepped down as president of SAG, just as Dwight D Eisenhower was elected President of the United States. Reagan wrote frankly about his opinion of the Vice President-elect, "Pray as I am praying for the health and long life of Eisenhower because the thought of Nixon in the White House is almost as bad as that of "Uncle Joe." … Nixon is a hand picked errand boy with a pleasing façade and naught but emptiness behind...he is less than honest and he is an ambitious opportunist completely undeserving of the high honor paid him."

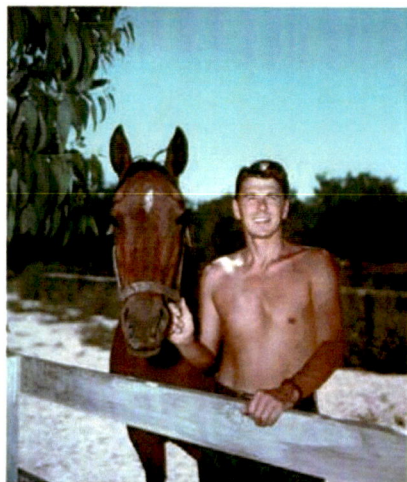

# Chapter Eight

## 1953-1962

### The Advent of Television

By the start of 1953 his career at Warner Bros was fading fast and Reagan was regarded as yesterday's man by studio and fans alike. He sensed himself that he could not perpetually play handsome romantic leads. He needed more grown-up roles in heavyweight productions and he wanted to move into outdoor films, possibly Westerns. He had certainly developed the craggy face of the Westerner, but he was no John Wayne or Jimmy Stewart. Unlike either of those super stars, he had nothing of the isolated loner about him and he simply didn't have an adequate range of talent to demonstrate the self-sufficient toughness a real Western hero must have, and lacking their overwhelming screen presence he found he had to settle for modest affairs like *Cattle Queen of Montana*.

The movie co-starred Barbara Stanwyk, was directed by one of the Hollywood greats, Allan Dwan, and was produced by Benedict Bogeaus. Reagan, who usually thrived on location work, was not happy during filming, "Everything is hectic and upset." Nancy hadn't gone with him because Patti was only two years old and Reagan wrote to his wife from Glacier National Park that both the producer and Miss Stanwyck, (or "Lady S" as he referred to her), were proving difficult to be around. He felt Barbara Stanwyck already believed the film would turn out to be poor and therefore was making no effort on it or investing much of her famed energy into it. His view of her is at odds with her highly respected reputation in the industry, although they later became friends. Admittedly, the picture was a low budget project and perhaps that irked all the players and crew involved and on July 17th 1954 Reagan wrote, "This has been the longest week in world history. I don't know how the picture is going. We started in confusion and have managed to develop that characteristic to an unusual degree. BB (the producer) is still defending his script, I'm still feeding suggestions to Allan Dwan and those two then huddle and argue. I'm quite interested to see what happens. Barbara Stanwyck just goes on her merry way in the exclusive company of two hairdressers and her maid. I wonder what picture she's making."

On the back of this film insiders began to whisper loudly that he would have to go to TV more regularly if he was to survive the industry crisis, but right then he didn't think that was all too bad, "This is my first crack at picture making since the big switch to TV film work…it bears out everything we've ever said. First of all-getting a crew was a case of rounding up who you could find. The industry, as we have so often said, literally forced our technicians to seek work in TV and now we reap the harvest. Ben said there was a scramble to get enough guys for this crew-with no thought whatsoever of picking and choosing. Let's just put it this way, they and these horses have a lot in common." Reagan knew exactly what direction he had to move in and he prepared a proposal for a TV series, *Yearling Row*, a drama based on his ranch in the Malibu Hills.

Although the idea was not taken up, he had made some prudent investments and he and Nancy were far from destitute. He had made a down payment in 1951 on his $65,000, 290-acre ranch in Malibu Canyon. In 1966, just after being elected Governor of California, he sold most of the holding on to Twentieth Century-Fox studios for what was then a staggeringly high $1,900,000. He also had some other irons in the fire.

And the optimist was far from downhearted. In February 1954 he signed up as an MC for a variety act in Las Vegas where he told Irish jokes along with a group of performers called the Continentals. The date had originally been scheduled for two weeks and was seen by many, including himself, as a long way down from his box office glory days. He hadn't wanted to go, and he took himself off to Vegas with his suitcase stuffed with books expecting a boring time. However, unexpectedly, the show became a sell-out smash with people lining up to get in. He enjoyed working with the Continentals and they all received warm standing ovations. His contract was extended.

As Hollywood's golden years began to fade, and TV's rose, Reagan somehow managed to turn bad to good once again, realizing a swift, smooth and outstandingly successful transfer from the big screen to the small. Just when everything had seemed lost, he sensed he was only just beginning. He was in the first wave of Hollywood stars to make the transition, and by making the switch he revived his acting career. In biographies his television work during the second half of the 1950's is largely glossed over with the note, "Ronald Reagan acted on TV" – Interestingly he had as many acting roles on TV over a fifteen year period as he had big screen parts. Five times he acted opposite his wife, and on one of the GE Theatre shows he co-hosted with her, he also introduced his children Patricia, then eight, and young Ronald, just two.

More often than not though his young family was left behind as he traveled the country alone. That was never to his liking and he wrote home to Nancy from his hotel in New York's Sherry-Netherland, "Back at the hotel I put in the call to you and then tried for Lew Wasserman-not in town! Sonny Werblin-away on vacation! Nancy Poo Pants Reagan-away out yonder! Eight million people in this pigeon crap encrusted metropolis and suddenly I realized I was alone with my thoughts and they smelled sulphurous."

He let Nancy know how much he missed her, but refused to admit to any concern for his future, and with good reason as his new career moved swiftly along. He had made his TV acting debut on the CBS dramatic anthology series called *Nash Airflyte Theatre* on July 12, 1950, before they married, playing Tommy Blunt, half of a detective team, Tuppence and Blunt (Cloris Leachman was Tuppence), in Agatha Christie's *The Case of the Missing Lady* (sometimes called *The Disappearance of Mrs Gordon*).

His TV works after this run included, Hollywood Opening Night: *The Priceless Gift* (29th December 1952) for NBC.

Ford Theater: *First Born* (May 2nd 1953) for NBC, with Nancy Davis, Nancy Guild and Tommy Rettig.

Chrysler Medallion Theater: *A Job for Jimmy Valentine* (8th July 1953) for CBS with Dorothy Hart.

Schlitz Playhouse of Stars: *The Doctor Comes Home* (31st July 1953) CBS, with Barnara Billingsley.

Lux Video Theater: *Message in a Bottle* (3rd September, 1953) CBS, with Maureen O'Sullivan.

Revlon Mirror Theater: *Next Stop Bethlehem* (5th December, 1953) CBS, with Charles Bickford.

Ford Theater: *And Suddenly You Know* (10th December, 1953) NBC, with Teresa Wright and Lee Aacker.

Lux Video Theater: *A Place in the Sun* (28th January, 1954)CBS. Reagan hosted only.

Schlitz Playhouse of Stars: *The Jungle Trap* (19th February, 1954) CBS. Starred with Barbara Billingsley.

Schlitz Playhouse of Stars: *The Edge of Battle* (26th March, 1954) CBS, with Neville Brand.

Ford Theater: *Beneath These Waters* (20th May 1954) NBC, with John Baer.

Soon after the successful Las Vegas tour ended Reagan's agent rang him to say General Electric wanted him to host their new television program and on 12th September 1954 he began hosting *General Electric Theater* for CBS on Sunday evenings. He would introduce each episode and star in four programs a year. They also wanted him to act as corporate ambassador for the company and would pay him to say over and over, wherever he went, "Progress is our most important product."

Reagan had been promised the show would be prestigious and his screen persona would not be harmed through his involvement in it, and in fact, with the help of the lead-in audience from the Ed Sullivan Show, it was soon the nation's top rated weekend program and his fame and fortune, far from suffering, grew accordingly. It was a massive turning point in his career. He had always had a sense of historical significance and a talent for using it to his best advantage, for being in the right place at the right time. Like other Hollywood film stars he had been aware of, and worried by, the rapid ascendancy of television, but his fears hadn't prevented him making his early small-screen debut on CBS's *Nash Airflyte Theatre* at the start of the fifties.

On July 23rd 1952, as President of SAG, he signed a blanket waiver, allowing his own talent agency, MCA, to operate as a television producer. This action went against SAG's whole history of insisting that agents stay out of production. Now MCA could hire its own actors and shoot its own shows, completely uncontrolled by any studio.

Naturally Lew Wasserman, president of MCA, was the main beneficiary of the deal, and there was always a chance that he would remember to reward his generous client in the future. However, there is no hard evidence that Reagan ever profitted personally from the waiver he pushed through, and it is also documented that SAG board members gave him unanimous authority to sign the deal on their behalf. The big studios had been loath to spend good money on celluloid for TV but Wasserman predicted it would be a profitable exercise in the long run, saying he would be able to offer the advertisers a consistent product.

Reagan says he agreed to sign the waiver because he feared all the best film and TV deals would be snapped up by the "live" studios in the East. He saw that his duty was to his Hollywood colleagues and he wanted to increase the rapidly diminishing number of roles available on the West Coast. Meanwhile his power and authority increased following the waiver and he began appearing more often on national television.

Apart from hosting the GE Theater series he also acted in: *The Long Way 'Round* (10th October, 1954) with Nancy Davis; *Out of the Night* (12th December, 1954) with James Dunn; *The Martyr* (23rd January, 1955) with Brian Aherne and Lee Marvin; *War and Peace on the Range* (13th March, 1955); *Bounty Court Martial* (9th October, 1955), with Raymond Massey; *Prosper's Old Mother* (20th November, 1955) with Ethel Barrymore and Charles Bronson; *Let it Rain* (18th December, 1955) with Cloris Leachman; *Try to Remember* (26th February, 1956) with Kim Hunter and Angie Dickinson; *The Lord's Dollar* (22nd April, 1956); *Professor Beware* (30th September, 1956); *The Orphans* (2nd December, 1956) with Kim Hunter; *No Skin Off Me* (3rd February, 1957); *Bargain Bride* (7th April, 1957) with Eva Bartok and Edgar Buchanan; *A Question of Survival* (19th May, 1957) with Kevin McCarthy; *Father and Son Night* (13th October, 1957) with Bobby Clark, Jack Albertson and Keith Larson; *The Coward of Fort Bennett* (16th March, 1958) with Neville Brand and John Dall; *No Hiding Place* (6th April, 1958) with Geraldine Page and Pernell Roberts; *The Castaway* (12th October, 1958) with Robert Fuller; *A Turkey for the President* (23rd November, 1958) with Nancy Davis and Ward Bond; *Deed of Mercy* (1st March, 1958) with Carole Lynley and Agnes Moorhead; *Nobody's Child* (10th May, 1959) with Diane Brewster; *Signs of Love* (8th November, 1959); *The House of Truth* (13th December, 1959) with Phyllis Thaxter; *So Deadly, So Evil* (13th March, 1960) with Peggy Lee; *Goodbye My Love* (16th October, 1960) with Anne Baxter; *Learn to Say Goodbye* (4th December, 1960) with Coleen Gray and Michael Burns; *The Other Wise Man* (25th December, 1960), with Nancy Davis and the Reagan children, Ronald Sr hosted this Christmas tale about the fourth Magus, absent from the Nativity; *The Devil You Say* (22nd January, 1961); *The Iron Silence* (24th September, 1961); *Money and the Minister* (26th November, 1961); *The Wall Between* (7th January, 1962) with Stephen Boyd; *Shadow of a Hero* (4th February, 1962) with David Janssen; *My Dark Days* (18th and 25th March, 1962) a two-part finale to the GE series.

Reagan also starred in Dick Powell's Zane Grey Theater; *The Long Shadow*
(19th January, 1961) CBS, an episode directed by Budd Boetticher.

The Dick Powell Show; *Who Killed Julie Greer* (26th September, 1961) for
NBC.

Wagon Train; *The Fort Pierce Story* (23rd September, 1963), ABC.

Kraft Suspense Theater; *Cruel and Unusual Night* (4th June, 1964) for NBC.
From 1963-1965, succeeding Stanley Andrews, he worked as host on the
series Death Valley Days and occasionally acted in episodes, including;
*Tribute to the Dog* (1964), *Raid on the San Francisco Mint* (1965), *The
Battle of San Francisco Bay* (1965), *No Gun Behind His Badge* (1965),
*Temporary Warden* (1965), *The Lawless Have Laws* (1965), *A City is Born*
(1965), *No Place for a Lady* (1965). When he left the show, his friend,
Robert Taylor, took over hosting duties for two seasons.

For many years he was criticized for selling his soul to GE to cement his
own future. Actually, all he had done in spring 1954 was allow MCA to
lease his voice and body out to the New York advertising agency Batten,
Barton, Durstine & Osborn. It had been BBD&O that offered him to GE as
"program supervisor" for a Sunday night series, 13 half-hour dramas, to be
produced by Revue. The agency had also suggested that Reagan make
personal appearances at GE facilities across the country, assuring GE bosses
that he could be relied on to improve plant morale and would also be willing
to become involved in PR work on their behalf.

General Electric Theater debuted on September 26, 1954 and was
instantly popular. Reagan said, "I am seen by more people in one week than
I am in a whole year in movie theaters."

By 1955 he had become established as one of Americas most
relaxed and attractive hosts on air. BBD&O were paying him on a sliding
scale, starting at $125,000 per annum. They expected a lot back from him
in return for his five year contract, including a 16 week per year traveling

clause. All the Reagans found the schedule punishing. Throughout the time he traveled for General Electric he still refused to fly, which made every journey an incredible logistical exercise. Nancy wrote, Ronnie would leave California in the late afternoon, take the Super Chief train all the next day and night to Chicago, then take the Twentieth Century to New York. He'd visit plants, make speeches, shake hands, tape episodes of *General Electric Theater*, and then begin the long train ride back."

By summer 1955 he calculated that he had met a hundred thousand GE workers in 185 facilities, and in his final estimate after 8 years of corporate spokesmanship, he said, "I was on my feet in front of a mike for about 250,000 minutes." Whilst this routine would have been unacceptable to most actors, and was difficult for him, Reagan seemed to thrive on it. The tours changed him. He delighted in his increasing national power and this proved that he was at last becoming more politician than actor, he was beginning to instruct as well as entertain, and he was brilliantly successful at it. He received enthusiastic standing ovations everywhere he went.

By 1958 a survey found him to be one of the most recognized men in the country! All his childhood fantasies were finally coming to full fruition and he soon became a fully integrated member of the GE institution. In his communication with his new audiences he also learned a new trick, he began to listen to what other people had to say, he started to hear what was in the hearts and minds of his fellow Americans, fellow workers.

Later, opponents under estimated him, attacking him unimaginatively with the old, "He's just an actor!", an amateur who lacked political experience. What a mistake they made when they failed to see that although he had not spent much time in the traditional political arenas, he had picked up skill and vast experience in what was to become the politics of the televisual age. He was actually way ahead of what turned out to be a new game plan, already "enjoying every whizzing minute of it." He polished his delivery, his intimate tone, his sincere air, his wry chuckle and his well-timed burst of fervor and enthusiasm.

He was also in the privileged position to be able to achieve something that perhaps they couldn't do when he toured the country for GE and listened to his vast audiences. The format of his meetings enabled the conversation to go both ways and, as he traveled the country, he took on board a powerful sense of what the general public thought, hoped for and wanted in the future. Reagan said, "That did much to shape my ideas. These employees I was meeting were a cross section of America, and damn it, too many of our political leaders, our labor leaders, and certainly a lot of geniuses…on Madison Avenue, have underestimated them. They want the truth, they are friendly and helpful, intelligent and alert." Over the years he would devise slogans that the experts felt were simplistic…on the other hand he already knew, the voters responded to them, "Government is not the solution to the problem. Government is the problem.", "Government causes inflation, and government can make it go away. The best social program is a job." He repeated the phrases until the doubters began to believe him.

The very continuity of television display meant that, with even a modest amount of understanding of what he took in through his tours, Reagan could parlay over the course of a few seasons of strolling persuasively out every Sunday night, a power that could be felt right back in Washington. His popularity was being erected on public esteem, and there was no better measure of his success than the viewer ratings. In 1929 the chairman of GE had been considered too important to run for President of the United States. Thirty years later that man could not match his own spokesman in recognizability and glamour. Ralph Cordiner was known to a few thousand people, Reagan, "Mr Progress" was the intimate of millions. For the whole family the GE years were ones of security, and despite the long separations involved, the Reagans grew closer together and were more settled and content than ever before.

He and Nancy tried to have another child and after suffering a miscarriage, Nancy finally became pregnant again. Ron was born on May 20th, 1958.

In 1959 SAG charged Reagan with the responsibility of negotiating a new contract with the major studios on behalf of its members. His stake in *General Electric Theater* should have disqualified him from the task, but perhaps SAG members considered that at least he was still spending plenty of time in front of a camera, any camera, and they were desperate. Film roles were increasingly scarce and the producers were refusing to grant the actors residual rights in the sales of their old movies to television. If anyone could represent them in the looming chasm at the start of 1960, it was Reagan; actor-producer-TV star-politician.

Whether he did so to the benefit of his former colleagues remained a matter of heated debate and 21 years later SAG chose to deny him a lifetime achievement award! Eventually the union members were forced to concede all pre-1960 performance rights to the producers, in exchange for a $2.26 million pension and welfare fund package. Some actors believed he traded away their residuals, but when he announced his strike-settlement package to a mass meeting of the membership on April 18th 1960, he received a landslide approval vote of 6,299 to 259.

In 1960 Reagan regarded JFK's acceptance speech of his nomination to stand for President at the Democratic National Convention as a frightening call to arms, "Mr Kennedy's bold new imaginative program…under the tousled boyish hair cut, it is still old Karl Marx-first launched a century ago."

Richard Nixon stood against Kennedy and American citizens voted pretty that year. Film imagery and celebrity had become an overriding factor in politics. This of course was good news for Reagan and his own date with destiny.

In 1955 when the Reagans had started construction of their new house at Pacific Palisades, 1669 San Onofre, a grateful GE decided to turn it into a showcase for all their latest electrical appliances and built for them the "House of the Future". It was fully equipped with General Electric gadgets; more refrigerators, ovens and special lighting than they could possibly use. It had a zebra skinned foyer, a sunken living room, triple car port, a climate changer, pool and patio. Each glass fronted room overlooked the sea. So much energy was consumed that the house had to be fitted with a special switch box of its own, and the local children delighted in pulling the plugs so that eventually the Reagans paid to be reconnected to the power source.

Reagan had drawn a heart with his and Nancy's initials in the wet cement of the patio and the pair always posed as model parents when it came to family photo opportunities. In fact all four of Reagan's children found him to be a remarkably disengaged father. He rarely bothered about any of them and Michael said, "I was real proud when Dad came to my high school commencement. He was guest of honor, and I was with him as we posed for pictures in caps and gowns. After the picture he introduced himself to all of us and came up to me and said, "Hi, my name's Ronald Reagan. What's yours?" he was looking right into my face. I took off my cap and said, "Dad it's me. Your son. Mike."

On July 25th, 1962 his mother died of a cerebral hemorrhage, aged 79. Like Jack before, she was buried without a headstone.

# Chapter Nine

## 1962-1966

### General Electric to Governor Reagan

When he traveled around the country on GE business Reagan became increasingly disturbed as he listened to the worries and fears of his audiences; particularly their often repeated complaint about high taxation. He understood exactly how they felt. It had not been so long before that the government had been clawing back up to ninety percent of his own earnings in tax. Apart from his disillusionment with Warner Bros and the films they had been asking him to work in, there had been little financial incentive for him to go to work at all, and he claimed that this was often the real reason he rejected certain pictures.

As he began to realize that his own concerns exactly mirrored those of the employees in the GE plants that he visited, his speeches became shorter, his question and answer sessions longer, and the talks he did give became more overtly political in their tone.

He complained, just as the workers making toasters did, that excessive government regulation was draining the economy of the free enterprise spirit upon which the country had been built. He had entered into his contract with General Electric as a Democrat, but now his own politics underwent a dramatic change with emerging views that caused a split with his employers and a race for the Governorship of California and then on to the ultimate prize.

His bosses at GE were unhappy and felt Reagan had become too preoccupied with politics and was too distracted by dangerous world events including the erection of the Berlin Wall in mid- august and Russia's detonation of a 58 megaton bomb. He warned at a speech in Pasadena on January 4th, 1962, that JFK's policies, including giving aid to pro-Communist governments abroad, would lead to social slavery at home. The stakes involved for GE were too high when he began to make such high profile public comments on their behalf. Several company executives were already under federal indictment for price-fixing, and a prosecutor appointed by Attorney General Robert Kennedy was about to grill dozens of witnesses, including Reagan himself. They couldn't afford to cause any further offence nor draw more unwelcome notice to themselves.

When Reagan was called before a grand jury inquiring into the SAG-MCA "blanket waiver" of 1952 GE suddenly realized it would have to get rid of its spokesman, or risk open warfare with Washington. Paradoxically, by 1962, Reagan was too powerful and popular a celebrity to attack openly. According to statistics of the day only former President Eisenhower had more prestige and value on the lecture circuit. At first he was simply asked to curb his political comments, after all, he was not paid to give his opinions, and they wanted him to concentrate instead on the commercial promotion he was employed for.

On February 5th 1962, when he gave his evidence to the jury, he was accused of selective amnesia, and the stinging criticism meant that Reagan had become too heavy a liability for GE to bear. BBD&O rang him to give him the bad news and he was told, more forcefully this time, to confine himself to plugging company products or GE would pull the plug and cancel the show. When he refused to co-operate GE decided that he had outlived his usefulness and fired him immediately. Reagan always denied that he cried on hearing the news, others state that he begged to keep the job. Whatever the truth of the matter, and although he didn't know it at the time, he had much bigger fish to fry.

The Reagans spent that Easter with Dr and Mrs Loyal Davis and the ex-television presenter was unusually quiet. He mentioned getting back into movies and writing his memoir. He had plenty of other pressing matters on his mind.

Even before he had been fired a group of California Republicans had asked him to run against Senator Thomas Kuchel in the spring primary. He had refused at the time, explaining that he was still a registered Democrat, but he did agree to support the Richard Nixon campaign. That commitment clearly demonstrated that he was now a Republican in everything but name. Whilst he talked to a number of rich Republicans about his political leanings he also confessed, "Like any actor, I keep thinking that the big part is still ahead." He definitely wanted to get back into the familiarity and security of the movie world and Hollywood's executive elite was largely Democratic. If he kept quiet, he might still be considered by casting directors. In the early 60's he attempted to be all things to all men, and was ably assisted by Nancy.

Even though he had always taken great care never to offend the producers, even though they all liked him and knew he was easy to work with, he still got no offers of work from any of them. Wasserman sent his updated resume to every studio and production company, but the photographs attached to it now reflected a fiftyish actor of no particular talent or box-office appeal. Wasserman confessed, "You've been around this business long enough to know that I can't force someone on a producer if he doesn't want to use him."

Reagan took the news badly and was convinced that Wasserman, an ardent supporter of Kennedy, had dropped him because of his changing politics. He felt betrayed by a man he had stuck with throughout his career, a man he had put his head on the block for.

The summer of 1962 was one of fast maturing ideologies for Reagan, who, despairing of reviving his acting career, finally registered as a Republican and began an all-out campaign of support for John Rousselot, a far-right Congressman running for re-election from ultra-conservative Orange County. Rousselot was the public relations director for the John Birch Society- an extreme, socially paranoid organization. The Cuban missile crisis and violent student riots made their fears seem reasonable to Reagan at the time. He also fully endorsed Nixon's campaign following the assassination of President Kennedy. Reagan spent much of his time and energy in the political arena and was greeted by an almost simultaneous wave lifting him to prominence in return. He was much in demand and when the conservatives rallied behind the presidential campaign of Senator Barry Goldwater in 1964, his oratorical gift proved to be one of the highlights of the doomed campaign. As faculty and students argued at Berkley, Reagan was asked by Holmes Tuttle, the owner of a successful Ford dealership based in Los Angeles, to record an emergency television address in support of the Goldwater campaign. Reagan wrote the speech himself and the brilliance of his half-hour performance was beamed nationwide by NBC on October 27th. Reagan told his audience, "You and I have a date with destiny. We can preserve for our children this, the last best hope of man on earth, or we can sentence them to take the first step into a thousand years of darkness. If we fail, at least we can let our children, and our children's children, say of us we justified our brief moment here. We did all that could be done."

The speech raised more than $8 million as cash flooded into the Republican coffers, more funds than had ever been brought in for any candidate before. The whole country was talking about his appearance and of course his background meant that he knew how to work an audience better than almost anyone else around. He was transformed overnight into a serious contender for the governorship of California himself. When Goldwater flopped in a landslide, (capturing only six states) and been consigned to the political scrap heap, Holmes Tuttle put together a committee to persuade Reagan to run for governor. At first he coyly refused, saying that he was a concerned citizen, not a politician, that he was happy doing what they wanted him to do, and was willing to drive around campaigning for others. Still, he had been quick to spot the opportunity in the problems on the college campus at the University of California and in the sense of general unrest everywhere, which might afford the Republicans the chance to grab hold of middle class discontent and use it to their own

130

ends. He finally agreed to become their candidate in 1966 and vowed "To clean up the mess at Berkeley."

His Hollywood years had not quite ended, but the focus of his life in the movie capital certainly had. Now primarily a politician, his earlier existence was not proving to be a hindrance as the fifty three year old actor began to clearly articulate the aspirations of rich California Republicans. He stated that he was frightened by the extent of their political ambitions for him, and affected a lack of interest in high office. For the rest of his life he claimed that he only yielded to their hopes out of a sense of civic duty. His brother helped get him a television contract as the new host of the syndicated television series, *Death Valley Days,* and had he only been an actor he might have happily stayed right there and settled down to more television work. But Reagan had moved on, he was now much more than just an actor and he quipped, "If only I could think of it as a script that would run for four years."

*Hellcats of the Navy*, made back in 1957 would have been Reagan's last feature film if his next picture, *The Killers*, made for television, had not been considered too violent for home screening. It was a strange, atypical role for him, and the only one of his career to present him as a thoroughly unpleasant character.

In 1946 Universal produced *The Killers* in a screenplay by Anthony Veiller. It was an expansion of a short story by Ernest Hemingway, which briefly tells the story of two men waiting in a diner for a man they have been hired to kill. The man is aware of them, but seems not to care and Hemingway's story is an exercise in fatalism. No reason is ever given for the man being marked for death.

The television production of the material lacked the plausibility of the earlier film that starred Burt Lancaster, and whilst Don Siegel's direction is pacy and the photography is good, the film was largely ignored due to its unpleasant tone. Critics agreed that Reagan gave a convincing account of the brutal, calculating crook, but most felt it was too difficult after so many years of seeing Reagan as a pleasant civilized fellow, to accept him as a villain now.

On the whole *The Killers* was not a fitting end to his film career, but it had never been intended for the big screen. He would rather have been remembered for his portrayals of George Gipp or Drake McHugh. He also knew playing that kind of role could harm his campaign work, and in his run for Governor, he didn't want to suffer from mis identification or misunderstanding.

So by 1965 he had been fully transformed from Actor into Politician. When he arrived anywhere to give a talk people lined up to meet him, to shake his hand. Many felt it was Nancy who pushed him now, but she replied, "Nothing could be further from the truth, and saying that shows a real misunderstanding of Ronnie. For the fact is-and this is something that nobody, oddly enough, has ever picked up on-Ronnie has always been a very competitive person. He has never needed to be pushed."

Nancy was exactly correct. Everything Reagan wanted, he got. He wanted to be a radio announcer, he wanted to be a film star, he wanted to be a politician, he wanted to become President, and he pushed his way to achievement, none of those things would simply land in someone's lap. They couldn't have happened by sitting back and waiting for life to bestow its gifts. Ronald Reagan knew perfectly well how to hold his own, he enjoyed the challenge and didn't back away from difficulty, and he played every game to win. Nancy may have made things easier for him by offering her devoted and unstinting support, but she simply couldn't have pushed him all the way to the White House had he not wanted to go.

One thing she did have to persuade him into was getting onto a plane again. He hadn't flown for many years, but once he had decided to run for governor, and he needed to be traveling constantly, he wrote, "I've always known that someday my ground hog days would end, and now these political shenanigans have made "someday" come around." Being deeply religious he had to accept that God had a plan for him, and that included getting back onto a plane.

There were more important transformations happening right across America. The country witnessed positives turning rapidly and shockingly into negatives; the Alabama riots, Malcolm X, the first combat troops being sent out to Vietnam and open urban warfare. Reagan appeared still to be tentative about his acceptance of the candidacy and he stated, though probably didn't mean, that he was happy to return to his private life if the Republicans found another, more suitable candidate. He drove around the state, attended party rallies, talked to ordinary people and attempted to adjust his big-business philosophy to theirs. He had never been the best listener; the qualities that made him a great speaker served him ill in conversation. Gore Vidal said Reagan was by far, "Hollywood's most grinding bore. Ronnie never stopped talking, even though he never had anything to say except what he had just read in the *Reader's Digest*."

On January 4th 1966 Reagan formally announced his candidacy for the Governorship of California. Millions of Californians saw him as "the nice guy" thanks to late night re-runs of his old movies on television and on November 8, 1966 a huge majority of them voted for him. He defeated incumbent Governor Brown by nearly a million votes, sweeping all but three of the state's fifty eight counties, with overwhelming majorities in Los Angeles and throughout southern California.

He and Nancy went out to dinner on election night and they heard the results come in on the car radio. Both were delighted by his victory.

All through 1966 and '67, their new house was under construction at 1669 San Onofre, it was all wood, glass and stone and built on the southern slope of the Santa Monica Mountains with a panoramic view of the surrounding country. But as governor he and the family had to move into a new "home" in Sacramento. When the wife of Reagan's predecessor Governor Pat Brown took Nancy on a tour of the official residence, she told her the noise of traffic was so bad that they would have to sleep at the back of the house to get any peace. There was nowhere for the children to play, all the windows were painted shut and the house had been declared a fire hazard!

Nancy refused to stay in the house so they moved to one on Forty Fifth Street, which was too small for entertaining, but was at least safe. It had a large pool and when they did invite guests over it was to a swim party. Sometimes the pool was covered over and Jack Benny or Red Skelton came up to perform. Reagan had been a lifeguard and was always alert to any poolside danger. At one of the parties, without a word to anyone he suddenly raced, fully dressed, into the pool to rescue a little girl who was in difficulties. He carried her to the side and placed her carefully on the edge and held her hand whilst she caught her breath before being restored to her mother. No one else there had even noticed her drowning.

The Reagans had to pay their own rent for the house, which they wouldn't have needed to do if they had remained in the governor's mansion. Nancy at least didn't begrudge the money saying that they could lead a normal family life at the smaller one. Reagan built a tree house for the children and they had new friends over all the time.

Reagan sold his prized ranch when they went to Sacramento because he would have to pay more tax on it than he was going to earn as governor. He did however insist on keeping the new house at Pacific Palisades. The family went back home to Los Angeles at the weekends.

# Chapter Ten

## Finding Grace

Life changed for everyone but extremely dramatically perhaps for Reagan. He had been a movie actor and, more than that, he had been a fan with a great capacity for the world of illusion. He had been both a creator and a consumer of make-believe, now the camera angle had moved and he worked for a different production team, but perhaps his reality, as he left the world of entertainment and marched into the political arena was actually not so very different after all.

Throughout the SAG presidency, the Governorship and later, when he was Leader of the Free World, those who heard the silver-soft voice, learned to stop worrying; there was a hero in charge. Could that be an illusion, delusion, a film star playing his role? In post-war American life and western culture generally, it was accepted that acting was a profession, demanding training, discipline, and sobriety, and was on an equal footing with lawyers, doctors and politicians. Of course Reagan had no formal training to be either actor or politician.

With the decline of the studio contract system in Hollywood, actors were free to pursue other projects, to express themselves on public issues and take life a little more seriously than before. Perhaps it was ironic that it turned out to be Ronald Reagan, the least serious of actors, a man no one ever took seriously as a major talent, who turned out to be the biggest beneficiary of the change as he helped shape a new order in America.

Some have attempted to make light of Reagan's extraordinary success in politics, saying he got by because he was "just an actor". Others argue he was not even a good actor-which actually seems to make his political success even more startling. As Governor of California did he simply read his lines, follow a script cobbled together by some mysterious screenwriter, did he use dubious and previously unrecognized, theatrical skills, as President? Or did a man lacking the depth for great roles in pictures somehow acquire a knack for filling the most responsible role in the world?

It would be nice for the scholars if Reagan fitted comfortably into the standard explanation for success in America; natural talent, solid training, honorable conduct in an honorable line of work. Nice if he turned out to be a man who won the respect of peers and public, after translating his gifts into a great Presidency.

Well, clearly, Reagan never climbed into the ranks of distinguished actors. He could be respectable or incompetent, but all too often he was mildly acceptable. He demanded nothing of his audience. He said *Kings Row* left him "wrung out" emotionally, but viewers of his movies would rarely have left the theater feeling equally wrung by the experience.

Neither is there much early evidence that he possessed a genius for political gesture. He did what he could in areas that he knew would have some meaning for the voter, he was also surprisingly pragmatic and, as it turned out, regularly successful. He was politically savvy. He shrewdly entertained returning Vietnam prisoners of war and visited wounded soldiers in hospital, and he understood how to take full advantage of the resulting positive publicity.

In the year he became governor he also celebrated his fifteenth wedding anniversary. Nancy believed her job was to support her husband through thick and thin, without question and that role invariably involved ensuring his comfort. She skillfully converted the California governor's office into a pleasant place to work and said, "Ronnie was just delighted. I took a huge jar of Jelly Belly beans that a friend had sent to Ronnie and put it on his desk. I noticed that it was the first thing that people went for when they came into the office to meet with him."

Reagan had a well-documented passion for jellybeans and after he became President, even had a specially designed holder to protect them on

Air Force One after he became President. He confirmed, tongue in cheek, "You can tell a lot about a fellow by his way of eating jellybeans!" He personally preferred the liquorice flavor and would sometimes have jars made up of just the black beans. He wrote, "its gotten to the point where we can hardly start a meeting or make a decision without passing around a jar of jellybeans."

The extraordinary lengths he went to in satisfying his candy craving sheds a peculiar light on the inner drive of a man who tended to appear terminally laid back and go a little way in explaining his astonishing success in two careers that would have defeated men of far higher qualification and far more ferocious ambition.

It is difficult to grasp the full extent of his many triumphs. The fact that he survived so long in a notoriously fickle Hollywood, managing his lengthy film career, despite his shortcomings, refusing to act in the theatrical sense of the word, is astonishing. He had refused to impose himself at the studio and was largely successful because he correctly saw his movie career as a lucky opportunity proffered him by rich and powerful men. All he had to do, as he saw it, was to go along with them, show up on time, learn his lines, submit to the publicity process, and above all, not question their decisions. He became a winner, not necessarily a stunner. Richard Schickel explained that life for Reagan was, "A collage, a juxtaposition of materials not normally brought into close congress…he is simply borne along through his days on the stream of his consciousness."…he just sort of dreamed himself to fame and fortune despite his strong pragmatic streak. Looking back on his Hollywood years, it is clear that acting was only an extension of reality for him, he could never work comfortably beyond his limited natural range of characterization.

He had seen his movie career as one great film in which he had been lucky enough to have had the starring role, "He seems to have found life around the studio fun, and both his own accounts and those of others show him in those days to be a young man of no temperament and no image of himself as an actor at all. This had been his salvation in the days when Warner Bros was in turmoil and faced with rebellion from its major stars." James Cagney, Bette Davis, Olivia De Haviland, Bogart and Flynn were all in conflict with Jack Warner. Reliable Reagan got on with the work. They all sought better parts, more money, and demanded to choose their own roles. Warner hardly heard a peep out of young Reagan. He had been unassuming and fully prepared to grind out whatever features he was assigned to.

The real actors with box-office appeal, the quick-change artists, were notoriously difficult for studios to manage. Reagan was neither. The limits he worked within were not a problem before the war; whilst he was still attractive, young and pleasant. After the war things were markedly different. Genre films lost their hold on the public. Actors were required to bring something new and subtle to their performances. Reagan found himself in a an uncomfortable spot, particularly when first wife, Jane Wyman, seemed to grasp the need for subtlety very early. Before the war they were both working in the B's at Warners, but Wyman had instinctively understood both the changes that were taking place and the opportunities they offered. By 1945 she had starred in *The Lost Weekend* and by 1947 her first Oscar nomination for *The Yearling*, just one year later she won the award for *Johnny Belinda,* and Reagan was left far behind in her wake; he quipped bitterly, "I should name Belinda as correspondent in my divorce." She found and rushed headlong into the world of imagination, he never managed it.

In his movie decline, he was a fader, not a faller and, undoubtedly, the gods of fortune smiled down on him. His mentors accumulated no grievances against him, he had never given any of them reason to besmirch a weakened star. Studio bosses tried to help him, because they liked him. Unlike most actors, he was always polite, subservient, amiable, respectful and steady. He had been loyal to Warner, and, more importantly, he had remained faithful to the only agency he ever had, Lew Wasserman's MCA.

With their help he had hung on in pictures for a while, and had been given plenty of nice guy parts in minor pictures. When he turned forty it was apparent to all of them that his future didn't rest in these little films and may even have already recognized that the television sit-com would soon render them obsolete. In his last movie, the lamentable *The Killers*, it was abundantly clear that he could not get away with playing out of his range either. He hinted at off-screen sadism in his relationship with Angie Dickinson, but he could not menace, nor project sexual banditry successfully.

By the time he made *The Killers,* he was already staring at his salvation, his solution. And, as the arc lights dimmed, he was pointed in the direction of political illusion, where he might again be a winner by turning up on time and learning his lines.

He was a hugely gifted member of the generation that came of age along with the movies. His cronies were those on which the myth-making power of the movies shone with the piercing power of the new. Sitting in exactly the right time and place, Reagan had had a wonderful capacity to project himself into those fantastic narratives, to turn his personal history into wish fulfillment of the kind that movies were conventionalizing. His was a story that the masses could read easily and eagerly. So powerful had been his ability to create starring roles for himself in his own mind that it had survived his rise within the moviemaking community and then later into the political arena.

He had arrived as governor slap bang in the middle of intensely difficult and restless times and he was never simply an incumbent, he was the hero- that was the way he saw it and played it for all his worth. He was light on his feet, always one step ahead, throughout the student rebellions of the sixties and seventies, which were difficult times for all concerned. The California Campuses were in flames and firebombs were landing everywhere, but Reagan went to talk to the enraged students directly and with his own brand of humor. He once went to a potentially hazardous meeting with them. They lined up in silence along the sidewalk as he approached. He walked slowly past the line, face inscrutable, then, when he reached the end, he turned, smiled, put a finger to his lips and said, "shhh!" He had lifted the sense of threat in the air and the meeting went ahead without bloodshed or further trouble.

No matter how inflamed people around him became, he rarely rose to the bait and hardly ever responded with anger or loss of composure. Nancy believed he didn't have it in him, saying the only way people would ever guess he was really mad was when he took his glasses off and threw them across the desk of his office, "That's about as bad as things ever got." He once said himself that he wasn't the type to stamp his feet.

His quick wit and lack of temperament weren't his only strengths however, and one of his major attributes was his fresh approach to the people he met. Once when a student said he had grown up in a different world from them and therefore must be out of touch, "Today we have television, jet planes, space travel, nuclear energy, computers..." Reagan interrupted, "it's true we didn't have those things when we were young. We invented them."

If he had never complained about his movie career, as governor, he found nothing to concern him either; life was hectic but it swung along gently. He never lost sleep, recreation or social time. When he worked he was full of energy and he won plenty of respect from his colleagues. Even when he had been the leader of SAG, where it was usually the has-beens who looked after union matters, Reagan had not been seen in that light by the other stars. Olivia De Havilland said "What comes to mind is his affability and his gift for conducting Screen Actors Guild meetings with adroitness and good humor. I think he was always an instinctive politician, and a genial one."

140

It had been as SAG President that he had first begun substituting agreeableness for authority, letting the mantle of office fall comfortably across his shoulders. He had been reaching to find a way to play politics that was within his range. His grasp of the complex issues confronting his SAG presidency had not been subtle. Seeking the lowest common denominator, he simplified matters such as the Communist penetration of the unions, as he applied B movie logic to the issues.

He had been instrumental in granting SAG waiver rights that permitted his own agency, MCA, to enter film and TV production, thus facilitating its rise to its present eminence as the most powerful, and stable, institution in the moving-image industry. Ultimately it was MCA who arranged the real estate transactions that provided him with the wealth to run for the presidency. But those who witnessed his SAG presidency decided his performance was better than adequate; if it played for professionals like Olivia De Havilland, it would certainly work for a broader and less demanding audience.

Regan didn't object to moving further into politics. Those who had been so good to him for so long were pushing him along another road. Why fight to be something he never was? Why not relax into a more comfortable world. And they were right. His too-temperate nature, lack of imaginative fire that had so limited his screen career, were exactly what was needed in different, TV and political venues.

"His picture ran longer and prospered better than our mind's eyes ever contemplated. And none of us, it need hardly be said, had plot devices to match the boldness of his; a mental movie in which the star becomes a real movie star? And then President?"-Schickel.

If anything, public admiration grew for him through the years of his retirement, partly perhaps because of the effort of his admirers to exalt him, partly because of the sympathy the public felt for him and Nancy when he declared that he was suffering from Alzheimer's disease. Americans love a winner. The excellent health that had served him through life had the effect of prolonging his death. His fading mind was supported by an energy it no longer required. In his last years he spent hours raking leaves out of the pool. He never knew his secret service agents then spent hours quietly replacing them.

Throughout his life he clung to Hollywood's unchanging vision of America, the shaded village life, freckle-faced young boys going fishing, hard work rewarded, the hero, the America Americans wanted to believe in. Reagan became the epitome of the dream. His movie career generated the hero, and his decline in the industry coincided exactly with his own increasing interest in Hollywood's labor unrest. Deeply involved in the workings of the guilds and trade unions and the perceived threat of Communism, he became adept at picking his way through the minefield. It was in that dangerous area that he acquired new skills, made influential friends and formed the personal politics that carried him to his next career. If anyone doubted the way motion pictures influenced American and Western society they need go no further than look at Ronald Reagan turning his Hollywood dreams into reality.

When a Reagan movie airs on television, the Reagan who disappeared in 1965 is seen, and perhaps we watch it with disinterest because he went on to much greater things. Could he have made it all the way to the presidency without the movie career behind him? When he turned to the glitter of politics from the gold dust of Hollywood he became a glorious has-been, but how did his films actually measure up against the myth that was created because he moved into the political arena, that he couldn't act or that he was never given a chance in unworthy pictures, "They didn't want them good, they wanted them Thursday."?

He carried the image of loser or an also-ran in the vast majority of his pictures...he was perennially, "the other guy." When he ran for the governorship of California a wit cracked, "James Stewart for governor,

Ronald Reagan for best friend." (Of course, it all went wrong; the best friend ran, won and successfully served for eight years.)

Within his range he had been a credible performer; reviewers had always praised his pleasing personality and liked the healthy boy, incapable of malice. His had been the appeal of the natural, but he had never exuded daring in his ventures. He had no talent for dialect and sprang from no theatrical tradition. He was no Brando or Cagney. He was unremarkable, wholesome, handsome and dull…but occasionally good enough to let us know he may have been underestimated throughout his Hollywood years. Perhaps the Washington years prove that.

**"If he were not the greatest President, he was the best Actor of the Presidency we have ever had."**
**(John Adams on George Washington)**

# THE FILMS OF RONALD REAGAN

# Love Is On the Air

**release date: October 2, 1937**         **running time: 58-61 minutes**

**Cast:**    Ronald Reagan, June Travis, Eddie Acuff, Ben Welden, Robert Barrat, Addison Richards, Raymond Hatton, Tommy Bupp, Dickie Jones, Willard Parker, William Hopper, Spec O'Donnell, Herbert Rawlinson, Lynne Roberts (aka Mary Hart), Jack Mower, Harry Hayden, Sonny Bupp, Glen Cavender, Alan Davis, John Dilson, John Elliott, Frank Mayo,

Jack Richardson, Cliff Saum, Lee Shumway, Edwin Stanley, Elliott Sullivan, Jerry Tucker, Billy Wayne, Jack Wise, Don Deering, Marianne Edwards, Priscilla Lyon, Johnnie Pirrone, Jr., Henry Hanna, George Billings, Margaret Davis, John Harron, Johnny Morris, Ann Howard, Fern Barry, Julia Perkins, Ray Nichols

**Credits:**          **First National-Warners**

*Executive Producers* Jack L. Warner, Hal B. Wallis; *Producer*
Bryan Foy; *Director* Nick Grinde; *Screenplay* Morton Grant,
George Bricker; *Story* Roy Chanslor; *Additional Dialogue* Pat C.
Flick; *Original Music* Howard Jackson; *Cinematography* James
Van Trees; *Art Director* Max Parker; *Assistant Director* Marshall
Hageman; *Editor* Doug Gould; *Wardrobe* Howard Shoup; *Sound*
Leslie Hewitt; *Unit Manager* Carrol Sax

## Synopsis:

Andy McCain (Reagan) is a crusading senior radio announcer at a
smalltown radio station. He finds himself called into manager, JD
Harrington's (Robert Barrat), office after his sponors complain
about his reports on local criminals. McCain casually smokes one
of his bosses cigarettes and merely shrugs when JD cautions him
again about his habit of editorializing on the air.

Reformist business leader, Roy Copelin, has vanished with $250,000
of cooperative funds; Nicey Ferguson, the city's chief racketeer and
EE Nichols, a retail tycoon, have been suspiciously quick to call it a
case of embezzlement. McCain has publicly challenged their claim
and promised to broadcast the full inside story... no wonder Nichols
has leaned on JD to get him fired.

Instead JD reassigns him to the daily *Kiddie's Hour*! While Jo
Hopkins (June Travis), producer of the KDTS children's
programming, is promoted over his head. She is resentful about
having McCain thrust into her area at first, but it isn't long before
she is on his side.

McCain resolves to uncover the connections between the racketeers,
local businessmen and the politicians who provide protection for
profit. He has a lead from a local youth that Copelin might have
been murdered.

Andy transforms his new show into a popular junior news magazine.
The racketeers are finally tricked into exposing themselves before
Andy's hidden microphone.

"And the hero of this story" Jo announces proudly, seizing the mike herself, "is your radio commentator, Andy McCain, who proved he can think as fast as he can talk."

## Reviews:

"A modest little comedy-drama" *New York Times* (November 12, 1937)*; "*One of those refreshing pictures which proves that quality does not depend upon names or the amount of money poured into the production . . . *Love Is On the Air* presents a new leading man, Ronald Reagan, who is a natural, giving one of the best first picture performances Hollywood has offered in many a day . . . (He) was found announcing from a Des Moines, Iowa, station (and is) completely at home in the role of Andy, but demonstrated an ability which will not confine him to radio-announcer roles." *Hollywood Reporter* (September 1937)*; "*Nick Grinde has turned in a good directing job, and has built suspense and a bit of excitement." *Daily Variety* (September 1937)*; "*Ronald Reagan, whom Warners is trying to build up into a juve lead...Reagan before the camera almost all the way, gives rather an in-and-out performance. He's best when in fast physical action." *Variety* (September 15, 1937)

## Notes:

Filming on the three week shoot began on June 7, 1937 at the Warner backlot in Burbank.

Budgeted at $119,000 the film ended production at a negative cost of $97,000. Warners earned $270,000 in worldwide rentals ($193,000 came from the domestic market and the balance from overseas theaters). By the early 1940's the average budget for a "B" film at Warners had soared to $180,000.

Working title of the production was, *Inside Story,* with Reagan cast as a radio announcer. The original plot was shot three years earlier under the title, *Hi, Nellie* with Paul Muni in the lead role.

Ronald Reagan, in his first starring role, received $200 a week. On April 20, 1937 he signed a standard seven year, player contract with the studio. As a contract player he would be evaluated every six months, with the studio having the option of either renewing or dropping him. The contract guaranteed Reagan a minimum of nineteen weeks work within the twenty-six week option period. At Warners, during this period, competing for the same type of roles as Reagan were fellow contract actors Wayne Morris and Dennis Morgan.

As preparation for the role, Reagan spent exactly one-day with a dialogue coach and was in rehearsals for three consecutive days.

Chicago-born leading lady June Travis (1914- ) appeared in thirty-one films, all of the B-variety, twenty-nine of which were released between 1935 and 1939. She made her screen debut in *Stranded* and ended her career with a cameo in *Monster a-Go-Go* (1965).

Third-billed, Missouri-born Eddie Acuff (1903-1956), between the early 1930's and 1951, appeared in over 235 films.

During the thirties, Nick Grinde (1893-1979), was one of Warners most prolific programmer directors for the Saturday matinee crowd. Starting as an assistant director in the mid-1920's, Grinde helmed his first feature, the Tim McCoy western, *Riders of the Dark,* in 1928. By the mid-thirties he was churning out B-films in a number of genres including crime, action, western, and mystery.

Producer Bryan Foy (1896-1977) was, for more than two decades, in charge of all "B" productions at Warners. His combined output as both a director and producer exceeded two-hundred productions. Foy, once known as one of the original "Seven Little Foys" a Vaudeville act, started directing in 1924. He turned to the production end in 1928 with the feature, *The Lights of New York.* Towards the end of his career he produced some big projects including the 3D thriller *The House of Wax* (1953), and his last motion picture project highlighting the wartime exploits of John F. Kennedy, *PT109* (1963).

Released in Britain under the title, *The Radio Murder Mystery.*

The film opened in New York City on November 27, 1937 at the Palace Theater at the bottom-half of a double bill that featured Katherine Hepburn and Ginger Rogers in *Stage Door.*

# Sergeant Murphy

**release date: November 18, 1937**          **running time: 57 minutes**

**Cast:**   Ronald Reagan, Mary Maguire, Donald Crisp, Ben Hendricks, Jr., William B. Davidson, Max Hoffman, Jr., David Newell, Emmett Vogan, Tracy Layne, Edmund Cobb, Ellen Clancy, Janet Shaw, Rosella Towne, Joan Valerie, Sam McDaniels, Raymond Brown, James D. Green, Alec Harford, Boyd Irwin, Edward Keane, Lloyd Lane, Wilfred Lucas, Fred Miller, Walter Miller, Art Mix, Kansas Moehring, Artie Ortego, Henry Otho, Lee Prather, Jack Richardson, Jack Shannon, Reginald Sheffield, John Graham Spacey, Cyril Thornton, David Thursby, Chad Trower, Douglas Wood, William Worthington, Helen Valkis, John Dilson, Jimmy Adamson

**Credits:**                **Warner Bros.**

*Executive Producers* Jack L. Warner, Hal B. Wallis; *Associate Producer* Bryan Foy; *Director* B. Reeves Eason; Screenwriter William Jacobs; *Story* Cy Bartlett; *Original Music* Howard Jackson, M.K. Jerome, Jack Scholl; *Cinematography* Ted D. McCord; *Editor* James Gibbon; *Art Direction* Hugh Reticker; *Costumes* Howard Shoup; *Dialogue Director* Frank Beckwith; *Assistant Director* William Kissel; *Set Decorator* Abem Finkel; *Sound* Charles Lang; *Unit Manager* Carrol Sax

## Synopsis:

The title of the film refers to a horse. Reagan plays a cavalry private devoted to the horse, an animal with a gift for jumping. It is so sensitive however that the sound of artillery makes him unreliable for army duty. The soldier spares the horse heavy duty, trains him and later gains posession of him.

He is aided in his efforts by the post colonel's (Donald Crisp) daughter, (Mary Maguire). She falls in love with the soldier and the horse. Once the horse is mustered out of the army, the three share a variety of adventures, some almost tragic. But eventually the horse wins acclaim in national shows and is smuggled to England where it is entered into the Grand National.

## Reviews:

"Film moves briskly, aided competently by the trio of featured players...Reagan and Miss Maguire...loom as another of Hollywood's ballyhooed romantic teams by their youthful zest and fresh interpretations" *Variety* (December 22, 1937); "Ronald

Reagan is coming along as a screen actor. He has gained noticeably in ease, in sureness of gesture, and in the ability to get his thoughts and emotions into the camera." *Hollywood Spectator* (December 18, 1937); *"...forgettable programmer....Ronnie is a lowly private."* *Leonard Maltin's 2000 Movie & Video Guide* (Penguin Putnam 1999);

## Notes:

Location filming started on July 12, 1937 (six days after completion of Reagan's debut film, *Love Is On the Air)* at the home of the 11th Cavalry, the Fort Ord military reservation, at the Presidio, on the Monterey Peninsula in northern California. Some second-unit filming was also done at San Pedro Harbor, the Providencia Ranch, Warners Calabasas Ranch, Santa Anita Racetrack and in Santa Barbara. The production was allotted eighteen days for the shoot and went five days over budget.

Budgeted at $147,000 the final negative cost of the production came in at $163,000. The picture returned $211,000 in domestic rentals for Warners and a further $68,000 from overseas markets.

Based on the story *Golden Girl,* screen-rights were secured by the studio for $3,250.

Reagan, an expert equestrian and reserve officer in the United States cavalry, performed most of his own stunts and all of his riding. He was again paid $200 a week. Director Eason was paid $3,033 while the cost for the entire cast came to $12,060. The owner of the title horse and its' double received $100 a week for the rentals of both animals.

With the intention of making this an "A" feature, Warners originally offered the lead role to one of its top stars, James Cagney

One sequence filmed at Fort Ord consisted of a parade of 1100 mounted soldiers riding past the podium.

While making this film Reagan was living in a furnished unit at the Montecito Apartments at the corner of Franklin and Whitley in Hollywood.

Leading lady, Mary Maguire (1917- ) hailed from Australia, arrived in the United States as a child, and entered films as a teenager. Her total screen output, from 1935 to 1942, consisted of less than twenty features, all of the "B" variety. With five films in release, 1937 was her most productive year. After a minor role in *This Was Paris,* she retired from acting.

By contrast, London-born Donald Crisp (1880-1974), in the capacity of actor or director, worked in the industry for fifty-five years. He started at the Biograph Studios in 1908, appeared as General Grant in Griffith's *The Birth of a Nation,* directed more than sixty-five films in the teens and twenties, and became a familiar and versatile character actor in scores of films of the thirties. By the time he retired, after his role in *Spencer's Mountain* in 1963, his screen credits exceed one-hundred and fifty.

B. (William) Reeves Eason (1886-1956), with his quick wit and efficiency of movement, was one of the foremost action directors of the 1930s and 1940s. The director of 125 features started out in the industry in 1915 as an actor, writer, and assistant director. He received universal acclaim for his staging and filming of the chariot scene in *Ben Hur* (1925), and was also assigned the formidable task of filming the burning of Atlanta in Technicolor, for David O. Selznick's epic *Gone With the Wind* (1939).

# Submarine D-1

**release date: November 27, 1937**                    **running time: 100 minutes**

**Cast:**  Pat O'Brien, George Brent, Wayne Morris, Doris Weston, Frank
McHugh, Henry O'Neill, Dennis Moore, Veda Ann Borg, Regis
Toomey, John Ridgely, Owen King, Wally Maher, Jerry Fletcher,
Walter Clyde, Broderick Crawford, Ronald Reagan, Fern Barry,
Donald Briggs, Allan Caven, Loia Cheaney, Gordon Clifford, Don
DeFore, Ralph Dunn, John Elliott, Jim Farley, Eddie Fetherston, Pat
Flaherty, Dick French, Sol Gorss, Allan Kenward, Mike Lally, Walter
Miller, Eric Pettit, Lee Phelps, Jeffrey Sayre, John Shea, Don Turner,
Billy Vincent, Dick Wessell, John Tyrell, Frank Bingman,

Robert Homass, Paul Barrett, Huey White, Jack Hatfield, Max
Hoffman, Jr., Kenneth Harlan, Allen Matthews, Wilfred Henry, Pat
O'Malley, Gordon De Main, Elliott Sullivan, Walter Young, John
Harron, Rosella Towne, Eddie Roberts, Billy Wayne, Hal Craig, Jack
Gardner, Frank Marlowe, John Marston, Nena Quartaro, Renee
Torres, Nina Berget, Alfonso Perroza, Harry Strang, Ted Oliver, Anna
Demetrio, Frank Orth, Glen Cavender, Ed Keane, Fred McKaye,
Philip Morris, Emmett Vogan, Clyde Dilson, David Newell

# Credits:    Cosmopolitan Pictures-First National-Warners

*Executive Producers* Hal B. Wallis, Jack Warner; *Producer* Louis F. Edelman; *Director* Lloyd Bacon; *Assistant Director* Dick Mayberry; *Cinematography* Arthur Edeson; *Writers* Warren Duff, Lawrence Kimble, Frank Wead; *Additional contract writer* William Wister Haines; *Original Music* Max Steiner; *Editor* William Holmes; *Special Effects* Byron Haskin, Hans F. Koenekamp; *Musical Director* Leo F. Forbstein; *Art Director* Esdras Hartley; *Wardrobe* Howard Shoup; *Sound* Alexander and Robert B. Lee; *Technical Advisor* Commander G.W.D. Dashiells

## Reviews:

"An interesting and, as far as it goes, apparently authentic document study of the Navy's undersea arm." *New York Times* (December 20, 1937);

## Notes:    *"All of the film I shot ended up on the cutting room floor."*

In production from late June to August 11, 1937 under the working title *Submarine 262*. Scenes were shot on location at the navy base on Coronado Beach in San Diego (3 weeks), the submarine base in New London, with second-unit work at the Panama Canal Zone and off Catalina Island. Reagan worked on the film for one week and in May joined the cast on their trip to Connecticut to the headquarters of the Atlantic submarine fleet.

Negative cost of the film was $857,000. Warners earned $992,000 from the domestic market and an additional $505,000 from overseas markets.

During previews Reagan was listed sixth in the cast billing. Final editing to highlight the action over the human drama, eliminated all of Reagan's scenes in the film. He was still being paid $200 a week by the studio.

Chicago-native, female lead Doris Weston (1917-1960) had a career which consisted of only nine films over three years (1937-1939).

Second-lead George Brent (1899-1979) was born in Ireland and came to Hollywood in the late 1920s. He appeared in over 85 films from 1930 to 1956, and made a last screen appearance, as a judge in *Born Again* (1978).

This would be the first of six films that Wayne Morris (1914-1959) worked in with Reagan. In 1936 the Los Angeles graduate of the Pasadena Playhouse was signed to a contract by Warners. For his ninth film the boxing story *Kid Galahad* (1937), he received top billing and much critical acclaim. Before entering the Navy as a fighter pilot on carriers, the tall, blond actor appeared in four 1941 releases: *I Wanted Wings, Bad Men of Missouri, 3 Sons O' Guns,* and *The Smiling Ghost.* Returning from the war with a chest full of medals and seven confirmed enemy plane "kills," Morris was never able to regain the momentum he had generated before the war.

Screenwriter Frank Wead (1895-1947) was a former Navy commander who turned to writing plays and stories for the screen after an accident left him with very limited use of his legs. Some of the more familiar of his more than thirty screenplays were *Dirigible* (1931), *Hell Divers* (1931), *Ceiling Zero* (1936), *Test Pilot* (1938), *I Wanted Wings* (1941) and for his friend John Ford, *They Were Expendable* (1945). In 1957 John Ford brought the life of Wead to the screen with John Wayne as the writer who overcame adversity, in *Wings of Eagles,* with Maureen O'Hara as his long-suffering wife.

In the Los Angeles area this film was shown as part of a double-bill with *Adventurous Blonde.*

Competition at the nation's theaters came from: *Navy Blue and Gold* (MGM) with Robert Young and James Stewart, Cary Grant and Irene Dunne in the romantic-comedy *The Awful Truth* (Columbia) and David O. Selznick's screwball comedy *Nothing Sacred* with Carole Lombard and Frederic March.

# Swing Your Lady

**release date: January 8, 1938**      **running time: 72-79 minutes**

**Cast:**  Humphrey Bogart, Frank McHugh, Louise Fazenda, Nat Pendleton, Penny Singleton, Allen Jenkins, Leon Weaver, Frank Weaver, Elviry Weaver, Ronald Reagan, Daniel Boone Savage, Hugh O'Connell, Tommy Bupp, Sonny Bupp, Joan Howard, Sue Moore, Olin Howlin, Sammy White, Irving Bacon, Tex Driscoll, June Gittelson, Roger Gray, John 'Skins" Miller, Spec O'Donnell, George Ovey, Frank Pharr, Victor Potel, Cliff Saum, Georgia Simmons, Foy Van Dolsen, Eddie Acuff

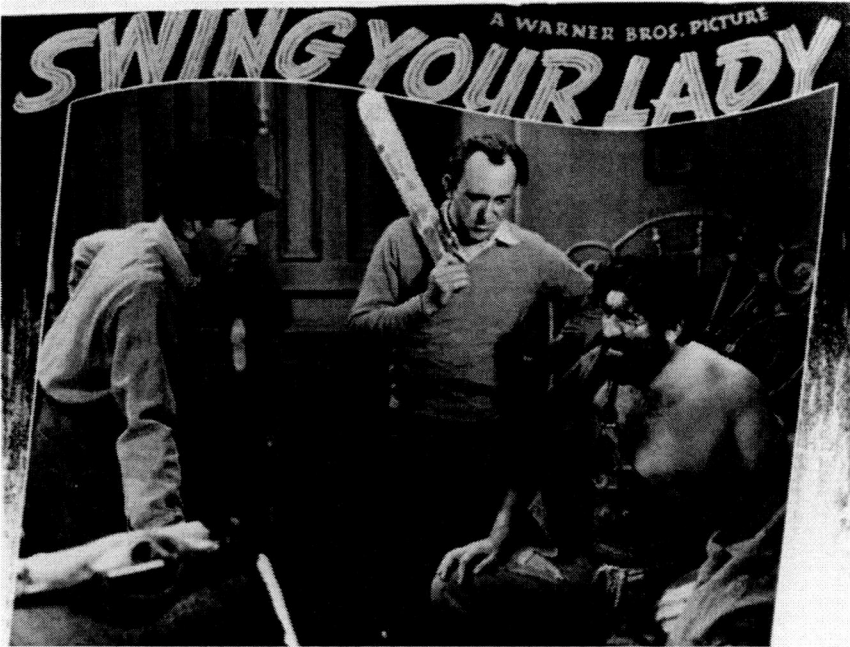

**Credits:**               **Warner Bros.**

*Executive Producers* Jack L. Warner, Hal B. Wallis; *Associate Producer* Samuel Bischoff; *Director* Ray Enright; *Cinematography* Arthur Edeson; *Writers* Maurice Leo, Kenyon Nicholson, Charles Robinson, Joseph Schrank; *Editor* Jack Killifer; *Original Music and Songs* Adolph Deutsch, M.K. Jerome, Jack Scholl; *Art Direction*

Esdras Hartley; *Costumes* Howard Shoup; *Assistant Director* Jesse Hibbs; *Sound* Charles Lang; *Musical Director* Leo F. Forbstein; *Orchestrations* Hugo Friedhofer; *Miscellaneous Musical* Bobby Connolly; *Dialogue Director* Jo Graham; *Unit Manager* Louis Baum; *Songs* "Mountain Swingaroo," "The Old Apple Tree," "Swing Your Lady," "Dig Me A Grave In Missouri" and "Hillbilly from 10th Avenue."

## Synopsis:

*Swing Your Lady* sees Reagan as Jack Miller, a glib tongued sports reporter. Ed Hatch (Humphrey Bogart) seethes with indignation as a slick promotor down on his luck, stranded in a small Kentucky town. His main asset is dim hulking wrestler Joe Skopapoulos (Nat Pendleton).

Hatch is impressed by the town's lady blacksmith, Sadie Horn (Louise Fazenda), and he plots to match her against his wrestler. The wrestler unfortunaately falls in love with Sadie and refuses to fight.

Hatch's dilemma is solved when the Sadie's hillbilly suitor arrives back in town and objects to the proposed match.

A new fight is arranged between the suitor and wrestler and the winner gets the girl. Joe wins but leaves his mentor in favor of small town life.

## Reviews:

"Sam Bischoff's entire production crew has done a good job, notably on the casting....To Ray Enright, the director, goes a lot of credit in guiding the comedy along over its dangerous spots and through its most laughable portions." *Variety* (January 23, 1938); "...another vulgar, ludicrous, irresponsible and yet, we firmly believe, anthropologically valuable study of Americana." *The New York Times* (January 27, 1938); "A bit of Ozark idiocy..." *Bogart: A Life in Hollywood* Jeffrey Meyers (Houghton-Mifflin, Boston, 1997); "It is difficult to understand the thinking behind *Swing Your Lady*, let alone be charitable about it." *Bogart.* Terrance Pettigrew (Proteus, London, 1977); "...a riotous hillbilly farce....No Mack Sennett Keystone was ever more down to earth fun...." *The Los Angeles Examiner* (Louella O. Parsons, February 9, 1938)

# Notes:

In production from September 8 to October 29, 1937, the film ran 14 days over schedule. Shot on Stage 8 and the backlot at Warners Burbank facilities.

Completed filming at a negative cost of $498,000 with a cast and crew of 85. Warners realized $410,000 in domestic rentals and a further $112,000 from the foreign markets.

Based on a Broadway play written by Kenyon Nicholson and Charles Robinson. Warners secured the screen-rights for $27,500.

Reagan paid $467 (at the rate of $200 a week). Ray Enright earned $17,500 for directing; Frank McHugh was paid $16,100, Humphrey Bogart $4,200; Allen Jenkins $6,300; Nat Pendleton $7,000; Louise Fazenda $2,500 ($1250 a week); Dorothy McNulty $350/week; Tommy Bupp $200/week; and Daniel Boone Savage received $500/week.

Original choice for the female lead was to have been Glenda Farrell.

Humphrey Bogart (1899-1957), after five years of bit-roles, had finally become a minor star due to his magnetic performance in *Petrified Forest* (1935). *Swing Your Lady* was one of six films he was assigned to by Warners in 1938. In later years he would remark that this was the worst film he ever appeared in. At the time of his death he was one of Hollywoods biggest stars and had over seventy-five screen credits. Reagan and Bogart also appeared together in *The Amazing Dr. Clitterhouse* and *Dark Victory.*

Leading lady Louise Fazenda (1895-1962), was, at the time of the making of this film, married to producer Hal Wallis. Making a name for herself as a deft comedienne, she had appeared in films since at least 1913. She retired in 1939. Fazenda and Wallis would stay married (1927-1962) until her death from a brain hemorrhage.

Ray Enright (1896-1965), a director of seventy-three motion pictures, started in the industry in the mid-teens as a cutter and editor of early comedy shorts for Mack Sennett then Thomas Ince before joining Warner Bros. where, in 1927, he was afforded the opportunity to direct his first film the Rin Tin Tin adventure *Tracked by the Police.* He worked on six films with Reagan and in the 1940s some of his better efforts included: the John Wayne-Marlene Dietrich-Randolph Scott western *The Spoilers* (1942), *The Iron Major* (1943) starring Pat O'Brien, *Gung Ho!* (1943) with Randolph Scott and *China Sky* (1945). He retired in 1953 after directing the Italian produced, George Raft mystery-drama *The Man From Cairo.*

The film had two premieres, one in Dallas in January 1938 and the other in Hannibal, Missouri in February.

The Weaver Brothers and their sister were a vaudeville team that played throughout the nation for several decades.

Cast members Nat Pendleton and Daniel Boone Savage were professional wrestlers.

In the Los Angeles area the film was part of a double-bill with the low-grade John Farrow directed, Boris Karloff horror entry *The Invisible Menace.*

In competition for the filmgoers dollar were Mae West's *Everyday is a Holiday* from Paramount and *Lady Behave,* a Republic B-film featuring Sally Eilers and Neil Hamilton.

Reagan with Louise Fazenda,
Penny Singleton and Humphrey Bogart

# Hollywood Hotel

**release date: January 15, 1938**          **running time: 100-109 minutes**

**Cast:**  Dick Powell, Rosemary Lane, Lola Lane, Benny Goodman, Raymond Paige, Hugh Herbert, Ted Healy, Glenda Farrell, Johnnie Davis, Louella Parsons, Alan Mowbray, Mabel Todd, Frances Langford, Jerry Cooper, Ken Niles, Duane Thompson,Allyn Joslyn, Grant Mitchell, Edgar Kennedy, Curt Bois, Benny Goodman Orchestra, Susan Hayward, Carole Landis, Teddy Wilson, Eddie Acuff, Don Barclay, Sonny Bupp, Leonard Carey, Georgia Cooper, William B. Davidson, Sarah Edwards, Betty Farrington, Fritz Feld, Jerry Fletcher, Eddie Graham, Harrison Greene, Lionel Hampton, Robert Homans, Paul Irving, Harry James, Gene Krupa, Ethelreda Leopold, Wally Maher, Frances Morris, Jack Mower, David Newell, Spec O'Donnell, Jean Perry, Ronald Reagan, John Ridgely, Joseph Romantini, Clinton Rosemond, Jeffrey Sayre, Janet Shaw, Libby Taylor, Perc Westmore, Marianne Edwards, David Leo Tillotson, Jackie Morrow, Billy Wayne, Harry Fox, Allen Fox, Lester Dorr, John Harron, Patsy Kane, Sidney Perlman, Bobby Watson, Allan Conrad, Edward Earl Ray, Owen King, George O'Hanlon, Jean Maddox, George Offerman, Jr., Helen Dickson, George Guhl, Jerry Mandy, Demeris Emanuel, John Sheehan, William Mansell, Rosella Towne, Dina Smirnova, Alan Davis, Al Herman, Al Shean, Milton Kibbee, Pearl Adams, Helen Valkis, Ellen Clancy, Don Wolheim

**Credits:**     **Warner Bros.-First National**

*Executive Producers* Jack L. Warner, Hal B. Wallis; *Director* Busby Berkeley; *Associate Producers* Sam Bischoff, Bryan Foy; *Screenplay* Jerry Wald, Maurice Leo, Richard Macauley; *Original Story* Jerry Wald, Maurice Leo; *Cinematography* George Barnes, Charles Rosher; *Editor* George Amy; *Art Director* Robert Haas; *Sound* Oliver S. Garretson, David Forrest; *Unit Manager* Bob Fellows; *Music* Richard A. Whiting, Phil Baxter, Ray Heindorf, Heinz Roemheld; *Musical Director* Leo F. Forbstein; *Assistant Dance Director* Matty King; *Lyricist* Johnny Mercer; *Costumes* Orry-Kelly; *Stunts* Vivian Austin; *Dialogue Director* Gene Lewis; *Assistant Director* Russ Saunders; *Song* "Satan's Holiday" by Joe Venuti, Benny Goodman, "Can't Teach My Heart New Tricks," I'm A Ding Dong Daddy from Dumas," "I'm Like A Fish Out of Water," I've Hitched My Wagon to a Star," "Let that be A Lesson to You," "Silhouetted in the Moonlight," "Sing You Son of a Gun," "Hooray For Hollywood," "California Here I Come" and "Dark Eyes."

## Synopsis:

Ronnie Bowers (Dick Powell), a saxophone player with Benny Goodman's Band, wins a talent competition and a trip to Hollywood. He becomes increasingly frustrated as he tries to get into the movie world. Eventually, with the help of Virginia (Rosemary Lane), he manages to snare an appearance on Louella Parson's stellar radio show. He wins immediate success.

## Reviews:

"A fairly good entertainment" *New York Times* (January 13, 1938); "...lively music and amusing story....Warners has assembled an excellent cast..." *Variety* (December 22, 1937); "Spectacular, eye-filling and crammed with hit tunes from start to finish . . . has everything that makes for top entertainment. . . .It has perfectly caught the spirit of the famous radio hour of the same name . . . (Dick Powell) turns in one of his best performances...Busby Berkeley, the director . . . deserves a bow for the fast pace and smoothness of his direction." *The Los Angeles Examiner* (Dorothy Manners, January 28, 1938);

"... a frantic kind of diversion with less pattern and more movement, sound and fury than the usual film-musical. .... If it is disjointed in story thread, it has the counterbalance of freshness and verve which seems like improvisation by the many performers involved." *Daily Variety (December 21, 1937);* "...a knockout show for any man's theater and for any audience. It is, by all manner of means, the greatest piece of entertainment with music ever turned out at that plant (Warners), and can be stacked up against any ever made at any studio." *The Hollywood Reporter* (December 21, 1937)

## Notes:

Negative cost of the production was $1,141,000. It returned domestic rentals of $1,094,000 to the studio and a further $255,000 from overseas markets.

Reagan paid $200 a week.

Director Busby Berkeley (1895-1976) was the preeminent choreographer of movie musicals of the 1930s and early 1940s. His staging of extravagant dance numbers with large indoor sets and unique camera angles (overhead shots) set the standard for decades and were enormous audience favorites during the Depression. Berkeley learned his craft as an army officer during World War I.

On Broadway he worked creating dance numbers and movements for Florence Ziegfeld. At the suggestion of Eddie Canter and Samuel Goldwyn he moved to Hollywood in 1930 and worked on the Canter films *Whoopee!* (1930), *Palmy Days* (1931), *The Kid from Spain* (1932) and *Roman Scandals* (1933).

Vincent Sherman directed the sequences with Reagan. Reagan had just played the lead in a Warner Brothers film, a B, yet he now found himself slotted into the finale of Hollywood Hotel and not even given a screen credit!

Reagan appears at the scene of the broadcast and plays one of Louella's staff. He appears pleased but nervous, as might well be the case…he had only very recently himself been a sports announcer on a radio show, and now found himself surrounded by a glittering array of the nation's biggest radio personalities.

Filmed from early August to early November 1937. Shot at the Warners backlot with some location work at the Glendale Grand Central Airport Terminal.

At one time Bette Davis was scheduled to headline the film.

Based on the radio program of the same name. Gossip columnist Louella Parsons, made her debut as an actress in this film.

Female-lead Rosemary Lane (born Mullican; 1914-1974) was one of the three acting Lane sisters. She also appeared with Lola and Priscilla in the popular *Four Wives* (1939) and its sequel *Four Mothers* (1941). Between 1937 and the time of her retirement from the screen in 1945 the actress appeared in twenty films. Some of her better known entries included: *Blackwell's Island* (1939) opposite John Garfield, *The Oklahoma Kid* (1939) which starred James Cagney and Humphrey Bogart.

Fourth-billed Chicago native Benny Goodman (1909-1986) was the man most responsible for creating the "Swing Era." Playing the clarinet and leading one of the most popular big bands of the 1930s and 1940s, Goodman recorded records, played on radio, and toured the world giving concerts for almost fifty years. In 1926 knowing what kind of sound he wanted to achieve, he made his first recording then in 1934 formed his own big-band orchestra. *Hollywood Hotel* would be the second of his eight screen appearances. His first role was in *The Big Broadcast of 1937* (1936).

The film faced competition at the nation's theaters from: *Mannequin* (MGM) with Joan Crawford and Spencer Tracy, Fox's *In Old Chicago* with Tyrone Power and Alice Faye and the screwball comedy from Howard Hawks *Bringing Up Baby* with Cary Grant and Katharine Hepburn.

# Accidents Will Happen

**release date: April 9, 1938**                    **running time: 60-62 minutes**

**Cast:** Ronald Reagan, Sheila Bromley, Dick Purcell, Addison Richards, Anderson Lawler, Gloria Blondell, Hugh O'Connell, Janet Shaw, Spec O'Donnell, Elliott Sullivan, Kenneth Harlan, Don Barclay, Max Hoffman, Jr., John Butler, Jeffrey Sayre, Fern Barry, Allan Cavan, Ralph Dunn, Earl Dwire, Betty Farrington, Jimmy Fox, Al Herman, Stuart Holmes, Richard Kipling, Wilfred Lucas, Betty Mack, Pat O'Malley, Willard Parker, Ralph Peters, Clinton Rosemond, Loretta Rush, Cliff Saum, Frank Shannon, Edwin Stanley, Myrtle Stedman, Bernard Suss, Monte Vandergrift, Max Wagner, Jack Wise, William Worthington, Ellen Clancy, Mary Doyle, Frank Shannon, John Harron, George Guhl, Allan Conrad, Milt Kibbee

**Credits:**     **First National-Warners**

*Executive Producers* Jack L. Warner, Hal B. Wallis; *Producer* Bryan Foy; *Director* William Clemens; *Writers* George Bricker, Anthony Coldeway, Morton Grant; *Story* George Bricker *(contract to treatment* Victor Rose); *Cinematography* L. William O'Connell; *Editor* Thomas Pratt; *Music* Howard Jackson; *Art Direction* Charles Novi; *Costumes* Howard Shoup; *Sound* Charles Lang; *Assistant Director* Bob Ross; *Technical Advisor* Victor Rose; *Dialogue Director* Vincent Sherman

## Synopsis:

*Accidents Will Happen*, grapples with the increasing manipulation of insurance companies by fraudulent claims, a practice, prevalent in 1938.

Eric Gregg (Ronald Reagan) is a naïve insurance adjustor married to Nora (Sheila Bromley). Nora has a taste for material pleasures which he can't afford. Her ethics do not match his and she fiddles his accounts.

He loses his job. Nora gives false evidence against him and joins the gang under investgation.

Eric's despair is lightened by Patricia Carmody (Gloria Blondell), a cigar stand girl. The two begin to gather evidence against the gang. They call in the police. Eric gets his job back, together with a new girl.

## Reviews:

"A fair but not very exciting program item." *The New York Times* (April 5, 1938); "This is an unsuccessful attempt to cash in on the news headlines. . . . The cast does a pretty good job, the direction is good, but the action stuff is not particularly impressive." *Variety* (April 23, 1938); "A strictly formula plot...A workmanlike production that is typical of the B product turned out under Bryan Foy. . . . Reagan carries his assignment with earnestness and fluency, and evidences the personality for a histrionic climb." *The Hollywood Reporter* (February 17, 1938); "Ronald Reagan playing the youthful, domestically harassed insurance company adjuster." *Daily Variety* (February 17, 1938)

## Notes:

In production from September 1 to early October 1937.
Negative cost of the production was $106,000. The studio earned

$178,000 in domestic rentals and $72,000 from the overseas markets. Reagan's salary was $200 a week.

Director William Clemens (1905-1980) started in the industry as an editor in the early 1930s. By the time his career ended in 1947 he had been at the helm of forty low-budget films including several entries in the Torchy Blane, Nancy Drew and Falcon series. Over that eleven year period some of his better known films included: *Man Hunt* (1936), *Footloose* (1937), *The Dead End Kids on Dress Parade* (1939), *Devil's Island* (1940) and *The Thirteenth Hour* (1947).

Leading-lady Sheila Bromley (1911-2003) was also billed as Sheila Manners, Sheila Mannors and Sheila Le Gay. Between 1930 and 1967 she made appearances in over 75 films including three low-budget entries with John Wayne. In the 1950s and 1960s she frequently worked in series television but still found time to be in an occasional picture such as *Hotel* (1967) and *Nightmare Circus* (1973).

Third-billed Dick Purcell (1908-1944) had roles in 74 films over a fifteen year period from 1930 until the time of his early death in 1944. He could be seen in" *Ceiling Zero* (1935), *Bullets or Ballots* (1936), *Navy Blues* (1937), *Nancy Drew-Detective* (1938), *The Bank Dick* (1940), *In Old California* (1942) and the serial *Captain America*. It was during the making of this chapterplay, in which he had the title role, that Purcell suffered a heart attack which killed him almost immediately.

Cinematographer L.William O'Connell besides filming *Accidents Will Happen* had seven other films released in 1938. He started in the industry as an assistant director in the mid-1910s then began filming motion pictures in 1918.

Competition on the nation's screens included: *The Adventures of Robin Hood* starring Errol Flynn in the title role, *Jezebel* with Bette Davis as a tempestuous southern belle and Roy Rogers' first starring effort, *Under Western Skies*.

# Cowboy From Brooklyn

**release date: July 9, 1938**                    **running time: 80 minutes**

**Cast:**  Dick Powell, Pat O'Brien, Priscilla Lane, Dick Foran, Ann Sheridan, Johnnie Davis, Ronald Reagan, Emma Dunn, Granville Bates, James Stephenson, Hobart Cavanaugh, Elisabeth Risdon, Dennis Moore, Rosella Towne, May Boley, Harry Barris, Candy Candido, Donald Briggs, Jeffrey Lynn, John Ridgely, William B. Davidson, Mary Field, Mary Gordon, Eddie Graham, John Harron, Sam Hayes, Dorothy Vaughan, Jack Wise, Brooks Benedict, John Butler, Eddy Chandler, Jimmy Fox, Neal Hart, Ben Hendricks, Jr., George Hickman, John Hiestand, Leyland Hodgson, Stuart Holmes, Don Marion, Frank Mayo, Bruce Mitchell, Clayton Moore, Jack Mower, John T. Murray, Wendell Niles, James Nolan, Cliff Saum, Monte Vandergrift, Emmett Vogan, Jack Moore, James Nolan

**Credits:**          **Cosmopolitan Productions/Warner Bros**

*Executive Producers* Jack L. Warner, Hal B. Wallis; *Associate Producer* Louis F. Edelman; *Director* Lloyd Bacon; From the play, *Howdy, Stranger* by Robert Sloane, Louis Pelletier Jr.; *Screenplay* Earl Baldwin; *Cinematography* Arthur Edeson; *Editor* James Gibbon; *Art Direction* Esdras Hartley; *Music* Harry Warren, Richard A. Whiting, Adolph Deutsch, Leo F. Forbstein; *Costumes* Milo Anderson; *Assistant Director* Richard Mayberry; *Sound* Charles David Forrest, Dolph Thomas; *Lyricist* Johnny Mercer, Richard A. Whiting; *Songs* "Howdy, Stranger," "I've Got A Heartful of Music," "I'll Dream of You Tonight," "Ride Tenderfoot, Ride"

## Synopsis:

Elly Jordan (Dick Powell) is the cowboy drifter of the title. He is a city dude with a fear of animals-even chickens and gophers. He is terrified of horses. He gets thrown off a train while traveling through the West.

He stumbles across a dude ranch and the owners take pity on him, and they offer him a job when they discover he has a nice singing voice.

He does well whilst he stays away from the livestock. Slick showbiz promotor, Roy Chadwick (Pat O'Brien) and his partner Pat Dunn (Reagan) arrive. They are down on their luck and are quick to spot a chance after hearing Elly sing. They decide to turn him into a radio singing cowboy. Their scheme works and Elly becomes an airways favorite. This is fine until he is asked to appear at rodeos.

Jane Hardy (Priscilla Lane), daughter of the rancher, tries to help him with hypnosis. Whilst he is under the trance he is able to perform well. Unfortunately he slips in and out of the state and is revealed as a coward.

He eventually performs as a cowboy hero at Madison Square Garden, thanks to the support of his love Jane.

## Reviews:

"The billing gives it top spot in the dials, but it will need strong support. . . . Lloyd Bacon has directed better films. This one gets a fair amount of laughs from hackneyed situations." *Variety* (June 14, 1938); "The film works best as a satire on the singing cowboy phenomenon." *The Overlook Film Encyclopedia: The Western* Phil Hardy (Overlook press, 1983); "...the finished results were pitiful." *The Warner Bros. Story* Clive Hirschhorn (New York, Crown, 1979); "...fast-moving, hilarious...filled with sweet music, a succession of laughs and a novel story...the picture is entertainment plus." *The Los Angeles Examiner* (Erskine Johnson, July 22, 1938)

## Notes:

In production from mid-January to mid-February 1938 under the working titles *Dude Rancher, Howdy, Stranger,* and *The Brooklyn Cowboy*.

The film's negative cost was $572,000. It returned $588,000 in domestic rentals for the studio and a further $179,000 from overseas markets.

Reagan's salary was $200 a week.

The film's lead, Dick Powell was the 7th biggest box-office star in the nation in 1935 and was ranked 6th in 1936.

Based on the Broadway play, *Howdy Stranger* by Robert Sloane and Louis Pelletier Jr. that opened in January 1937.

Lloyd Bacon (1890-1955) who amassed over 100 director credits, started as a stage actor during the early years of the second decade of the 20th century. Switching to films he soon found employment as a villain menacing Charlie Chaplin and other comedians in several early two-reelers. By the 1920s he was working in comedies for Mack Sennett and Lloyd Hamilton. In 1928 he earned a place in history by directing *The Singing Fool* (1928) the first all-talking film starring Al Jolsen. In the 1930s he collaborated with Busby Berkeley on a number of musicals including *42nd Street* (1933), *Footlight Parade* (1933) and *Gold Diggers of 1937.* Working at both Warners and Fox for the next decade, he helmed: *Knute Rockne, All American* (1940), *Navy Blues* (1941), *Action in the North Atlantic* (1943), *The Sullivans* (1944), the uproarious comedy *The Good Humor Man* (1950), *The Frogman* (1951) and *The French Line* (1954) with Jane Russell for RKO.

At this time, fifth-billed Ann Sheridan (1915-1967) was being groomed for stardom by Warner Bros. The Texas native, born Clara Lou Sheridan, was a beauty contest winner who had been signed to a film contract by Paramount in 1933. Between 1934 and 1935 the studio inserted her, as an extra or in bit roles, in over 20 features. When she was dropped by Paramount in 1936, Warner Bros. immediately picked up her contract and began promoting her as the "Oomph Girl." The actress who was featured in 80 motion pictures would star in an unsuccessful comedy-western television series before retiring from the industry.

Fourth-billed Dick Foran (born John Nicholas Foran, 1910-1979), was the wealthy son of a New Jersey state senator. He started his professional career by singing in bands and on the radio then in 1936 was signed by Warner Bros. to headline, over a two-year period, a series of 12 singing westerns.

From 1949 to 1957 (with the exception of one year off due to salary issues) Clayton Moore (1914-1999) who was uncredited as the rodeo timekeeper, became a hero to the first generation of children growing up in front of their television sets and their parents. This one-time B-actor became famous as television's masked man, *The Lone Ranger.* Throughout the 1940's, prior to donning his white Stetson and mounting his white steed, Silver, he had appeared at Republic as a heavy in many of their serials, Westerns and melodramas.

Released in Britain with the title, *Romance and Rhythm.*

Warners remade the film in 1948 as *Two Guys From Texas* with Dennis Morgan and Jack Carson in the leads.

Competition at the nation's screens included: *Algiers* (United Artists) starring Charles Boyer and Hedy Lamarr, *Marie Antoinette* with Norma Shearer in the lead role from MGM, Mickey Rooney in the latest installment of the Andy Hardy series, *Love Finds Andy Hardy* and *Alexander's Ragtime Band.*

# The Amazing Dr. Clitterhouse

**release date: July 20, 1938**                    **running time: 87 minutes**

**Cast:**   Edward G. Robinson, Claire Trevor, Humphrey Bogart, Allen Jenkins, Donald Crisp, Gale Page, Henry O'Neill, John Litel, Thurston Hall, Max 'Slapsie Maxie' Rosenbloom, Bert Hanlon, Curt Bois, Ward Bond, Vladimir Sokoloff, Billy Wayne, Robert Homans, Irving Bacon, Edgar Dearing, Susan Hayward, Frank Anthony, Wade Boteler, Sidney Bracey, Georgia Caine, Romaine Callender, Glen Cavender, Loia Cheaney, Hal Craig, Ray Dawe, Hal K. Dawson, Earl Dwire, Frank Fanning, Mary Field, Edward Gargan, William Haade, Winifred Harris, John Harron, Thomas E. Jackson, Mike Lally, Vera Lewis, Al Loyd, Bruce Mitchell, Edmund Mortimer, Jack Mower, Ronald Reagan, Bob Reeves, Frank Reicher, Ky Robinson, Ruth Robinson, Eric Stanley, Larry Steers, Libby Taylor, Monte Vandergrift, Joyce Williams, William Worthington

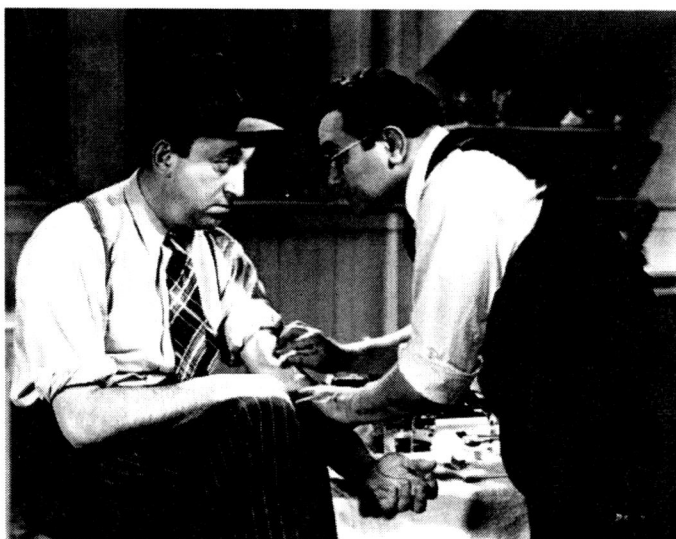

**Credits:**                    **First National-Warners**

*Executive Producers* Jack L. Warner, Hal B. Wallis; *Producers* Anatole Litvak, Gilbert Miller; *Associate Producer* Robert Lord; *Director* Anatole Litvak; *Screenplay* John Wexley, John Huston; *Based on the play* "The Amazing Dr. Clitterhouse" by Barre Lyndon;

*Music* Leo F. Forbstein , Max Steiner; *Cinematography* Tony Gaudio; *Editor* Warren Lowe; *Art Direction* Carl Jules Weyl; *Sound* C.A. Riggs; *Assistant Director* Jack Sullivan; *Orchestrations* George Parrish; *Wardrobe* Milo Anderson; *Dialogue Director* Jo Graham; *Technical Advisor* Dr. Leo Morton Schulman; *Supervisor* Robert Lord

## Reviews:

"...an unquestionable winner...Litvak's direction opens at a nice clip and holds a steady pace, with suspense well developed and light comedy relief adequately spotted." *Variety* (June 21, 1938);

## Notes:

In production from February to early-April 1938.

The film had a negative cost of $536,000 and returned $783,000 in domestic rentals to the studio and an additional $434,000 from overseas markets.

Reagan paid $250 a week but his part was edited out.

Adapted from both the same London and New York stage hit of 1937.

Carl Laemmle Jr secured the screen-rights for a sum in excess of $50,000. Laemmle then transferred the rights to Warners in exchange for the loan-out of Paul Muni to play the lead role in *The Hunchback of Notre Dame*.

# Boy Meets Girl

**release date: August 27, 1938**                    **running time: 86 minutes**

**Cast:**   James Cagney, Pat O'Brien, Marie Wilson, Ralph Bellamy, Frank McHugh, Dick Foran, Bruce Lester, Ronald Reagan, Paul Clark, Penny Singleton, Dennie Moore, Harry Seymour, Bert Hanlon, James Stephenson, Clem Bevans, Curt Bois, Sidney Bracey, Loia Cheaney, Eddie Conrad, Hal K. Dawson, Otto Fries, William Haade, John Harron, George Hickman, Jan Holm, Bert Howard, Nanette Lafayette, Carole Landis, Vera Lewis, Peggy Moran, James Nolan, John Ridgely, Cliff Saum, Janet Shaw, Bill Telaak, Rosella Towne, Dorothy Vaughan, Pierre Watkin, Paul Clark

**Credits:**                    **First National-Warners**

*Executive Producers* Jack L. Warner, Hal B. Wallis; *Producer* George Abbott; *Director* Lloyd Bacon; *Writers* Bella Spewack, Sam Spewack*; Cinematography* Sol Polito; *Editor* William Holmes; *Associate Producer* Sam Bischoff; *Music* M.K. Jerome, Jack Scholl, Al Dubin, Ray Heindorf, Howard Jensen Harry Warren; *Art Direction* Esdras Hartley; *Costumes* Milo Anderson; *Makeup* Perc Westmore; *Sound* Dolph Thomas; *Assistant Director* Dick Mayberry; *Music Supervisor* Leo F. Forbstein; *Lyricists* M.K. Jerome, Jack Scholl, Johnny Mercer; *Song* "With A Pain In My Heart"

## Synopsis:

The film is set in Warner's Burbank Studio. Many interesting shots of picture-making activity of the day are included. Robert Law (James Cagney) and JC Benson (Pat O'Brien) are a pair of screenwriters in need of an idea for a picture. Their studio supervisor, C Elliott Friday (Ralph Bellamy), has lost all patience with them, but is constantly up against it whenever he tries to get rid of them. The studio's cowboy star, Larry Toms (Dick Foran), needs a good picture to save his career at the studio. The writers devise a typical boy-meets-girl story for him.

They invent a part for the infant son of studio waitress, Susie (Marie Wilson), and build the role until the cowboy star becomes jealous.

The project is a big success, especially for the baby.

Reagan plays the part of a radio announcer in the last reel.

## Reviews:

"It does not approximate the ripsnorting click of the play . . . the picture version of this comedy classic is a little more than adequate . . . Ronald Reagan, as the radio announcer. . . makes his brief opportunity register." *Variety* (August 28, 1938); "Nearly all the lines which the script could least afford to spare have been dropped, presumably because of conflict with the delicately casuistical Hayes code of morals. A curious pale of unreality hangs over the scenes." *The New York Times* (August 27, 1938);

## Notes:

In production from early March to early April 1938.

Negative cost of the film was $591,000. It returned $561,000 in domestic rentals to the studio and a further $93,000 from overseas markets. North American theatergoers paid slightly in excess of $1,100,000 to see the production.

Reagan's salary was $200 a week while Warners paid Pat O'Brien just under $4,000 a week and James Cagney nearly $5,000 a week. In November 1939 after much acrimony, Cagney's salary was raised to $12,500 a week.

Based on the play *Boy Meets Girl* by Bella and Samuel Spewack. The original casting choices were the comedy team of Olsen and Johnson for the male leads with Marion Davies for the top-lining female. Warners wanted George Abbott to direct.

Female-lead Marie Wilson (1916-1972) would make a career out of playing ditzy blondes. The astute comedienne started out as a dancer on Broadway then headed to Hollywood in 1933. Under contract to Warner Bros. in the late 1930s the actress would appear in up to four films a year for the studio. In a career that extended from 1934 to 1962 she made over 50 films.

With his distinguished looks and bearing Ralph Bellamy (1904-1991) had a long career that spanned almost sixty years (1931-1990) and included appearances in over 120 films, 5 television series, and a dozen mini-series made for television movies.

The film's lead, James Cagney was the number nine star at the box-office for 1939.

Also appearing at the nation's theaters at the same time were the Laurel & Hardy comedy, *Blockheads* (MGM), the Joe E. Brown laugher, *The Gladiator* (Columbia), *Alexander's Ragtime Band, Love Finds Andy Hardy* and *Four Daughters*.

# Girls On Probation

**release date: October 22, 1938**          **running time: 60-65 minutes**

**Cast:**   Jane Bryan, Ronald Reagan, Anthony Averill, Sheila Bromley, Henry O'Neill, Elisabeth Risdon, Sig Rumann, Dorothy Perterson, Esther Dale, Susan Hayward, Larry Williams, Arthur Foyt, Peggy Shannon, Lenita Lane, James Nolan, Janet Shaw, Joseph Crehan, Pierre Watkin, James Spottswood, Brenda Fowler, Kate Drain Lawson, Maude Lambert, Lane Chandler, John Hamilton, Carole Landis, Marian Alden, Fern Barry, Nat Carr, Glen Cavender, Paulette Evans, Jan Holm, Clara Horton, Reid Kilpatrick, Sally Sage, Jack Mower, George Offerman Jr., Ed Keane, Art Miles, Dickie Jones, Emory Parnell, Max Hoffman, Jr., Dick Rich, Sol Gorss, Cliff Saum, Stuart Holmes, Hal Craig, Ed Stanley, Marian Alden, Vera Lewis, Lew Harvey, Ralph Sanford

**Credits:**                   **First National-Warners**

*Executive Producers* Jack L. Warner, Hal B. Wallis; *Producer* Bryan Foy; *Director* William C. McGann; *Screenplay* Crane Wilbur; *Music* Howard Jackson; *Cinematography* Arthur L. Todd; *Editor* Frederick Richards; *Art Direction* Hugh Reticker; *Costumes* Howard Shoup; *Assistant Director* Elmer Decker; *Sound* Leslie G. Hewitt; *Dialogue Director* Harry Seymour

## Synopsis:

Connie Heath (Jane Bryan), is a nice, innocent girl. Her troubles begin when a guest at a party, Gloria Adams (Susan Hayward), accuses her of stealing the evening gown she is wearing. Connie is arrested. The gown had been loaned to her by a friend, Hilda Engstrom (Sheila Bromley), who works in the dry cleaning shop with Connie. Although the guest drops the charges, the insurance company decides to prosecute and Connie is tried for grand larceny.

Bright young attorney, Neil Dillon (Ronald Reagan), believes her story and he gets her off with a suspended sentence.

Her father, Roger Heath (Sig Rumann) is not so understanding and he orders her to leave home.

Connie gets another job in another town where she once again runs into Hilda, who is now involved in a bank robbery with her lover, Tony Rand (Anthony Averill). During the robbery, Connie hets pushed into the getaway car and when the robbers are caught by the police she is charged as an accomplice. She is given a probated sentence of 3 years. She returns home and gets a job with Neil, but doesn't warn him about what has happened. Connie and Neil fall in love and plan to wed. Then Hilda shows up and blackmails Connie. Connie co-operates with the police and Hilda's boyfriend is brought to justice.

Connie finds happiness in the arms of her lover

## Reviews:

"Ronald Reagan seems a little lightweight as a D.A., and is perhaps a little too soft for that kind of job, but otherwise, especially romantically, he serves well. The story . . . is routine but moves along swiftly. . ." *Variety* (October 26, 1938); "Human and interesting" *Photoplay* (February, 1939); "...packs a strong moral feeling. . . . Ronald Reagan is neatly cast as a casual young lawyer. . . . Director William McGann made strong visual and verbal use of his story and cast..." *The Hollywood Reporter* (August 19, 1938); "In the attorney's part Ronald Reagan is especially well cast. . . . William McGann's direction stresses the action without sloughing character and motivation, holding the narrative to good pace." *Daily Variety* (August 19, 1938)

## Notes:

In production from May 2 to early June 1938.

The negative cost for this entry was only $158,000. It returned a profitable $441,000 in rentals from the domestic market and a further $91,000 from overseas theaters.

Reagan paid $300 a week.

It has been reported that Carol Landis was to have had a starring role in the feature, but dropped out before production began.

Crane Wilbur also wrote the scripts for the earlier crime melodramas, *Crime School* and *Alcatraz Island*.

Pittsburgh native William C. McGann (1893-1977) between 1930 and 1944 directed 52 films, almost all of the B-variety. Learning the art of motion picture photography, he started in the industry in the mid-teens. By 1919 he was a full-fledged cinematographer who in 1920 would shoot the Douglas Fairbanks classic swashbuckler *The Mark of Zorro*. After only nine films as head of photography the inquisitive McGann moved on to become a second unit and assistant director. By 1930 he was directing his first film, the Rin Tin Tin adventure *On the Border*. He then spent much of 1931 in Mexico working on Spanish productions before returning to the States in 1932 for seven consecutive B-releases during that year. In 1939 he directed the critically praised John Garfield drama *Blackwell's Island* and at Republic in 1942 helmed the John Wayne western *In Old California*. After filming the low-budget western *Trial by Trigger* he once again changed career pursuits and became a Special Effects expert for Warner Bros. where he worked on some notable films including: *A Stolen Life* and *The Big Sleep* (1946), *Cheyenne* and *Life with Father* (1947), *Key Largo* and *Johnny Belinda* (1948), *The Fountainhead* (1949), John Wayne's *Operation Pacific* and *On Moonlight Bay* (1951).

Top-billed Jane Bryan (1918-  ) born in Hollywood, was being groomed by Warner Bros. in the mid-1930s to become one of their top-tier female talents. The actress had other ideas when in 1940, after 18 films and completing her role in *Brother Rat and A Baby* she married wealthy industrialist Justin Dart (of Walgreen drugstore fame) and left the industry. A quarter of a century later, Dart would be one of the California millionaire industrialists who oversaw the rise of Ronald Reagan as a politician and force to be reckoned with on a national level. After completing *Girls on Probation* Bryan joined Ronald Reagan for the filming of *Brother Rat* (1938).

Third-billed, St. Louis born Anthony Averill's (1911-1982) film career lasted only two years (1938-39). He appeared in thirteen films, all of the "B" variety including *Torchy Blane in Panama, Racket Busters, Heart of the North* (all 1938), *The Phantom Creeps,*

*Blackwell's Island* and *Torture Ship* (1939). Averill also worked with Reagan on *Secret Service of the Air* (1939).

Matronly-looking character actress Elisabeth Risdon (1887-1958), was born in London, performed on the stage, then worked in over 40 British silents before coming to Hollywood and establishing herself in such popular films as *Crime and Punishment* (1935), *Dead End* (1937), *The Adventures of Huckleberry Finn* (1939), *Abe Lincoln in Illinois* (1940), *High Sierra* (1941), *Random Harvest* (1942), *Tall In the Saddle* (1944), *Life with Father* (1947) and her last feature *Scaramouche* (1952). She made over 140 films in a forty year screen career.

In the Los Angeles market the co-feature on the program was *Secrets of an Actress* with Kay Francis and George Brent.

Playing at the nation's theaters at the same time: *Angels With Dirty Faces* (Warners) starring James Cagney, Pat O'Brien, Humphrey Bogart, and the Dead End Kids and MGM's *Boy's Town* with Spencer Tracy and Mickey Rooney.

# Brother Rat

**release date: October 29, 1938**          **running time: 90 minutes**

**Cast:**   Priscilla Lane, Wayne Morris, Johnnie Davis, Jane Bryan, Eddie
Albert, Ronald Reagan, Jane Wyman, Henry O'Neill, Gordon Oliver,
Larry Williams, William Tracy, Jessie Busley, Olin Howlin, Louise
Beavers, Isabel Withers, Allan Cavan, Don DeFore, Jerry Fletcher,
Mildred Gover, Fred Hamilton, Oscar 'Dutch' Hendrian, Wilfred
Lucas, Cliff Saum, Robert E. Scott, Howard Leeds, Hugh McArthur,
Jerry Cecil, Frank Coghlan Jr, Tommy Seidel, William Orr, George
O'Hanlon, Eddie Bracken

**Credits:**                    **First National-Warners**

*Producer* George Abbott; *Executive Producers* Jack L. Warner, Hal
B. Wallis; *Associate Producer* Robert Lord; *Director* William
Keighley; Screen*writers* Richard Macauley, Jerry Wald; *Based on
the play* "Brother Rat" by John Monks, Jr. and Fred F. Finklehodde;
*Cinematography* Ernest Haller; *Music* Heinz Roemheld; *Musical
Director* Leo F. Forbstein; *Editor* William Holmes; *Art Direction* Max
Parker; *Costumes* Milo Anderson; *Production Manager* Carroll Sax;
*Assistant Director* Chuck Hansen; *Sound* Oliver S. Garretson;

*Technical Advisor* Frank McCarthy; *Property* Bill Kuehl, E. Edwards; *Mixer* Oliver Garretson; *Gaffer* Charlie Alexander; *Best Boy* Jake Goldenhar; *Grip* S.E. Young

## Synopsis:

The title refers to the fond pet name cadets of the Virginia Military Institute have for each other. In the last few weeks before graduation, wild trio, Billy (Wayne Morris), Dan (Ronald Reagan) and Bing (Eddie Albert) attempt to get themselves into shape in order to pass muster. Billy is by far the wildest, and Dan runs a close second. Between them they break most of the Institute rules, especially those about staying up after hours and leaving the grounds to visit girlfriends. Bing has a more disturbing problem-he is secretly married, although this is forbidden. He receives news that his bride is pregnant. Bing becomes increasingly nervous although his friends do their best to cover for him. Since they are already involved in a variety of stunts on and off campus, their best usually leads to further complications.

Dan makes his life at the academy even more fraught when he starts romancing the commandant's daughter, Claire Adams (Jane Wyman). Things become difficult when pregnant bride Kate (Jane Bryan), appears for the end of term football game and prom.

Eventually everything gets worked out and all the cadets win their sheepskins.

## Reviews:

"All of the wholesome drama, comedy, and laugh-lines of the original play have been retained in the film version. . . . Ronald Reagan is fine as the third member of the group." *Variety* (October 19, 1938); "He (Reagan) was the rugged, good-natured all-American youth." *Warner Brothers Presents: The Most Exciting Years- from The Jazz Singer to White Heat*. Ted Sennett (New York; Arlington House, 1971); ". . . an amusing and diverting farce. . . . memorable for its outstanding cast." *Magill's American Film Guide* New Jersey; Salem Press, 1980); "fast-moving panorama of comedy, excitement and even romance . . . filled with laughs. . . . Priscilla Lane is . . . one of the best young actresses to be discovered this year . . . Reagan has a likeable personality and gives a good account of himself." *The Los Angeles Examiner* (Louella O. Parsons, October 28, 1938)

# Notes:

In production from April 27 to July 1938. Location work at the Virginia Military Institute in Lexington, Virginia lasted from April 27 to May 3rd. In California outdoor sequences were shot at the 30 Acres Ranch. Retakes filmed at Warners in mid-August. The shooting schedule was 33 days.

Budgeted at $582,000, the film ended production with a negative cost of $544,000. It reported domestic rentals of $1,183,000 and a further $134,000 from overseas markets.

During production Hal Wallis wanted to rename the production *Brother Cadet*. Other alternate titles included: *Call to Arms* and *About Face*.

Reagan earned $300 a week while in production. He was selected over Jeffrey Lynn for the role. Other salaries: Eddie Albert was paid $750 a week; Olin Howland $650 a week; Jessie Busley $600/week; Louise Beavers $600/week; Gordon Oliver $300 a week; Robert Scott $250 a week. Susan Hayward was originally sought for the role of Kate that went to Jane Bryan.

Based on the Broadway play of 1936 that was produced by George Abbott and partially bankrolled by Warners.

Eddie Albert (born Edward Albert Heimberger, 1908- ) in his film debut, was the only member from the Broadway cast who re-created his original role on the screen. After graduating from the University of Minnesota he joined a circus as a trapeze artist, then became a stage and radio performer. The veteran of over 100 films was twice nominated for Best Supporting Actor: *Roman Holiday* (1953) and *The Heartbreak Kid* (1972). Prior to joining the Navy during World War II Albert appeared in 17 features including the sequel to *Brother Rat, Eagle Squadron* (1942) and *Bombardier* (1943).

Director William Keighley (1889-1984) was born in Philadelphia and after a short stint as a stage actor, came to Hollywood in the late 1920s. At the start of his career he worked at Warners as an assistant director, dialogue director and actor before helming the first of his eventual 79 features the crime drama, *The Match King* (1932) with Warren William and Lili Damita. After completing *The Master of Ballantrae* with Errol Flynn in 1953, he retired from the industry.

This was the first film that Reagan and Jane Wyman appeared together on the screen. 7th billed Wyman (Sarah Jane Mayfield, 1914- ) came to Hollywood in the early 1930s and worked as an extra and bit-player in several films until Warners signed her to a term contract in 1936. Over the course of her film career, which extended from 1932 until 1969, she made appearances in over 80 films, won the Oscar for Best Actress for her role in *Johnny Belinda* (1949), and was nominated on three other occasions for her acting in *The Yearling* (1946) *The Blue Veil* (1951) and *Magnificent Obsession* (1954). In the medium of television she, for five years, served as hostess and sometimes actress in the *Jane Wyman Presents the Fireside Theater,* and for almost nine years was the matriarch of the family in the night-time soap opera *Falcon Crest* (1981-1990). Some of her other better known motion pictures included: *My Favorite Spy* (1942), *The Lost Weekend* (1945), *Magic Town* (1947), *The Glass Menagerie* (1950), *So Big* (1953), *Lucy Gallant* (1955), Miracle In the Rain *(1956), Pollyana* (1960) and *Bon Voyage!* (1962).

In a career that spanned over four decades (1920-1966), cinematographer Ernest Haller (1896-1970) worked on over 175 features. Averaging over five films a year in the 1930s, some of his better efforts included: *International House* and *Emperor Jones* (1933), *Captain Blood* (1935) with Errol Flynn, Bette Davis' *Jezebel* (1938), *The Roaring Twenties* and *Gone With the Wind* (1939). Although his output in the 1940s decreased to 29 films, they did include: *The Bride Came C.O.D.* (1941), Jack Benny's comedy classic *George Washington Slept Here* (1942), Joan Crawford's Oscar winner *Mildred Pierce* (1945) and the Gary Cooper-Ingrid Bergman drama *Saratoga Trunk* (1946). His later noteworthy motion pictures included: *Dallas* (1950), James Dean's *Rebel Without A Cause* (1955), *Man of the West* (1958), *Whatever Happened to Baby Jane?* (1962) starring Bette Davis and Joan Crawford and *Lilies of the Field* (1963).

World premiere held at the State Theater in Lexington, Virginia. While playing in Los Angeles the second feature on the program was *Broadway Musketeers* with Margaret Lindsay, Ann Sheridan and Marie Wilson.

Also at the nation's theaters: *Young Dr. Kildare* (MGM) with Lew Ayres and Lionel Barrymore, *Beau Geste* starring Gary Cooper and Ray Milland, *You Can't Take It With You* Frank Capra's delightful comedy with James Stewart, Jean Arthur and Lionel Barrymore.

# Going Places

release date: December 31, 1938        running time: 84-85 minutes

**Cast:**   Dick Powell, Anita Louise, Allen Jenkins, Ronald Reagan, Walter
Catlett, Harold Huber, Larry Williams, Thurston Hall, Minna
Gombell, Joyce Compton, Robert Warwick, John Ridgely, Joe
Cunningham, Eddie 'Rochester' Anderson, George Reed, Louis
Armstrong, Maxine Sullivan, Brooks Benedict, Ward Bond, Eddy
Chandler, Dorothy Dandridge, Jesse Graves, John Harron,
Ferdinand Munier, Jack Richardson, Janet Shaw, Rosella Towne,
Leo White, Sidney Bracy, Frank Mayo


**Credits:**                **Cosmopolitan Production**
                        **First National-Warners**


*Producer* Hal B. Wallis; *Director* Ray Enright; *Writers* William
Collier Sr., Sig Herzig, Maurice Leo, Victor Mapes, Jerry Wald;
*Cinematography* Arthur L. Todd; *Original Music* Harry Warren,
Heinz Roemheld; *Stock Music* Sam Perry; *Editor* Clarence Kolster;
*Art Direction* Hugh Reticker; *Sound* Robert B. Lee; *Costumes* Howard
Shoup; *Dialogue Director Hugh Cummings; Musical Director* Leo
F. Forbstein*; Music Arrangers* Ray Heindorf, Frank Perkins;
*Lyricists* Johnny Mercer, Harry Warren; *Songs* "'Say It With A
Kiss," "Oh, What A Horse was Charles," "Mutiny In the Nursery"
and "Jeepers Creepers."

## Synopsis:

Peter Mason (Dick Powell) is a sporting goods salesman posing as
a famous gentleman jockey in order to infiltrate the home of a
wealthy Maryland horseman, Colonel Withering (Thurston Hall).
His pleasing personality enables him to become a member of the
wealthy horsey set, which includes the colonel's dashing son, Jack
Withering (Ronald Reagan) and his neice Ellen Parker (Anita
Louise).

His success becomes a problem when he falls in love with Ellen,
and is then expected to ride the colonel's horses. Of course, he
doesn't know how to ride. By fluke, he manages to perform well on
the ride, which leads to him being chosen to perform in a race on
the colonel's prize horse, Jeepers Creepers.

The horse is all but wild and can be pacified only when he hears its song sung by his groom.

The groom becomes indespensible to Mason's hopes of not being discovered.

The race is won by having the groom and his musician friends ride in a truck along the racetrack, leading Jeppers Creepers to victory.

## Reviews:

". . . should prove satisfactory, though not smash boxoffice. . . . Ronald Reagan has a minor assignment that is taken care of satisfactorily." *Variety* (January 6, 1939); "After *Cowboy from Brooklyn* and *Hard to Get*, Dick Powell became a three-time loser with *Going Places*." *The Warner Bros. Story.* Clive Hirschhorn *(New York; Crown, 1979);* ". . . a boisterous comedy. . . . Picture makes no pretensions beyond entertainment bid for average audience . . . Ray Enright keeps up a hot directorial pace and goads his troupe to play it to the hilt." *Daily Variety* (December 17, 1938);

## Notes:

In production from early August to late September 1938.

Negative cost was placed at $571,000. It earned domestic rentals of $470,000 and a further $199,000 from the overseas markets.

Reagan paid at the rate of $300 a week.

Based on the hit play, *The Hottentot* by Victor Mapes and William Collier Sr. (March 1920). This was the third filmed remake. First done in 1923 by First National with Douglas MacLean in the lead. Remade in 1929, with sound, by Warners with Edward Everett Horton in the starring role. In 1936 the nucleus of the story again reached the screen in the Joe E. Brown comedy, *Polo Joe* (Warners). Female lead Anita Louise (born Anita Louise Fremault, 1915-1970), began her career in films at the age of seven. A year earlier she had been performing on Broadway in the play *Peter Ibbeston*. Signing a contract with Warners in 1934, she was assigned to an average of five films a year throughout the remainder of the decade including the costume epics *Madame DuBarry* (1934) as Marie Antoinette, Titania in *A Midsummer Night's Dream* (1935) and as Princess DeLambelle in *Marie Antoinette* (1938). After more then 70 motion pictures, she ended her acting career with a recurring role in the television series *My Friend Flicka* (1956). From 1940 until the time of his death in 1960, Louise was married to producer and Fox executive Buddy Adler.

A born character actor, Allen Jenkins (Alfred McGonegal, 1900-

1974), attended the American Academy of Dramatic Arts, appeared on Broadway, then journeyed to Hollywood in 1930 and became a charter member of the unofficial Warners' stock company. Between 1931 and 1974 he appeared in over 110 motion pictures, many as a comedy relief and some as a member of a gang of heavies.

Eddie Anderson (1905-1977) achieved his greatest fame as Jack Benny's personal valet first on radio (1937) then into television (1950-1965). Known for his trademark raspy voice which was the result of an injury to his vocal cords as a child, Anderson, referred to as Rochester by Benny, started out in vaudeville with his older brother in "The Three Black Aces" singing group. His film career spanned four decades and included appearances in over sixty films. In the Los Angeles market the second feature on the bill was *Devil's Island* with Boris Karloff.

National release on January 9, 1939. The film faced competition from the Fox A-Western *Jesse James* (Fox-color) with Tyrone Power and Henry Fonda, RKO's *Gunga Din* with Cary Grant, Douglas Fairbanks, Jr. and Victor McLaglen and *Wings of the Navy.*

# Secret Service of the Air

**release date: March 4, 1939**                **running time: 60-61 minutes**

**Cast:**   Ronald Reagan, John Litel, Ila Rhodes, James Stephenson, Eddie Foy Jr., Rosella Towne, Larry Williams, John Ridgely, Anthony Averill, Bernard Nedell, Frank M. Thomas, Joe Cunningham, Morgan Conway, John Harron, Herbert Rawlinson, Raymond Bailey, Richard Bond, Sidney Bracey, Nat Carr, Glen Cavender, Eddy Chandler, Lane Chandler, Davison Clark, Hal Craig, Edgar Edwards, Sol Gorss, Duke Green, John Hamilton, Harry Hollinsworth, Stuart Holmes, Al Lloyd, Frank Mayo, Carlyle Moore Jr., Alberto Morin, Jack Mower, Pat O'Malley, Henry Otho, Paul Panzer, Jack Richardson, Cliff Saum, Jeffrey Sayre, John Sinclair, George Sorel, Don Turner, Guy Usher, Pierre Watkin, Jack Wise, Albert Lloyd, Jack Goodrich, Dave Roberts, Emilio Blanco, Jack Woody

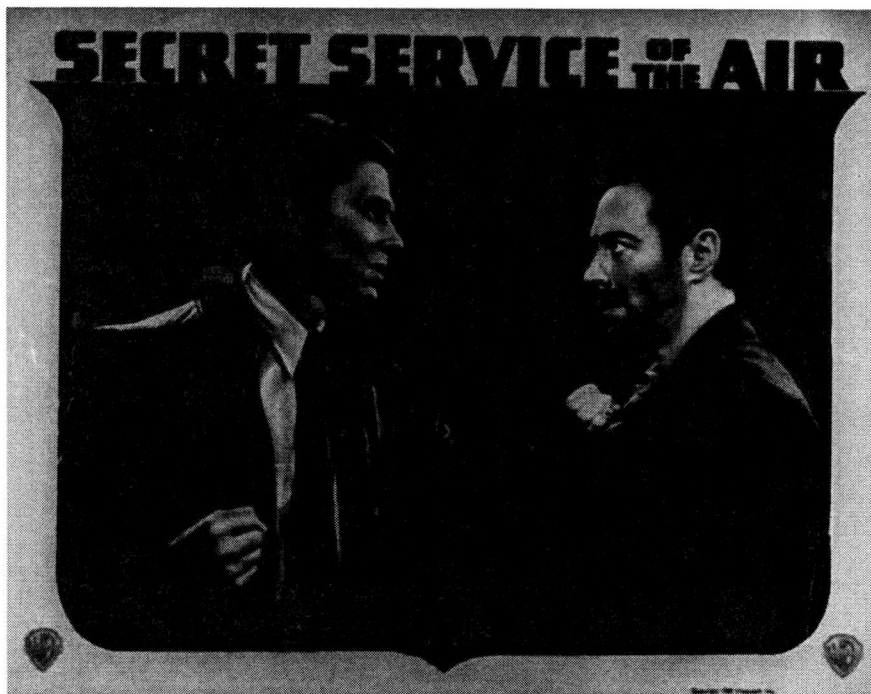

**Credits:**                **First National-Warners**

*Executive Producers* Jack L. Warner, Hal B. Wallis; *Associate Producer* Bryan Foy; *Director* Noel M. Smith; *Screenplay* Raymond L. Schrock; *Based on material compiled by* W.H. Moran; *Cinematography* Ted D. McCord, Arthur Edeson; *Original Music & Orchestrations* Bernhard Kaun; *Editor* Doug Gould; *Art Direction* Ted Smith; *Costumes* Howard Shoup; *Sound* Dolph Thomas; *Musical Director* Leo F. Forbstein; *Dialogue Director* Frank Beckwith; *Assistant Director* Elmer Decker; *Makeup* Charles Dudley; *Hair Stylist* Helen Turpin; *Grip* Owen Compton; *Best Boy* Bert Alan; *Gaffer* Rex Story

## Synopsis:

The hero of the picture is Lieutentant Brass Bancroft (Ronald Reagan), a former army air corps flyer who now makes a living as a commercial pilot. He joins the Secret Service, but his reasons for this are not made clear.

Once in the employ of the Government, Brass plunges into assignments with equal amounts of courage and energy. His first task is to uncover the villains operating an airborne smuggling ring, bringing aliens into the United States. To do this he poses as a counterfeit money agent.

In the climax, Bancroft grapples with the villain in the cockpit of the plunging plane. The villain tries to open the cockpit hatch

## Reviews:

"Considerable melodramatic ado about nothing." *The New York Times.* (March 2, 1939). "A satisfactory booking for secondary theaters . . . . (T)he picture, a well-made B, is based on a better than average story . . . and arouses considerable interest through the exciting action, fighting, flying etc. It doesn't lag at any point. . . . Ronald Reagan impresses as the G-Man. He handles his fists for fullest results. . . ." *Variety* (March 8, 1939); "lukewarm drama with a tired plot line." *The Warner Bros. Story.* Clive Hirschhorn (New York; Crown, 1979)

**Notes:**  *"I became the Errol Flynn of the B's."*
In production from September 26 to October 20, 1938 under the title *Murder Plane.* It took four additional days for process and special effects shots while retakes took place between November 15 and November 29th.

Allotted filming schedule was 16 days. The production spent one day (October 4th) at the airfield in Newhall, several days at Glendale Airport (Grand Central Airport), and a week at the Providencia Ranch, just south of the Warner Bros. studio complex. Interiors were filmed on Warner soundstages 5, 6, 12 and 17. It took 20 days to complete shooting with the principals.

The negative cost of the production was $145,000. The film earned rentals of $211,000 in the domestic market and an additional $101,000 from overseas sources.

While Reagan earned $1675 for appearing in this film, his co-star John Litel was paid $3,000, the female lead Rhodes earned $375 a week, sidekick Eddie Foy was paid at the rate of $500 a week as was other cast member Frank Thomas. Sixth-billed Rosella Towne was on the production payroll at $150 a week while director Noel Smith received $1250 for his efforts. For his cinematography, veteran cameraman Ted McCord was paid $9622.

Based on the story, *Murder In the Air* and materials supplied by former Secret Service Chief, W.H. Moran.

Reagan as Lieutenant 'Brass' Bancroft, in the first of a series of four films.

Second-billed John Litel (1892-1972) went to Europe and enlisted in the French army at the start of World War I. Returning to America with a chest full of medals he enrolled in the American Academy of Dramatic Arts and was soon performing on Broadway. In 1929 he appeared in the first of more than 160 films. Part of the stable of Warner character actors in the 1930s and 1940s, Litel was often assigned roles in up to 15 features a year.

Little is known about leading lady Ila Rhodes. It is alleged that she was engaged to Reagan before he met Wyman. The actress' film career consisted of only five films, all released in 1939. In her first feature *Off the Record* she was cast as a telephone operator and did not receive a credit. Her second film *Women in the Wind* had her playing the part of an aviatrix. The actresses' last two motion pictures *Dark Victory* and *Hell's Kitchen*, also featured Reagan.

California-born Noel Smith (1895-1955) directed over 100 films between 1917 and 1952, wrote the stories for 21 others, and at the end of his career between 1947 and 1952, served as a second unit director on four features. Nearly all of Smith's films were of the B-variety with low budgets, lean shooting schedules, and on the bottom bill at movie houses.

In his forty-five year career Ted McCord (1921-1966) was the cinematographer on over 145 films including *So Big (1924), Ride*

*Him, Cowboy* (1932), *Action in the North Pacific* (1943), *The Treasure of Sierra Madre* and *Johhny Belinda* (both 1948), *Flamingo Road* (1949), *Rocky Mountain* (1950), *East of Eden* (1955), *The Hanging Tree* (1959) and *The Sound of Music* (1965). Warner Bros.' biggest hits of 1939 were *Dark Victory, Angels With Dirty Faces* and *Dodge City.*

The weekly salaries, in 1939 for Warners biggest stars were: Jimmy Cagney $12,500; Paul Muni $11,500; Edward G. Robinson $8,000; Claude Rains $6,000; George Raft $5,000; Errol Flynn $5,000; Bette Davis $4,000; Pat O'Brien $4,000; John Garfield $1,500; Olivia DeHavilland $1,250.

Competition at the nation's screens included: *Blackwell's Island* (Warners) with John Garfield and Rosemary Lane, *Blondie Meets the Boss* (Columbia) starring Penny Singleton in the title role, *Bachelor Mother* (RKO) featuring Ginger Rogers, *Charlie Chan In Reno* (Fox) and *Children of the Wild* (Grand National).

# Dark Victory

**release date: April 22, 1939**                    **running time: 104-105 minutes**

**Cast:**   Bette Davis, George Brent, Humphrey Bogart, Geraldine Fitzgerald, Ronald Reagan, Henry Travers, Cora Witherspoon, Dorothy Peterson, Virginia Brissac, Charles Richman, Herbert Rawlinson, Leonard Mudie, Fay Helm, Lottie Williams, Marian Alden, Wilda Bennett, Diane Bernard, Richard Bond, Sidney Bracey, Nat Carr, Glen Cavender, Mary Currier, Frank Darien, Edgar Edwards, Paulette Evans, Jack A. Goodrich, Eddie Graham, John Harron, Leyland Hodgson, Stuart Holmes, Alexander Leftwich, Frank Mayo, Will Morgan, Jack Mower, David Newell, Wedgwood Nowell, Ila Rhodes, John Ridgely, Speirs Ruskell, Cliff Saum, Jeffrey Sayre, Rosella Towne, William Worthington, Maris Wrixon,

**Credits:**                    **First National-Warners**

*Executive Producer* Hal B. Wallis; *Associate Producer* David Lewis; *Director* Edmund Goulding; *Screenwriter* Casey Robinson; *Based on the play* "Dark Victory" by George Emerson Brewer, Jr., and Bertram Bloch; *Cinematography* Ernest Haller; *Editor* William Holmes; *Original Music* Max Steiner, Howard Jackson; *Other Music* Edmund Goulding, Elsie Janis; *Orchestra Arrangements* Hugo Friedhofer; *Art Direction* Robert M. Haas; *Costumes* Orry-Kelly;

*Unit Manager* Robert Ross; *Second Unit Director* Frank Heath; *Musical Director* Leo F. Forbstein; *Technical Director* Dr. Leo Schulman; *Sound* Robert B. Lee; *Song*: 'Oh, Give Me Time for Tenderness'

## Synopsis:

This highly crafted soap opera sees Judith Traherne (Bette Davis), a wealthy Long Island socialite given up to a heady social life. She is confident about her affluence and the power she has over men. She is unprepared for the tragedy that strikes in the form of a brain tumor.

The underlying honesty and courage with which she faces this affliction eventually prove her a woman of real substance.

Among her friends is Ann King (Fitzgerald), her secretary and dashing young Alex Hamm (Ronald Reagan). Hamm, a rich and frequently drunk member of the set, loves Judith, but makes no great impression on her. Still, he and Ann get their friend to see brain specialist Dr Frederick Steele (George Brent). The doctor diagnoses that the tumor will be fatal and that she has only about a year to live.

Judith falls in love with the doctor and accepts his proposal of marriage until she realises how short a time she has left. She assumes that Steel's offer was born out of pity and she rejects him to return to the social whirl.

She is concerned about her thoroughbred horse whose trainer (Bogart) candidly points out her false pride. Judith now realises she does have a last chance for happiness and she marries the doctor.

They enjoy an idyllic few months together before Judith's sight begins to fail. When Steele goes off to attend a medical conference she feins good health and she spends her last hours alone, but she is comforted by the feeling that she has achieved a measure of victory over the darkness dealt her.

## Reviews:

"One of the sensitive and haunting pictures of the season." *The New York Times* (April 21, 1939). "Intense drama, with undercurrent of tragedy ever present. . . . Picture is studded with seve      ˜se sequences that are tear-jerkers of ultra caliber." *Variety* 1939); "A gem of a picture...this poignant dram⁄ engrossing. . . The two-time Academy Award winner hold any audience with her superb performance. Edmund Golding. . . captured the mood of the

194

unerring in his judgment in handling each difficult moment . . . ranks high as artistic entertainment" *The Los Angeles Examiner* (Louella O. Parsons, May 19, 1939); "Here is drama so engrossing that it will hold its audience breathless for its entire length." *The Hollywood Reporter* (March 8, 1939); "(Ronald Reagan) is very effective in the film, and it was instrumental in furthering his career." *Jane Wyman.* Joe Morella and Edward Z. Epstein (Delacorte Press. New York, 1985)

**Notes:**                              *"A truly fine movie."*

In production at locations in the west San Fernando Valley, from early October to late November 1938.

Budgeted at $517,000 the film ended production at a negative cost of $597,000. It earned domestic rentals of $1,165,000 and a further $538,000 from the overseas markets.

While Reagan was paid $300 a week, the film's star Bette Davis was earning $3500 a week. Her pay from Warners for making four films in 1939 came to $147,000 or $36,750 per feature. Davis was the 9th biggest star at the box-office in 1940, 8th in 1941 and 10th in 1944.

Nominated for three Oscars: Best Picture, Best Actress (Davis), and Best original score Music (Steiner).

Based on a relatively unsuccessful play that opened on Broadway on November 9, 1934 with Tallulah Bankhead in the lead.

Screen-rights originally secured by David O. Selznick with the hope of signing Greta Garbo and Frederic March for the leads. In 1936 Selznick offered the lead role to Merle Oberon. After several years, Warners purchased the rights from the producer for $27,000 and a percentage of the profits. For the leads the studio envisioned Kay Francis and Spencer Tracy.

Bette Davis made four films with director, Goulding. The other three: *That Certain Woman* (1937), *The Old Maid* (1939), and *The Great Lie* (1941).

*The Stolen Hours,* a 1963 United Artists release starring Susan Hayward, was based on the play.

Director, screenwriter, actor, composer and playwright, Edmund Goulding (1891-1959) was born in England, worked on the London stage, fought and was wounded in World War I, emigrated to the United States in 1921 and after several years of writing screenplays, was signed by MGM as a combination director and screenwriter. Over the course of his American career he directed over 35 films and wrote the scenarios for over 65. With the release of *Grand Hotel* (MGM) in 1932, Goulding's reputation as a director of competence was assured. Some of his better known motion pictures include: *The Dawn Patrol* (1938), *'Til We Meet Again* (1940), *The Razor's Edge* (1946) and *Nightmare Alley* (1947). After directing the Pat Boone musical *Mardi Gras (1958)* he retired and within a year, despondent over finances, committed suicide.

After appearing in bit parts in at least twelve films dating back to 1934, this was Dublin-born Geraldine Fitzgerald's (1913- ) first major screen role. She was then signed to appear in the classic tearjerker *Wuthering Heights* (1939). Some of the better known of her more than 40 films were: *Till We Meet Again* (1940), *Watch on the Rhine* (1943), *Wilson* (1944), *O.S.S.* (1946), *Ten North Frederick* (1958), *The Pawnbroker* (1964), *Harry and Tonto* (1974) and *Poltergeist II* (1986).

New Orleans native Cora Witherspoon (1890-1957) had a career that extended over two decades (1931-1954) and consisted of almost fifty screen appearances. She was in the original *Frankie and Johnny* (1936), and had character roles in *Madame X* (1937), *Marie Antoinette* (1938), *Dodge City* (1939), as W.C. Fields wife in *The Bank Dick* (1940), *I've Always Loved You* (1946) and *The Mating Season* (1951).

Writer Casey Robinson (1903-1979) was one of Warners best script doctors in the 1930s and 40s. Although he did not always receive credit for his work, between 1927 and 1975 he had a hand in writing or "fixing" over 75 film scripts. Robinson is credited with the screenplays for Errol Flynn's *Captain Blood* (1935), Reagan's *Kings Row* (1942) and *This Is the Army* (1943), *Saratoga Trunk* (1946), *The Snows of Kilimanjaro* (1952) and *While the City Sleeps* (1956). He also worked on *The Pride of the Yankees* (1942), *Casablanca* (1942) and *Adventure* (1945). Between 1944 and 1975 the talented Robinson also produced seven films.

Remade in 1976 as a made-for-television movie with Elizabeth Montgomery in the Bette Davis role.

# Naughty But Nice

**release date: June 23, 1939**　　　　　　　**running time: 89-90 minutes**

**Cast:**　Ann Sheridan, Dick Powell, Gale Page, Helen Broderick, Ronald Reagan, Allen Jenkins, Zasu Pitts, Max 'Slapsie Maxie' Rosenbloom, Jerry Colonna, Luis Alberni, Vera Lewis, Elizabeth Dunn, William B. Davidson, Granville Bates, Halliwell Hobbes, Jimmy Conlin, Tom Dugan, Sidney Bracey, Daisy Bufford, Nat Carr, Maurice Cass, Hobart Cavanaugh, Elise Cavanna, Glen Cavender, Sol Gorss, William Gould, Eddie Graham, Harrison Greene, Bert Hanlon, John Harron, Peter Lind Hayes, Al Herman, Stuart Holmes, Selmer Jackson, Al Loyd, Jerry Mandy, Frank Mayo, Edward McWade, Jack Mower, David Newell, William Newell, Wedgewood Nowell, Garry Owen, Herbert Rawlinson, John Ridgely, Sally Sage, Cliff Saum, Bobby Sherwood, Larry Steers, Grady Sutton, Leo White, Ernest Wood, Gary Owen

**Credits:**            **First National-Warners**

*Executive In Charge of Production* Jack L. Warner; *Executive Producer* Hal B. Wallis; *Associate Producer* Samuel Bischoff; *Director* Ray Enright; *Screenplay* Richard Macaulay, Jerry Wald; *Cinematography* Arthur L. Todd; *Editor* Thomas Richards; *Original Music* Harry Warren, Heinz Roemheld; *Non-Original Music by* Franz Liszt, Wolfgang Amadeus Mozart, Michael William Balfe, Franz Schubert, Robert Schumann, Richard Wagner, Ludwig van Beethoven; *Art Director* Max Parker; *Costumes* Howard Shoup; *Assistant Director* Jesse Hibbs; *Sound* Charles David Forrest, Francis J. Scheid; *Dialogue Director* Hugh Cummings; *Musical Director* Leo F. Forbstein; *Music Arranger* Ray Heindorf; *Songs* "In A Moment of Weakness," "Hurray for Spinach," "I'm Happy About the Whole Thing," "I don't Believe in Signs" and "Corn Pickin," *words and music by* Harry Warren, Johnny Mercer

## Synopsis:

The Professor (Dick Powell), attempts to get his symphonic composition published.

He is badly equipped to meet the kind of sharks who manipulate music in New York's Tin Pan Alley. He has been coddled by three maiden aunts, who believe he is a genius. In fact his music, whilst not brilliant has enough merit to make it acceptable in a pop format. His main work is stolen and turns up as a jive song, "Hooray for Spinach", performed by Ann Sheridan.

She works on the Professor for her own ends, but a lovely lyricist played by Gale Page falls in love with him.

Also on the Professor's side is honest music publisher, (Ronald Reagan).

The picture is a mildly amusing satirization of how pop merchants can lift material from the classics.

## Reviews:

"Pretty flat, even down to the borrowed music." *The New York Times* (June 23, 1939); "It has a good quota of laughs and is generally bright, despite a plot at which the cynical Tin Pan Alley habitués might look askance." *Variety* (June 28, 1939); "Like a nice dish of warm weather variety? Mix equal portions of Ann Sheridan's 'oomph' and Dick Powell's voice. That's *Naughty But Nice*. . . . as neat a title as I've come across in days. . . breezy comedy and good direction." *The Los Angeles Examiner* (Dorothy Manners, July 14, 1939)

**Notes:**

In production from late-October to mid-December 1938 under the working titles *The Professor Steps Out* and *Always Leave them Laughing.*

The production had a negative cost of $399,000. It brought in domestic rentals of $445,000 and an additional $152,000 from overseas markets.

Reagan's salary was $300 a week.

After seven years, this was Dick Powell's last film for Warner Bros. Not happy with their star leaving for another studio, Warners lowered Powell to second billing, in support of Ann Sheridan, who was getting the "oomph" buildup by the Publicity Department.

Third-billed Gale Page (born Sally Perkins Rutter, 1913-1983) appeared on radio as a singer and actress before signing as a contract player at Warners in 1938. Her entire film career consisted of appearances in only 16 pictures. She also appeared with Reagan in *The Amazing Dr. Clitterhouse* (1938) and as the coach's wife in *Knute Rocke-All American* (1940). After completing her part in *Anna Lucasta* (1949) she retired from the screen only to return for one more role in *About Mrs. Leslie* (1954).

Cast member Helen Broderick (1891-1959), a veteran of over 35 films, was better known as the mother of actor Broderick Crawford. After a role in the Deanna Durbin musical *Because of Him* (1946), Broderick left the screen. The elderly actress was instrumental in making Reagan aware of the politics within the Screen Actors Guild (SAG) which would eventually lead to his growing interest in governmental politics.

Comedian Jerry Colonna (1904-1986) is best known for his appearances on the screen, television and radio in support of Bob Hope. When Hope entertained servicemen throughout the world, Colonna was usually at his side. Between 1935 and 1962 the veteran comedian appeared sporadically in motion pictures with appearances in nearly 30 films. He worked with Hope and Bing Crosby in *Road to Singapore* (1940), *Road to Rio* (1947) and *The Road to Hong Kong* (1962).

Cast member Peter Lind Hayes (1915-1998) was primarily a band leader. As a technical sergeant during World War II he was featured in the war film *Winged Victory* (1944). Throughout the 1950s and early 1960s he hosted several television series: *The Peter Lind Hayes Show* (1950), *Star of the Family* (1951-1952), and *Peter Loves Mary* (1960).

In the Los Angeles market this film was released as the upper part of a double-bill with another Reagan film *Hell's Kitchen.*

Other films playing throughout the nation at the time of *Naughty But Nice's* release included *Man In the Iron Mask* (United Artists) with Louis Hayward and Joan Bennett, *Good Girls Go to Paris* (Columbia) starring Melvyn Douglas and Joan Blondell, *Stronger Than Desire* (MGM) featuring Virginia Bruce and Walter Pidgeon and the 12-chapter serials *Dare Devils of the Red Circle* (Republic) and *Flash Gordon Conquers the Universe* (Universal) with Buster Crabbe as the hero.

# Hell's Kitchen

**release date: July 8, 1939**　　　　　**running time: 81-82 minutes**

**Cast:**　Billy Halop, Bobby Jordan, Leo Gorcey, Huntz Hall, Gabriel Dell, Bernard Punsly, Margaret Lindsay, Ronald Reagan, Stanley Fields, Frankie Burke, Grant Mitchell, Frederic Tozere, Arthur Loft, Vera Lewis, Robert Homans, Charley Foy, Raymond Bailey, Clem Bevans, George Irving, Ila Rhodes, Robert Strange, Joe Devlin, Jack Gardner, Sol Gorss, Max Hoffman Jr., Stuart Holmes, Jack Kenney, Reid Kilpatrick, Jimmie Lucas, Jack Mower, Louis Natheaux, Larry Nunn, George Offerman, Jimmy O'Gatty, George O'Hanlon, Lee Phelps, Dick Rich, Ruth Robinson, Cliff Saum, Ernie Stanton, Charles Sullivan, Elliott Sullivan, Don Turner, Lotie Williams, Tom Wilson, Jack Wise, Sonny Noisom

**Credits:**　　　　　　**First National-Warners**

Producers Bryan Foy, Mark Hellinger; *Directors* Ewald Andre Dupont, Lewis Seiler; *Assistant Director* William Kissell; *Writers* Fred Niblo Jr., Crane Wilbur; *Original Story* Crane Wilbur; *Cinematography* Charles Rosher; *Original Music* Ray Heindorf, Heinz Roemheld; *Editor* Clarence Kolster; *Production Design* Hugh Reticker; *Costumes* Milo Anderson; *Sound* Dolph Thomas; *Dialogue Director* Hugh Cummings

## Synopsis:

*Hell's Kitchen* finds the Dead End Kids having graduated from reform school and assigned to a "Boy's Town" type shelter. The shelter is run by crooked superintendent, Crispin (Grant Mitchell). He is assisted by ex-racketeer Buck (Stanley Fields), who is now on probation himself. This tough character tries to straighten the kids out and joins together with them to try to get Crispin kicked out of his job.

Also on hand to try to run the shelter are two social workers, Jim (Ronald Reagan) and Beth (Margaret Lindsay). Their tentative romance is railroaded into the real thing through the efforts of the kids.

**Reviews:**

"Margaret Lindsay and Ronald Reagan are nicely teamed as co-workers attempting to run the boys' school right." *Variety* (July 1, 1939); "Entertaining enough but negligible as social comment." *The Warner Bros. Story*. Clive Hirschhorn (New York, Crown, 1979); "(The Dead End Kids) take the audience from laughing cheers to sobs and tears." *The Los Angeles Examiner* (Dorothy Manners, July 14, 1939); "Starting out with real promise, *Hell's Kitchen* rapidly loses itself in its own plot entanglements. . . . (an) unconvincing picture. . . . drags in every possible meller element from love to murder. . . . Ronald Reagan aids Miss Lindsay in providing romantic interest." *Daily Variety* (July 13, 1939); ". . . slotted for second billing in the dualers and for those spots which want their melodrama broad if not too believable....stocked with implausible incident and guilty of pulling its punches woefully in the clinches. . . . Reagan and Margaret Lindsay show to advantage in the thinly developed romantic sub-plot." *The Hollywood Reporter* (July 13, 1939)

**Notes:** *"An experience similar to going over Niagara Falls in a barrel the hard way-upstream."*

In production from January 13 to early February 1939.
The film had a negative cost of $303,000. It returned $481,000 to the studio in domestic rentals and an additional $205,000 from overseas markets.
Reagan paid $300 a week. Lead actor Billy Halop received $750 a week. The real-life manners of the young actors who made up the team of screen delinquents had caused other actors to refuse to work with them. James Cagney had warned Reagan, "Just tell them you look forward to working with them but you'll slap hell out of them if they do one thing out of line."
Another *Dead End Boys* melodrama taking notice of the success of *Boys Town* at MGM. The first feature with the gang of juvenile delinquents known as the *Dead End Kids,* was *Dead End* (1937), which was based on the smash Broadway play *(1935)*. Young Leo Gorcey (1915-1965) appeared on stage and recreated his role when it transitioned to the screen. Because of complaints from the Parent Teacher Association, this was the last Dead Ends Kids film dealing with gangsters in a somewhat positive light.
Over a thirty year period from 1932 to 1963 Margaret Lindsay (1910-1981) appeared in more than eighty films of all genres from the "B" mystery series Ellery Queen and Crime Doctor to bigger

budgeted features, *Jezebel* (1938), *The House of the Seven Gables* (1940), *Cass Timberlane* (1947) and the Doris Day comedy hit *Please Don't Eat the Daisies* (1960). After appearing in the Noel Coward Fox entry *Cavalcade* (1933), Lindsay signed a term contract with Warner Bros. and was inserted into an average of five films a year by the studio. In the 1950s and 1960s, as good film roles dried up, the actress was a frequent guest on series television. New York City-born Billy Halop (1920-1976) was the leader of the original Dead End Kids. Halop and other teenage members of the cast were summoned to Hollywood in 1937 to reprise their stage role in the very successful *Dead End* for producer Samuel Goldwyn. The film was a smash hit and lead to several sequels and spinoffs. Over the next twenty years, at different studios (Universal, Monogram, Allied Artists), the gang's name and faces changed first to the East Side Kids then the Bowery Boys. Halop had minor, often un-credited roles in over two dozen films, work more frequently on television, and eventually, in the 1960s he became a registered nurse in the Los Angeles area. Another Dead End Kid, the studious one, Bernard Punsly (1923-2004), never comfortable in front of the cameras, joined the army during World War II, then went to medical school on the GI Bill and become a medical doctor. He was the last of the original New York gang of teenagers to die.

In the Los Angeles market this film ended up on the bottom half of a double bill that featured another Reagan film *Naughty But Nice*. Competition at the nations screens came from *The Old Maid* with Bette Davis and Miriam Hopkins and MGM's *The Women* starring Norma Shearer and Joan Crawford.

# The Angels Wash Their Faces

**release date: August 26, 1939**         **running time: 76-87 minutes**

**Cast:**   Ann Sheridan, Billy Halop, Bernard Punsly, Leo Gorcey, Huntz
Hall, Gabriel Dell, Bobby Jordan, Ronald Reagan, Bonita
Granville, Frankie Thomas, Henry O'Neill, Eduardo Ciannelli,
Berton Churchill, Bernard Nedell, Dick Rich, Jackie Searl,
Margaret Hamilton, Marjorie Main, Minor Watson, Cy Kendall,
Grady Sutton, Aldrich Bowker, Robert Strange, Egon Brecher,
Sarah Padden, Nat Carr, John Hamilton, Claude Wisberg, Frankie
Burke, Glen Cavender, Eddy Chandler, Jack Clifford, Frank
Coghlan Jr., Eddie Graham, Sibyl Harris, John Harron, Howard C.
Hickman, Max Hoffman Jr., Stuart Holmes, William Hopper,
Edward Keane, Lon McCallister, Jack Mower, Garry Owen, Paul
Panzer, Lee Phelps, Jack Richardson, John Ridgely, Cliff Saum,
Harry Strang, Charles Trowbridge, Jack Wagner, Tom Wilson

**Credits:**         **First National-Warners**

*Executive Producers* Jack L. Warner, Hal B. Wallis; *Associate
Producer* Max Siegel; *Director* Ray Enright; *Screenplay* Michael
Fessier, Niven Busch, Robert Buckner; *Story Idea* H. Jonathan
Finn; *Cinematography* Arthur L. Todd; *Original Music* Adolph

Deutsch; *Non-Original Music* Al Feldman; *Performed by* Ella Fitzgerald; *Editor* James Gibbon; *Art Director* Ted Smith; *Costumes* Milo Anderson; *Sound* Dolph Thomas; *Assistant Director* Jesse Hibbs; *Music Director* Leo F. Forbstein; *Music Arranger* Ray Heindorf; *Dialogue Director* Hugh Cummings; *song:* A-Tisket A-Tasket

## Synopsis:

When one of the gang, Gabe Ryan (Frankie Thomas) is framed as an arsonist and indicted by an insurance company, his friends, The Termites, decide to help clear him. They become model ctizens and co-operate fully with district attorney, Mr Remsen (Henry O'Neill) and his son, Pat (Ronald Reagan). Pat is in love with Gabe's sister, Joy Ryan (Ann Sheridan).

One of the gang, Billy Shafter (Billy Halop) becomes mayor during Boy's Week. He appoints his friends to various civic posts. They gather the evidence that enables the District Attorney to nab the real arsonists. Gabe is cleared and his sister and Jim are marched to the alter to the loud cheering of The Termites

## Reviews:

". . . sacrifices plausibility for action . . . terrific meller pace makes it the sort of fare the average audience will eat up. . . . Ray Enright has directed with an eye for the spectacular." *Variety* (August 30, 1939); "An ablutional sequel to *Angels With Dirty Faces*" *The New York Times* (September 4, 1939); "Cracking good entertainment and action all the way . . . suffers no scripting loopholes that let audience interest down . . . Reagan is another to whom Warners has given careful training through appearances in a series of supporting roles. His work here justifies the company's faith in him, and his likeable personality and easy and natural style mark him worthy of important assignments. . . . The script is well written, packing some exceptionally punchy dialogue." *The Hollywood Reporter* (October 6, 1939); "It's good entertainment. . . . It's the director's picture . . . not quite the sockeroo its predecessor was . . . Ronald Reagan as Miss Sheridan's vis-à-vis is satisfactory." *Daily Variety* (October 6, 1939)

## Notes:

In production from March 13 to April 15, 1939, under the working title, *(The) Battle of City Hall.*

The production had a negative cost of $380,000 and earned domestic rentals of $495,000. Foreign sources added a further $283,000 to the worldwide take for the studio.

By contrast the earlier filmed sequel *Angels With Dirty Faces,* budgeted at $602,000, had a final negative cost of $633,000. It reported worldwide rentals for Warner Bros. of a stunning $2,334,000.

Reagan paid $300 a week for playing the role of the deputy district attorney. Ann Sheridan's salary for 1939 had been elevated to $5000 a week. Within a month Reagan had a new agent when he signed to be represented by MCA and Lew Wasserman.

The fourth film in the *Dead End Kid* series following *Dead End* (1937), *Angels with Dirty Faces* (1938), and *Hell's Kitchen* (1939). James Cagney had scored a great hit in 1938 playing a mean-hearted gangster in *Angels With Dirty Faces* in which he starred along with The Dead End Kids. *Angels Wash Their Faces* was a follow-up, but it did not match the impact of Cagney's picture and it became purely a Dead End Kids picture.

Petite Bonita Granville (1923-1988) was a former child star who began appearing on stage before the age of five, and hit the screen at nine in the B-programmer *Westward Passage* (1932). Signed to a contract by Warner Bros., by 1937 she would be earning $500 a week. The actress is best known for appearing as the title character in four Nancy Drew detective stories. The biggest box-office hit of her over fifty films was the very-low budgeted *Hitler's Children* (1943). In 1947 Granville married industrialist Jack Wrather who bought the rights to The Lone Ranger and Lassie characters. Retiring from the screen after an appearance in *The Lone Ranger* (1956) she remained active behind the cameras working as an executive on both long running television series (*The Lone Ranger* 1949-1957 and *Lassie* 1954-1974).

Actor Frankie Thomas (1921- ) had a comparatively short film career, lasting less than a decade (1934-1942) and included under twenty features. As a child and teenager he had roles in *Wednesday's Child* (1934), *Dog of Flanders* (1935), *Boys Town* (1938), four episodes of the Nancy Drew series and several Dead End Kids comedies. In 1949 he turned to the small screen and had roles in three short-lived television series including that of the title character in *Tom Corbett, Space Cadet* (1950).

Screenwriter Niven Busch (1903-1991), who is most famous for writing the novel *Duel In the Sun,* between 1932 and 1955 also wrote the scenarios for over twenty-five motion pictures. His first screen credit was for the Howard Hawks directed James Cagney starrer *The Crowd Roars*. His other collaborations for the screen included *College Coach* (1933), *Babbitt* (1934), *In Old Chicago* (1937), the Gary Cooper Western *The Westerner* (1940), *Belle Starr* (1941), the Lana Turner-John Garfield suspense-melodrama *The Postman Always Rings Twice* (1946), and Glenn Ford's *The Man from the Alamo* (1953).

In March 1939 Warner Bros. received an unsolicited request to allow their contract player, Reagan, to work as an announcer for the radio broadcasts of the local minor league baseball team. Reagan was eager to accept the job which would pay $100 a week, but was overruled by studio executives.

Competition on the nations screens came from: *These Glamour Girls* (MGM) Lew Ayres, Lana Turner; Gary Cooper's *The Real Glory* (United Artists); *The Rains Came* (Fox); *Golden Boy* (Columbia) and *Rio* (Universal)

# Code of the Secret Service

**release date: May 27, 1939**              **running time: 58-61 minutes**

**Cast:**   Ronald Reagan, Rosella Towne, Eddie Foy Jr., Moroni Olsen, Edgar Edwards, Jack Mower, John Gallaudet, Joe King, Steve Darrell, Sol Gorss, Frank Mayo, George Regas, Dick Botiller, Glen Cavender, Rafael Corio, Demetrius Emanuel, Antonio Filauri, June Gittelson, John Harron, Stuart Holmes, Chris-Pin Martin, Ted Offenbecker, Frank Puglia, Theodore Rand, Pedro Regas, Jack Richardson, Julian Rivero, Cliff Saum, Wally West, Maris Wrixon, Martin Garralaga, Theodore Rand, Paul Panzar, Jerry Gomez, Jose Luis Tortosa, Jack Wise, Al Loyd, Tom Wilxon, Jack Richardson, George Offerman

**Credits:**              **First National-Warners**

*Executive Producers* Jack L. Warner, Hal B. Wallis; *Producer* Bryan Foy; *Director* Noel M. Smith; *Writers* Lee Katz, Dean Franklin; *Original Music & Orchestrations* Bernhard Kaun; *Cinematography* Ted D. McCord; *Editor* Frederick Richards; *Art Direction* Charles Novi; *Costumes* Milo Anderson; *Sound* Dolph Thomas; *Assistant Director* Marshall Hageman; *Dialogue Director* John Langan; *Comedy Construction* Lex Neal

## Synopsis:

For his second time out as Lt Brass Bancroft of the Secret Service, Ronald Reagan is sent into a remote part of Mexico to discover the operations of a band of American counterfeiters. After plates are stolen from the United States Mint, Brass traces them to a mountain hideaway but there, gets snared by the theives. They pin the blame on him for the death of a fellow agent and Brass is slated for execution.

He breaks out of jail but again falls into the hands of the counterfeiters along with Elaine (Rosella Towne), the daughter of an American rancher. The pair seem doomed to be blown up, along with all the counterfeiting evidence.

Brass overpowers a guard and escapes, taking Elaine along. He then lures the smooth leader of the gang, Friar Parker (Moroni Olsen), back across the United States border. There he arrests him.

## Reviews:

"Reminiscent of the wild and wooly melodramatics of the early Pearl White serials. . . . Plot structure is illogical, dialog is strained, and futile attempts made at comedy." *Variety* (May 13, 1939); "A weakling sequel to the previous release . . . It is formula stuff throughout, oafishly hung together and plotted . . . Ronald Reagan's ingratiating efforts are largely lost in this hokus-pocus. . ." *The Hollywood Reporter* (May 15, 1939)

## Notes:

Second in the B-series of action films highlighting the secret service exploits of Ronald Reagan as Lieutenant 'Brass' Bancroft. Filmed in December 1938 at locations in the Iverson Ranch in Chatsworth. Negative cost of the production was $133,000. It earned domestic rentals of $164,000 and $88,000 from the overseas markets.

Reagan received $300 a week in salary. He hated the picture so much he begged Warner Bros not to release it. They compromised and released it everywhere except in Los Angeles.

Working title, *Smashing the Money Ring.*

Over a period of seven years (1937-43), Ohio-born Rosella Towne (1919- ) appeared in more than thirty-five films of which eight included Ronald Reagan. She came to Hollywood as a teenager in the early 1930s and was signed to a contract by Warner Bros. who inserted the young actress (often uncredited) in up to fifteen B-features a year. After a supporting role in *A Gentle Gangster* (1943) she retired from the screen.

Imposing character actor Moroni Olsen (1889-1954) was born in Utah and by the mid-1920s was a seasoned performer on the Broadway stage. Journeying to Hollywood in the early 1930s, after four years of un-credited and bit roles, Olsen received co-star billing as Porthos in *The Three Musketeers* (1935). Over the next twenty-three years he appeared in more than 100 films and played such historical luminaries as Buffalo Bill to Barbara Stanwyck's *Annie Oakley* (1935), John Knox opposite Katharine Hepburn in *Mary of Scotland* (1936), Robert E. Lee in Errol Flynn's *Santa Fe Trail* (1940) and Sam Houston in *Lone Star* (1952).

Screenwriter Dean Franklin (born Dean Riesner in New York City, 1918-2002) started in the industry as Dinky Dean child actor. Among the nearly dozen silents he acted in were *Peck's Bad Boy* (1921) and *The Pilgrim* (1923) starring Charlie Chaplin. As he drifted away from acting, *Code of the Secret Service* written under the name Dean Franklin, was his first effort under contract to the studio. In the 1950s and 60s, while still writing for the screen, he had ample time to pen episodes of the television series' *Lawman, Rawhide, Bonanza, Ben Casey, The Outer Limits* and *Twelve O'Clock High.* For Clint Eastwood he helped write the screenplays to *Coogan's Bluff* (1968), *Play Misty For Me* (1971), *Dirty Harry* (1971), *High Plains Drifter* (1973) and *The Enforcer* (1976). Riesner is credited with writing the following immortal dialogue for "Dirty" Harry Callahan, "Do you feel lucky? Well, do you punk?"

The top tunes played on the radio in May 1939 were: "And the Angels Sing," "Don't Worry 'Bout Me," "Night Must Fall," "Three Little Fishes" and "Our Love."

Opened in New York on November 6, 1939.

The film faced competition at the nation's screens from *Goodbye Mr. Chips* starring Robert Donat in his Oscar winning role, *Young Mr. Lincoln* from John Ford, Garbo's *Ninotchka, Calling Dr. Kildare* (MGM) with Lew Ayres and Lionel Barrymore and the B-series entry *Torchy Blane Runs For Mayor* (Warners) with Glenda Farrell and Barton MacLane.

# Smashing the Money Ring

**release date: October 21, 1939**            **running time: 57-61 minutes**

**Cast:**   Ronald Reagan, Margot Stevenson, Eddie Foy Jr., Joe Downing, Charles D. Brown, Elliott Sullivan, Joe King, Charles C. Wilson, William B. Davidson, John Hamilton, Sidney Bracey, Jack Wise, Jack Mower, Don Turner, Oscar 'Dutch' Hendrian, Bob Perry, John Ridgely, Nat Carr, Glen Cavender, George Cheseboro, Donald Douglas, Ralph Dunn, Milton Frome, Sol Gorss, Fred Graham, John Harron, Edward Hearn, Al Herman, Max Hoffman Jr., William Hopper, Frank Mayo, Louis Natheaux, Frank O'Connor, Pat O,Malley, Paul Panzer, Lee Phelps, George Reeves, Dick Rich, Ralph Sanford, Cliff Saum, Charles Trowbridge, Monte Vandergrift, Tom Wilson, Jim Pierce

**Credits:**            **First National-Warners**

*Executive Producers* Jack L. Warner, Hal. B. Wallis; *Associate Producer* Bryan Foy; *Director* Terry O. Morse; *Writers* Anthony Coldeway, Jonathan Finn, Raymond L. Schrock; *Cinematography* James Van Trees, Lou O'Connell; *Original Music* Bernhard Kaun; *Editor* Frank Magee; *Production Design* Charles Novi; *Costumes* Milo Anderson; *Sound* Dolph Thomas; *Assistant Director* Arthur Lueker; *Technical Advisor* Charles Perry; *Dialogue Director* Arthur Ripley; *Orchestrations* Bernhard Kaun

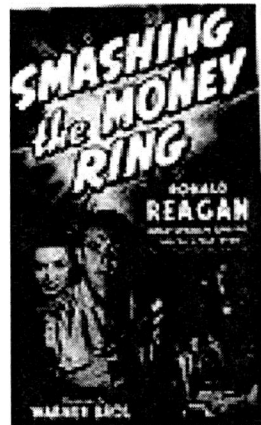

## Synopsis:

Brass and his sidekick Gabby Watters (Eddie Foy Jr), are assigned to track a gang of counterfeiters who are flooding the country with bad notes. Following up a tip from the underworld, Brass again goes undercover as a counterfeiter. He has himself thrown into prison and there discovers that the gang is printing the bogus bills right on the premises, on the prison press!

Brass engineers a jail break and leads government colleagues to the source of the operation.

## Reviews:

"Tells an obvious story fast and gets it over with." *The New York Times* (November 17, 1939); "A program picture . . . production values measuring up to this classification. Makes satisfactory dual support because of highly melodramatic content. . . . Reagan is about the same as in previous vehicles in this group." *Variety* (November 16, 1939); "It is a distinct improvement over the first of Warner's Secret Service series . . . it advances Ronald Reagan an other step toward stardom . . . (He) again adds to a picture with his affable, natural style. He is equally good in fast action shows such as this, or in a sophisticated part such as he had in *Dark Victory."* *The Hollywood Reporter* (October 23, 1939)

## Notes:

In production from June 26 to early July 1939 under the working title *Queer Money.*

Negative cost of the film was $126,000. It earned $186,000 in domestic rentals for the studio and a further $78,000 form overseas markets.

Based on the story, *Murder In Sing Sing.*

Reagan earned $400 a week. For the third time the actor played G-Man Lieutenant 'Brass' Bancroft.

During his career in Hollywood which extended from the mid-1920's to 1969, Terry O. Morse (1906-1984) was as comfortable being a film editor as he was a director of B-films. On a number of features he often served in both capacities. The St. Louis native edited over sixty motion pictures and directed eighteen low-grade films. *Smashing the Money Ring* was only his fifth directorial effort. In 1956 Morse was assigned the task of taking a Japanese science-fiction film, *Godzilla, King of the Monsters* and making it marketable for the American audience by directing and editing sequences with Raymond Burr. The flick proved to be an immense hit. Morse also edited Elvis Presley's *Blue Hawaii* (1961), and served in a dual capacity on the Nick Adams-Robert Conrad gangster feature *Young Dillinger* (1965).

This film marked leading-lady Margot Stevenson's (1914- ) first co-starring role. Her total film output consisted of less than twenty entries. By the end of 1940 she had been relegated to uncredited bit-parts.

4th billed Joe Downing (1903-1975), born in New York City, entered films as a bit-player in the early 1930s and by the time he retired in 1957 had accumulated over fifty screen appearances.

Almost all of his roles were in low-budget films including *The Lady in the Morgue* (1938), *Racket Busters* (1938), *Angels With Dirty Faces* (1939), *Torchy Runs for Mayor* (1939), *Each Dawn I Die* (1939), *Another Thin Man* (1939), *Belle Starr* (1941) and *Lucky Jordan* (1942). His last role was in the crime-drama *Slaughter on Tenth Avenue* (1957).

Character actor John Hamilton (1886-1958) played on Broadway, appeared in touring companies across the nation, worked in over 300 films, yet will be best remembered for playing newspaper editor Perry White during the 1950s in television's *The Adventures of Superman*. Hamilton who was generally typecast as a military officer, judge, law enforcement official or warden worked with Reagan in six Warner Bros. films.

Bit-player and extra Fred Graham (1908-1979), for much of the 1940s acted as a stuntman and double for John Wayne. Between 1931 and the late 1960's he appeared in nearly 200 motion pictures. The top-five tunes played on the nation's radios during the fall of 1939 were: "Last Night," "South of the Border," "Are You Having Any Fun?" "My Prayer" and "What's New."

Plays appearing on Broadway included *Key Largo* with Paul Muni and *The Man Who Came To Dinner*. Playing on the nation's screens were the Columbia B-film *Scandal Sheet* starring Otto Kruger, Edward Norris and Ona Munson, the low-budget comedy *Beware Spooks* (Columbia), *Disputed Passage* (Paramount) starring Dorothy Lamour and *20,000 Men A Year* (Fox) with Randolph Scott.

The annual survey by the Roper organization revealed that the top ten male stars for 1939 were: 1) Spencer Tracy 2) Clark Gable 3) Tyrone Power 4) Wallace Beery 5) Lionel Barrymore 6) Paul Muni 7) Robert Taylor 8) Gary Cooper 9) William Powell 10) Nelson Eddy. For the women the rankings were: 1) Bette Davis 2) Myrna Loy 3) Jeanette MacDonald 4) Irene Dunne 5) Norma Shearer 6) Shirley Temple 7) Janet Gaynor 8) Ginger Rogers 9) Claudette Colbert 10) Joan Crawford.

# Brother Rat and A Baby

**release date: January 17, 1940**          **running time: 87 minutes**

**Cast:** Priscilla Lane, Wayne Morris, Jane Bryan, Eddie Albert, Jane
Wyman, Ronald Reagan, Peter B. Good, Arthur Treacher, Moroni
Olsen, Jessie Busley, Larry Williams, Berton Churchill, Nana
Bryant, Paul Harvey, Mayo Methot, Edward Gargan, Irving Bacon,
Granville Bates, Wade Boteler, Tommy Bupp, Glen Cavender,
Eddy Chandler, Cliff Clark, Richard Clayton, Michael Conroy,
John Deering, John Dilson, William Gould, Eddie Graham, John
Hamilton, John Harron, Alan Ladd, Douglas Meins, Carlyle Moore
Jr., Ted Osborne, Sally Sage, Cliff Saum, George Sorrell, Elliott
Sullivan, Emmett Vogan, Billy Wayne, Dave Willock, Claude
Wisberg, Allan Chaney, Harlan Briggs, Jeffrey Sayre, Ed Cecil

**Credits:**                    **First National-Warners**

*Executive Producer* Hal B. Wallis; *Director* Ray Enright; *Associate
Producer* Robert Lord; *Cinematography Charles Rosher;* Writers
*Earl Baldwin, Fred F. Finklehoffe, Richard Macaulay, John Monks
Jr., Jerry* Wald*; Editor* Clarence Kolster; *Original Music* Heinz
Roemheld, Howard Jackson; *Art Direction* Robert M. Haas;
*Costumes* Milo Anderson; *Makeup* Perc Westmore; *Executive In
Charge of Production* Jack L. Warner; *Assistant Directors* Jesse
Hibbs, Russell Saunders; *Sound* Stanley Jones; *Special Effects*
Byron Haskin, Willard Van Enger; *Dialogue Director* Hugh
Cummings; *Musical Director* Leo F. Forbstein; *Musical Arranger*
Ray Heindorf

## Synopsis:

Dan Crawford (Ronald Reagan) spends his time continuing the
courtship of the Colonel's daughter, Claire (Jane Wyman). He
manages to incur the wrath of the Colonel by keeping Jane out until
dawn.

Bing (Eddie Albert), wants a job as a sports coach at the Virginia
Military Institute. His buddies try to help out but fail. They
persuade Bing and Kate (Jane Bryan) to bring baby (Peter B Good),
to go to New York. The wild ideas of Billy (Wayne Morris) get
them all into trouble and in one of his many moments of
desperation over lack of money, he steals a violin and pawns it.

Somehow, the improbable adventure works out, and Billy plants the baby on an airplane bound for a goodwill tour of Peru.

The resultant publicity gets Bing his job at VMI, Dan wins his girl and Billy winds up in the arms of a lovely southerner, Joyce Winfree (Priscilla Lane).

## Reviews:

"Picture swings more to comedy side than its predecessor and should attract profitable biz . . . a wholesome and effervescing comedy built on a fragile story structure. . . . Reagan is a serious and plodding illustrator" *Variety* (January 4, 1940); "a feeble attempt to draw on the same vein of humor." *Warner Brothers Presents: The Most Exciting Years-From The Jazz Singer to White Heat.* Ted Sennett (Arlington House, 1971); "Scoring top honors in the acting department are pert Jane Wyman and Ronald Reagan . . . Miss Wyman is particularly effective in her comedy scenes and . . . Reagan is exceptionally good." *The Los Angeles Examiner* (January 19, 1940)

## Notes:

Filmed from October 3 to November 7, 1939. Sequel to the previous years *Brother Rat* with the same principal six actors repeating their earlier roles. This production, that started filming less than eighteen months after the first film, was allotted a budget of only 40% of the original and a shooting schedule of 24 days. It took 30 days to complete principal photography.

Shot on stages 8, 12A and 14 on the Warners lot and at the Alhambra Airport.

Although budgeted at $332,000, the final negative cost of the production was $318,000. It earned the studio $716,000 in domestic rentals and a further $85,000 from the overseas markets.

Reagan was paid $400 a week.

In 1940 Warner Bros. released 45 features.

Associate Producer Robert Lord (1900-1976) is credited with writing the scenarios or screenplays for seventy-one features (1925-1940), and acting as a Producer on forty-seven films (1932-1951). As a writer he worked on the memorable *Little Caesar* (1931), *So Big!* (1932), *20,000 Years in Sing Sing* (also produced, 1932), *Black Legion* (1937) and *'Til We Meet Again* (1940). His production credits include *The Prince and the Pauper* (1937), *The Amazing Dr. Clitterhouse* (1938), *Dodge City* and *The Private Lives of Elizabeth and Essex* (both released in 1939 with Errol Flynn), *The Letter*

(1940), *Dive Bomber* (1941) and Humphrey Bogart's *Sirocco* (1951).

Eighth-billed, British-born Arthur Treacher (1894-1975) seemed to always be playing the quintessential English butler. With his imposing height and arrogance he supported Shirley Temple in *Curley Top* (1935), *Stowaway* (1936) and *Heidi* (1937). To a generation of television viewers Treacher served as the announcer and confidant of Merv Griffin on the later's talk show from 1962 until his death in 1975.

Character actor Paul Harvey (1882-1955) between 1928 and 1955 appeared in nearly 200 films. Some of his better known features included *The House of Rothschild* (1934), Bogart's *The Petrified Forest* (1936), *The Plainsman* (1937), Shirley Temple's *Rebecca of Sunnybrook Farm* (1938), *Arizona* (1940), *High Sierra* (1941), Hitchcock's *Spellbound* (1945), *Father of the Bride* (1950), and *Calamity Jane* (1953). Harvey also appeared in Reagan's *John Loves Mary* (1949).

Reagan as the character Dan Crawford, is fifth billed, just behind Jane Wyman. After the completion of principal photography in mid-November 1939 Reagan and Wyman announced their engagement. Within a week Reagan, Wyman, Susan Hayward and other performers would become part of Louella Parsons' six-week stage revue, national tour- *Hollywood Stars of 1940 On Parade*. They journeyed north to San Francisco for the first leg of the engagement. Other cities on the tour which ended in Washington D.C. on January 15, 1940 included Chicago, Baltimore and Philadelphia. For the duration of the tour, both Reagan and Wyman were paid $300 a week. The clever Parsons earned $3,000 a week and reams of positive publicity. Parsons, the "Queen" of Hollywood gossip columnists had a nationwide readership of 17,000,000 while her nearest competitor, Hedda Hopper was read by nearly 6,000,000 daily. On January 26, 1940, now back in Hollywood, the engaged couple wed.

In November, Warners increased contract player James Cagney's salary from $5000 to $12,500 a week.

Released in Great Britain under the title, *Baby Be Good*.

While playing in the Los Angeles area the program also included Boris Karloff and Margaret Lindsay in the low-budgeted feature *British Intelligence*.

Competition at the nation's theaters included: *Remember the Night* (Paramount) with Barbara Stanwyck and Fred MacMurray, *The Fighting 69th* (Warners) with James Cagney and Pat O'Brien,

*Green Hell* (Universal) starring Douglas Fairbanks Jr., the Western *Geronimo* (Paramount) starring Preston Foster, *Swanee River* (Fox) with Don Ameche in the lead, *The Cisco Kid and the Lady* (Fox) with Cesar Romero in the title role and the classic *Rebecca* (United Artists) toplining Laurence Olivier and Joan Fontaine.

# An Angel From Texas

**release date: April 27, 1940**                    **running time: 69-71 minutes**

**Cast:**    Eddie Albert, Rosemary Lane, Wayne Morris, Jane Wyman, Ronald Reagan, Ruth Terry, John Litel, Hobart Cavanaugh, Ann Shoemaker, Tom Kennedy, Eddie Acuff, Ralph Dunn, Edward Gargan, Holmes Herbert, George Irving, Jack Kennedy, Ethan Laidlaw, Joe Levine, Vera Lewis, Murdock MacQuarrie, Mira McKinney, Paul Phillips, Al Stedman, Milburn Stone, Elliot Sullivan, Ferris Taylor, Emmett Vogan, Lottie Williams, John Deering, Dudley Dickerson, Dorothy Vaughan, Billy Wayne, Frank Mayo, Johnnie Albright, Claude Wisberg, Michael Conroy, Richard Clayton, Jack Mower, William Gould, Gus Glassmire, Charles Costello, Jimmy Fox

**Credits:**                    **First National-Warners**

*Executive Producer* Jack L. Warner; *Associate Producer* Robert Fellows; *Director* Ray Enright; *Screenplay* Bertram Milhauser, Fred Niblo Jr.; *Based on the play* The Butter and Egg Man *by George S. Kaufman; Cinematography* Arthur L. Todd; *Editor* Clarence Kolster; *Art Direction* Esdras Hartley; *Costumes* Milo Anderson; *Original Music* M.K. Jerome, Jack Scholl, Howard Jackson; *Sound* Charles Lang; *Makeup* Perc Westmore; *Musical Director* Howard Jackson; *Assistant Director* Jesse Hibbs; *Dialogue Director* Hugh Cummings

## Synopsis:

Eddie Albert plays a mild young Texan who sends his girlfiend (Rosemary Lane) off to New York where she hopes to become an actress. Instead, she becomes a secretary to glib producer (Wayne Morris) and his partner (Ronald Reagan). The producers need backing for their new show, and as the innocent arrives in town with his mother's savings of $20,000, with plans to invest it in a hotel, he is talked into putting it in the play instead.

Albert makes the condition that his girlfriend gets the main role. The producers have a problem as they had already offered the part to Valerie Blayne (Ruth Terry). She threatens them with a visit from her gangster friends if she doesn't get the part. Eventually she backs down and leaves the way open for the Texan.

The play, written as a heavy drama, was so silly that it draws laughs and the show is eventually turned into a sucessful farce.

## Reviews:

". . . Provide(s) its audience with light comedy fare that will tend to take their minds off these troublesome and hectic times . . . Pleasing performances are given by Wayne Morris and Ronald Reagan as the Broadway producers. . . . Director Ray Enright keeps the story moving at a fast clip." *The Hollywood Reporter* (June 6, 1940); ". . . falls almost as flat as some of its gags. It was a much more entertaining offering when it hit the screen as a silent under the First National banner in 1928....an anemic screenplay . . . Most lasting impression that will be garnered by audiences is that Associate Producer Robert Fellows attempted to set up some sort of production record in turning out 'Angel.' *Daily Variety* (June 6, 1940)

## Notes:

In production from February 8 to early March 1940.

The negative cost of the film was $234,000. It earned domestic rentals of $295,000 and a further $75,000 from overseas theaters. Reagan earned $400 a week.

The original source material for the film appeared on Broadway in September 1925 under the title, *Butter and Egg Man*. It first reached the screen in 1928 and then again in 1936 with the title *Song and Dance Man*.

Four of the leads in this film also appeared in the earlier hit *Brother Rat*.

Reagan and Jane Wyman are husband and wife in this story. Just before filming started, on January 26, 1940, they married in real life.

Between 1937 and 1947 actress Ruth Terry (1920- ) appeared in 32 films. She had minor roles in *Alexander's Ragtime Band* (1938) and *The Hound of the Baskervilles* (1939), and bigger parts in several B-pictures including *Blonde Goes Latin* (1941), *Pistol Packin' Mama* (1943) and *Three Little Sisters* (1944). After an unbilled role in *The New Interns* (1964), she retired from the screen.

Kansas-born Milburn Stone's (1904-1980) total film count exceeded 150. He started in the early-1930s and finally left the big screen in 1955 for a role that would endear him to millions of weekly viewers. As Doc Adams in one of television's all-time great and durable series *Gunsmoke,* he served as friend and mentor to Matt Dillon (James Arness). Stone remained with the series until its cancellation in 1975.

Associate producer Robert Fellows (1903-1969) started in films as a second unit and assistant director in the mid-1920s. In 1940 he was promoted to associate producer on Warner Bros. Errol Flynn Western *Virginia City*. Besides *Angel in Texas* he also, in 1940, made *Knute Rockne All American* and *Santa Fe Trail*. Fellows again worked with Flynn on *They Died With Their Boots On* (1942). He also served in the production capacity on the Marlene Dietrich-Randolph Scott-John Wayne action film *Pittsburgh* (1942) as well as Wayne's *Tall In the Saddle* (1944). In the early 1950s Fellows joined with John Wayne to form Wayne-Fellows Productions. They reached agreement with Warner Bros. to distribute their celluloid output which included *Big Jim McLain* (1952), *Hondo* (1953) and *The High and the Mighty* (1954).

Also playing at the nation's theaters during the early summer of 1940 were Warner's *Brother Orchid* which had been released into 314 theaters, Paramount's Bob Hope comedy *The Ghost Breakers* and Republic's *Gangs of Chicago* with Lloyd Nolan, Barton MacLane and Lola Lane.

# Murder In the Air

**release date: June 1, 1940**                    **running time: 55 minutes**

**Cast:**  Ronald Reagan, John Litel, Lya Lys, James Stephenson, Eddie Foy Jr., Robert Warwick, Victor Zimmerman, William Gould, Kenneth Harlan, Frank Wilcox, Owen King, Dick Rich, Charles Brokaw, Helen Lynd, Jeffrey Sayre, Lane Chandler, Cliff Clark, Richard Clayton, Alan Davis, John Deering, John Hamilton, Selmer Jackson, Reid Kilpatrick, Mike Lally, Alexander Lockwood, Frank Mayo, John 'Skins' Miller, Carlyle Moore Jr., Jack Mower, David Newell, Wedgewood Nowell, Paul Panzer, Paul Phillips, Charles Sherlock, Garland Smith, Edwin Stanley, Julie Stevens, Claude Wisberg, Donald Curtis, Charles Marsh

**Credits:**                    **First National-Warners**

*Executive Producers* Jack L. Warner, Hal B. Wallis; *Producer* Bryan Foy; *Director* Lewis Seiler; *Assistant Director* William Kissell; *Screenplay* Raymond L. Schrock*; Cinematography* Ted D. McCord; *Original Music* William Lava; *Editor* Frank Magee; *Art Direction* Stanley Fleischer; *Costumes* Howard Shoup; *Sound* Robert B. Lee; *Dialogue Director* Harry Seymour

## Synopsis:

The last, and best, of Reagan's Secret Service pictures sees Brass assigned by his boss Saxby (John Litel) to bring into custody a suspected spy named Joe Garvey (James Stephenson). The agency has been unable to obtain any information or evidence against the character. When a well known spy is killed in a train wreck the death is covered up and Bancroft assumes the dead man's identity. Brass meets Garvey who tells him to board the United States Navy dirigible Mason to examine a new device called "The Inertia Projector", a death ray that can bring down airplanes within a radius of four miles.

Bancroft discovers that one of the officials on the ship is working with Garvey and is intent on stealing the blueprints of the invention.

Brass saves the projector from destruction, but during a storm at sea, the enemy agent escapes with the plans.

Once back on land Brass uses the machine to bring down the plane in which Garvey is attempting to escape.

Brass has saved his country from the forces of evil.

## Reviews:

"This is intended to be a spy thriller, but it gets badly tangled up in its own super-melodramatics at the finish for a silly and unsatisfactory ending. *Variety* (July 10, 1940); ". . . highly incredible melodramatic incident. . . . Mr. Reagan . . . handles his role of counter-espionage agent with the customary daring." *The New York Times* (July 8, 1940)

## Notes:

In production from mid-September to mid-October 1939.

Negative cost of the film was $113,000. It generated $155,000 in domestic rentals and a further $77,000 from overseas markets.

Some location work filmed at the Glendale Airport.

Fourth and last of the series of the Secret Service adventures with Reagan again in the role of Lieutenant 'Brass' Bancroft. He earned $400 a week.

Leading lady Lya Lys (1908-1986) was born in Berlin, Germany, appeared in several features in her native country in the late 1920s then came to Hollywood in 1931 to continue her film career. With her thick accent, the going was rough. *Murder In the Air* was the last of her eleven motion pictures. Of this number she had minor, often uncredited roles in *The Lives of the Bengal Lancers* (1935), *The Young In Heart* (1938) and *Confessions of a Nazi Spy* (1939).

Sixth-billed Robert Warwick (1878-1964) with his strict demeanor and stern face was often assigned the role of judge, doctor, political official or military officer. The actor with over 200 screen credits started out in films in 1914. By the coming of sound he had already appeared in 140 motion pictures. Some of his better-known films include: *I Am A Fugitive From a Chain Gang* (1932), *The Three Musketeers* (1933), Claudette Colbert's *Cleopatra* (1934), *Hop-Along-Cassidy* (1935), *Mary of Scotland* (1936), *The Adventures of Robin Hood* (1938), *The Sea Hawk* (1940), *Gentleman's Agreement* (1947), *Tarzan and the Slave Girl* (1950) and Yul Brynner's *The Buccaneer* (1958). He retired from films after completing a role as a Congressman in the comedy *It Started With a Kiss* (1959).

Lane Chandler (Robert Chandler Oakes, 1899-1972) was a real cowboy from South Dakota who drifted to Hollywood in the mid-1920s and found work as an extra and stuntman. Paramount signed the tall (6'4") former cowboy to a contract to headline some low-budget Westerns. The studio also inserted him into contemporary films opposite some of the top leading ladies of the day including Greta Garbo, Clara Bow and Betty Bronson. By the early 1930s Chandler's star had fallen dramatically, relegating him to supporting roles in B-westerns and melodramas. He is credited with having appeared in over 315 films including such diverse fare as *Roman Scandals* (1933), the Gene Autry science-fiction Western *The Phantom Empire* (1935), Cecil B. DeMille's *The Plainsman* (1937), *The Lone Ranger* (1938), DeMille's *Union Pacific* (1939), *My Little Chickadee* (1940) with W.C. Fields, Gary Cooper's *Sergeant York* (1941), DeMille's *Reap the Wild Wind* (1942), *Along Came Jones* (1945) again with Gary

Cooper, *Saratoga Trunk* (1946), *Unconquered* (1947), *Samson and Delilah* (1949), *The Indian Fighter* (1955), and *Requiem for a Gunfighter* (1965). He appeared in three films with Reagan.

Competition at the nation's screens included: *All This and Heaven Too* (Warners) starring Bette Davis and Charles Boyer, MGM's *Waterloo Bridge* featuring Robert Taylor and Vivien Leigh and *Private Affairs* (Universal) with Nancy Kelly and Robert Cummings in the leads.

# Knute Rockne All American

**release date: October 4, 1940**          **running time: 97-98 minutes**

**Cast:**  Pat O'Brien, Gale Page, Ronald Reagan, Donald Crisp, Albert Bassermann, Owen Davis Jr., Nick Lukats, Kane Richmond, William Marshall, William Byrne, John Litel, Henry O'Neill, John Qualen, Dorothy Tree, Johnny Sheffield, Howard Jones, Glen 'Pop' Warner, Amos Alonzo Stagg, William 'Bill' Spaulding, Eddy Chandler, Pat Flaherty, William Haade, Frank Mayo, John Ridgely, Erville Alderson, Rudolph Anders, Peter Ashley, Evelyn Atchinson, Tommy Baker, Tommy Bennett, Georgie Billings, Wade Boteler, Egon Brecher, David Bruce,

Cliff Clark, Richard Clayton, Frank Coghlan Jr., Joe Cunningham, Donald Curtis, Billy Dawson, Edgar Dearing, Dudley Dickerson, David Dickinson, Lucille Fairbanks, James Flavin, Bunky Fleischman, John Gallaudet, Peter B. Good, Sol Gorss, Jack Grant Jr., Billy Gratton, Creighton Hale, Harry Harvey Jr., Michael Harvey, Harry Hayden, Patricia Hayes, George Haywood, Oscar 'Dutch' Hendrian, William Hopper, George Irving, Danny Jackson, Lois James, Dickie Jones, Brian Keith, Owen King, Marilyn Kinsley, Lois Lindsay, Carlyle Moore Jr., Paul Panzer, Steve Pendleton, Lee Phelps, George Reeves, Sam Rice, Ruth Robinson, Jeffrey Sayre, Billy Sheffield, Edwin Stanley, Phil Thorpe, Ruth

Tobey, Charles Trowbridge, Frederick Vogeding, David Wade, Pierre Watkin, Gary Watson, Charles C. Wilson, Robert Winkler, Jack Wise, Maris Wrixon, the Moreau Choir of Notre Dame

## Credits:            First National-Warners

*Executive Producer* Hal B. Wallis; *Associate Producer* Robert Fellows; *Director* Lloyd Bacon; *Executive in Charge of Production* Jack L. Warner; *Writer* Robert Buckner; *Cinematography* Tony Gaudio; *Original Music* Heinz Roemheld; *Non-Original Music* Walter Donaldson, John F. Shea, Michael J. Shea, Samuel A. Ward; *Editor* Ralph Dawson; *Art Direction* Robert M. Haas; *Costumes* Milo Anderson; *Makeup* Perc Westmore; *Assistant Directors* Don Alvarado, Frank Anthony, Jesse Hibbs; *Sound* Charles Lang; *Special Effects* Byron Haskin, Rex Wimpy; *Musical Director* Leo F. Forbstein; *Technical Advisors* J.A. Haley, Nick Lukats; *Orchestrations* Ray Heindorf; *Montage* Don Siegel; *Valuable Assistance* Bonnie Skiles Rockne

## Synopsis:

The Warner tribute to famed Notre Dame football coach, Knute Rockne, shows Rockne's (Pat O'Brien), life from his childhood in Norway and his teenage years around Chicago through to his coaching days and premature death in a plane crash and his moving funeral oration in Notre Dame Chapel.

Rockne works his way through Notre Dame as a postal clerk, staying on to teach and coach. He marries his sweetheart, Bonnie Skiles (Gale Page).

The film shows the inception of the famous Rockne passing attack, devised with Gus Dorais (Owen Davis Jr) and his tactical staff. It also focuses on his relationship with George Gipp (Ronald Reagan) and the legendary Notre Dame Four Horsemen. The succession of gridiron victories is spoiled by Rockne's affliction with phlebitis. Still, the disease does not dampen his spirit and his dedication to sportsmanship.

Gipp appears in only one powerful reel of the picture, encompassing an appealing entrance, solid middle and touching death scene when the young footballer succumbs to pneumonia. On his death bed he tells Rockne, "Some day when things are tough, maybe you can ask the boys to go in there and win just once for the Gipper."

At the end of the film, when Notre Dame are on the verge of defeat to the Army team, Rockne electrifies their sagging spirit by calling on them to "win one for the Gipper."

## Reviews:

". . . carries both inspirational and dramatic appeal on a wide scale . . . one of the best biographical pictures ever turned out. . . . Picture is more than a historical document of football during the past three decades-it's an inspirational reminder of what this country stands for. And decidedly timely." *Variety* (October 9, 1940); "Impressive and exciting...stirring film . . . well knit story . . . an inspiring record of an outstanding American." *Screenland* (December 1940); ". . . swift-moving episodic fashion. . . . There is so much meat to this entire picture that we couldn't even begin describing it." *The Exhibitor* (October 1940); "...a wealth of excitement. . . It reels off with the snap and persuasibility of a fight talk from 'Rock' himself." *The New York Times* (October 21, 1940); "...one of those pictures that happen too seldom and it is so inspiring that I would like to suggest here that every young boy be shown the story. . . . The performance that gave me happiness was that of Ronald Reagan as George Gipp . . . Ronnie who wanted to play this role more than anything else, does an outstanding job and I am very proud of him. . . Lloyd Bacon has directed some fine pictures but this tops anything he has ever done, it is his masterpiece." *The Los Angeles Examiner* (Louella O. Parsons October 5, 1940); "This film should be preserved forever in the archives of the Museum of Modern Art, New York-for this one reason of- truthfully and vividly recording a current phenomenon. . . One of the superlative biographical creations of the epoch. . . " *Chicago Daily News* (October 15, 1940)

## Notes:

In production from April 2 to May 13, 1940 on location at The University of Notre Dame in South Bend, Indiana, Loyola University's Carter Field in Culver City, California and the studio lot under the working titles *All American, The Spirit of Knute Rockne, The Story of Knute Rockne, The Fighting Irish, Laughing Irish Hearts* and *The Life of Knute Rockne*. Although the film was allotted a 36-day shooting schedule, principal photography was completed in 32 days. Final 2nd Unit work and retakes were completed on May 28th. This was accomplished despite the repeated delays at Loyola due to airplane noise from planes taking off and landing from the nearby Howard Hughes airfield and factory.

Negative cost of the film was $646,000. It returned $1,516,000 in domestic rentals to the studio and a further $128,000 from overseas markets.

For working in this film Reagan earned $2,667. The star, Pat O'Brien received $30,000. Character actor Donald Crisp was paid $13,000 and lead actress Gale Page got $4,000. Director Bacon earned $11,375 and producer Robert Fellows received $20,292.

After MGM let its screen-rights to the production lapse, Warner Bros. paid $30,500 for the story and assigned Robert Buckner to write a scenario.

Screenwriter Buckner (1906-1989), besides penning 32 films, was also a Producer of over a dozen box-office hits. Buckner received his first writing credit for his work on the modest feature *Gold Is Where You Find It* (1938). With his second writing assignment *Jezebel* (1938) he became much in demand at Warner Bros. Having a knack with Westerns the studio gave him the responsibility for writing the scenarios for *The Oklahoma Kid* and *Dodge City* (both 1939), *Virginia City* and *Santa Fe Trail* (both 1940) as well as James Cagney's musical tribute *Yankee Doodle Dandy* (1942), *Sword in the Desert* (1949), Elvis Presley's first film *Love Me Tender* (1956) and the Don Murray Western *From Hell to Texas* (1958) for which he also served as a producer. The first film to bear Buckner's name as producer was the Errol Flynn boxing picture *Gentlemen Jim* (1942). Others soon followed including *Mission to Moscow* (1943), *God Is My Co-Pilot* (1945) and *Life With Father* (1947).

Within weeks of the start of production, director William K. Howard was replaced by Lloyd Bacon.

London-born, Oxford-educated, slight-of-build, Donald Crisp (1882-1974) was not only a director of over sixty silent motion pictures in the teens and twenties, but was one of the better known and successful character actors of the thirties and forties. In a career that spanned 55 years (1908-1963) he appeared before the cameras in more than 150 productions including D.W. Griffith's *The Birth of a Nation* (1915), *Mutiny on the Bounty* (1935), *The Charge of the Light Brigade* (1936), *Wuthering Heights* (1939), *Lassie Come Home* (1943), *The Man From Laramie* (1955) and *Spencer's Mountain* (1963). In 1941 he won an Academy Award for his role in John Ford's *How Green Was My Valley.*

Leaving his native Germany, after spending several decades in motion pictures and on the stages of theaters throughout Europe, Albert Bassermann (1867-1952) arrived in Hollywood in 1939 to continue his distinguished acting career. Over the next eight years he appeared in 25 films, was nominated for an Oscar for his role in Alfred Hitchcock's *Foreign Correspondent* (1940). The actor died in an airplane crash.

University of Minnesota graduate Kane Richmond (born Fred W. Bowditch, 1906-1973) was a film booker and theater manager when discovered by a Universal executive on a trip to Hollywood. He began his new film career in 1929 and nearly twenty years later (1948) had starring or supporting roles in over 90 films or serials. Some of his better known films included *The Adventures of Rex and Rinty* (1936), *Mars Attacks the World* (1938), *Charlie Chan in Reno* (1939), *Spy Smasher (serial, 1942)*. The actor was married to Marion Burns who had a brief career in the 1930s as heroine to several cowboys stars including John Wayne.

Son of actor Reginald Sheffield, California born Johnny Sheffield (1931- ), who played Rockne at age seven, was a child actor on Broadway, then, in 1939 was chosen by Johnny Weissmuller to make his film debut as Tarzan's son 'Boy' in *Tarzan Finds A Son.* He appeared in eight Tarzan adventures for MGM then RKO. In the late 1940s and early 1950s he starred in his own low-budget series of films based on the popular character Bomba, the Jungle Boy. In all, Sheffield appeared in 27 Hollywood films.

In July 1939 Warners announced that James Cagney would play the role of Knute Rockne. Also, at one time, John Payne was considered for the lead role. Notre Dame, which had a say in the casting process, refused to allow Cagney to play the legendary coach. Warner executives considered the following for the role of George Gipp: John Wayne, William Holden, Robert Young, and Robert Cummings. Reagan and Dennis Morgan did a screen test.

Football coaching legends, Howard Jones, Glenn 'Pop' Warner, Alonzo Stagg, and William Spaulding briefly appeared in this film. Both O'Brien and Reagan recreated their roles for the *Lux Radio Theater Broadcast* of the film. While this film was in production Columbia expressed an interest in borrowing Reagan for a leading role in an upcoming Irving Briskin film.

At the time of the making of the film, Reagan and Jane Wyman were both represented by agent Lew Wasserman of MCA.

World premiere held on October 4th at the University in South Bend, Indiana with both O'Brien and Reagan in attendance.

In Britain, released under the title, *A Modern Hero.*

Competition at the nation's theaters came from: John Ford's *Long Voyage Home* (United Artists), *They Knew What They Wanted* (RKO) with Carole Lombard and Charles Laughton, the elaborate

Korda fantasy *The Thief of Bagdad* (United Artists) with Sabu, the Johnny Mack Brown B-Western, *Law and Order* (Universal) and the Technicolor musical, *Down Argentina Way* (Fox) starring Betty Grable the top female box-office star of the 1940s.

In 1962 MGM made a television version of the motion picture.

# Tugboat Annie Sails Again

**release date: October 18, 1940**          **running time:  75-77 minutes**

**Cast:**  Marjorie Rambeau, Alan Hale, Jane Wyman, Ronald Reagan, Clarence Kolb, Charles Halton, Paul Hurst, Victor Kilian, Chill Wills, Harry Shannon, John Hamilton, Sidney Bracey, Jack Mower, Margaret Hayes, Josephine Whittell, Neil Reagan, Granville Bates, Glen Cavender, George Meader, Leon Belasco, George Campeau, Lucia Carroll, Eddie Conrad, Edward Gargan, Eddie Graham, Frank Hagney, Creighton Hale, Winifred Harris, Al Lloyd, Jack Richardson, Don Turner, Leo White, Dana Dale, Tim Wilson

**Credits:**                    **First National-Warners**

*Producer* Edmund Grainger; *Executive In Charge* Jack L. Warner; *Director* Lewis Seiler; *Screenplay* Walter DeLeon; *Based on characters created by* Norman Reilly Raine; *Cinematography* Arthur Edeson; *Original Music* Adolph Deutsch, Max Steiner; *Editor* Harol McLernon; *Art Direction* Ted Smith; *Costumes* Howard Shoup; *Sound* Oliver S. Garretson; *Makeup* Perc Westmore; *Assistant Director* Russell Saunders; *Musical Director* Leo F. Forbstein; *Dialogue Director* Bert Hanlon

## Synopsis:

Annie (Marjorie Rambeau), is a widow running a vessel called the Narcissus in the port of Secoma. Her main rival in the business is Captain Bullwinkle (Alan Hale). He harries her at every turn. The company for whom Annie works needs a loan of $25,000, and she manages to get it for them. This brings her the job of towing a dry dock to Alaska, but she is forced to give it over to another captain. She goes along for the ride and is able to save the day when he runs into difficulties.

## Reviews:

"Picture is a standard programmer. . . . Story runs along familiar lines, and displays neither freshness nor originality in its unfolding...Picture suffers from static direction . . . Jane Wyman and Ronald Reagan provide romantic interest." *Variety* (October 23, 1940): "Marjorie Rambeau is....giving out with little more than a broad imitation of the late and beloved Marie Dressler. . . . (T)he story is a clumsy lot of business and the humor is generally forced . . . Ronald Reagan and Jane Wyman make a pleasant pair of incidental love birds . . . There is too much slack in its towline." *The New York Times* (November 9, 1940);

## Notes:

In production from June 10 to mid-July 1940.

Negative cost of the film was $289,000. It generated $392,000 in domestic rentals and a further $172,000 from overseas markets.

Just before the start of production Reagan's salary was raised to $500 a week.

This was the much-publicized sequel to the original *Tugboat Annie* (MGM, 1933) which was directed by Mervyn LeRoy and starred Marie Dressler and Wallace Beery who, at the time were both top-ten box-office stars when the film was released.

Prior to the signing of Rambeau for the lead, the studio had considered casting Elsa Maxwell. San Francisco-born Marjorie Rambeau (1889-1970) was a considerable star on the Broadway of the 1910s and 1920s. Although she had appeared in nearly a dozen films prior to 1920, it was not until 1930 that she began to make her mark on the screen. By accepting character roles she was able to appear in over fifty sound features and be nominated for an Oscar twice for her portrayals in The *Primrose Path* (1940) and as Joan Crawford's mother in *Torch Song* (1953).

Prolific character actor, Texas-born Chill Wills (1903-1978) had a career that spanned over four decades and included more than 100 films. He and his musical group the Avalon Boys were signed by RKO to supporting roles in several 1936-7 B-westerns. After a year of indecision Wills split from his group and decided to go solo by becoming a sidekick to George O'Brien in a number of 1939 Westerns. He then moved on to more substantial roles in the A-productions *Boom Town* and *The Westerner* (both 1940), *Western Union, Billy the Kid* and *Honky Tonk* (all 1941), *Tarzan's New York Adventure* (1942), the Judy Garland musical *Meet Me in St. Louis* (1944), as Buck Forrester in *The Yearling* (1946) and *Tulsa* (1949). In 1950 Universal signed him as the voice of Francis the Talking Mule. The film was so popular with audiences in the heartland that the studio released five sequels. Also in 1950 Wills, for the second time, appeared with John Wayne, in John Ford's last of the cavalry trilogy *Rio Grande*. His subdued performance as Uncle Bawley Benedict in *Giant* (1956) was superb, as was his rollicking roles in Wayne's *The Alamo* (1960) and *McLintock!* (1963). For his performance in the former he was nominated for his only Oscar.

Writer Norman Reilly Raine (1894-1971) created the characters of Tugboat Annie and her waterfront companions in 1931. He helped bring them to the screen in 1933 and also wrote either the screenplays or stories for, among other films, *White Woman* (1933), *China Clipper* (1936), *The Life of Emile Zola* (1937), *Each Dawn I Die* (1939), *Eagle Squadron* (1942), *A Bell for Adano* (1945) and *The Sea of Lost Ships* (1954). Raine is credited with having input on over thirty feature films.

The characters were also the basis for a television series *The Adventures of Tugboat Annie* (1957) which starred Minerva Urecal in the title role.

World premiere held on October 18, 1940 in Tacoma, Washington with Reagan, Wyman, Rambeau and Hedda Hopper in attendance

This was the only film that Neil Reagan appeared in with his brother.

Competition at the nation's theaters came from *The Golden Fleece* (MGM) a comedy starring Lew Ayres and Rita Johnson, *A Little Bit of Heaven* (Universal) romantic-musical starring Gloria Jean and Robert Stack and *Meet the Wildcat* (Universal) with Ralph Bellamy and Margaret Lindsay.

# Santa Fe Trail

**release date: December 13, 1940**                    **running time: 110 minutes**

**Cast:**   Errol Flynn, Olivia deHavilland, Raymond Massey, Ronald Reagan, Alan Hale, William Lundigan, Van Heflin, Gene Reynolds, Henry O'Neill, Guinn 'Big Boy' Williams, Alan Baxter, John Litel, Moroni Olsen, David Bruce, Hobart Cavanaugh, Charles D. Brown, Joe Sawyer, Frank Wilcox, Ward Bond, Russell Simpson, Charles Middleton, Erville Alderson, Spencer Charters, Susan Peters, William Marshall, George Haywood, Cliff Clark, Edmunc Cobb, Louis Jean Heydt, William Hopper, Edward Peil Sr., Addison Richards, Harry Strang, Emmett Vogan, Arthur Aylesworth, Roy Barcroft, Trevor Bardette, Al Bridge, Jess Lee Brooks, Georgia Cane, Lucia Carroll, Eddy Chandler, Lane Chandler, Mildred Coles, Harry Cording, Joseph Crehan, Neal Dodd, Jim Farley, Mildred Grover, Mitzi Green, Creighton Hale, Henry Hall, Theresa Harris, Edward Hearn, Russell Hicks, Sclmer Jackson, Victor Kilian, Richard Kipling, Wilfred Lucas, Frank Mayo, Tom McGuire, Lafe McKee, Mira McKinney, John Meyer, Edmund Mortimer, Jack Mower, Nestor Paiva, Bernice Pilot, Alex Proper, Clinton Rosemond, Napolean Simpson, Walter Soderling, Grace Stafford, Libby Taylor, Eddy Waller, Ernest Whitman, Maris Wrixon

**Credits:**           **First National-Warners**

*Director* Michael Curtiz; *Executive In Charge of Production* Jack L. Warner; *Producers* Robert Fellows, Hal B. Wallis; *Cinematography* Sol Polino; *Writer* Robert Buckner*; Editor* George Amy; *Music* Max Steiner, Hugo Friedhofer, M.K. Jerome, Jack Scholl; *Art Direction* John Hughes; *Costumes* Milo Anderson; *Makeup* Perc Westmore; *Unit Manager* Frank Mattison; *Assistant Director* Jack Sullivan; *Sound* Robert B. Lee; *Special Effects* Byron Haskin, Hans F. Koenekamp; *Stunts* John Epper; *2nd Unit Director* Bun Haskin; *Musical Director* Leo F. Forbstein; *Music Arranger* Hugo Friedhofer; *Dialogue Director* Jo Graham; *Battle Hym of the Republic* lyricist & music by Julia Ward Howe and William Steffe; *The Arkansas Traveler* by William Lucho

**Synopsis:**

The story of the abolitionist crusade of John Brown (Raymond Massey) just prior to the Civil War, and also the successful campaign to track him down and hang him.

JEB Stuart (Errol Flynn) graduates from West Point in 1854. George Amstrong Custer (Ronald Reagan) is also seen receiving his commission. (At the time Custer was a fifteen year old Ohio schoolboy and in fact Suart and he were Civil War adversaries and never met.)

The movie also falsely parades Philip Sheridan, James Longstreet, George Pickett and James Hood (all Civil War generals) as 1854 graduates.

As an adventure yarn the movie is more acceptable and it begins when Stuart and Custer are assigned to the Second United States Cavalry, stationed at Fort Leavenworth, Kansas. They both fall in love with Kit Halliday (Olivia de Havilland), daughter of frontier businessman, (Henry O'Neil).

The job of patrolling the frontier brings them into conflict with John Brown, his family and followers. In an attempt to free the slaves, Brown causes much bloodshed and bitterness.

To make his campaigns more tactical, Brown hires cashiered West Point cadet (Van Heflin), which causes growing concern in the army. But it is this cadet, possibly to save his own skin rather than out of a sense of duty, who eventually informs on Brown, reporting his movements to the army.

When Brown takes over the town of Harpers Ferry, Virginia, a military force under the command of Colonel Robert E Lee (Morini

Olsen) is sent to defeat him. Stuart, under a white flag, is ordered to confer with Brown, but when the fanatical abolitionist refuses to surrender he is attacked and his forces beaten.

He is tried for treason and hanged.

When last seen, Stuart and Custer are on a train and Stuart is married to Kit.

## Reviews:

". . . stacks up as an outstanding film . . . swiftly moving yarn by director Michael Curtiz.....Raymond Massey makes the John Brown role the film's outstanding characterization. Ronald Reagan is another who impresses." *Variety* (December 18, 1940); "A solemn, highly inaccurate biography of the early years of Confederate General Jeb Stuart." *The Overlook Film Encyclopedia: The Western* Phil Hardy (Overlook Press, 1983); "It's history twisted far beyond recognition: oversimplified theme, overcomplicated plot, hokey slapstick, juvenile nonsense" *Western Films: A Complete Guide* Brian Garfield (Da Capo, 1982); "It has about everything that a high-priced horse-opera should have-hard riding, hard shooting, hard fighting, a bit of hard drinking and Errol Flynn." *The New York Times* (December 21, 1940); "There's enough action to satisfy any audience composed of red-blooded men and there's enough romance to satisfy any audience composed of romantically inclined women." *The Exhibitor* (December 25, 1940); "Errol Flynn . . . this is one of his best parts. . . . Of almost equal importance is Ronald Reagan, whose George Custer is one of the highlights . . . It does my heart good to see Ronny get the chance which he deserves." *Louella O. Parsons* (December 16, 1940); "Vivid, exciting and dramatic. . . . (An) impressive, thrilling adventure. . . . Reagan as George Custer is splendidly cast . . . " *Los Angeles Examiner* (January 1, 1941)

## Notes:

In production from July 19 to September 17, 1940 at the Warner outdoor ranch in Calabasas, Iverson Ranch, Providencia Studio, and at Lasky Mesa in the Canoga Park section of the San Fernando Valley. Some second-unit work done in Sonora, California. The film was allotted a 48 day shooting schedule. Working title was *Diary of the Santa Fe.*

Budgeted at $926,000 the final negative cost of the film came to $1,115,000. It generated domestic rentals of $1,748,000 and an additional $785,000 from overseas markets. Its' worldwide box office gross exceeded $5,500,000.

Director Curtiz earned $39,600. Errol Flynn was paid $66,667 while co-star Olivia DeHavilland earned $7,722. Reagan received $500 a week or $5,000. Other salaries of the cast: Raymond Massey $5,000 a week with a five week guarantee; Alan Hale $10,000; William Lundigan $2,333; Van Heflin $1,000 a week; Guinn "Big Boy" Williams $750 a week; Ward Bond $750 a week; Alan Baxter $750 a week; Joe Sawyer $500 a week; Russell Simpson $500 a week; Gene Raymond, on loan from MGM, was paid $1,000 for two weeks while his home studio also received $1,000 for his services.

This western was a follow-up to the very successful *Dodge City* with the same leading actors and much of the supporting cast.

In the early stages of casting Jack Warner had originally wanted John Wayne for the role of Custer. Reagan actually replaced Wayne Morris in the Custer role after Morris had already spent two days working in the film. Reagan had completed his role in *Knute Rockne* only one day before being called to work on this production.

Canadian-born Raymond Massey (1896-1983) who portrayed abolitionist John Brown, played him again fifteen years later in the western, *Seven Angry Men* (1955). The veteran of World War I debuted on the London stage in the early 1920s, then started appearing in films in 1929. He appeared in the classic British science-fiction epic *Things To Come* (1936), played Black Michael in *The Prisoner of Zenda* (1937); was the villain in Cecil B. DeMille's *Reap the Wild Wind* (1942), played Nazi officers in *Desperate Journey* (1942) and *Hotel Berlin* (1945), and was featured in the Ayn Rand novel *The Fountainhead* (1949). Some of his other popular motion pictures include *David and Bathsheba* (1951), *Battle Cry* (1955), *The Naked and the Dead* (1958) and *MacKenna's Gold* (1969).

With over 65 screen credits William Lundigan (1914-1975) was initially groomed for stardom by Universal Pictures in the late 1930s. Despite his best efforts, he was rarely offered starring roles except in low-budgeters, and had to settle for supporting roles in major films such as *Dodge City* (1939), *The Fighting 69th* (1940), *Salute to the Marines* (1947), *Pinky* (1949) and *Riders to the Stars* (1954).

Actress Susan Peters (1921-1952) who had the role of Jefferson Davis' daughter, the young woman meant for the Reagan character, was on the verge of stardom when tragedy struck. At the age of nineteen she signed a term contract with Warner Bros. and began making minor appearances in numerous features including James Cagney's *The Strawberry Blonde* (1941) and the Gary Cooper vehicle *Meet John Doe* (1941). Although losing one of the main roles to Betty Field in *King's Row* (1941), within a few months she rebounded by receiving fourth billing opposite Humphrey Bogart in *The Big Shot* (1942). By the end of the year the actress had moved to MGM and was being offered bigger roles in some major films including *Random Harvest* (1942), for which she was nominated for a Best Actress Oscar. For her work in 1943 she was named a "Star of Tomorrow" by the nation's theater-owners. On New Year's Day 1945 while on a hunting trip with her husband, actor Richard Quine, she accidentally discharged her rifle. The bullet entered her spine and left her permanently paralyzed. Using a wheelchair she appeared in *The Sign of the Ram* (1948) and the television series *Miss Susan* (1951). Neither venture was successful, leaving the actress morbidly depressed and a recluse. She died at the age of 31 from the combined effects of starvation, pneumonia, and kidney failure.

On December 11th a train full of Warner stars and executives left Pasadena for the world premier of *Santa Fe Trail* in Santa Fe, New Mexico that was scheduled for December 13.

Competition at the nation's screens came from: *One Night in the Tropics* (Universal) the first screen teaming of Bud Abbott and Lou Costello, *Victory* (Paramount) a brooding drama starring Frederic

March and Betty Field and the Western *Trail of the Vigilantes*
(Universal) with Franchot Tone, Warren Williams and Broderick
Crawford.

ERROL FLYNN and OLIVIA De HAVILLAND in "SANTA FE TRAIL"- A Warner Bros-First National Picture

# The Bad Man

**release date: March 28, 1941**                    **running time: 70 minutes**

**Cast:**   Wallace Beery, Lionel Barrymore, Laraine Day, Ronald Reagan, Henry Travers, Chris-Pin Martin, Tom Conway, Chill Wills, Nydia Westman, Charles Stevens, Joe Dominguez, Artie Ortego, Daniel Rea,

**Credits:**                    **Metro-Goldwyn-Mayer**

*Director* Richard Thorpe; *Producer* J. Walter Ruben; *Cinematography* Clyde De Vinna; *Screenplay* Wells Root; *Original Music* Franz Waxman; *Editor* Conrad A. Nervig; *Set Decoration* Edwin B. Willis; *Costumes* Gile Steele, Dolly Tree; *Makeup* Sydney Guilaroff; *Assistant Director* William Ryan; *Art Directors* Cedric Gibbons, John S. Detlie; *Sound* Douglas Shearer; *Technical Advisor* Ernsto A. Romero; *Based on the play* "The Bad Man" by Porter Emerson Browne; *Stage Play Presenter* William Harris Jr.

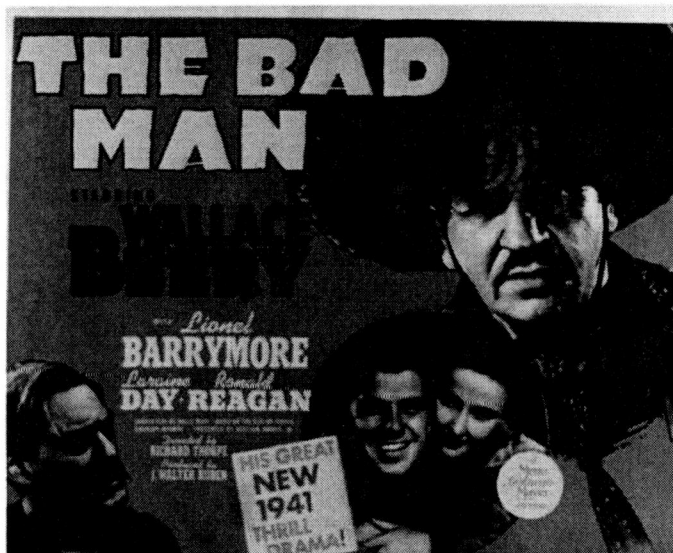

## Synopsis:

Loveable Mexican bandit, Pancho Lopez (Wallace Beery) is a blustering border bandit who briefly dons the Robin Hood guise in order to help young man, Gil Jones (Ronald Reagan), who had once saved his life.

Jones and his wheelchair ridden Uncle Henry (Lionel Barrymore) face the possible loss of their ranch due to a failure to meet mortgage payments. Gil's childhood sweetheart Lucia Pell (Larraine Day) arrives at the ranch with her husband Morgan (Tom Conway) for a visit. They are not a happy couple, and when Lopez arrives with his band of cattle rustlers, the old bandit takes matters into his own hands. He raises the money for the mortgage and sends the husband packing, leaving Lucia free to rekindle her romance with Gil.

## Reviews:

". . . handicapped chiefly by an antiquated and inadequate treatment of the play. . . . Reagan plays his role with well-regulated reserve. . ." *Variety* (April 2, 1941); ". . . this one is bolstered by the energetic performance of Barrymore. . . ." *Western Films: A Complete Guide.* Brian Garfield (Da Capo, 1982); "(T)he most static and loquacious Western we've encountered in a long time. . . . (T)he actors just talk on and on, and what they have to say is, unfortunately uninteresting. . . . Ronald Reagan makes an ineffectual hero." *The New York Times* (April 4, 1941); "Lionel Barrymore has the best role . . . Pretty Laraine Day seems wasted . . . Ronald Reagan has a better chance to shine as the hero." *The Los Angeles Examiner* (Dorothy Manners, March 26, 1941); "The weirdest thing that has come off the MGM lot in some years, utterly impossible to classify. It is not comedy nor drama, neither adventure film nor character study. . . . There are, by actual count, three short action scenes. The rest is played on two indoor sets, a porch and a patio." *The Hollywood Reporter* (March 26, 1941);

## Notes:

In production from November 11 to December 18, 1940 with additional sequences (retakes) shot from February 11 to 28, 1941. Filmed at Flagstaff, Arizona, Gallup, New Mexico, and Red Rock Canyon in California.

Third film adaptation of the play that opened in New York on September 30, 1920, and had a run that reached 342 performances. Holbrook Blinn played the lead character Pancho Lopez, on both the stage and in the first screen adaptation. In the second remake, the lead was Walter Huston.

Warners loaned Reagan to MGM for this film project. They paid him $500 a week while receiving $1500 a week from MGM for his services.

A week before filming started, actor Henry O'Neill bowed out of the production.

One of the most prolific directors in the history of Hollywood with 186 screen credits, Richard Thorpe (1896-1991) was active in the industry from 1920 to 1967. He started out as an actor, learned editing techniques, wrote seventeen screenplays and survived the grind of directing up to seventeen silent films a year in the 1920s, to emerge as one of MGM's most dependable and cost-conscious directors of the 1940s and 1950s. Along the way Thorpe directed four exciting Tarzan films: *Tarzan Escapes* (1936), *Tarzan Finds A Son* (1939), *Tarzan's Secret Treasure* (1941) and *Tarzan's New York Adventure* (1942). His other notable features included *Ivanhoe* (1952) with Robert Taylor and Elizabeth Taylor in the leads, *Knights of the Round Table* (1953) with Robert Taylor and Ava Gardner, and two Elvis Presley films: *Jailhouse Rock* (1957) and the musical-comedy *Fun In Acapulco* (1963).

Utah-born leading lady Larraine Day (1917- ) had a career which encompassed 40 films with the vast majority being released between 1938 and 1949. The actress hit her stride in the mid-1940s when she appeared opposite such stalwarts as Cary Grant, Gary Cooper and John Wayne. After a bit-part in *Stella Dallas* (1937) Day as Laraine Johnson was signed to work with George O'Brien in three B-westerns. She then joined MGM, had her last name changed to Day and was cast in the role of Nurse Mary Lamont in seven of the Dr. Kildare low-budget entries (1939-1941). At this time Alfred Hitchcock signed Day to co-star opposite Joel McCrea in the thriller *Foreign Correspondent* (1940). In 1942 Day's star rose further as she was assigned to bigger-budgeted films including *Journey for Margaret* (1942), *Mr. Lucky* (1943), *The Story of Dr. Wassell* (1944), *The Locket* (1946) and *Tycoon* (1947). In the 1950s the actress appeared in only five films with the most notable being a cameo role in John Wayne's *The High and the Mighty* (1954). From 1947 to 1960 she was married to volatile former baseball player and manager Leo Durocher.

Tucson, Arizona born actor Chris-Pin Martin (born Ysabel Ponciana Chris-Pin Martin Piaz, 1893-1953) was the stereotypical Mexican in nearly 125 Hollywood films. The short, rotund Martin began appearing in films in the early 1920s. In 1925 he had a bit part in Charlie Chaplin's *The Gold Rush* and four years later he received a

screen credit for his role in the first sound Western *In Old Arizona* (1929). Relegated to working almost entirely in Westerns he had featured roles in the large-screen *Billy the Kid* (1930), and in the role of Gordito, began a long association with *The Cisco Kid* (1931). The success of the Cisco Kid character would lead to seven sequels in the early 1940s. The intentionally comic actor worked right up to the time of his death from a heart attack.

Opened at Grauman's Chinese Theater in Hollywood. On the bottom-half of the bill was the B-film *Blonde Inspiration* with John Shelton and Virginia Grey.

Released in Britain under the title, *Two-Gun Cupid.*

Competition at the nation's screens included: *I Wanted Wings* (Par) Ray Milland, William Holden, Wayne Morris. *Dead Men Tell* (Fox), *Pot O' Gold* (United Artists) starring James Stewart and Paulette Goddard, and Gene Autry's musical-Western *Back In the Saddle* (Republic).

# Million Dollar Baby

**release date: May 31, 1941**                    **running time: 100-102 minutes**

**Cast:**   Priscilla Lane, Jeffrey Lynn, Ronald Reagan, May Robson, Lee
Patrick, Helen Westley, George Barbier, Nan Wynn, John Qualen,
Walter Catlett, Fay Helm, Richard Carle, John Ridgely, Maris
Wrixon, James Burke, Charles Halton, Johnny Sheffield, Nat Carr,
Eddie Graham, Stuart Holmes, Tony Hughes, Vera Lewis, Wilbur
Mack, Jean Maddox, Jack Mower, Charles Sullivan, Jack Wise, Jean
Ames, Peter Ashley, Irving Bacon, Mary Brodel, George Campeau,
Glen Cavender, David Clarke, Georgia Cooper, Pedro de Cordoba,
Garrett Craig, George Davis, Peggy Diggins, Charles Drake, Edgar
Edwards, Paulette Evans, William Forrest, Edward Gargan, Inez
Gay, Kenneth Harlan, Arthur Hoyt, George Humbert, Jack Kenney,
Donald Kerr, Charles Marsh, Greta Meyer, Will Morgan, David
Oliver, Frank Otto, Steve Pendleton, Garland Smith, Ted
Thompson, Dorothy Vaughan, Herb Vigran, Nella Walker, Billy
Wayne, Leo White, Lottie Williams, Douglas Wood

**Credits:**                    **First National-Warners**

*Executive Producer* Hal B. Wallis; *Director* Curtis Bernhardt;
*Associate Producer* David Lewis; *Screenplay* Casey Robinson,
Richard Macaulay, Jerry Wald; *Story* Leonard Spigelgass; *Original
Music* Frederick Hollander, Howard Jackson; *Cinematography*
Charles Rosher; *Editor* Rudi Fehr; *Art Direction* Robert M. Haas;
*Costumes* Orry-Kelly; *Makeup* Perc Westmore; *Assistant Director*
Chuck Hansen; *Sound* Charles Lang; *Musical Director* Leo F.
Forbstein; *Dialogue Director* Hugh Cummings; *Lyricists* Mort
Dixon  Billy Rose; *Music* "Fantastic Impromptu" by Frederic
Chopin; *Songs* "Who is in Your Dreams Tonight?," "I Found a
Million Dollar Baby-in a Five and Ten Cent Store"

## Synopsis:

Peter Rowan (Ronald Reagan) is a struggling concert pianist.
Young attorney James Amory (Jeffrey Lynn) visits millionairess
Cornelia Wheelwright (May Robson), who has been living abroad
for the past thirty years, and reveals to her that her late father
obtained his vast fortune by defrauding his partner.

Faced with the unpleasant truth, she decides to visit America and make restitution. She meets granddaughter of the partner, Pamela McAllister (Priscilla Lane), and, in order to get to know the girl, moves into the same modest rooming house. Miss Wheelwright makes a gift of a million dollars to the girl, who is confused and delighted.

Her happiness is disturbed when she is rejected by her pianist boyfriend, Peter, who does not want to benefit by marrying money. Somewhat improbably, the love of the scrupulous musician is won back when the girl donates all the money to charity.

In the meantime the old lady meets many ordinary Americans and her own life is broadened.

## Reviews:

"Good mass entertainment. It has comedy, romance, music, and human interest, as well as fast-moving action and snappy dialogue. . . " *Harrison's Report* (May 31, 1941); ". . . an unbelievable and tedious strain on both the imagination and the seat of the pants . . . sourpuss piano-player Ronald Reagan." *Variety* (May 28, 1941); "(I)t seems to be put together like a prefabricated house, strictly according to blueprint. . . It is one of the most formula-made pictures ever to come along . . . the comedy is much too pat and suspiciously familiar. . . . Here is Ronald Reagan re-enacting the same character that John Garfield played in *Four Daughters.*" *The New York Times* (June 12, 1941); "This is the sort of show which audiences will enjoy tremendously...the pace as a whole is very fast...The direction is tops, and a tricky bright musical score helps matters along." *The Exhibitor* (May 28, 1941); ". . . a happy, refreshing comedy . . . entertainment for all of us who like comedy (and) romance. . ." *Louella O. Parsons* (May 22, 1941); "refreshing, rollicking comedy with plenty of human interest and heart appeal . . . Reagan . . . wonderful as the young composer." *The Los Angeles Examiner* (Pauline Gallagher, May 30, 1941)

## Notes:

In production from January 2 to February 1941 under the working title, *Miss Wheelwright Discovers America.*

Negative cost of the film was $451,000. It generated domestic rentals of $699,000 and overseas markets contributed an additional $219,000 to the Warner Bros. coffers.

Reagan was paid $500 a week.

The Priscilla Lane role was originally conceived for Irene Dunn then Ann Sheridan and later Olivia DeHavilland.

Director Curtis Bernhardt (1899-1981) fled his native Germany in 1939 after directing nearly 20 films. Signed by Warner Bros. his first American efforts were *My Lover Come Back* starring Olivia DeHavilland with Jane Wyman in a supporting role and *Lady With Red Hair* (both 1940). He also directed Reagan in *Juke Girl* (1942).

2nd billed Jeffrey Lynn (born Ragmar Lind, 1909-1995) made the preponderance of his thirty-odd films in the 1940s. Warner Bros. had groomed him for stardom in the early 1940s but by the time he returned from service with the Army-Air Corps during World War II, his star had dimmed considerably, and he was never able to regain the momentum he had before the war. Of the six 1939 movies he appeared in, *The Roaring Twenties* was the most successful. A year earlier the actor received much acclaim for his portrayal of Felix Deitz in *Four Daughters.*

In the post-WWII era, Lynn gave his best performances in *Whiplash* (1948) and *A Letter to Three Wives* (1949). In the 1950s and 1960s he often appeared as a guest on television programs and was a regular on two daytime soap operas (*The Secret Storm* and *The Edge of Night).* On the big screen he had minor roles in Elizabeth Taylor's *Butterfield 8* (1960) and Frank Sinatra's *Tony Rome* (1967).

Australian-born May Robson (born Mary Jeannette Robinson, 1858-1942) has the distinction of being the earliest-born actress to receive an Oscar nomination. She was nominated for a Best Actress Oscar for her portrayal in *Lady For A Day* (1933). By the time she made her screen debut in the mid-teens she was nearly sixty. Nevertheless, Robson recorded appearances in over sixty films including the original *King of Kings* (1927), *Alice of Wonderland* (1933) wherein she played The Queen of Hearts, as Countess Vronsky in *Anna Karenina* (1935), Aunt Polly in *The Adventures of Tom Sawyer* (1938) and the Howard Hawks comedy classic *Bringing Up Baby* (1938) with Cary Grant and Katharine Hepburn. After *Million Dollar Baby* she made only two more films before passing away at the age of 84.

Days after the film completed production, on February 9th Reagan received his Draft notice. Warners obtained a draft deferment for their star.

In the Los Angeles area the film was double-billed with *Singapore Woman* starring Brenda Marshall and David Bruce.

Competition at the nation's screens included: *Billy the Kid* (MGM) starring Robert Taylor in the title role; *Blood and Sand* (Fox) with Tyrone Power, Linda Darnell and Rita Hayworth; *Affectionately*

*Yours* (Warners) with Merle Oberon and Dennis Morgan; *Caught In the Draft* (Paramount) a Bob Hope and Dorothy Lamour comedy; *In the Navy* (Universal) starring Abbott and Costello with Dick Powell and The Andrew Sisters; and *Love Crazy* (MGM) featuring William Powell and Myrna Loy.

# International Squadron

**release date: August 13. 1941**          **running time: 85-87 minutes**

**Cast:** Ronald Stephenson, William Perry, Julie Andrews, Reginald Herbert, Selmer Reagan, James Olympe Bradna, Lundigan, Joan Bishop, Tod Cliff Edwards, Denny, Holmes Charles Irwin, Jackson, Jean Ames, Frank Baker, Sonny Bupp, Shirley Coates, Eddie Conrad, Helmut Dantine, Leslie Denison, Ann Edmonds, Frank Faylen, Gerald Gavin, Frederick Giermann, Brenda Henderson, Leyland Hodgson, William (De Wolfe) Hopper, Hugh Huntley, Crauford Kent, Knud Kreuger, Marten Lamont, Ernest Lennart, Harry Lewis, Doris Lloyd, John Meredith, Ivan Molnar, Ottola Nesmith, Pat O'Hara, Addison Richards, John Ridgely, Henry Rowland, Tom Skinner, Tom Stevenson, Cyril Thornton, David Thursby, Richard Travis, Marjorie Whatley, Alice Talton, Will Stanton, Lowden Adams, Louise Brien, Harry Harvey, Jr., Tony Marsh, Gerard Calvin, Shirley Coats, Marjorie Whately, Ernest Lenart, George Kirby

**Credits:**          **First National-Warners**

*Associate Producer* Edmund Grainger; *Directors* Lewis Seiler, Lothar Mendes; *Writers* Kenneth Gamet, Barry Trivers; *Suggested by the play* "Ceiling Zero" by Frank Wead; *Music* William Lava; *Cinematography* Ted D. McCord, James Van Trees; *Editor* Frank

Presented by WARNER BROS. Pictures Inc.

INTERNATIONAL SQUADRON

Magee; *Costumes* Howard Shoup; *Special Effects* Robert Burks; *Stunt Pilot* Paul Mantz; *Dialogue Director* Harold Winston; *Assistant Director* Jesse Hibbs; *Art Director* Esdras Hartley; *Sound* Robert B. Lee; *Makeup* Perc Westmore; *Technical Advisor* Byron F. Kennerly

## Synopsis:

Jimmy Grant (Ronald Reagan) is a crack stunt pilot who accepts the job of flying a bomber to England, to deliver it to the RAF. Once there he finds two old friends in British uniform, one squadron commander Charles Wyatt (James Stephenson) and the other fighter pilot Reg Wilkins (William Lundigan).

They try to persuade him to join the service, but the fun-loving American shows no interest, until he is involved in a London air raid. When he sees a child killed he changes his mind and decides to help in the fight against Fascism.

Jimmy likes Jeanette (Olympe Bradna), the girlfriend of French pilot, Michele Edme (Tod Andrews). He is so smitten with her that he fails to report for a mission and the friend who stands in for him is killed in action.

Jimmy, who has already alienated many of the other pilots with his brashness, comes to his senses and he decides to make up for what he has done. When the French pilot is assigned to a dangerous mission,

Jimmy knocks him out and takes his place. In carrying out the mission Jimmy dies a heroic death.

## Reviews:

". . . combat as well as air-raiding scenes, are depicted realistically . . . the action is breezy, the dialogue natural and at times, amusing, and the romantic interludes, are well handled. . ." *Harrison's Reports* (August 16, 1941); ". . . a higher bracket B programmer, displaying plenty of action and drama in the air and ground sectors. . . . Exciting tempo provides topnotch meller entertainment. . . . Reagan is excellently spotted as the expert flyer who leaves a girl at every airport, and the picture will elevate his audience standing." *Variety* (August 13, 1941); "Reagan's performance is tops, in breezy, even style. . . . He carries the starring burden and proves he can shoulder it." *The New York Post* (November 14, 1941); "Ronald Reagan is excellent as the slap-happy hell-diver who finally pays for his moral failures with his own death in combat . . . a boisterous, stripped-for-action melodrama." *The New York Times* (November 14, 1941); "Although obviously sincere and well-acted . . . will probably have a tough time as a single feature in the bigger situations . . . the story is much too familiar-with most of the scenes cut from the usual war-film pattern . . . the entire marquee strength of the film rests with Ronald Reagan, whose name is not yet big enough to mean much." *The Exhibitor* (July 1941); ". . . better than *Ceiling Zero* for it is exciting and the characterization of the light-hearted soldier of fortune is good movie drama. . ." *The Los Angeles Examiner* (Louella O. Parsons, October 31, 1941); ". . . a moderately exciting war drama. . . . Reagan doesn't jell as the dashing Romeo. . . . Reagan isn't convincing as the light-hearted kid who hurts his friends only unintentionally." *Daily Variety* (August 13, 1941); ". . . a tense exciting aviation drama that can hold its own in any company. . . . Reagan continues his march forward, turning in an exuberant performance that fairly sparkles." *The Hollywood Reporter* (August 13, 1941)

**Notes:**

In production from late-March to May 6,1941 under the working title *Flight Patrol*. Some retakes shot on June 15 and July 20th. Sequences shot at Van Nuys and Alhambra Airports.

Negative cost of the film was $384,000. It generated domestic rentals of $829,000 and an additional $521,000 from the overseas markets.

The studio, remaking the earlier film *Ceiling Zero,* envisioned Errol Flynn and John Wayne as the film's leads. When neither star expressed interest in the project, Humphrey Bogart and Dennis Morgan were given screen tests. Eventually, the budget for the production was lowered and Reagan was signed for the lead.

Reagan was paid $500 a week.

In 1941 the nation's theater owners voted Ronald Reagan as one of the top-ten "Stars of Tomorrow." He rated in the fifth position behind (1) Laraine Day (2) Rita Hayworth (3) Ruth Hussey (4) Robert Preston, but ahead of John Payne, Jeffrey Lynn, Ann Rutherford, Dennis Morgan, and Jackie Cooper. In 1942, his wife, Jane Wyman ranked number three on the "Stars of Tomorrow" listing.

This was James Stephenson's (1889-1941) fifth and last film with Reagan and his last production ever. Within a month after retakes were completed he died from a massive heart attack. Over a period of five years the English-born actor appeared in 39 motion pictures including *The Perfect Crime* (1937), *Nancy Drew-Detective* (1938), *Devil's Island, Beau Geste* and *Confessions of A Nazi Spy* (1939), *The Sea Hawk* (1940) and *Shining Victory* (1941).

Parisian-born leading lady Olympe Bradna (1920- ) appeared in only fifteen American films (1933-41). Her first notable screen role was in the thriller *The Last Train from Madrid* (1937) which was soon followed by a part in the Gary Cooper-George Raft gripping adventure feature *Souls at Sea* (1937). After completing her 4th-billed role in the B-film *Highway West* (1941), she retired from acting.

Frank Wead wrote the original play *Ceiling Zero* (April 1935), which was made into the 1936 film starring James Cagney and Pat O'Brien under the direction of Howard Hawks.

Lewis Seiler replaced Lothar Mendes as director during filming.

The studio actually shot real footage of air-raids and battles over Britain between English Spitfires and German Messerschmitts and Heinkels.

Co-director Lothar Mendes (1894-1974) was born in Berlin and spent a decade making movies, as a writer, actor and director, in his native Germany. He migrated to the United States in 1928 and along with Merian C. Cooper directed the often filmed adventure tale *The Four*

*Feathers* (1929). *International Squadron* was only his 17th. American production. After directing *The Walls Came Tumbling Down* (1946), he moved to London and retired from filmmaking.

Colorado-born Julie Bishop (born Jacqueline Wells, 1914-2001) started as a child actress in Hollywood of the early 1920s then as an adult worked as a second-lead or character actress in dozens of features. When she appeared in her last film *The Big Land* in 1957, she had accumulated more than 85 screen credits. *International Squadron* was one of five films she made in 1941.

*International Squadron* reminded audiences of two other similarly themed films of the time, Universal's *Eagle Squadron* and the Fox release *A Yank in the RAF.*

In the Los Angeles market the film was double-billed with the Warner Bros. feature *Smiling Ghost* starring Wayne Morris and Brenda Marshall.

Opened at the Warner Theater on Leicester Square in London on November 2, 1941.

Competition at the nation's theaters came from: *The Little Foxes* (Goldwyn-RKO) with Bette Davis, *Navy Blues* (Warners) starring Ann Sheridan and Jack Oakie, *Life Begins For Andy Hardy* (MGM) with Mickey Rooney and *Sunset In Wyoming* the latest Gene Autry B-Western from Republic.

# Nine Lives Are Not Enough

**release date: September 20, 1941**          **running time: 63-64 minutes**

**Cast:**   Ronald Reagan, Joan Perry, James Gleason, Howard Da Silva, Faye Emerson, Edward Brophy, Peter Whitney, Charles Drake, Vera Lewis, Ben Welden, Howard C. Hickman, Cliff Clark, Tom Stevenson, Paul Phillips, Joseph Crehan, John Maxwell, Hank Mann, Glen Cavender, Eddy Chandler, Billy Dawson, Creighton Hale, Thurston Hall, John Hamilton, Stuart Holmes, Olaf Hytten, Joan Leslie, Al Lloyd, Theodore Lorch, Frank Mayo, Jack Mower, Jimmy O'Gatty, Sam Rice, Jack Richardson, John Ridgely, Walter Soderling, Leo White, Jack Wise, Mary Brodel

**Credits:**                    **First National-Warners**

*Director* A. Edward Sutherland; *Executive Producer* Hal B. Wallis; *Producer* Bryan Foy; *Associate Producer* William Jacobs; *Cinematography* Ted D. McCord; *Screenwriter* Fred Niblo Jr.; *Based on the novel* "Nine Lives Are Not Enough" by Jerome Odlum; *Original Music* William Lava; *Editor* Doug Gould; *Art Direction* Stanley Fleischer; *Costumes* Howard Shoup; *Makeup* Perc Westmore; *Assistant Director* Philip Quinn; *Sound* Charles Lang; *Musical Director* Leo F. Forbstein; *Dialogue Director* Harry Seymour

## Synopsis:

Matt Sawyer (Ronald Reagan) is a brash young newspaperman full of energy and dauntless curiosity.

He writes an expose of gangster Moxie Karper (Ben Welden). Moxie clears himself and slaps the newspaper with a libel suit.

Matt is demoted by tough boss Murray (Howard da Silva). He is assigned to two police men, Sergeant Daniels (James Gleason) and Slattery (Edward Brophy). They trust him and decide to help him prove the gangster's guilt.

They find the body of a missing millionaire, who everyone believes committed suicide. Matt reports it to the newspaper as a murder and the story is printed. The coroner insists it was suicide and Matt is fired. This only serves to make him more determined to prove the case.

He is now also helped by the millionaire's daughter (Joan Perry).

Matt survives various attempts on his life before finally proving the millionaire was murdered by his partner Colonel Andrews (Howard Hickman), who is in league with the very racketeer Matt had tired to expose.

The millionaire's daughter buys the newspaper out and gives Matt the job of editor. She is in love with him.

## Reviews:

"A fairly entertaining program picture. . . . Plot is routine, the action is fast-moving . . . the performances are good, and some of the dialogue quite amusing." *Harrison's Reports* (September 6, 1941); ". . . crammed with lively action, comic situations and vivid characterizations. It opens with a wallop, has headlong pace and closes with an explosive climax . . . a blazing whodunit, with suspense piled up and action so fast that the average spectator won't have time for the moment of calm thought . . . Ronald Reagan . . . hilariously scatter-brained and devilishly resourceful . . . Reagan gives a superbly helter-skelter performance." *Variety* (September 3,

1941); "...an amalgam of practically every second-rate thriller that springs to mind." *The Warner Bros. Story.* Clive Hirschhorn (New York; Crown, 1979); "(T)he film could have been done in three minutes......In this case nine lives are nine too many." *The New York Times* (October 30, 1941); " The picture's theme and treatment have served many times since 'Front Page' and "Five Star Final' which set the style for this type of melodrama.....the film offers satisfying value." *The Exhibitor* (September 1941)

**Notes:**

In production for twenty-one shooting days during June 1941. Reagan paid $600 a week.

Negative cost of the film was $164,000. It generated domestic rentals of $211,000 and a further $89,000 from the overseas markets.

Leading-lady Joan Perry (1911-1996) retired from the screen after making this film, her nineteenth, and married the infamous Harry Cohen, head of Columbia Pictures. Her career began in 1935 after she arrived in Hollywood and signed a term contract with Columbia Pictures. Cast only in B-films she made appearances in such low-budget items as *The Mysterious Avenger* and *Meet Nero Wolfe* (both 1936), *The Lone Wolf Strikes* (1940), *Maisie Was A Lady* (1941) and at Warner Bros. *International Squadron with Reagan* (1941). She remained married to Cohen until his death in 1958. In 1962 the former actress married Laurence Harvey. They were divorced in 1972.

Louisiana-born Faye Emerson (1917-1983) appeared in 27 films but is best known as one of the first television personalities. Between 1948 and 1956 she starred in five different small screen series. The actress broke into films in 1941 and was cast in seven features including *Affectionately Yours, Bad Men of Missouri* and

*Manpower*. She also worked with Reagan in *Juke Girl* and had minor supporting roles in *Air Force* (1943), *Destination Tokyo* (1943) and *The Mask of Dimitrios* (1944). In 1944 Emerson made headlines by marrying President Roosevelt's son, Elliott. The marriage ended in 1950, just about the time that her popularity was approaching its zenith.

Due to creative differences, original director Ben Stoloff was replaced by Sutherland. A. Edward Sutherland (1895-1973) was brought to America from England by his parents in the first decade of the 20$^{th}$ century. While still in his teens he worked as an actor in over 30 films including *Tillie's Punctured Romance* (1914), *The Sea Wolf* (1920) and *The Witching Hour* (1921). Although still acting until 1929, by 1925 he had already decided that being a director was his life's calling. Between 1925 and 1956 he directed over 50 features including *International House* (1933), *Diamond Jim* (1935), W.C. Fields' *Poppy* (1936), the Laurel and Hardy classic *The Flying Deuces* (1939), *One Night in the Tropics* (1940) with the emerging comedy team of Abbott and Costello and *Abie's Irish Rose* (1946). After helming *Bermuda Affair* (1956) he turned to television and directed two less than successful series.

Competition at the nation's theaters included: *Birth of the Blues* (Par) starring Bing Crosby and Mary Martin, *Belle Starr* (Fox) with Randolph Scott and Gene Tierney, *When Ladies Meet* (MGM) featuring Joan Crawford and Robert Taylor and *My Life with Caroline* (RKO) with Ronald Coleman and Anna Lee getting top-billing.

In 1941 Warner Bros. released 37 feature-length films.

# King's Row

**release date: April 18, 1942**          **running time: 126-130 minutes**

**Cast:**  Ann Sheridan, Robert Cummings, Ronald Reagan, Betty Field, Charles Coburn, Claude Rains, Judith Anderson, Nancy Coleman, Kaaren Verne, Maria Ouspenskaya, Harry Davenport, Ernest Cossart, Ilka Gruning, Pat Moriarity, Minor Watson, Ludwig Stossel, Erwin Kalser, Egon Brecher, Ann E. Todd, Scotty Beckett, Douglas Croft, Mary Thomas, Julie Warren, Mary Scott, Leah Baird, Walter Baldwin, Henry Blair, Joan Duvalle, Eden Gray, Ludwig Hardt, Herbert Heywood, Danny Jackson, Fred Kelsey, Hank Mann, Frank Mayo, Frank Milan, Jack Mower, Hattie Noel, Emory Parnell, Bertha Powell, Thomas W. Ross, Hermine Sterler, Elizabeth Valentine

**Credits:**                    **First National-Warners**

*Director* Sam Wood; *Executive Producer* Hal B. Wallis; *Associate Producer* David Lewis; *Screenplay* Casey Robinson; *Based on the*

*novel* "Kings Row" by Henry Bellamann; *Cinematography* James Wong Howe; *2nd Cameraman* Wesley Anderson; *Original Music* Erich Wolfgang Korngold; *Editor* Ralph Dawson; *Production Design* William Cameron Menzies; *Art Direction* Carl Jules Weil; *Sound* Robert B. Lee; *Costumes* Orry-Kelly, Rvdo Loshak, Martha Giddings; *Makeup* Perc Westmore, Joe Stintoni; *Hair* Helen Stinton; *Unit Manager* Frank Mattison, Eugene Bush; *Special Effects* Robert Burks; *Props* Dutch Renfsnerder, G.W. Bernsten; *Musical Director* Leo F. Forbstein; *Orchestrators* Hugo Friedhofer, Ray Heindorf, Bernhard Kaun, Milan Roder; *Assistant Director* Sherry Shourds; *2nd Assistant Director* Emmett Emerson; *Set Dresser* George Hopkins; *Publicist* Don King; *Best boy* Cliff Hutchinson; *Grip* Warren Yaple; *Gaffer* Edward Rike; *Stills* Madison Lacy

## Synopsis:

Screen writer Casey Robinson turned the central theme of incest between Dr Alexander Tower (Claude Raines) and his daughter Cassandra (Nancy Coleman), into a matter of insanity and their relationship is only hinted at in the film. Cassandra is portrayed as insane and her father is unable to cure her.

A group of children going home from school. Parris Mitchell (Robert Cummings) takes his sweetheart Cassandra swimming and then goes home to his grandmother who reminds him he has two party invitations, Cassandra's and one from Louise (Nancy Coleman), the daughter of Dr and Mrs Henry Gordon (Charles Coburn and Judith Anderson).

Parris goes to Cassandra's.

Many years pass and the children have now grown up.

Parris is a medical student taking instruction from Cassandra's father. Cassandra is neurotic.

Louise meanwhile is in love with Drake McHugh (Reagan), but has been warned off him by her parents. Randy (Ann Sheridan) is also in love with Drake.

Cassandra and Parris are still in love.

His grandmother dies of cancer. He is about to go off to medical school, but is loath to leave the now pregnant Cassandra.

She is killed by her father who also commits suicide.

Previously very rich, decadent Drake is suddenly left with no cash after the bank is embezzled. He has to go to work on the railway and is involved in an accident.

Both legs are amputated unnecessarily by Dr Gordon

Drake decides he will not let it ruin his life

## Reviews:

"A powerful but somewhat depressing drama. . . . Both direction and acting are excellent, and the production is praiseworthy. It is tender and inspiring in some situations, and interesting as a whole." *Harrison's Reports* (December 27, 1941); ". . . an impressive and occasionally inspiring, though overlong picture . . . steadily engrossing and plausible. . . . Ronald Reagan does a continuously believable job. . ." *Variety* (December 24, 1941); "Reagan gave the best performance of his career." *Ronald Reagan: His Life and Rise to the Presidency* Bill Boyarsky (Random House, 1981); "Gives you that rare glow which comes from seeing a job crisply done, competently, and with confidence." *The New Yorker* (February 1942); "A triumphant example of its expertise and theatrical flair applied to a literary source. . . . An arresting film . . . Scene after scene demonstrates a high gloss of professionalism." *Warner Brothers Presents: The Most Exciting Years-from The Jazz Singer to White Heat.* Ted Sennett (New York; Arlington House, 1971); "The acting . . . was splendid and confounded the cynics, who had assumed that Ronald Reagan . . . and Ann Sheridan . . . were the lightweights for their roles." *The Warner Bros. Story.* Clive Hirschhorn (New York; Crown, 1979); "Warner Brothers bit off a great deal more than they could chew when they tried to make a cogent motion picture out of (the) gloomy and ponderous novel . . . one of the bulkiest blunders to come out of Hollywood in some time . . . . There are moments of pathos . . . and occasionally it strikes a sharp nostalgic note. But on the whole it accumulates no impulse." *The New York Times* (February 3, 1942); ". . . loses none of its flavor on the screen. . . . The magnificent direction of Sam Wood and the screenplay by Casey Robinson plus several great performances , mark *Kings Row* as a spectacular and dramatic motion picture...Reagan fulfill(s) every promise . . . This is really Ronnie's big chance and he makes the most of it by turning in a superior performance." *The Los Angeles Examiner* (Louella O. Parsons, April 2, 1942); "The expertness of David Lewis' production, the sustained direction of Sam Wood, the eloquent art of James Wong Howe's camera and the truly great performances of some of the players make the picture a likely contender for Academy honors....Reagan has never appeared to such excellent advantage." *Daily Variety* (December 23, 1941); "All the dramatic impact of one of the more important novels published in our times reaches the screen in a picture that taxes critical superlatives . . . is a rare, engrossing emotional experience. . . . The writing by Robinson is inspired. The direction by Wood in faithful key with the spirit of the story...the director is in magnificent command throughout..." *The Hollywood Reporter* (December 23, 1941)

**Notes:**              *"The finest picture I've ever been in."*

In production from July 14 to early October 1941. Some location work shot at Saugus, California, twenty miles north of the studio. Reagan started filming his scenes in August.

Negative cost of the production was $1,092,000. The film earned domestic rentals of $2,281,000 and a further $997,000 from overseas markets. Its' worldwide box office receipts were slightly in excess of $6,400,000.

On August 25, 1941 Reagan's contract was renegotiated. He signed a new three-year contract which upped his weekly salary to $1650 a week. He was guaranteed a paycheck for 40 weeks a year or $66,000 minimum per annum. Jane Wyman's contract had also been renegotiated and upped to $1500 a week with the same yearly guarantee.

Nominated for three Oscars: Best Picture, Best Director, and Best Cinematography (black & white).

Warner Bros. secured the screen rights for the book, in June 1940, for $35,000. In doing so they outbid Fox who had wanted to make the film with Henry Fonda in the lead. David O. Selznick offered Warners $75,000 for the screen rights.

Ronald Reagan's 1965 autobiography titled *Where's the Rest of Me?* Came from one of his lines of dialogue in this film.

Alternate casting: for the Betty Field role: Ida Lupino, Olivia De Havilland, Bette Davis, Katharine Hepburn, Marsha Hunt, Laraine Day, Susan Peters, Joan Leslie and Gene Tierney. Before Reagan was signed for the role of Drake McHugh, the studio considered John Garfield. For the Robert Cummings role they sought the services of Tyrone Power. Fox would not loan Power out, forcing Warners to borrow Cummings from Universal.

Due to his involvement with this film, Reagan received his second deferment from the Draft Board.

Director Sam Wood (1883-1949) between 1920 and 1949, directed 81 feature-length films. Although he helmed up to four motion pictures a year, he did not hit his stride until the mid-1930s with such box-office hits as *A Night at the Opera* (1935) and *A Day at the Races* (1937), both with the zany Marx Brothers. His other big hits included *Madame X* (1937), *Goodbye, Mr. Chips* (1939), *The Devil and Miss Jones* (1941), *The Pride of the Yankees* (1942) with

Cooper as the Yankee immortal, *For Whom the Bells Tolls* (1943). Second-billed Robert Cummings (1908-1990), equally adept at light comedy and drama, over a career that spanned forty-five years, appeared in 67 films and starred in four television series. The Joplin, Missouri native was a godson of Orville Wright and learned to fly from the pioneer aviator. During World War II Cummings was an aviator with the Army-Air Corps. Starting out in films as an extra in 1933 his breakout year came in 1937 with roles in three top films: *The Last Train From Madrid, Souls at Sea* and *Wells Fargo.* He displayed his comedic talent by acting in *The Devil and Miss Jones* and *Moon Over Miami* (both 1941). Besides *King's Row,* in 1942 he also had a starring role in Alfred Hitchcock's suspense thriller *Saboteur* (1942). Cummings is best known for his role of Bob Carson, the woman-chasing photographer on *The Bob Cummings Show* (aka *Love That Bob* 1955-1959).

Boston-born Betty Field (1913-1973) trained at New York's prestigious Academy of Dramatic Arts, appeared on Broadway, then took her stage triumph as Barbara Pearson in *What A Life* (1939) to the screen to serve as her film debut. Over the next decade she had memorable roles in *Of Mice and Men* (1939), opposite John Wayne in *Shepherd of the Hills* (1940), *Flesh and Fantasy* (1943), *Tomorrow, the World* (1944), *The Southerner* (1945) and as Daisy Buchanan in *The Great Gatsby* (1949). In the 1950s and 1960s she had supporting roles in *Picnic* (1955), *Bus Stop* (1956), *Peyton Place* (1957), *Butterfield 8* (1960), and opposite Clint Eastwood in her last screen appearance *Coogan's Bluff* (1968).

China-born James Wong Howe (Wong Tung Jim, 1899-1976),

came to America at the age of five, was a boxer and assistant to a photographer as a teenager in 1917, and entered the motion picture industry as an apprentice in the editing department. Within three years he was working at an odd assortment of jobs for Cecil B. DeMille before settling in the camera department to learn the art of photographing movies. In 1922 he received his first of 132 credit as director of photography on a full-length feature film. The winner of two Academy Awards for his work on *The Rose Tattoo* (1955) and *Hud* (1963) also was responsible for the photography on many other memorable films including *The Trail of the Lonesome Pine* (1923), *Peter Pan* (1924), *Chandu the Magician* with Bela Lugosi *(1932), The Thin Man* (1934), *The Prisoner of Zenda* (1937), *Abe Lincoln in Illinois* (1940), *Yankee Doodle Dandy* (1942), *Objective, Burma!* (1945), *Body and Soul* (1947), *Come Back, Little Sheba* (1952), *Picnic* (1955), *The Last Angry Man* (1959), *Hombre* (1967) and Barbra Streisand's debut film, *Funny Lady* (1975).

Competition on the nation's screens came from: *Hellzapoppin'* (Universal) with Olsen and Johnson; *The Man Who Came To Dinner* (Warners) Bette Davis and Ann Sheridan. *Dr. Kildare's Victory* (MGM) with Lew Ayers and Lionel Barrymore and *The Prime Minister* (Warner Bros.) with John Gielgud.

In 1955 Warners announced plans for a remake of the film. It was to have starred Montgomery Clift, Frank Sinatra, Eva Marie Saint, and Ronald Reagan. The project never materialized. What did come to fruition was a television series based on the movie in 1955, that lasted just one season.

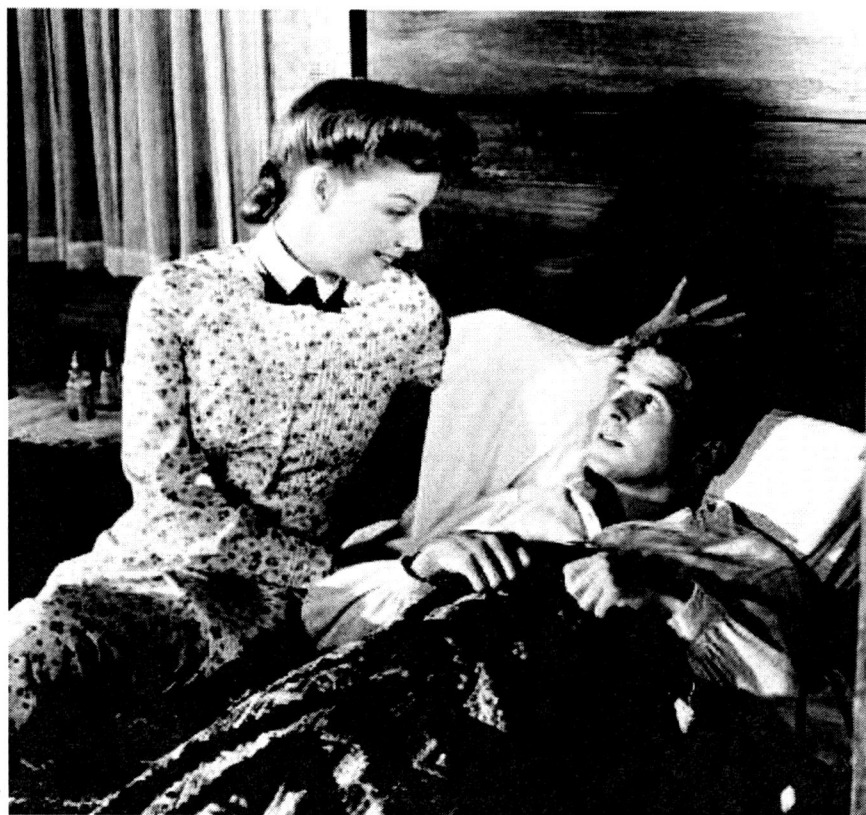

# Juke Girl

**release date: April 8, 1942**                    **running time: 90 minutes**

**Cast:**    Ann Sheridan, Ronald Reagan, Richard Whorf, George Tobias, Gene Lockhart, Alan Hale, Betty Brewer, Howard Da Silva, Donald MacBride, Willard Robertson, Faye Emerson, Willie Best, Fuzzy Knight, Spencer Charters, William B. Davidson, Frank Wilcox, William Haade, Irving Bacon, Al Bridge, Paul E. Burns, Clancy Cooper, Frank Darien, William Edmunds, Hank Mann, Jack

Mower, Don Turner, Cliff Saum, Paul Panzer, Glen Cavender, James Flavin, Jean Fitzgerald, Pat Flaherty, Jack Gardner, Sol Gorss, William Gould, Kenneth Harlan, William (De Wolfe) Hopper, Fred Kelsey, Milton Kibbee, Frank Mayo, Patrick McVey, Edward Peil Sr., Frank Pharr, William 'Bill' Phillips, Dewey Robinson, Glenn Strange, Forrest Taylor, Ray Teal, Eddy Waller, Dan White, Guy Wilkerson, Victor Zimmerman

**Credits:**                    **Warners**

*Executive Producer* Hal B. Wallis; *Associate Producers* Jerry Wald, Jack Saper; *Director* Curtis Bernhardt; *Screenplay* A.I. Bezzerides; *Adaptation* Kenneth Gamet, Theodore Pratt; *Cinematography* Bert Glennon; *Editor* Warren Low; *Music* Adolph Deutsch, M.K. Jerome, Jack Scholl, Heinz Roemheld; *Musical Director* Leo F. Forbstein; *Art Direction* Robert M. Haas; *Costumes* Milo Anderson; *Makeup*

Perc Westmore; *Sound* Charles Lang; *Orchestrators* Hugo Friedhofer, Jerome Moross; *Assistant Director* Jesse Hibbs; *Dialogue Director* Hugh Cummings; *Songs* "Found Me A Bluebell," "No One Talks To No One No More" and Slaphappy Pappy."

## Synopsis:

Ugly conflict between management and labor flares in the world of itinerant crop pickers in Florida.

Drifters Steve Talbot (Reagan) and Danny (Richard Whorf) arrive to pick up work in the tomato fields. Their friendship is strained when a dispute erupts between the owner of the fruit farm and the packing plant, Henry Madden (Gene Lockhart) and a farmer Nick Garcos (George Tobias), who resents the low prices paid for his crops. Steve sides with the farmer and Danny sees his opportunity with the owner. The tense situation comes to a head one night in a juke joint, where girls are employed to entertain the field workers. Anger over low wages and long hours explodes into a brawl. Lola Mears (Ann Sheridan) joins with Steve and the campaign for the farmers. They set out to break the monopoly, and even though they achieve their goal, killings and mob justice follow swiftly.

## Reviews:

". . . result is as grade B as the title would seem to indicate. It's loaded with fist-flying action, but that's about the most to be said for this story . . . Reagan..is a sincere and capable performer. . ." *Variety* (April 8, 1942); "(A) gritty melodrama . . . erratic direction . . . much fast and furious action." *Warner Brothers Presents: The Most Exciting Years-from The Jazz Singer to White Heat.* Ted Sennett (New York; Arlington House, 1971); "(T)here is a routine deliberateness about this one which keeps it from seeming real. . . . Mr. Reagan is staunch as the young hero . . . the whole smacks too much of the synthetic." *The New York Times* (June 19, 1942); ". . . cram-packed with action and color. . . . Director Curtis Bernhardt has done a rather, admirable job merely by controlling the sweep of his material . . . a man-sized evening of entertainment." *The Los Angeles Examiner* (Neil Rau, May 28, 1942); ". . . the picture has more than its share of interesting performances and well staged, however untimely, excitement. . . . Reagan does another outstanding personable character." *The Hollywood Reporter* (April 7, 1942); "Miss Sheridan, Ronald Reagan and Richard Whorf handle the top roles with conviction and a persuasive romantic warmth . . . Curtis Bernhardt does an excellent piece of initial feature direction." *Daily Variety* (April 7, 1942)

**Notes:** *"I discovered how nervous fatigue can creep up on you"*

In production from early October to December 12, 1941 under the title *Jook Girl*. Shot at the Burbank Studio and the outdoor lot at the Calabasas Ranch. Some second unit work shot in California's central San Joaquin Valley.

Negative cost of the film was $751,000. It earned domestic rentals of $1,281,000 and a further $262,000 from overseas markets.

Based on the article "Land of the Jook" by Theodore Pratt which appeared in the April 26, 1941 issue of *The Saturday Evening Post*. Ida Lupino was the original choice for the role played by Ann Sheridan. This was the fifth and last film that Reagan and Sheridan appeared in together.

Third-billed Richard Whorf (1906-1966), a high school dropout, was not only an actor but a director, writer and producer. He made his Broadway debut in 1927. Appeared in one film in 1934 then signed a standard contract with Warner Bros. in 1940. As a director he made *Blonde Fever* (1944), *Till the Clouds Roll By* (1946), *It Happened in Brooklyn* (1947) and *Champagne for Caesar* (1950). Two of his producer credits were for the features *Burning Hills* (1956) and *Bombers B-52* (1957). In the 1950s and 60s Whorf directed hundreds of episodes of series television including *Gunsmoke, Wagon Train,* and *The Beverly Hillbillies*.

Not much is known about second female lead Betty Brewer (sometimes billed as Ilene Brewer). Starting around 1938 she appeared in the first of what would be fifteen films, then in the very early 1950s was a regular on two different television shows. Brewer's first major role was in *Rangers of Fortune* (1940). Over the next few years she would alternate between Westerns (*The Roundup*) and dramas or comedies (*The Devil and Miss Jones*). After *Juke Girl* the actress had smaller roles in a succession of films including *The Pride of the Yankees* (1942). In 1950, for one season, she worked with Don Ameche on the *Holiday Hotel* television series and performed as a regular singer on *The Bill Cullen Show* a variety program that started in 1953.

Cinematographer Bert Glennon (1893-1967), while attending Stanford University, was already working in the industry as an assistant cameraman. During this early period he was also hired as an actor in several films including, as the scarecrow in *The Patchwork Girl of Oz* (1914). *Ramona* released in 1916 was the first of 110 films that Glennon photographed. He was a favorite of both John Ford and Cecil B. DeMille.

New York City-born George Tobias (1901-1980) was part of the Warner Bros. stock company of supporting players from the late 1930s through the 1940. In his heyday he could be seen in such entertaining features as: *The Hunchback of Notre Dame* and *Ninotchka* (both 1939), *Torrid Zone* (1940), *The Strawberry Blonde* and *Sergeant York* (1941), *Yankee Doodle Dandy* (1942), *Air Force* (1943), *Objective, Burma!* (1945), *Sinbad the Sailor* (1947), *Rawhide* (1951), *The Glenn Miller Story* (1953) and *Bullet for a Badman* (1964).

During the making of this film Reagan received his third deferment from the Draft Board. In January 1942 he obtained a 4th and last deferment.

Competition at the nation's screens came from: *The Spoilers* (Universal) with Marlene Dietrich, Randolph Scott and John Wayne; Orson Welles' *The Magnificent Ambersons; Tarzan's New York Adventure* (MGM); *This Gun For Hire* (Paramount) with Veronica Lake, Robert Preston and Alan Ladd; *Reap the Wild Wind* (Paramount) Cecil B. DeMille sea epic starring Ray Milland, John Wayne and Paulette Goddard.

# Desperate Journey

**release date: August 18, 1942**          **running time: 107-109 minutes**

**Cast:**  Errol Flynn, Ronald Reagan, Nancy Coleman, Raymond Massey, Alan Hale, Arthur Kennedy, Ronald Sinclair, Albert Bassermann, Sig Ruman, Patrick O'Moore, Felix Basch, Ilka Gruning, Elsa Basserman, Charles Irwin, Richard Fraser, Rudolph Anders, Robert O. Davis, Henry Victor, Bruce Lester, Lester Matthews, Eugene Gericke, Frank Alten, Louis V. Arco, John Banner, Barry Bernard, Walter Bonn, Sven Hugo Borg, Walter Brooke, Harold Daniels, William Yetter, Helmut Dantine, Carl Harbaugh, Arno Frey, Eddie Hall, Ludwig Hardt, William Hopper, Jurt Katch, Rudolph Steinbeck, Harry Lewis, Rolf Lindau, Jack Lomas, Frank Mayo, Don Phillips, Otto Reichow, Henry Rowland, Richard Ryen, Ferdinand Schumann-Heink, Hans Schumm, Hans Twardowski, Lester Sharpe, Bob Stevenson, Sigfrid Tor, Philip Van Zandt, Roland Varno, Douglas Walton, Rex Williams, Charles Flynn, William Vaughn Kurt Katch, Victor Zimmerman, Rudolf Myzet, Fred Vogeding, Hans von Morhart, Ray Miller, Carl Ekberg, Fred Giermann, Erno Verebes, James Harker, Peter Michael, Leslie Denison, Pat O'Hara

**Credits:**            **Warners-First National**

*Producer* Hal B. Wallis*; Associate Producer* Jack Saper; *Director* Raoul Walsh; *Cinematography* Bert Glennon; *Screenplay* Arthur T. Horman; *Additional Writing* Vincent Sherman, Julia & Philip Epstein; *Music* Max Steiner, Hugh Friedhofer; *Musical Director* Leo F. Forbstein; *Orchestrations* Hugo Friedhofer; *Editor* Rudi Fehr; *Art Direction* Carl Jules Weyl; *Costumes* Milo Anderson; *Makeup* Perc Westmore; *Sound* C.A. Riggs; *Assistant Directors* Claude Archer, Russell Saunders; *Special Effects* Edwin B. DuPar, Byron Haskin, Nathan Levinson; *Stunts* Buster Wiles; *Technical Advisor* Owen Cathcart-Jones; *Dialogue Director* Hugh MacMullan

## Synopsis:

In this tale of the adventures of an RAF bomber on a mission to Germany. Flight Lieutenant Terrence Forbes (Errol Flynn) is an Australian pilot, Flying Officer Jed Forrest (Arthur Kennedy) is his Canadian navigator, Flight Sergeant Kirk Edwards (Arthur Hale) is a Scottish veteran of the First World War, Flight Sergeant Lloyd Hollis (Ronald Sinclair) is an Englishman and Flying Officer Johnny Hammond (Ronald Reagan) is one of Hollywoods favourite characters, the brash, amusing , irreverant, brave Yank in the RAF. The crew of the Flying Fortress, D-for-Danny, take flight, after much good natured bantering at the briefing, for a bombing run over Germany. After dropping their bombs they are shot down and tracked by a German army unit under Major Otto Baumeister (Raymond Massey).

The major is in charge of a secret Messerschmidt plant.

The boys easily outwit the major and escape, making their way across war time Germany, heading for the north coast, in one amazing scene in stolen Nazi uniforms, (the only instance when an American president has been photographed wearing fascist livery). They engage in much sabatage as they go and face violent conflict. Edwards and Hollis are killed.

Eventually the survivors are aided by an anti-Nazi German family headed by Doctor Mather (Albert Basserman) and his daughter Kaethe (Nancy Coleman).

They help the boys to fight back and they eventually reach the coast, steal a German bomber, machine gun the chasing Major and take off to fly back across the English Channel. The Australian pilot Forbes quips, "Now for Australia and a crack at the Japs!"

## Reviews:

"...nerve-tingling adventure, excellently done, and will ring up heavy grosses everywhere...Reagan, who has come along splendidly under the Warner coaching in the past year or so, is excellent as usual, combining plenty of thespic talent with his air of freehand cocksureness." *Variety* (August 19, 1942); "...The three musketeers idea packed with action, shorn of romance and utilizing the Third Reich for terrain." *The Motion Picture Herald* (August 1942); "Moves with the speed of a cross-country express, alive with action, thrills and topical interest....lightning pace, bristling dialogue and countless thrills...Director Raoul Walsh deserves credit for keeping the story lively, fast, and so full of thrills...Reagan, in a second role, all but steals the show. It is worth note that in this film Mr. Reagan makes his last appearance on the screen as a Hollywood actor, having bowed out of movies to join Uncle Sam's forces." *The Los Angeles Examiner* (Sara Hamilton, September 28, 1942); "Bright dialog almost compensates for the story's continuation past the point of greatest effectiveness. . . Reagan scores solidly as the wise-cracking American volunteer flying officer." *The Hollywood Reporter* (August 14, 1942); "High action and topical interest for all....The suspense is maintained at a gripping pace...Standout is Ronald Reagan, the cocky, wisecracking American member of the R.A.F., milking a fat part of every value." *Daily Variety* (August 14, 1942)

## Notes:

In production from late January to mid-April 1942, under the working title *Forced Landing.* Scenes shot at Metropolitan Airport in Los Angeles, Sherwood Lake, and the Warner Ranch in Calabasas.

Negative cost of the film was $1,209,000. It earned domestic rentals of $2,029,000 and a further $1,951,000 from overseas markets. Its' worldwide box-office receipts exceeded $8,800,000.

Reagan paid $1650 a week. Errol Flynn was earning $6,000 a week. During the making of the film Flynn, beset by an assortment of ailments, saw his weight drop to 165 pounds. Called by the Selective Service, he was given a complete medical evaluation by the Draft Board and learned that besides having the existing conditions of sinusitis, emphysema and gonorrhea he had contracted tuberculosis in his right lung. In 1939 Flynn was the 8th biggest star at the nation's box-offices.

On April 10, 1942 Warners announced that Humphrey Bogart would replace Reagan as the star of their upcoming prestige production,

*Casablanca*. Nine days later Reagan entered the army, at Fort Mason, California, as a second lieutenant in the cavalry. Due to his very poor eyesight he was reclassified and sent to Culver City to work at "Camp Roach" which turned out instruction films for the military. Just prior to leaving for the service Reagan and Warner Bros. reached an agreement for the studio to hire the actor's mother, at a salary of $75 a week, to answer his fan mail. This amount was deducted from his weekly salary, as soon as he returned from the Army and went back on the studio payroll.

Many critics took note of the remarkable similarity of this war film with the earlier released British/Canadian production, *The Invaders* (Columbia).

In 1942 Hollywood released a record 488 feature-length films.

*Desperate Journey* was nominated for an Academy Award for "Best Special Effects."

While performing on the Los Angeles stage, character actor and Carnegie Institute of Technology graduate Arthur Kennedy (1914-1990) was discovered by James Cagney who inserted the young actor into his next film *City of Conquest* (1940), in the role of his younger brother. From 1940 to 1990, his film career consisted of over eighty motion pictures including *High Sierra* (1941), *They Died With Their Boots On* (1942), *Air Force* (1943), *Champion* (1949), *Bend of the River* (1952), *Peyton Place* (1957), *Elmer Gantry* (1960), and *Cheyenne Autumn* (1964). He was nominated for four best supporting Oscars (*Champion, Trial, Peyton Place, Some Came Running*) and one Best Actor Oscar for his role in *Bright Victory* (1951). During World War II Kennedy flew and served as an instructor on B-17 bombers.

With close to 200 screen credits, Alan Hale (born Rufus Alan McKahan, 1892-1950) was one of the busiest character actors in the Hollywood of the 1930s and 40s. Before the advent of sound he had already made appearances in over 130 productions including the 1922 version of *Robin Hood*. He also played the Little John character in the Errol Flynn version *The Adventures of Robin Hood* (1938) and again reprised the role in his last screen work *Rogues of Sherwood Forest* (1950). The large, rotund actor worked with Flynn in eight films including *Dodge City* (1939), *Virginia City* and *Santa Fe Trail* (both 1940) and *Gentleman Jim* (1942). Hale made five films with Reagan.

Everett, Washington born Nancy Coleman (1912-2000), worked with Reagan in *King's Row* (1941) but never appeared in a major film after her appearance in *Mourning Becomes Electra* (1947).

Busy in the medium of television throughout the 1950's and 1960's, the actress was a regular in the daytime soap operas, *The Edge of Night* (1967) and *Ryan's Hope* (1976).

Film editor Rudi Fehr (1911-1999) was born in Berlin, Germany and worked in both the German and British film industry before leaving for the United States in 1939. Between 1940 and 1985 he edited 32 films including his first the Warner Bros. drama *My Love Came Back* (1940), the Errol Flynn Western *Rocky Mountain* (1950), *House of Wax* (1953) and Hitchcock's *Dial M for Murder* (1954). Fehr also edited Reagan's *Million Dollar Baby, The Voice of the Turtle* and *The Girl from Jones Beach.* He received an Oscar nomination for his collaborative work on the Jack Nicholson film *Prizzi's Honor* (1985).

Competition at the nation's theaters included: *Across the Pacific* (Warners) starring Humphrey Bogart; *Now Voyager* (Warners) with Bette Davis and Paul Henreid and *Manila Calling* (Fox) featuring Lloyd Nolan and Carole Landis.

# This Is the Army

**release date: July 29, 1943**          **running time: 113-121 minutes**

**Cast:** George Murphy, Joan Leslie, George Tobias, Alan Hale, Charles Butterworth, Dolores Costello, Una Merkel, Stanley Ridges, Rosemary DeCamp, Ruth Donnelly, Dorothy Peterson, Frances Langford, Gertrude Niesen, Kate Smith, Ronald Reagan, Joe Louis, Alan Anderson, Ezra Stone, Tom D'Andrea, James Burrell, Ross Elliott, Alan Manson, John Prinze Mendes, Julie Oshins, Earl Oxford, Robert Shanley, Philip Truex, James MacColl, Herbert Anderson, Ralph Magelssen, Tilestone Perry, John Cook Jr., Larry Weeks, The Allon Trio, Murray Alper, Warner Anderson, Irving Bacon, Leah Baird, Louis Bednarcik, Irving Berlin, Dick Bernie, Jackie Brown, Angelo Buono, Jimmy Butler, Frank Coghlan Jr., Jimmy Conlin, Richard Crane, Belmonte Cristiani, James Cross, John Daheim, Gayle DeCamp, Alan Dexter, John Draper, Geno Erbisti, Richard Farnsworth, Martin Faust, Sgt. Fisher, Ross Ford, Art Foster, Ilka Gruning, Eddie Hall, Hank Henry, Richard Irving, John James, Jerry Jarrett, Henry Jones, Fred Kelly, J.P. Mandes, Pinkie Mitchell, Victor Moore, Patsy Moran, Gene Nelson, Allen Pomeroy, Richard Reeves, Sydney Robin, William Roerich, Hayden Rorke, Arthur Space, Arthur Steiner, Ernest Truex, Pierre Watkin, Doodles Weaver, Jack Young, Gene Berg, William Wyckoff, Bill Kennedy, Harry McKim, John L. Murphy, Robert McDonald, Robert Adams, Peter O'Neill, Jack Dillon, Bert Spencer, Lee Harmon, Alexis Sousloff, Jack Riano, Peter I. Burns, Byron Shores

**Credits:**                                        **Warners**

*Producers* Jack L. Warner, Hal B. Wallis; *Director* Michael Curtiz; *Screenplay* Irving Berlin, Casey Robinson, Claude Binyon; *Contract writers* Philip G. Epstein, Julius J. Epstein; *Original Music* Irving Berlin, Ray Heindorf, Max Steiner; *Cinematography* Bert Glennon, Sol Polito; *Assistant Cameramen* Benny Cohan, George Nogle; *Editor* George Amy; *Art Directors* John Hughes, John Koenig; *Set Decoration* George James Hopkins; *Costumes* Orry-Kelly, Leon Robicheau; *Makeup* Perc Westmore, Ward Hamilton; *Sound* C.A. Riggs; *Assistant Directors* Frank Heath, Jack Sullivan; *2nd Assistant Directors* Fred Scheld, John Lucas; *Special Effects* Jack Cosgrove; *Stunts* Richard Farnsworth; *Assistant Art Director* John Beckman; *Lyricist* Irving Berlin; *Musical Director* Leo F. Forbstein; *Orchestrations* Ray Heindorf; *Dialogue Directors* Hugh Cummings, Eddie Blatt; *Color Director (Technicolor)* Natalie Kalmus, Richard Mueller; *Montage* James

Leicester, Don Siegel; *Technical Advisor* Frank T. McCabe; *Production Number Stagers* LeRoy Prinze Robert Sidney; *Stills* Fred Morgan; *Gaffer* Claude Hutchinson; *Props* Herbert Pews; *Unit Manager* Al Alleborn; *Grip* Owen Crompton; *Best Boy* Percy D. Burt; *Unit Publicist* Cameron Shipp; *Clerk* Gloria Fayth.

*Songs* "Your Country and My Country," "My Sweetie," "Poor Little Me, I'm on K.P.," "We're On Our Way to France," "God Bless America," "What Does He Look Like?" "Oh How I Hate To Get Up in the Morning," "This is the Army Mr. Jones," "I'm Getting Tired So I Can Sleep," "Mandy," "Ladies of the Chorus," "Well-Dressed Man in Harlem," "How About A Cheer for the Navy," "I Left My Heart at the Stage Door Canteen," "With My Head In the Clouds," "American Eagles" and "This Time Is the Last Time."

## Synopsis:

The story starts with a favorite star of Broadway, Jerry Jones (George Murphy), being drafted and put in charge of an Army show. The show is a success and at the final performance, the cast marches out of the theatre and off to the real war.

At the outbreak of World War Two Jerry is a producer and his son Johnny (Ronald Reagan), his assistant. Johnny joins the army and is the author of *This is the Army*. At the final performance in Washington before the President, he takes time out to marry his sweetheart played by Joan Leslie.

At the same show Jerry and some friens from Yip, Yip, Yaphank appear to do a nostalgic number about their days in the army-together with Berlin himself-"Oh How I Hate to Get Up in the Morning".

There is no mention anywhere that Berlin is the author of all the material for both shows, but his musical brought a huge contribution to America's war effort.

## Reviews:

"A magnificent job is this tremendous film." *Photoplay* (January 1944); "Everything about it is, box-office boff....socko entertainment . . . it's showmanship and patriotism combined to a super-duper Yankee Doodle degree...socko Berlin songs-17 of 'em." *Variety* (August 4, 1943); "This is really comparable to some of the finest work turned out by the Warner studios, and is an excellent production." *The Exhibitor* (August 1943); ". . . is still the freshest, the most endearing, the most rousing musical tribute to the American fighting man that has come out of World War II . . . buoyant, captivating, as American as hot dogs or the Bill of Rights." *The New York Times* (June 29, 1943); "(A) rich and potent entertainment stimulating as a military band and twenty times as colorful." *The Motion Picture Exhibitor* (June 1943); ". . . is the best motion picture dealing with any phase of the war that has come out of Hollywood. . . . It is the extraordinary spirit of the film that makes it great. . . . Lieutenant Ronald Reagan is his usual ingratiating self. . ." *The Los Angeles Examiner* (Louella O. Parsons August 18, 1943)

**Notes:**    *"It was a thrill for me to get away from the desk and feel once again that I was part of the picture business."*

In production from February 24 to May 13, 1943 at a negative cost of $1,870,000. The film was originally budgeted at $1,400,000. Locations included the Warner Ranch in Calabasas and Camp Cook in central California.

From a domestic boxoffice gross in excess of $20,000,000, the film earned rentals of $8,301,000, of which $1,951,045 was turned over to the Army Relief Fund. Foreign markets added an additional $2,144,000 in rentals.

In May 1942 Paramount began negotiating for the screen rights to Irving Berlin's stage musical. In July of 1942 Warner Bros. paid $250,000 to Irving Berlin to bring the play to the screen. Berlin also received 50% of any profits generated.

After the Broadway run, on September 29, 1942 the national road tour of the show began in Washington D.C. The tour ended in Los Angeles where many of the performers including personnel in military uniform, repeated their roles for the screen.

Reagan on the army payroll while making this film, was paid the standard rate for a first lieutenant- $250 a month. He began shooting his scenes on February 24, 1943. While in the service, primarily stationed in Culver City, Lieutenant then later Captain Reagan was involved in the making of over 400 training films.

Before George Murphy signed for the lead role, others believed in contention included Pat O'Brien, Fred Astaire, Joseph Cotton and Walter Huston. Ginger Rogers, who had significant box office appeal at the time, was considered for the role assigned to Joan Leslie. Murphy received $28,333.33 for his starring role. The grand finale and production employed five-hundred actors.

Top-billed George Murphy (1902-1992) dropped out of Yale to pursue a career in dancing. Eddie Cantor called him to Hollywood and offered the 32 year old the role of his screen son in the film adaptation of *Kid Millions* (1934). From 1934 until 1952 Murphy danced or acted his way through 45 films including the well-known entries *Little Miss Broadway* (1938) with Shirley Temple, *A Girl, a Guy, and a Gob* (1941), *The Navy Comes Through* (1942), and the stirring war entry *Bataan* (1943). From 1944 to 1946 Murphy was President of The Screen Actors Guild (SAG) and from 1964 to 1975 was a United States Senator from California.

Female-lead and girlfriend of Reagan in the film, Joan Leslie (born Joan Brodel, 1925- ) began as a child actor with bit roles in several films including Garbo's *Camille* (1936) and *Nancy Drew, Reporter* (1939). Signed by Warner Bros. in late 1939 the teenager was cast as the young girl with the "bad" leg in Humphrey Bogart's breakout film *High Sierra* (1941). In the same year she was the love interest of Gary Cooper in the huge box-office hit *Sergeant York* and had a role in *The Male Animal.* She appeared in over 20 other features but contract battles with Warner Bros. cost her substantial roles.

Irving Berlin (1888-1989), the prolific and popular songwriter, penned over 1000 songs and movie scores over fifty years, many of which remain firmly etched into the minds of generations of Americans. His most popular work *God Bless America,* was created as a tribute to the land he loved and continues to be performed at the beginning of sports events throughout the country. Berlin stipulated that all proceeds from the song would go to a foundation that funded several charities. Some of his other standards include *White Christmas, Blue Skies, Always, There's No Business Like Show Business, Easter Parade, Heat Wave* and *How Deep is the Ocean.* For the silver screen he scored the music for *Top Hat, Alexander's Ragtime Band, Holiday Inn, Blue Skies, Easter Parade* and *White Christmas.*

The general release in the United States was held on August 14, 1943. The film won the Oscar for *Best Music* (Ray Heindorf), and was nominated for two other Academy Awards: Best Sound and Best Art Direction.

World premiere held in New York on July 28, 1943. The cost of the top ticket for the premiere was $55.00.

In 1943 Warner Bros. was paying Humphrey Bogart $3500 a week with a minimum guarantee of 40 weeks.

Another Warner Bros. musical, *Yankee Doodle Dandy* starring James Cagney, with a domestic gross of $4,800,000 was also one of the biggest hits of the year.

Competition at the nation's theaters included: *I Dood It* (MGM) starring Red Skelton, *Watch on the Rhine* (Warners) with Bette Davis, *Jungle Woman* (Universal) featuring Evelyn Ankers in the title role and the dreary drama *Summer Storm* (United Artists) starring George Sanders and Linda Darnell.

# Stallion Road

**release date: April 12, 1947**          **running time: 97-98 minutes**

**Cast:**  Ronald Reagan, Alexis Smith, Zachary Scott, Peggy Knudsen, Patti Brady, Harry Davenport, Angela Greene, Frank Puglia, Ralph Byrd, Lloyd Corrigan, Fernando Alvarado, Matthew Boulton, Monte Blue, Nina Campana, Dan Dowling, Byron Foulger, Mary Gordon, Creighton Hale, Sam Harris, Reed Howes, Fred Kelsey, Douglas Kennedy, Elaine Lange, Leon Lenoir, Vera Lewis, Ralph Littlefield, Jack Mower, Oscar O'Shea, Paul Panzar, Dewey Robinson, Roxanne Stark, Bobby Valentine, Tom Wilson, Joan Winfield

*Executive Producer* Jack L. Warner; *Producer* Alex Gottlieb;
*Directors* James V, Kern, Raoul Walsh; *Writer* Stephen Longstreet;
*Cinematography* Arthur Edeson; *Music* Frederick Hollander;
*Editor* David Weisbart; *Art Direction* Stanley Fleischer; *Set
Decorator* Clarence Steensen; *Second Unit Director* Richard
Mayberry; *Sound* Stanley Jones; *Musical Director* Leo F.
Forbstein; *Orchestrations* Leonid Raab; *Dialogue Director*
Bretaigne Windust; *Special Effects* Willard Van Enger; *Montage*
James Leicester; *Makeup* Perc Westmore; *Wardrobe* Milo
Anderson, Leah Rhodes; *Stunts* Richard Farnsworth

## Synopsis:

The film title refers to a horse breeding ranch of that name, owned
by Larry Hanrahan (Reagan), who is also the area veterinarian.
Novelist, Stephen (Zachary Scott), pays his friend a visit and makes
notes about his lifestyle.

Larry is called out to care for an ailing prize mare belonging to local rancher Rory Teller (Alexis Smith). The horse doen't appear to be very sick and is quickly cured.

The horse then appears at a state fair jumping contest and beats the vet's own horse. Soon after it relapses into illness and dies. Rory blames Larry for negligence and for failing to come back out when she called for his help.

However, Larry had been fighting an outbreak of anthrax that had stricken a cattle herd.

With the vet distracted, romance flares between Rory and Stephen. He takes advantage of the rift and asks Rory to marry him.

The anthrax problem reaches greater proportions and it eventually becomes apparent to Rory that she was wrong to spurn Larry.

Larry perfects a serum treatment but becomes infected with anthrax himself. His doctor, (Harry Davenport) gives him up for lost, but Rory injects him with the serum and the gamble pays off. He recovers and their romance again blossoms. The novelist accepts defeat.

## Reviews:

"Its chief virtue was the way it looked-average entertainment." *The Warner Bros. Story.* Clive Hirschhorn (New York, Crown, 1979); ". . . (G)enerates considerable interest . . . Direction packs a lot of punch in the few action sequences . . . but falls short on understanding necessary to develop characters that people the plot." *Variety* (March 19, 1947); "Ronald Reagan performs the veterinarian in a conventionally stout-fellow style and Alexis Smith plays the lady horse-breeder with a sleek and monotonous haughtiness." *The New York Times* (April 5, 1947); "Three people, Ronald Reagan, Zachary Scott and Alexis Smith, stand out in clear focus above a story that veers to the hokumy and through sheer talent, personality and appeal keep interest high to the finish . . . Ronald in his first postwar role reminds again what a splendid and dependable actor he is." *The Los Angeles Examiner* (Sara Hamilton, April 5, 1947); "The picture should not be expected to do record business, but it gives full money's worth in entertainment . . . Ronald Reagan and Zachary Scott are excellent as the friendly rivals...The appearance of Reagan marks his first post-war role, and his performance is of a caliber to make one realize that he has been missed." *The Hollywood Reporter* (March 18, 1947)

## Notes:

In production from April 2 to July 6, 1946 with a 109 day shooting schedule. Some location work was done at Hidden Valley, a reclusive area with large estates, ranches, and many horses that is now part of Westlake Village, and located just north of Los Angeles. Several sequences were also shot at Griffith Park ten minutes south of the Warner Bros. studio complex.

Negative cost of the film was $2,040,000. It generated $2,091,900 in domestic film rentals and a further $687,000 from overseas markets.

Envisioned as a big-budget, color entry with original cast choices Errol Flynn then Bogart and Lauren Bacall. Bogart and Bacall were suspended by the studio after declining to work in the film. Raoul Walsh had been set to direct. When Bacall declined the role, studio looked at Eleanor Parker.

First Reagan picture after the War. His new contract with Warner Bros., signed on August 21, 1945, thirty days after his discharge from the army, guaranteed the actor a minimum of 43 weeks of salary a year, at $3500 a week or $150,500 per annum.

In 1946 Ronald Reagan earned $169,750.

Also in 1946 Warner Bros. paid Humphrey Bogart $432,000, Bette Davis $328,000, and Errol Flynn $199,999.

Director James V, Kern's (1909-1966) feature career consisted of only six unimpressive films. The former attorney was a screenwriter before helming his first motion picture *The Doughgirls* in 1944. *Stallion Road* was his third directorial effort. It was in television that Kern, with his quick shooting habits and organizational ability, excelled. He directed numerous episodes of *I Love Lucy* in the 1950s as well as episodes of *Topper, The Millionaire, The Gale Storm Show, Maverick, 77 Sunset Strip, My Three Sons* and *My Favorite Martian.*

Canadian-born female-lead Alexis Smith (1921-1993) was signed by Warner Bros. to a contract right out of college. The 5' 9" ravishing redhead was inserted into a succession of forgettable roles until she played opposite Errol Flynn in the biography of boxing champion *Gentleman Jim* (1942). In 1971 the fifty-year old actress appeared as the headliner on Broadway in the frantic musical *Follies,* and won a Tony award for Best Actress.

Often the second lead in a host of motion pictures, Zachary Scott (1914-1965) appeared on Broadway in the early 1940s and was personally signed by Jack L. Warner for the lead of *The Mask of Dimitrios* (1944). The film's success led to challenging roles in *The*

*Southerner* (1945), as Joan Crawford's husband in *Mildred Pierce* (1945), *Cass Timberlane* (1947) *Whiplash* (1948) and *Colt .45* (1950). Between 1945 and 1962 Scott was seen in more than 35 features. He died at the age of 51 from a malignant brain tumor.

On October 4, 1948 Reagan, Alexis Smith and Zachary Scott reprised their roles on the *Lux Radio Theater* program.

Competition at the nation's theaters came from: *Tarzan and the Huntress* (RKO); *The Mighty McGurk* (MGM) starring Wallace Beery and Dean Stockwell, Paramount's *My Favorite Brunette, The Locket*

# That Hagen Girl

**release date: November 1, 1947**        **running time: 83-84 minutes**

WARNER BROS. ~~~ RONALD REAGAN · SHIRLEY TEMPLE ~ THAT HAGEN GIRL·

**Cast:**  Ronald Reagan, Shirley Temple, Rory Calhoun, Lois Maxwell, Dorothy Peterson, Charles Kemper, Conrad Janis, Penny Edwards, Jean Porter, Harry Davenport, Nella Walker, Winifred Harris, Moroni Olsen, Frank Conroy, Kathryn Card, Douglas Kennedy, Barbara Brown, Tom Fadden, William B. Davidson, Florence Allen, Lois Austin, Donia Bussey, Gino Corrado, Rex Downing, William Edmunds, Sarah Edwards, Virginia Farmer, Ross Ford, Doris Fulton, Jane Hamilton, Billy Henderson, Joyce Horne, Boyd Irwin, Jessica Jordan, Kathryn Kane, Fred Kelsey, Ray Klinge, Gracille LaVinder, Kyle MacDonnell, Billy Mauch, Jack McGee, Lydia McKim, Claire Meade, Frank Meredith, John Michaels, Ray Montgomery, Jack Mower, Frank O'Connor, Robert Palmer, Milton Parsons, Constance Purdy, Ruth Robinson, William Roy, Ed Russell, Jack Smart, Walter Soderling, Helen Wallace, Anthony Warde, Paul Weber, Guy Wilkerson, Rhoda Williams, Billy Roy, Richard Wimer, Edward Murphy

That Hagen Girl

**Credits:**                    **Warner Bros.**

*Producer* Alex Gottlieb; *Executive Producer* Jack L. Warner; *Director* Peter Godfrey; *Screenplay* Charles Hoffman; *Based on the novel* "That Hagen Girl" by Edith Roberts; *Cinematography* Karl Freund; *Music* Franz Waxman; *Editor* David Weisbart; *Art Direction* Stanley Fleischer; *Set Decorator* Lyle B. Reifsnider; *Costumes* Travilla; *Makeup* Perc Westmore; *Assistant Director* Claude Archer; *Sound* Stanley Jones; *Special Effects* Wesley Anderson, William C., McGann; *Musical Director* Leo F. Fobstein; *Orchestrator* Leonid Raab; *Unit Manager* Frank Mattison; *Montage* James Leicester; *Dialogue Director* Herschel Daugherty

## Synopsis:

The story revolves around old-fashioned small town gossip. Mary Hagen (Shirley Temple) is an adoptee who hears rumors throughout her childhood and adolescence about her parentage, mostly that she is the illegitimate daughter of a demented heiress and a local war hero, Tom Bates (Ronald Reagan), who is now a lawyer. Mary is befriended by a teacher Julia Kane (Lois Maxwell), and romanced by young socialite Ken Frenesu (Rory Calhoun), but most of the people of the town shun her. Her forster mother Minta

Hagen (Dorothy Peterson) dies and she is expelled from school for provoking a brawl, which was not her fault.

Tom returns to town from Washington, where he has been decorated for his war service. He gradually falls in love with the girl, despite the rumors that he is her father.

He rescues Mary from a suicide attempt, and she accepts his propsal of marriage.

To ease her mind he proves that she comes from an orphanage in Evanston, Illionois, and that the gossip she has heard all her life is nonsense.

## Reviews:

"Will not perk up much boxoffice activity. Handicapped by shopworn screenplay...Reagan walks through his role without conviction. . . ." *Variety* (October 22, 1947); "Dull screenplay . . . This is the kind of heart-searing melodrama which flourished in the silent picture era, and no amount of modernization in dialogue or dress can hide its antiquity. . . . Both Shirley Temple and Ronald Reagan do their level best but under the circumstances they cannot help but show their confusion from time to time." *The Hollywood Reporter* (October 22, 1947); "Ronald Reagan keeps as straight a face as he can while doing what might have struck him as the silliest job of his career." *The New York Times* (October 25, 1947); ". . . it is a dated dud . . . there are moments of charm and appeal . . . Nevertheless, it is a dull and confusing mélange, so preposterous in theme for 1947 as to constitute an insult to the intelligence." *The Los Angeles Examiner* (Kay Proctor, November 27, 1947); "The film represents a nadir in Ronald Reagan's acting career." *Jane Wyman.* Joe Morella & Edward Z. Epstein (Delacorte Press, New York, 1985)

## Notes:          *"I tried to turn down the next script offering."*

Filmed from June 2 to August 9, 1947 under the working title *Mary Hagen*.

The day before production started Reagan and Jane Wyman appeared as guests on Louella Parsons' radio program to publicize their respective upcoming releases.

Negative cost of the film was placed at $1,327,000. It brought in domestic rentals of $1,818,000 and a further $301,000 from overseas markets.

During production Ronald Reagan was paid $3500 a week. Several weeks into the filming he developed viral pneumonia, was hospitalized with an elevated temperature of 104 degrees, lost 18 pounds which led to his absence from the set from June 19 to July 14. Long after filming was complete Reagan was so uncomfortable with the story that he petitioned Jack Warner to have the end changed so that Mary could finish up in the arms of her young boyfriend. The end was changed instead to Tom and Mary boarding a train together, and the audience is left unsatisfied, not knowing if they are married or just travelling together.

Warners signed Shirley Temple (1928-  ), on-loan from David O. Selznick Productions, at a reported $75,000. To get her, they also had to take on Rory Calhoun, who was also under an exclusive contract to Selznick. Temple was pregnant during the shoot. The actress who was the top box-office star in the nation as a child in the 1930s, only appeared in five more films (*Fort Apache, Mr. Belvedere Goes to College, Adventure in Baltimore, The Story of Sea Biscuit* and *A Kiss for Corliss*) before a short-lived career on television (1958).

Prior to the signing of the young actress, the producer and director had been seeking to sign either Anne Baxter or Teresa Wright.

In 1947 Reagan was elected President of the Screen Actors Guild (SAG).

London-born director Peter Godfrey (1899-1970) toiled in the British theater as an actor, director and writer through the 1920's. He migrated to Hollywood in the 1930s where he worked solely as an actor and was assigned to minor roles in *Blockade* (1938), *The Hunchback of Notre Dame* (1939) and *Edison the Man* (1940). In 1941 he served as Spencer Tracy's butler, Poole, in MGM's *Dr. Jekyll and Mr. Hyde*. Although he continued to act until 1947, by the mid-1940s he had moved behind the cameras. As a director he helmed 19 films including *Hotel Berlin* and *Christmas in Connecticut* (both 1945), *The Two Mrs. Carrolls* (1947), *Barricade* (1950) and *Please Murder Me* (1956). Godfrey also directed Reagan in *The Girl from Jones Beach* (1949).

Los Angeles native Rory Calhoun (born Francis Timothy McCown, 1922-1999) was discovered by famed Hollywood agent Sue Carol, the wife of actor Alan Ladd. Prior to landing in films, the high school drop-out was a lumberjack, boxer and truck driver. It was legendary producer David O. Selznick who changed his screen name to Rory Calhoun. While still a teenager the tall, lean Calhoun nicknamed "Smoky" worked in the first of more than 80 films with a bit part in the Henry Hathaway drama set against the backdrop of

Nazis in Africa, *Sundown* (1941). Although the preponderance of his films were Westerns, he did make some other features including *County Fair* (1950), *I'd Climb the Highest Mountain* (1951), *How To Marry a Millionaire* (1953) and *Flight To Hong Kong* (1956). In 1958 Calhoun became cowboy Bill Longley in the CBS television series *The Texan* and in 1982 began a five-year run in the role of a judge on the CBS daytime soap opera *Capitol.*

For her fourth-billed role, Lois Maxwell won the 1948 Golden Globe award for "Most promising newcomer." Maxwell (1927- ) born Lois Hooker in Ontario, Canada was a graduate of England's prestigious Royal Academy of Dramatic Arts. Her first screen role, in *Stairway to Heaven* (1946) was uncredited, and was followed by *That Hagen Girl* and several low-budget entries. From 1949 to 1952 she worked in half a dozen Italian films then appeared erratically in the British cinema until she was signed for the recurring role of Miss Moneypenny in the new James Bond series.

Competition at the nation's screens was supplied by *Man About Town* (RKO) musical starring Maurice Chevalier; the Roy Rogers B-western filmed in Republic's Trucolor, *On the Spanish Trail, The Unfinished Dance* (MGM) with Margaret O'Brien and Cyd Charisse and *The Fugitive* (RKO) starring Henry Fonda under John Ford's direction. Warner Bros. was also re-releasing the double-bills *The Sea Hawk* and *The Sea Wolf* and *Bad Men of Missouri* with *Each Dawn I Die* to well above average business.

On August 17, 1947 Reagan appeared as a guest on Dorothy Lamour's radio show which served to publicize the military services. Two months later, on October 13th. the actor and Irene Dunn presented a dramatized presentation of the popular Gary Cooper-Ingrid Bergman film *Saratoga Trunk* on the popular radio series *Cavalcade of America.* Both performers received $3500 for their services.

# Voice of the Turtle

**release date: December 25, 1947**          **running time: 103 minutes**

**Cast:**   Ronald Reagan, Eleanor Parker, Eve Arden, Wayne Morris, Kent Smith, John Emery, Erskine Sanford, John Holland, Alan Foster, Douglas Kennedy, Ernest Anderson, Lois Austin, Richard Bartell, Peter Camlin, Tristram Coffin, Bunty Cutler, Noel Delorme, Bernard DeRoux, Suzanne Dulier, Sarah Edwards, Ross Ford, William Gould, Doris Kemper, Joan Lawrence, Jack Lee, Philip Morris, Brian O'Hara, Nino Pipitone, Robert Spencer, Nick Stewart, Helen Wallace, Janet Warren, Frank Wilcox, Nicodemus Stewart, Juanita Roberts, Francine Bordeaux, Darlene Mohilef, Norma Fenton, Peter Gowland,

**Credits:**                 **Warner Bros.**

*Producer* Charles Hoffman; *Director* Irving Rapper; *Screenplay* John Van Druten, from his play; *Additional Dialogue* Charles Hoffman; *Cinematography* Sol Polito; *Music* Max Steiner; *Editor* Rudi Fehr; *Art Direction* Robert M. Haas; *Set Decoration* William L. Kuehl; *Costumes* Leah Rhodes; *Assistant Director* Lester D.

Guthrie; *Sound* Stanley Jones; *Special Effects* Harry Barndollar, Edwin B. DuPar; *Musical Director* Leo F. Forbstein; *Orchestrator* Murray Cutter; *Montage* James Leicester; *Dialogue Director* Richard Barr; *Makeup* Perc Westmore; *Music* "Londonderry Air."

## Synopsis:

Sally Middleton (Eleanor Parker), a New York actress, is a warm hearted girl who falls in love for the sake of love, and during wartime she is finding eligible men scarce. Her Producer stops dating her and she is depressed until Bill (Ronald Reagan) enters her life. He is in town to meet man-loving actress Olive Lashbrook (Eve Arden), but the over-booked Olive has forgotten Bill and starts dating a naval commander (Wayne Morris) instead.

Bill has nowhere to stay and Sally offers her apartment.

Bill soon has amorous feelings toward Sally. Although cautious at first she soon warms to him.

By this time Olive has rekindled her feelings toward Bill and is afraid of losing his affection.

She constantly phones the apartment, but finally has to give up.

## Reviews:

". . . strong comedy entertainment...an infectious, fluffy mirth-maker with sturdy box-office prospects. . . . Ronald Reagan doesn't miss any bets..in getting the most from his role" *Variety* (December 21, 1947); A frothy and amusing tale." *Warner Brothers Presents: The Most Exciting Years-from The Jazz Singer to White Heat.* Ted Sennett (New York, Arlington House, 1971); ". . . solid, intelligent direction." *The Warner Bros. Story.* Clive Hirschhorn (New York; Crown, 1979)' "Ronald Reagan turns in a pleasantly sensitive performance as the Marine sergeant." *Newsweek* (January 1947); "Choice of Ronald Reagan for the soldier's part was as good as any . . . It's a breeze for the ex air force captain who can wriggle his way in and out of comedy and drama with equal dexterity." *The Hollywood Reporter* (December 26, 1947)

## Notes:

In production from February 22 to May 5, 1947.

National release date was February 21, 1948.

Negative cost of the production was $2,380,000. It returned domestic rentals of $2,617,000 and an additional $499,000 from overseas markets.

Warner Bros. paid $500,000 plus 15% of the gross receipts for the screen rights to the play. In an unusual occurrence, the film hit the screen while the play was still on Broadway. It ran on the "Great White Way" from December 8, 1943 to January 3, 1948.

Reagan was paid at the rate of $3500 a week. In December 1946 director John Huston offered the actor a substantial part in his upcoming film *The Treasure of Sierra Madre*. He wanted to accept the offer, eagerly seeking to work with Bogart again, but was overruled by Warner Bros. who insisted that he take *The Voice of the Turtle* assignment as Bill Page, an army sergeant looking for love; Reagan felt that whilst it would make a pleasing comedy, it was not be a good vehicle for him. The role he coveted eventually went to Bruce Bennett.

London-born Irving Rapper (1898-1999) started in the industry as a second-unit director, moved up to a dialogue director in the mid-1930's and directed the first of his twenty-two features in 1941. His films include *Now, Voyager* (1942), *The Corn Is Green* (1945), *The Glass Menagerie* (1950), *Marjorie Morningstar (1958),* and *Born Again* (1978).

Eve Arden (born Eunice Quedens, 1908-1990), made a career of playing the wise-cracking, ever-knowledgeable friend of the female lead in many of her nearly 70 motion pictures. She made her first screen appearance in 1929 (*Song of Love*). By the late 1930s, after a stint on Broadway, she was in demand with substantial roles in several bigger films including the Marx Brothers' *At The Circus* (1939), *Comrade X* and *No, No, Nanette* (both 1940), *Ziegfeld Girl* (1941), *Cover Girl* (1944), her Oscar nominated role as friend to Joan Crawford in *Mildred Pierce* (1945), the Danny Kaye comedy *The Kid from Brooklyn* (1946) and *Tea for Two* (1950). In 1948 she signed for the signature role in the radio series *Our Miss Brooks*. When it came to television in 1952 the tall actress became America's favorite school teacher. The show ran for four seasons, earned Arden an Emmy for Best Actress and spawned a 1955 movie of the same name. She starred in two additional television series which had limited success and had supporting roles in the musical *Grease* (1978) and it's 1982 sequel.

The Eleanor Parker role was originally offered to Jean Arthur then Margaret Sullivan the star of the Broadway production. Reagan lobbied the studio to sign June Allyson, from MGM, for the female lead. Eleanor Parker (1922-  ), born in Ohio, had an active film career that spanned more than twenty-five years and included over 50 films. In 1944 she appeared opposite John Garfield in *Between Two Worlds* and during the same year was on the screen in

*Hollywood Canteen.* The actress also appeared in *Pride of the Marines* (1945), the remake of *Of Human Bondage* (1946) and *Caged* (1950) for which she received her first Oscar nomination. Four films later, for her role in *Detective Story* (1951) she was again nominated for an Academy Award. Some of her other features included *Scaramouche* (1952), *The Naked Jungle* (1954) with Charlton Heston, *Interrupted Melody* (1955, her third Oscar nomination), *The King and Four Queens* (1956) and *Return to Peyton Place* (1961). In 1965 she played the part of the Baroness in *The Sound of Music.* As film roles dried up, the actress turned to television appearing in made-for-television movies as well as guesting on numerous programs of the 1960s to the early 1990s.

After *Key Largo* and *My Wild Irish Rose, The Voice of the Turtle* was Warner Bros.' biggest grosser of 1947.

The studio's first choice for the role that eventually went to Reagan was either Cary Grant or Tyrone Power.

When reissued in the mid-1950s title was changed to *One For the Books.*

Competition at the nation's theaters included: *The Paradine Case* (RKO) with Gregory Peck and *A Double Life* (Universal) with Ronald Coleman. Reflecting the changing times, the Loews State Theater in New York City announced that for the first time in 26 years, it was dropping its four-a-day vaudeville show.

# John Loves Mary

**release date: February 4, 1949**     **running time:  96-98 minutes**

**Cast:**  Ronald Reagan, Jack Carson, Wayne Morris, Edward Arnold, Virginia Field, Katharine Alexander, Paul Harvey, Ernest Cossart, Patricia Neal, Russell Arms, Irving Bacon, Rodney Bell, Rudolf Friml, Creighton Hale, George Hickman, Douglas Kennedy, Philo McCullough, Ray Montgomery, Jack Mower, Nino Pipitone, Larry Rio, Lottie Williams, Tom Wilson

**Credits:**              **Warner Bros**.

*Producer* Jerry Wald; *Director* David Butler; *Cinematography* J. Peverell Marley; *Assistant Cameraman* Larry Cairns; *Writers* Henry Ephron, Phoebe Ephron, Norman Krasna; *Music* David Buttolph; *Editor* Irene Morra; *Art Direction* Robert M. Haas; *Set Decoration* William L. Kuehl; *Costumes* Milo Anderson, Henry Field, Martha Bunch; *Production Manager* Eric Stacey; *Makeup* Bill Cooley, Ray Forman, Perc Westmore; *Assistant Director* Philip Quinn; *2nd. Assistant Director* Mel Dellar; *Sound* Francis J. Scheid; *Dialogue Director* Herschel Daugherty; *Special Effects* Robert Burks,

William C. McGann; *Orchestrator* Leonid Raab; *Music* "Someone to Watch Over Me" by George Gershwin; *Script Supervisor* Alma Young; *Camera Operator* Ray Ramsey; *Gaffer* Ralph Owen; *Grip* Warren Yaple; *Still Photographer* Eugene Richee; *Props* G.W. Bernsten, Harry Goldman;

## Synopsis:

Mary McKinley (Patricia Neal) awaits the arrival of her fiance John Lawrence (Ronald Reagan) from England. He has been away serving in the army for some years. John, it appears, owes his friend Fred Taylor (Jack Carson) a favor for saving his life in battle. Repayment concerns Fred's London girlfriend Lilly Herbish (Virginia Field), who wants to go to the States to marry her soldier. She can't go as a single girl, so John marries her. They intend to get divorced when they reach America. John then plans to marry Mary. He is unaware that Fred is already married to a pregnant wife. Mary's father, Senator McKinley (Edward Arnold), arranges the marriage of his daughter to the returning soldier, but Lilly appears with her tale of woe, creating many complications.

Army lieutenant, O'Leary (Wayne Morris) unravels the problems when he reveals that he married Lilly in London and later noted himself as killed in action to escape the marriage...therefore John and Lilly are not really married at all...

## Reviews:

"Reagan, as John, and Jack Carson, as his ex-G.I. buddy, carry off the stars roles with a slick ease that sharpens the characters plenty." *Daily Variety* (January 25, 1949); "...Reagan' portrayal of John, the returning soldier, is a hep enactment, but broad enough for the baffling circumstances in which he finds himself." *Variety* (January 26, 1949); "A frail jape..." *Warner Brothers Presents: The Most Exciting Years-from the Jazz Singer to White Heat.* Ted Sennett (New York; Arlington House, 1971); "Ronald Reagan is fairly respectable a the young soldier...he manages to maintain a certain dignity.....Patricia Neal...shows little to recommend her to further comedy jobs." *The New York Times* (February 4, 1949); "Reagan, always as natural and unassuming as your favorite bank-teller, is perfectly cast as the discharged soldier and turns in another of his ingratiating portrayals." *The Los Angeles Examiner* (February 10, 1949); "....a rollicking version of the New York stage success that fairly bubbles with good humor and literally bristles with laughs....Reagan contributes an authentic portrait of a discharged

G.I., and he successfully endows the slap-happy part with the conviction it needs." *The Hollywood Reporter* (January 25, 1949)

## Notes:

In production from mid-January to late-February 1948. There was one day of retakes on March 4, 1948.

The film's negative cost was $1,346,000. Rentals from the domestic market were $1,668,000. The overseas run brought in an additional $354,000 to the studio.

Based on a popular Broadway play.

The Virginia Field role was to have originally been offered to Jane Wyman, but just prior to the start of filming, the couple separated. Reagan and Wyman were divorced in June 1948.

This motion picture marked Patricia Neal's film debut. In her first film, Warner Bros. paid the actress $1250 a week while Reagan earned $3500 a week.

Canadian-born, second-billed Jack Carson (1910-1963) was equally at home acting in dramas and comedies. Between 1937 and 1961 the husky Carson was seen in 94 films, often in as many as sixteen a year (1938). After minor appearances in *Mr. Smith Goes to Washington* and *Destry Rides Again* (1939), he moved to Warner Bros. in 1941 and was afforded better supporting roles in a number of their films including *The Strawberry Blonde* (1941), *The Male Animal* and *Gentleman Jim* (both 1942). His most popular films of the 1950s included *A Star Is Born* (1954) and *Cat on a Hot Tin Roof* (1958). The actor who was married to actress Lola Albright from 1952 to 1958 died of stomach cancer on the same date as fellow performer Dick Powell.

Female-lead Virginia Field (1917- ) was born in London, came to Hollywood as a teenager, and appeared in 45 films and dozens of episodic television series' before retiring in 1968. Some of her better known motion pictures included *The Primrose Path* (1934), *Little Lord Faunteroy* (1936), *Lloyd's of London* (1936), *Waterloo Bridge* (1940), and *A Connecticut Yankee in King Arthur's Court* (1949) with Bing Crosby and Rhonda Fleming.

Cinematographer J. Peverell Marley (1901-1964), in a career that spanned nearly forty years, was involved in the photography of over 100 Hollywood motion pictures. He worked for Cecil B. DeMille on the silent versions of *The Ten Commandments* (1923) and *King of Kings* (1927) as well as the well known sound features, *The House of Rothschild* (1934), *The Three Musketeers* (1935), *Alexander's Ragtime Band* (1938), *The Three Musketeers* (1939),

*Four Jills in a Jeep* (1944), *Life with Father* (1947), the 3D films *House of Wax* and *Charge at Feather River* (both 1953), *The Spirit of St. Louis* (1957) and his last feature *The Sins of Rachel Cade* (1961). Marley, who was married to actress Linda Darnell from 1944 to 1952, also shot Reagan's *Night Unto Night*.

Competition at the nation's screens included: *Shockproof* (Columbia) with Cornel Wilde; *The Life of Riley* (Universal) based on the radio program, with William Bendix in the lead; *The Bride* (MGM) with Robert Taylor and Ava Gardner and *Bad Boy* (Monogram) with Audie Murphy's first screen role.

Both Reagan and Neal performed an abbreviated version of their film roles on the June 19, 1950 episode of the *Lux Radio Theater.*

# Night Unto Night

**release date: May 14, 1949**          **running time: 94-95 minutes**

**Cast:**  Ronald Reagan, Viveca Lindfors, Broderick Crawford, Rosemary DeCamp, Osa Massen, Art Baker, Craig Stevens, Erskine Sanford, Ann Burr, Johnny McGovern, Lillian Yarbo, Ross Ford, Almira Sessions, Dick Elliott, Lois Austin, Irving Bacon, Bill Bletcher, Jack Mower, Paul Panzar, Larry Rio, Ramon Ros, Leo White, Jack Wise, Bing Conley, Joe Devlin, Dennis Donnelly, William Haade, Creighton Hale, Dick Johnstone, Philo McCullough, Lottie Williams

**Credits:**                    **Warner Bros.**

*Executive Producer* Jack L. Warner; *Producer* Owen Crump; *Director* Don Siegel; *Screenplay* Kathryn Scola; *Based on the novel* "Night unto Night" by Philip Wylie; *Cinematography* J. Peverell Marley; *Music* Franz Waxman; *Editor* Thomas Reilly; *Art Direction* Hugh Reticker; *Set Decorator* G.W. Bernstein; *Costumes* Leah Rhodes; *Production Manager* Louis Baum; *Sound* Oliver S. Garretson; *Makeup* Cherie Banks, Ward Hamilton, Perc Westmore; *Assistant Director* Oren Haglund; *Special Effects* Harry Barndollar, Edwin B. DuPar; *Musical Director* Leo F. Forbstein; *Orchestrator* Leonid Raab; *Camera Operator* George Gordon; *Dialogue Director* Jack Daniels; *Montage* James Leicester; *Script Supervisor* Rita Michaels; *Gaffer* Robert Neville; *Grip* Warren Yaple

## Synopsis:

John (Ronald Reagan) is an eplieptic biochemist. He is a sensitive man who takes up residence in a secluded house on Florida's Gulf Coast when he realizes his illness is chronic. In solitude he is able to rest and this allows him to carry on with his work. His beach house is rented from an attractive young widow, Ann (Viveca Lindfors).

They gradually fall in love, but John can't bring himself to tell Ann about his epilepsy. But she too has problems; whenever she entres the house she is haunted by the voice of her late husband.

John tries to convince her that the dead don't return. His own condition worsens until he has a violent fit.

Doctor Poole (Art Baker), tells John there is no hope, and he finally tells Ann. She refuses to give up and prevents him from committing suicide during a hurricane.

## Reviews:

"It fails to come off entirely but has the elements of appeal to the femme ticket buyer . . . Ronald Reagan's . . . performance suffers in comparison to his co-star's and lacks depth . . . Don Siegel's direction is strained and strives too much for dramatic effects . . ." *Variety* (April 20, 1949); "Viveca Lindfors obviously is a fine actress, but her role is so poorly written and directed that she appears to be over-emoting. Ronald Reagan walks through his part." *The Los Angeles Examiner* (Shirle Duggan, June 6, 1949); "Ronald Reagan and Vivica Lindfors play the two central roles sympathetically, though neither seems to get very far beneath the surface." *The*

*Christian Science Monitor* (June 15, 1949); " . . . nothing much happens….Reagan plays the role . . . with the abstracted air of a man who has just forgotten an important telephone number." *Time* (July 4, 1949); "(It) is a brave effort…but it is not entertainment, and even stalwart acting and capable direction fail to make it so." *Boxoffice* (May 28, 1949); "Interesting at times, but never good entertainment . . . A fine cast is wasted on a morbid and frequently unconvincing story . . . Reagan never seems quite at home in his difficult role, although he makes a valiant effort to make it convincing" *The Hollywood Reporter* (April 19, 1949)

## Notes:

In production from September 19 to January 18, 1947 with several additional pickup days in late January and February 1947. Filming took place in the midst of Hollywood's biggest labor strike when several unions set up picket lines at studio gates. In part due to the strike, and lacking a final, polished script, the film ran 54 days over the allotted schedule.

Budgeted at $1,200,000 the final negative cost of the film came in at $1,810,000. It was a total failure with domestic rentals of only $449,000 and foreign receipts of just $249,000. The production went on Warners financial statement as a loss in excess of $1,800,000. This film proved to be Reagan's biggest and costliest post-World War II flop.

Reagan paid $3500 a week; Broderick Crawford received $2500 a week; Art Baker $1250/week; Erskine Sanford $1000/week; Irving Bacon $1000/week; Osa Massen $750/week; Lillian Yarbo $500/week; Ann Burr $250/week.

For the Reagan role the studio had also considered Bogart, Flynn and Dennis Morgan, while for the Lindfors part casting agents had suggested, among others, Bette Davis, Joan Crawford, Barbara Stanwyck, Ann Sheridan and Ida Lupino.

Warners purchased the screen-rights to the novel on January 21, 1946. The Chicago-born, Cambridge University educated Don Siegel (1912-1991) started as an actor in the mid-1930s, then quickly segued behind the cameras in an assortment of positions. He started as an editor, went on to become a montage artist, second-unit director and finally a director and producer with solid credentials in both the medium of motion pictures and television. Known for his gritty style and creating a sense of realism, Siegel directed 35 feature-length films between 1945 and 1982, including the early minor classics *Riot in Cell Block 11* (1954), the low-budget science-fiction epic *Invasion of the Body Snatchers* (1956) and *Baby Face Nelson* (1957). He directed Elvis Presley in *Flaming Star* (1960), Ronald Reagan in his only role as a heavy in *The Killers* (1964), the Clint Eastwood films *Coogan's Bluff* (1968), *Two Mules for Sister Sara* (1970), *The Beguiled* (1971), *Dirty Harry* (1971) and *Escape from Alcatraz* (1979), as well as Walter Matthau's finest dramatic role, *Charley Varrick* (1973) and John Wayne's last film *The Shootist* (1976). After his divorce from Viveca Lindfors (married 1948-1953), whom he had fallen in love with during production, Siegel married actress Doe Avedon in 1957. In the early 1990's Siegel, in an interview, stated that the casting of Reagan for the lead role lead led to , "the most miscast picture of the century." After seeing the first rough cut, sensing a disaster in the making, Jack Warner wanted to shelve the film.

Swedish actress Viveca Lindfors (born Elsa Viveca Torstensdotter Lindfors, 1920-1995) appeared in more than a dozen of her native country's films before coming to Hollywood and signing a contract with Warner Bros. in 1946. Cast opposite Reagan in her American motion picture debut, studio officials had hoped that the European import would become another Garbo or Ingrid Bergman. As the film remained on the shelf for several years, two of her later motion pictures *(To the Victor* and *Adventures of Don Juan)* were released in the interim. The actress appeared in over 50 American films including *Dark City* (1950), *I Accuse!* (1958), *The Story of Ruth* (1960), *The Way We Were* (1973) and *Welcome to L.A.* (1976). Appearing on television and in Europe, Lindfors remained active right up until the time of her death from rheumatoid arthritis complications.

Known for his raspy voice and gruff manner, actor Broderick Crawford (1911-1986) won an Academy Award for best actor, appeared in several prestigious films, spent most of his professional life acting in forgettable roles, and achieved his greatest fame starring as a police lieutenant for four years on the much loved *Highway Patrol* television series (1954-1958). Philadelphia-born Crawford first rose to stardom in 1937 when he played the role of the slow-witted Lennie in John Steinbeck's *Of Mice and Men* on Broadway. Although not selected to recreate the role on the screen, he did manage to be cast in supporting roles, in several notable films of the late-1930s and early 1940s including the Gary Cooper action flicks, *Beau Geste* and *The Real Glory* (both 1939), as Bob Dalton in the Western *When the Daltons Rode* (1940), as Bob Holliday in *Badlands of Dakota* (1941) and the crime drama

*Larceny, Inc.* (1942). In 1949 the role of a lifetime came along. When John Wayne and several other major boxoffice stars refused the lead, Crawford took over the role of southern politician Willie Stark in *All the King's Men*. He would triumph over Wayne (*Sands of Iwo Jima)* and others to win the Oscar for Best Actor of 1949. Although the actor continued working on television and appeared in 40 additional films, he never matched the personal success he achieved in the releases of 1949-50.

Philip Wylie (1902-1971) who wrote the novel that was adapted for the screen, from 1938 to 1966, authored a total of 17 screenplays including *Island of Lost Souls* (1933), *Come on Marines* (1934), *Charlie Chan In Reno* (1939), *Springtime in the Rockies* (1942) and the sci-fi special effects extravaganza, *When Worlds Collide* (1951).

New York City-born Art Baker (born Arthur Shank, 1898-1966) had a film career exceeding fifty films spread over 29 years (1937-66). Some of the better-known features he appeared in were *Spellbound* (1945), *Abie's Irish Rose* (1946), *Beginning or the End* (1947), and his last two efforts, *Young Dillinger* (1965) and *The Wild Angels* (1966). From 1950 to 1958 he was the host of one of the first reality television program *You Asked for It*.

In 1949 weekly attendance at the nation's movie theaters averaged 87,500,000. These patrons would pay an average of forty-six cents for each of the 470 films released during the year.

The Reagan film faced competition from the re-edited version of Kirk Douglas' *Champion,* RKO's *Mighty Joe Young* with Terry Moore and Ben Johnson and the Republic serial *King of the Rocketmen.*

# Girl From Jones Beach

**release date: July 16, 1949**  **running time: 77-79 minutes**

**Cast:** Ronald Reagan, Virginia Mayo, Eddie Bracken, Dona Drake, Henry Travers, Lois Wilson, Florence Bates, Jerome Cowan, Helen Westcott, Paul Harvey, Lloyd Corrigan, Gary Gray, Myrna Dell, Dolores Castle, John Mylong, Lola Albright, Raymond Bailey, Richard Bartell, Andre Baruch, Oliver Blake, Lennie Bremen, Carol Brewster, Peter Camlin, Chester Clute, Lorraine Crawford, Antonio Filauri, William Forrest, Glen B. Gallagher, Jack Gargan, Karen X. Gaylord, Gregory Golubeff, Creighton Hale, Grayce Hampton, Carey Harrison, Henry Lblings, Joi Lansing, Vonne Lester, Kay Mansfield, Tony Merrill, Broderick O'Farrell, Robert

A. O'Neil, Paul Panzar, Angi O. Poulos, Jeff Richards, Dale Robertson, Buddy Roosevelt, Queenie Smith, Mary Stuart, Betty Underwood, Nancy Valentine, Joan Vohs, Alice Wallace, Billy Wayne, Eve Whitney, Guy Wilkerson, William Yetter Sr., Nick Thompson, Daniel de Jonghe, Sam Bernard, Sandra Gould, Bobby Barber, Alvin Hammer, Patricia Northrop, Glen Gallagher, Ray Montgomery, John Marstan, Eddie Garr, Wally Dean, Anthony Jochim, Luther Crockett, Henrietta Taylor, Philo McCullough, Jack Mower, Leah Baird, Maurice St. Clair, Grace Young

## Credits:                              Warner Bros.

*Producer* Alex Gotlieb; *Director* Peter Godfrey; *Writer* Allen Boretz from a story by I.A.L. Diamond; *Cinematography* Carl E. Guthrie; *Music* David Buttolph, Al Dubin, Harry Warren; *Editor* Rudi Fehr; *Art Direction* Stanley Fleischer; *Set Decoration* William L. Kuehl; *Production Manager* Eric Stacey; *Assistant Director* Arthur Lueker; *Sound* Dolph Thomas; *Costumes* Leah Rhodes; *Special Effects* Edwin B. DuPar, William C. McGann; *Makeup* Perc Westmore, Alma Armstrong, George Bau, Gordon Bau; *Orchestrator* Leonid Raub; *Lyricists* Eddie Seiler, Harry Warren, Sol Marcus; *Camera Operator* Lou Jennings; *Script Supervisor* Rita Michaels; *Still Photographer* Frank Bjeering; *Grip* Jack Brown; *Gaffer* Vic Johnson; *Dialogue Director* John Maxwell

## Synopsis:

Bob Randolph (Ronald Reagan) is an illustrator with a reputation as an artist who concentrates his talents on the ideal female form. He is famed for his many paintings of an ideal shape known as "The Randolph Girl". He is approached by a television company which offers to put his model on air. Randolph admits there is no one model, but that his work is a composite of dozens of girls.

The company's publicist Chuck Donovan (Eddie Bracken) decides to seek out a beauty who resembles the ideal.

Bob and Chuck search Jones Beach, where they find one girl who is close to the perfect Randolph Girl, Ruth Wilson (Virginia Mayo). She declines their offer to appear on television. She is a school teacher, more interested in improving minds than catering to their fancies.

Bob is fascinated by her and in order to get to know her better he enrolls in her citizenship class. He poses as a Czech immigrant, barely able to speak English.

Ruth, though charmed, soon realizes who he is.

Things hot up when a newspaper prints a picture of her in a glamorous bathing suit and she finds herself in trouble with the school board.

Ruth feels the board has invaded her private life and when they fire her, she takes them to court. Judge Bullfinch (Henry Travers) finds in her favor.

Bob and Ruth marry

## Reviews:

"Ronald Reagan was another of the film's plus factors, revealing himself to be a more than capable purveyor of such lightweight nonsense..." *The Warner Bros. Story.* Clive Hirschhorn (New York; Crown, 1979); "As a comedy actress, Miss Mayo is no better than a rather weak script." *The New York Times* (July 30, 1949); "...a bright, splashy little comedy with a cute story, several bathing suits, and honest-to-goodness laughs. . . . an excellent performance from Ronald Reagan."

*The Los Angeles Examiner* (Dorothy Manners, July 16, 1949); "..a lively farce comedy...The story is clever and amusing and the screenplay develops it with frothy, saucy humor....Ronald Reagan has a happy assignment...plays it with witty aplomb." *The Hollywood Reporter* (June 21, 1949); "A breezy, amiable piece of escapist filmfare....A lot of good chuckles and fun is developed along the way." *Daily Variety* (June 21, 1949)

**Notes:**

In production from mid-May to July 1, 1948. Due to a severe back injury, Reagan had to leave the feature for three weeks. He was paid $3500 a week.

Before starting work on this film Reagan on May 3, 1948, appeared on the Lux Radio Theater with the dramatization of the film *Cloak and Dagger*. He was paid $3500.

While the budget for this film was $901,000, Warners had allotted $2,500,000 to Alfred Hitchcock's *Under Capricorn* starring Ingrid Bergman and Joseph Cotton. The thriller, with rentals of just $1,210,000 in the United States and a further $1,458,000 from the rest of the world was the biggest disappointment of the year for the studio. By contrast, *The Girl from Jones Beach* earned $1,764,000 in domestic rentals and an additional $362,000 from overseas markets.

Lauren Bacall was originally assigned the female lead. When she balked at accepting the role the studio suspended her and she was forced to buy her way out of the studio contract. Original male lead choice was Dennis Morgan.

Female-lead Virginia Mayo (born Virginia Jones, 1920- ) was a St. Louis native who appeared in 53 films from 1943 to 1997.

She worked in a number of elaborate productions supporting leading men Bob Hope (*The Princess and the Pirate* 1944) and Danny Kaye (*Wonder Man, The Kid from Brooklyn, The Secret Life of Walter Mitty* and *A Song is Born*). Mayo was equally adept at performing in dramatic roles opposite James Cagney, Burt Lancaster, Gregory Peck and Joel McCrea. Her better-known films include *Up In Arms* (1943), *Wonder Man* (1945), *Colorado Territory* and *White Heat* (both 1949), *The West Point Story* (1950). *Captain Horatio Hornblower* (1951) and *Fort Dobbs* (1958). Mayo worked infrequently in the decades of the sixties through the nineties.

Second-male lead Eddie Bracken (1915-2002) returned to Hollywood in 1940 to reprise his stage role for the screen in the musical *Too Many Girls*. The veteran of show-business had been performing in front of audiences since the age of nine, was in several *Our Gang* comedy shorts and made his motion picture debut as an adult in *Brother Rat* (1938).

Dona Drake (born Rita Novella, 1914-1989) started in show-business in the mid-1930s, under the names Una Velon, Rita Shaw and Rita Rio, as a singer then bandleader of an all-girl orchestra. She migrated to films in 1935 and appeared in more than 25 features including *Moonlight and Melody* (1935), *Louisiana*

*Purchase* (1941), *Road To Morocco* (1942), the Claudette Colbert-John Wayne comedy *Without Reservations* (1946), *So This Is New York* (1948), *Kansas City Confidential* (1952) and *The Bandits of Corsica* (1953).

Character actor Lloyd Corrigan (1900-1969) often played the role of doctor, judge, politician, or military officer. Arriving in Hollywood from San Francisco in the early 1920s the well-educated Corrigan went to work acting in films as well as writing 27 screenplays. Between 1930 and 1937 he also directed 13 features, nearly all of the "B" variety. Some of his better-known films include *Young Tom Edison* (1940), *Men of Boys Town* (1941), *Hitler's Children* (1943), *She-Wolf of London* (1946), *When Willie Comes Marching Home* (1950), *Son of Paleface* (1952), *The Manchurian Candidate* (1962) and *It's a Mad Mad Mad Mad World* (1963). He also appeared with Reagan in *Stallion Road* and *The Last Outpost.*

Other members of the cast met with varying degrees of success in films. Joi Lansing (born Joy Rae Brown, 1929-1972) played the part of a model in this film. As a real-life model she had come to Hollywood in 1948 and was immediately typecast in a succession of features as a model. Her early motion pictures included *Take Me Out to the Ballgame* (1949), *FBI Girl* (1951), *Singing in the Rain* (1952), *The French Line* (1954), *Touch of Evil* (1958) and *Marriage on the Rocks* (1965).

Character actor Paul Harvey (1882-1955), between 1928 and his death, appeared in over 180 films, while William Forrest (1902-1989) had over 220 screen credits from 1931 to 1971. Buddy Roosevelt (1898-1973) started out in Hollywood as a stuntman in the mid-teens. He worked with William S. Hart in *Hell's Hinges* (1916) and turned to acting in the mid-1920s. The last of his more than 150 screen appearances, most of which were Westerns, was in John Ford's *The Man Who Shot Liberty Valance* (1962). Ohio-born Lola Albright (1925- ) came to Hollywood in the mid-1940s, worked as a bit-player in several films including *The Pirate* (1948) and secured her first big role opposite Kirk Douglas in the boxing film *Champion.* Although she appeared in over 30 features, she is best remembered for her role in television's *Peter Gunn* detective series (1958-1961). World War II army veteran Dale Robertson (1923- ) also started in films in 1948. The vast majority of his more then 30 motion pictures were Westerns and he is best remembered for his starring role in the 211 episodes of the television series *Tales of Wells Fargo (1957-1962).* Character actor Raymond Bailey

(1904-1980) between 1939 and 1975 appeared in just over 50 films, but will be remembered fondly for his role as tight-fisted banker Milburn Drysdale on television's *The Beverly Hillbillies*.
The biggest Warner Bros. performers at the box office for 1949 were *Flamingo Road, Johnny Belinda* and *Look for the Silver Lining*.
Competition on the nation's screens included: *Scene of the Crime* (MGM) drama starring Van Johnson and Arlene Dahl, *Come to the Stable* (Fox) with Loretta Young; *Rope of Sand* (Paramount) with Burt Lancaster; *In the Good Old Summertime* (MGM) with July Garland and Van Johnson and the British entry, *Christopher Columbus* with Frederic March in the title role.

# It's A Great Feeling

**release date:  August 1, 1949**                **running time: 84-85 minutes**

**Cast:**   Dennis Morgan, Doris Day, Jack Carson, Bill Goodwin, Irving
Bacon, Claire Carleton, Shirley Ballard, Mel Blanc, Carol
Brewster, Sue Casey, Nita Talbot, Joan Vohs, Eve Whitney, Jean
Andren, Lois Austin, Frank Cady, Jacqueline deWit, Dudley
Dickerson, Tom Dugan, Pat Flaherty, Errol Flynn, Buddy Gorman,
Sandra Gould, Wendy Lee, Georges Renavent, Jack Wise, The
Famous Mazzone-Abbott Dancers, Harlan Warde, Ray
Montgomery, Janet Barret, Cosmo Sardo, Robby Cherry, Ralph
Littlefield, Alfredo Nunez, Henry Mirelez, Ruben Yuriar, James
Holden, Mark Strong, Forbes Murray, Victor Holbrook, Al
Billings, Mickey McMasters, George Sherwood, Bunty Cutler,
Peter Meersman, Rod Rogers, Olan E. Soule, Jan Bryant, Edward
Clark, George Calliga, Carli Eleanor, Paul Bradley, Eugene
Beeday, Waclaw Rekwart, Albert Poillet, Marcel De La Brosse
**In cameos playing themselves:** David Butler, Gary Cooper, Joan
Crawford, Michael Curtiz, Sydney Greenstreet, Ray Heindorf,
Danny Kaye, Patricia Neal, Eleanor Parker, Maureen Reagan,
Ronald Reagan, Edward G. Robinson, King Vidor, Raoul Walsh,
Jane Wyman

**Credits:**                        **First National-Warners**

*Producer* Alex Gottlieb; *Director* David Butler; *Screenwriters* Jack
Rose, Melville Shavelson; *Story* I.A.L. Diamond; *Original Music*
Jule Styne, Howard Jackson; *Cinematography* Wilfred M. Cline;
*Film Editor* Irene Morra; *Art Direction* Stanley Fleischer*; Set
Decoration* Lyle B. Reifsnider; *Musical Director* Ray Heindorf;
*Costumes* Milo Anderson; *Makeup* Agnes Flanagan, Micki
Marcelino, Perc Westmore; *Production Manager* Frank Mattison;
*Assistant Director* Philip Quinn; *Sound* Charles David Forrest,
Dolph Thomas; *Special Effects* Hans F. Koenekamp, William C.
McGann; *Script Supervisor* Jean Baker; *Lyricist* Sammy Cahn;
*Choreographer* LeRoy Prinz; *Orchestrator* Leo Shuken; *Color
Consultants* Natalie Kalmus, Mitchell Kovaleski; *Stills* Pat Clark;
*Orchestrator* Sidney Cutner; *Dialogue Director* Herschel
Daugherty; *Camera Operator* Al Green; *Grip* Charles Harris;
*Gaffer* Charles O'Bannon; *Songs,* "It's A Great Feeling," "Blame
My Absent-Minded Heart," "At the Café Rendezvous," "That Was

A Big Fat Lie," "There's Nothing Rougher Than Love," "Give Me a Song With a Beautiful Melody," "Fiddle-dee-dee."

## Synopsis:

Full of guest celebrity appearances.

Ronald Reagan has a cameo part in picture in which Dennis Morgan and Jack Carson encounter difficulties finding a director for their upcoming picture. In the film, the idea of having to work with carson causes stars to faint and all directors refuse the job. Carson decides to direct it himself. He selects a waitress (played by Doris Day) as his co-star. She goes home to a small town to marry Jeff (who looks like, and is, Errol Flynn). Reagan's appearance comes when Carson sits in a barber shop moaning to the man in the next chair. It is occupied by a listening Reagan.

## Reviews:

"A gay, light-hearted session of fun kidding Hollywood and picture making....Writers set it up with funny dialog and situations and David Butler's direction belts it along at a fast pace to show off the broad antics...Ronald Reagan has his moments with (Jack) Carson." *Daily Variety* (July 26, 1949); "...a sparkling score with six bright new songs, and some fine dancing, could hardly fail to be good entertainment....it's lots of fun and should be successful in any location." *The Hollywood Reporter* (July 26, 1949); "Take a story about Hollywood, kid it, add a little ham, throw in handfuls of surprise seasoning, serve hot on tuneful platters and you've got a dish that can't miss." *The Los Angeles Examiner* (Sara Hamilton, August 20, 1949)

## Notes:

Filmed from August 20 to October 16, 1948 on the Warner lot.
Negative cost of the production was $1,452,000. It earned domestic rentals of $2,059,000 and an additional $654,000 from foreign markets. The total world box-office take was $5,900,000.
A musical-comedy taking place in the Warners commissary.
Ronald Reagan had a cameo, also as himself.
The title song was nominated for an Oscar.
Producer Alex Gottlieb (1906-1988) was born in the Ukraine, brought to the United States by his parents in the 1920s, and started in motion pictures by writing for the screen. He became an associate producer at Universal when the studio signed Abbott and Costello for a series of comedies. In 1941 he supervised the release

of the first three A&C comedies, *Buck Privates, In the Navy* and *Hold That Ghost*. All were tremendous hits throughout the nation and elevated the comedy team to the top position of most potent box-office stars for 1941. By the mid-1940s Gottlieb branched out to serve as Producer on other types of films including *Hollywood Canteen* (1944), *Cinderella Jones* (1946) and three Reagan features: *Stallion Road, That Hagen Girl* and *The Girl From Jones Beach*. Besides continuing to produce Abbott and Costello films in the 1950s (*Jack and the Beanstalk, Meet Captain Kidd*) he also worked on Bob Hope's *I'll Take Sweden* (1965), the Elvis Presley *Frankie and Johnny* (1966) and his last effort *The Great Sex War* (1969).

Dennis Morgan (born Stanley Morner, 1908-1994) came to Hollywood in 1935 and by the time he ended his active career thirty years later, had appeared in nearly 60 films. He sang in *The Great Ziegfeld* (1936) and had roles in *Navy Blue and Gold* (1937), *Men With Wings* (1938), *The Fighting 69th*. (1940), and opposite Ginger Rogers in *Kitty Foyle* (1940). It was Warner Bros. that changed his name to Dennis Morgan and cast him in assortment of supporting and starring roles in a succession of varied films that included *Bad Men of Missouri* (1941), *God Is My Co-Pilot* (1945) and *Christmas in Connecticut (1945)*. In the late 1940s Morgan and Jack Carson were teamed by the studio for several films in an effort to recreate the comedy chemistry that had served Bob Hope and Bing Crosby so well through their "Road" pictures. Morgan continued to act into the 1950s but the quality of assignments diminished until he retired in 1956 after a part in *Uranium Boom*. Over the next two decades Morgan would make an occasional appearance and was seen in a cameo in his last effort, *Won Ton Ton, the Dog Who Saved Hollywood* (1976).

# Hasty Heart

**release date: December 2, 1949**          **running time: 102-105 minutes**

**Cast:**  Ronald Reagan, Patricia Neal, Richard Todd, Anthony Nichols, Howard Marion-Crawford, Ralph Michael, John Sherman, Alfie Bass, Orland Martins, Sam Kydd

**Credits:      Associated British Pictures Corp.-Warner Bros.**

*Producer* Alex Boyd; *Director* Vincent Sherman; *Writer* Ranald MacDougall; *Based on the play* "The Hasty Heart" by John Patrick and *Produced* by Howard Lindsay and Russel Crouse;

*Cinematography* Wilkie Cooper; *Music* Jack Beaver; *Editor* Edward B. Jarvis; *Art Direction* Terence Verity; *Costumes* Peggy Henderson; *Sound* Harold V. King, Cecil Thornton; *Production Manager* Gerry Mitchell; *Makeup* Bob Clark, A.G. Scott; *Assistant Director* Terry Hunter; *Musical Director* Louis Levy; *Camera Operator* Arthur Graham; *Continuity* Joan Wyatt

## Synopsis:

*The Hasty Heart* is set in Burma, 1945. Young Scottish soldier Lachie (Richard Todd) is wounded in a Japanese ambush and is rushed to a field hospital. His doctor realises he has only a few weeks to live as his remaining kidney is failing-but he thinks it best not to tell him. Instead he asks Ward Sister Margaret Parker (Patricia Neal) to tell the other soldiers on the ward, and request that they make the boy's last few weeks as happy and fulfilled as possible. Unfortunately, "Lackie" is not an easy man to like or befriend. He's cold, dour, proud and aloof. He rebuffs all his fellow patient's offers of friendship. "Yank" (Ronald Reagan), who is recovering from an attack of malaria, and Sister Margaret, use all their ingenuity to reach "Lackie", who comes from a loveless and bleak background. He cannot relate to others, but an impromptu twenty first birthday party seems to do the trick. "Lackie" feels he has real friends around him for the first

time in his life when he is presented with a new Scottish uniform. Then he overhears that he is dying, and that his new friends have known all along. His happiness is shattered and he reverts to his former bitter self, resenting what he takes as pity from the other men. He is offered the choice of remaining in the hospital where he would die surrounded by friends, or of returning to Scotland where he could spend his remaining days alone. Even though Lackie has already made known, he has no one waiting for him back home, he decideds to leave anyway.

Yank explodes with anger, telling Lackie he is lucky to have anyone willing to stick with him at all.

Lachie's belief that "sorrow is born in the hasty heart" comes to see that he was too swift to reject the men and Sister Margaret. He stays in Burma to die amongst those who care about him.

## Reviews:

"Reagan and his fellow patients achieve an offhand naturalness that maintains them as distinct individuals." *Newsweek* (December 1949); "One of the most barefaced tearjerkers ever concocted." *The New Republic* (January 1950); "a good performance by Richard Todd and a notable appearance by Ronald Reagan in a British film." *Films and the Second World War* Roger Manvell (New Jersey; A.S. Barnes, 1974); "Ronald Reagan and Patricia Neal....are in good form. The former is naturally at home playing the part of a Yank ambulance driver." *Variety* (reviewed in England September 21, 1949); ". . . comes to the screen as a tremendously effective motion picture....Reagan plays the Yank with the exact amount of gusto such a character should have in a British outpost hospital." *Variety* (American review December 7, 1949); "Mr. Todd gives a deeply touching picture of a man whose short and lonely life is eventually enriched by fleeting friendships.....the film has a richness and vitality of characterization which gives it deep appeal." *The New York Times* (January 21, 1950); "This is a fine motion picture....Yank played so efficiently by Ronald Reagan...Ronnie's performance is compelling, likeable and warm...Ronnie is excellent...Humor and pathos go hand in hand." *Los Angeles Examiner* (Louella O. Parsons, December 15, 1949); "Reagan puts over the Yank patient with just the right amount of U.S. gusto. It's one of his best jobs to date." *Daily Variety* (December 1, 1949); "To a rare and beautiful story the film medium brings added depth, greater meaning and a more rounded background....a vital and valid drama...There is tremendous dignity to his (Vincent Sherman) work-and this, we think, is the salient feature of the fine picture...Reagan's performance of the American is a warm and human characterization, made so as much by the actor's persuasive talent as his own genial and likeable personality." *The Hollywood Reporter* (December 1, 1949)

## Notes:

Started filming on December 16, 1948 at Britain's Elstree Studios. In production for nine weeks (45 days) until March 31, 1949. Despite many problems during the shoot, it ran only five days over the allotted schedule.

Budgeted at $1,000,000 the final negative cost came to $934,000. The film returned domestic rentals of $1,315,000 and an additional $1,036,000 from foreign markets.

Reagan paid $3500 a week.

The original play, which opened on Broadway in January, had a six-month run in 1945.

In February 1945 the trades reported that MGM was buying the screen rights to the play and had Robert Montgomery set for the lead role.

Richard Todd was nominated for an Oscar in the Best Actor category. The film won Golden Globes for "most promising newcomer" Richard Todd and for "best film promoting international understanding." Todd was also nominated for a best actor Golden Globe. The Writers Guild of America (WGA) nominated Ranald MacDougall for his work on this production.

Dublin-born newcomer, Richard Todd (1919- ) had a film career that included 50 films over 40 years. After service in World War II as a paratrooper, the actor replaced Richard Basehart on Broadway in the stage production of *The Hasty Heart*. Before appearing in the film version of the stage play he made his screen debut in *For Them That Trespass* (1949). Based on his work in *The Hasty Heart* the actor was signed to appear in a succession of British and American films including *Interrupted Journey* (1949), Alfred Hitchcock's *Stage Fright* (1950) and *Flesh and Blood* (1950). Some of his other motion pictures were *The Story of Robin Hood and his Merrie Men* (1952) as Robin Hood, *The Sword and the Rose* (1953), *The Dam Busters* (1954), *A Man Called Peter* (1955), *D-Day the Sixth of June* (1956) and the all-star definitive war film *The Longest Day* (1962).

Director Vincent Sherman (1906- ) was born in Georgia, acted in nearly a dozen films in the early 1930s, turned to writing for the screen in 1938 and after having six of his stories turned into screenplays, became a director at Warner Bros. In 1939 with his first credit being *The Return of Doctor X*. Between 1939 and 1967 he directed 30 films including *The Man Who Talked Too Much* (1940), *All Through the Night* (1942), *Adventures of Don Juan* (1948), *Lone Star* (1952), *The Young Philadelphians* (1959) and *Ice Palace* (1960).

English-born, 4th billed Anthony Nicholls (1902-1977) who played Lt. Colonel Dunn, had nearly 50 screen credits in a career that ended with a part in *The Omen* (1976). The character actor began appearing in supporting roles after World War II and hit his stride in the early 1950s. Some of his better-known films include *Man on the Run* (1948), *The Woman With No Name* (1950), *Happy Ever After* (1954), *Dunkirk* (1958), *Seven Keys* (1961), *A Man for All Seasons* (1966), *Battle For Britain* (1969) and O Lucky Man! *(1979)*.

After this production, Reagan sought to star in the western, *Ghost*

*Mountain.* For years he had wanted to be the star of a big-budget Western and despite a great deal of lobbying by the actor, Warner Bros. decided to cast Errol Flynn for the oater that was released in 1950 under the title, *Rocky Mountain.* This was done despite the fact that Reagan "discovered" the script at the studio and personally made management aware of its potential.

Disturbed by the slight that was no reward for his loyalty to the studio, Reagan had his contract renegotiated allowing him to work at other film companies. His next project was to have been Universal's *Fugitive from Terror.* In June of 1949 a broken leg suffered at a charity baseball game, led to six weeks of hospitalization and forced the actor to bow out of the project. Due to the serious injury Reagan also lost out on the starring role in the Columbia comedy *And Baby Makes Three.*

In 1949 Reagan was elected chairman of the Motion Picture Industrial Council.

The British version at 107 minutes, was slightly longer than the American print.

The Hollywood premier was held on December 14, 1949.

Competition at the nation's screens included: *On the Town* (MGM) musical starring Gene Kelly and Frank Sinatra; *My Foolish Heart* (RKO) with Dana Andrews and Susan Hayward and *Malaya* (MGM) an adventure story with Spencer Tracy and James Stewart.

In the 1950s *The Hasty Heart* was adapted for television. It was first telecast on November 2, 1953 on the *Broadway Theater Television* program, then presented as a new production starring Don Murray and Jackie Cooper on the *Dupont Show of the Month* on December 22, 1958. In September 1983 a cable network presented a repeat showing of the 1982 Los Angeles stage production of *The Hasty Heart* that starred television actors Gregory Harrison and Cheryl Ladd.

# Louisa

release date: August 21, 1950          running time: 90 minutes

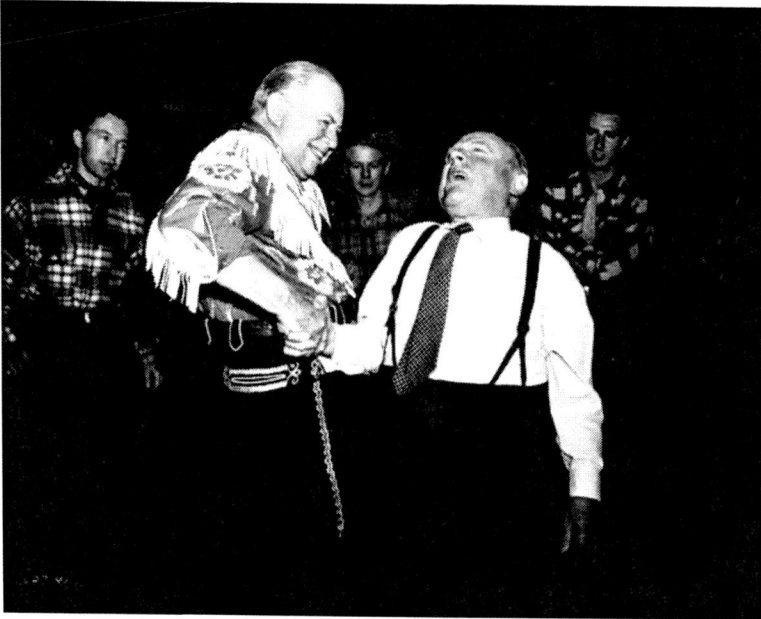

**Cast:** Ronald Reagan, Charles Coburn, Ruth Hussey, Edmund Gwenn, Spring Byington, Piper Laurie, Scotty Beckett, Jimmy Hunt, Connie Gilchrist, Willard Waterman, Marjorie Crossland, Martin Milner, Terry Frost, Dave Willock, Neal Dodd, Ann Pearce, Bill Clauson, Chuck Courtney, John Cullum, George Eldredge, Frank Ferguson, Scott Groves, Dell Henderson, Sherry Jackson, Howard Keiser, Richard Mickelson, Robert J. Miles, William Newell, Diana Norris, Donna Norris, Eddie Parker, Laura Kasley Brooks, William H. O'Brien, Barbara Wittlinger, George Washburn, Bob Bowman, Gay Gayle, Scotty Groves

**Credits:**          **Universal International Pictures.**

*Director* Alexander Hall; *Producer* Robert Arthur; *Cinematography* Maury Gertsman; *Writer* Stanley Roberts; *Music* Frank Skinner; *Editor* Milton Carruth; *Art Direction* Robert F. Boyle,  Bernard Herzbrun; *Set Decorations* Russell A. Gausman,  Ruby R. Levitt; *Costumes* Rosemary Odell; *Production Manager* Howard Christie; *Assistant Director* Joseph E. Kenney; *Makeup* Olga Collings, Joan

St. Oegger, Bud Westmore; *Sound* Glenn E. Anderson, Leslie I. Carey; *Special Effects* David S. Horsley; *Camera Operator* Harry Davis; *Script Supervisor* Dorothy Hughes; *Still Photographer* Bert Anderson; *Gaffer* John Brooks; *Grip* Russ Franks

## Synopsis:

Louisa Norton (Spring Byington) is a cheerful, fussy grandmother intent on the pursuit of a pair of elderley, but spirited swains.

Hal Norton (Ronald Reagan) is her son, a genial, middle-aged architect. He is happily married to Meg Norton (Ruth Hussey), has a pretty daughter, Cathy (Piper Laurie) and earns a good living. He is comfortable until his mother suddenly descends for a visit. The tension builds steadily. Hal suggests she joins a ladie's club, but when setting out to do so, she bumps into local grocer Mr Hammond (Edmund Gwenn). He charms her with his knowledge of gourmet cooking.

As romance blossoms between the elderly pair, Hal begins to object. He believes the grocer is after his mother's money. Nevertheless, he is invited to dinner and finds he has a rival for Louisa's affection, Mr Burnside (Charles Coburn).. Burnside is Hal's boss.

As Burnside makes inroads in his courting of Louisa, Mr Hammond becomes increasingly angry.

At a country club gathering the two rivals play competitive games. Burnside gets the upper hand at every turn. Louisa is unhappy, feeling Hal's boss is too rough on the gentle grocer. She consoles Mr Hammond.

Burnside hires a detective to investigate Hammond's past life and finds out that he has been married four times before. Eventually Louisa finds out that Mr Hammond loved his wife so much that they they had a marriage ceremony every ten years and called theselves by other names each time. This romantic disclosure beguiles Louisa and she agrees to become the second Mrs Hammond.

## Reviews:

"...a lot of fun for family audiences, particularly the middle-aged or older ticket buyers..." *Variety* (May 31, 1950); "A jovial little picture. . . a thoroughly congenial family comedy in this iconoclastic little film...Ronald Reagan is amusingly befuddled as the lady's anxious son...It's good fun for all." *The New York Times* (October 25, 1950); "Best little rib tickler to come along in months....Ronnie Reagan couldn't be more charming as the harassed son." *The Los Angeles Examiner* (Dorothy Manners, September 2, 1950); "...A young-in-heart delight dedicated to the dictum that life begins at sixty...genial, heart-warming story....Mercifully free of sentimentality." *The Universal Story.* Clive Hirschhorn (Octopus Books; London, 1983); "...a gay and different comedy whose novel subject matter alone should assure it of enthusiastic response...Ronald Reagan's genial make-believe in the part of the harassed young architect whose very career is shaken by his mother's love life is a decided factor in the success of *Louisa.*" *The Hollywood Reporter* (May 31, 1950)

## Notes:

Filming commenced in late January 1950 and ended thirty-five days later (on March 4th), at a cost of $792,954.

First film in new five year-five picture contract with Universal. Reagan was paid $75,000 a film or $7,500 a week for ten weeks. Co-star, Charles Coburn also received a salary of $75,000.

Reagan's first film for the studio was to have been a crime thriller with Ida Lupino (*Fugitive From Terror*). On June 18, 1949 while participating in a charity baseball game with other Hollywood celebrities, the actor broke his leg in six places and was in a hospital, in traction, for over three months.

Boston-bred Alexander Hall (1894-1968) whose film career extended from 1914 to 1956 started out in the industry working as both an actor and second unit director. In the mid-1920s, the man who was thrust on the stage at the age of four, and was a veteran of World War I, added editor to his resume. Hall devoted 24 years of his life to directing, helming 39 features and is best remembered for his urbane, sophisticated comedies. The one-time husband of actress Lola Lane had several notable films including Shirley Temple's *Little Miss Marker, Here Comes Mr. Jordan* and *Bedtime Story* (both 1941), *My Sister Eileen* (1942), *The Great Lover* (1949), *Up Front* (1951) and *Forever Darling* (1956).

Character-actor Charles Coburn (1877-1961) entered the world of motion pictures in 1933 at the age of 56. In the late teens and up to the mid-1930s the rotund Coburn with the perfect Southern demeanor acted on Broadway and other stage venues with his wife. He turned to film after her death. The actor appeared in 71 motion pictures, often in the part of a doctor. He won an Oscar for his supporting role in *The More the Merrier* (1943). Coburn's better-known films are *Yellow Jack* (1938), *The Story of Alexander Graham*

*Bell* (1939), *Edison, the Man* (1940), *The Devil and Miss Jones* (1941), *Heaven Can Wait* (1943), *Rhapsody in Blue* (1945), *Gentlemen Prefer Blondes* (1953) and his last substantial role *John Paul Jones* (1959). Coburn also appeared with Reagan in *King's Row* as the sadistic doctor who amputates both of the character's legs.

Third-billed Ruth Hussey (1914-  ) was signed by MGM for their B-films unit and made her film debut in 1937. The actress had supporting roles in episodes of the Andy Hardy, Maisie and Thin Man series and was nominated for an Oscar for Best Supporting Actress for her fast-paced characterization in *The Philadelphia Story* (1940). She also appeared in *Tennessee Johnson* (1943), *The Uninvited* (1944), *The Great Gatsby* (1949), and her last film *The Facts of Life* (1960).

Edmund Gwen (born Edmund Kellaway, 1875-1959), a native of the United Kingdom, made appearances in over 100 British and American films. A protégé of George Bernard Shaw, Gwen began performing on the London stage in 1895. After service in World War I he entered silent motion pictures and emigrated to the United States. Some of his better known films include *Sylvia Scarlett* (1935), *Anthony Adverse* (1936), *A Yank at Oxford* (1938), *Pride and Prejudice* (1940), *Foreign Correspondent* (1940), *Lassie Come Home* (1943) *The Keys of the Kingdom* (1944), and *Miracle on 34th. Street* (1947) in which he portrayed old Kris Kringle opposite a very young Natalie Wood. Gwen won an Oscar for his role as Kringle.

Spring Byington (1886-1971) began appearing in plays in 1900 in her native Colorado. Twenty years later she was brought to the Broadway stage by famed showman George S. Kaufman, and made her motion picture debut in 1931. By 1935 she was featured in up to eight films a year including Universal's *Werewolf of London* and MGM's *Mutiny on the Bounty*. The actress who had roles in over ninety motion pictures was nominated for an Oscar for her work in *You Can't Take It With You* (1938). Some of her better-known features include *Palm Springs* (1936), *Off to the Races* (1937), *Jezebel* (1938), *Meet John Doe* (1941), *Heaven Can Wait* (1943) and *Angels in the Outfield* (1951). As films roles decreased in the 1950s, the loveable matronly type switched to television to star in the long-running (1954-61) comedy *December Bride*.

This film marked the motion picture debut of Piper Laurie (born Rosetta Jacques, 1932- ). Universal signed the starlet right out of high school. The actress who appeared in over sixty features was nominated for three Academy Awards, the first for playing the role of Paul Newman's girlfriend in *The Hustler.*

The film was nominated for the Oscar for Best Sound.

World premiere held in Illinois on August 21, 1950. The film opened in Los Angeles on September 7th and went into general release on October 24th.

Competition at the nation's screens included: *The Good Humor Man* (Columbia) comedy with Jack Carson and Lola Albright; *The Happy Years* (MGM) comedy with Dean Stockwell and Darryl Hickman and the Warner Bros. Western *This Side of the Law* with Viveca Lindfors and Kent Smith.

Theater attendance in the United States for 1950, due largely to the effect of television, slipped by over 30% from the prior year to 60,000,000 a week.

# Storm Warning

release date: March 3, 1951                    running time: 93 minutes

**Cast:** Ginger Rogers, Ronald Reagan, Doris Day, Steve Cochran, Hugh
Sanders. Lloyd Gough, Raymond Greenleaf, Ned Glass, Paul E.
Burns, Walter Baldwin, Lynn Whitney, Stuart Randall, Sean
McClory, Lillian Albertson, Paul Brinegar, Chick Chandler, Leo
Cleary, Charles J. Conrad, Ned Davenport, Don Dillaway, King
Donovan, Ross Elliott, Gene Evans, Pat Flaherty, Alex Gerry,
Dabbs Greer, Harry Harvey, Edward Hearn, Len Hendry, Lloyd
Jenkins, David Le Grand, Frank Marlowe, Charles Marsh, David
McMahon, Charles Phillips, Grandon Rhodes, Dewey Robinson,
Joe Smith, Charles Sullivan, Dale Van Sickle, Anthony Warde,
Duke Watson, Charles Watts, Tom Wells, Robert Williams,Janet
Barrett, Walter Bacon, Bill Welsh, Tommy Walker, George Lloyd,
Fern Berry, Mike Donovan, Carl Harbough, Mary Hokanson, Joe
Dougherty, Dick Anderson, Bob Stevenson, Bob O'Neill, Lee
Roberts, Ed Peil Sr., Doug Carter, Norman Field, Michael McHale,
Howard Mitchell, Frank McCarroll, Mike Lally

**Credits:**                    **Warner Bros.**

*Director* Stuart Heisler; *Producer* Jerry Wald; *Cinematography* Carl E. Guthrie; *Writers* Richard Brooks, Daniel Fuchs; *Music* Daniele Amfitheatrof, Max Steiner; *Editor* Clarence Kolster; *Art Direction* Leo K. Kuter; *Set Decorator* G.W. Bernsten; *Sound* Leslie G. Hewitt; *Assistant Director* Chuck Hansen; *Costumes* Milo Anderson; *Makeup* Perc Westmore, Ray Forman, Frank Westmore; *Orchestrator* Maurice De Packh; *Musical Director* Ray Heindorf; *Script Supervisor* Howard Hohler; *Camera Operator* Lou Jennings; *Still Photographer* Eugene Ritchie; *Grip* Herschel Brown; *Gaffer* Vic Johnson

## Synopsis:

Focal character is New York fashion model Marsha Mitchell (Ginger Rogers), who visits her newly married sister, Lucy (Doris Day) in a small Southern town. Soon after her arrival on a night bus Marsha witnesses a group of Ku Klux Klan members dragging a man from jail and killing him. Two of the men remove their hoods and Marsha sees Charlie Barr (Hugh Sanders) and the killer Hank Rice (Steve Cochran). When she reaches her sister's home she discovers that Hank is Lucy's husband.

Pregnant Lucy, very much in love with Hank, begs her sister to forget the incident.

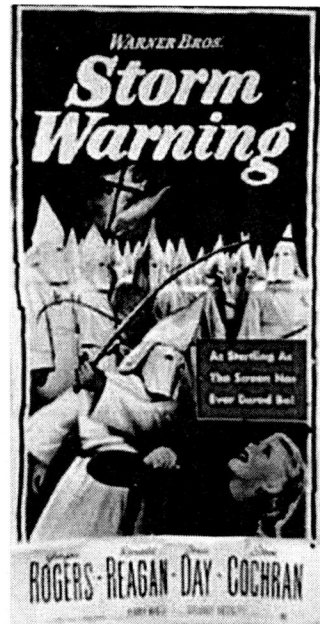

Marsha reluctantly agrees, but District Attorney Burt Rainey (Ronald Reagan) learns that Marsha witnessed the killing and subpoenas her to appear in court. Rainey is determined to wipe out the local KKK, but Marsha denies recognising any of the men.

The Klansmen celebrate their victory and Hank gets drunk. Marsha packs to leave. Hank makes a pass at her, and when Lucy intercedes he beats both women.

Marsha now knows just how violent Hank is and resloves to turn him over to the police.

He kidnaps her and takes her to a KKK meeting. Charlie Barr decides to have her flogged out of town.

Rainey arrives at the meeting just in time, accompanied by Lucy and the police.

Rainey is able to identify even the hooded members. Barr tells Rainey that the death of the man dragged from jail had been accidental, but that Hank fired the shot. Hank panics and fires his gun to stop Barr talking, but the bullet hits Lucy. Hank is gunned down. Barr is arrested and the rest of the Klansmen disappear from the meeting.

## Reviews:

". . . weaves a hard-hitting plot around violence, murder, and the Ku Klux Klan . . country prosecutor is given a lot of sock by Ronald Reagan." *Variety* (December 6, 1950) "This is an intelligent film, marked by the strong performances of the ensemble...Reagan is effective as the public defender...He is earnest without being self-righteous." *TV Guide;* "Mr. Reagan is as pat and pedestrian as any well-drilled stock company . . . may have some shocking impact, but it doesn't go into the more dramatic 'hows' and 'whys.' *The New York Times* (March 3, 1951); "Steve Cochran is brilliant in probably the most hateful characterization of the season....Reagan's District Attorney is more along the lines of the sturdy, upright young man we have come to expect of him. And that isn't bad." *The Los Angeles Examiner* (Dorothy Manners, January 27, 1951)

## Notes:

Filming started on November 15, 1949 in Corona, Calif.

While in production the feature was known as *Storm Center.*

Negative cost was $1,212,000. It generated $1,192,000 in domestic film rentals and a further $582,000 from overseas markets.

On May 10, 1949, dissatisfied with his selection of roles, Reagan re-negotiated his 4th contract with Warner Bros. He was now able to accept offers from other studios while appearing in only one film a year for the studio. This compromise reduced his guaranteed salary by 50% to $75,000 per feature (at the rate of $6250 a week for 12 weeks) and was structured to cover three motion pictures over a three year period. This new contract covered the actor's next three Warner entries: *Storm Warning, She's Working Her Way Through College* and *The Winning Team.* Within weeks the actor was free to sign a 5 year-$75,000 a film contract with Universal.

Doris Day (born Doris Mary Ann Von Kappelhoff, 1924- ) when teamed with leading men Cary Grant, Rock Hudson and James Garner in a succession of hit comedies (*Pillow Talk, Lover Come Back, That Touch of Mink, The Thrill of it All, Move Over, Darling, Send Me No Flowers* and *Do Not Disturb)*, became the biggest female box-office star of the decade of the sixties. A car accident as a teenager vanquished any thought of a career as a dancer and brought forth her singing talents. By the mid-1940s she was touring the country as the singer for the Bob Crosby and Les Brown Orchestras. Day signed with Warner Bros. in 1948 and became a credible actress and box-office attraction in the 1950s starring opposite Kirk Douglas in *Young Man With a Horn* (1950), James Cagney in *The West Point Story* (1950) and Gordon MacRea in *On Moonlight Bay* (1951). She starred as the title character in the Western-musical *Calamity Jane* (1953), was the doomed Ruth Etting in the biography *Love Me or Leave Me* (1955), played in Hitchcock's remake of *The Man Who Knew Too Much* (1956) with Jimmy Stewart and was seen opposite Clark Gable in *Teacher's Pet* (1958). After a 40 picture film career, Day retired from the screen in 1968 and immediately starred in her own comedy television series which ran for five years (1968-73), *The Doris Day Show.*

Director Stuart Heisler (1896-1979) started out as a film editor in the early 1920s then segued into directing in 1936. He is credited with having edited over 30 films and directed 25 for the big screen. As an editor Heisler worked on the original *Stella Dallas* (1925), *The Kid From Spain* (1932), *Roman Scandals* (1933) and *Kid Millions* (1934). Before turning to directing fulltime he also edited Mae West's *Klondike Annie* (1936) and the W.C. Fields comedy *Poppy* (1936). Some of his more popular directorial efforts were *Among the Living* (1941), *Along Came Jones* (1945) starring Gary Cooper, *Tulsa* (1949) with Susan Hayward, *Chain Lightning* (1950) and *The Lone Ranger* (1956). In the 1950s Heisler turned to television by directing numerous episodes of the Westerns *Lawman, Rawhide, The Virginian* and *The Dakotas.*

The role played by Ginger Rogers was initially offered to Lauren Bacall.

From 1945 to 1967 actor Steve Cochran (1917-1965) appeared in 40 films. Starting in the theater he was signed by Samuel Goldwin to come to Hollywood and menace Danny Kaye in the comedy *Wonder Man* (1945) and again work with the comedian in *The Kid from Brooklyn* (1946). In between the Goldwyn films, Cochran worked in two Boston Blackie B-detective mysteries and in 1949 worked with James Cagney in Warner Bros. crime classic, *White Heat*. Other notable features that he appeared in were *The Best Years of Our Lives* (1946), *Dallas* (1950), *Back to God's Country* (1953) and *Deadly Companions* (1961).

Stuntman and bit-player Dale Van Sickle (1907-1977), an All-American football player at the University of Florida, appeared in well over 200 films.

The film faced competition at the nation's screens from: *For Heaven's Sake* (Fox), a comedy with Clifton Webb and Joan Bennett; *The Killer That Stalked New York* (Columbia) low budget entry with Evelyn Keyes in the lead; *Halls of Montezuma* (Fox) with Richard Widmark, *Pagan Love Song* (MGM) starring Esther Williams and Howard Keel, and *The Great Missouri Raid* (Paramount), a western starring Wendell Corey and MacDonald Carey.

# The Last Outpost

**release date: April 8, 1951**          **running time: 89 minutes**

**Cast:**   Ronald Reagan, Rhonda Fleming, Bruce Bennett, Bill Williams, Noah Beery Jr, Peter Hansen, Hugh Beaumont, Lloyd Corrigan, John Ridgely, James Burke, Iron Eyes Cody, Richard Crane, Charles Evans, Terry Frost, Harold Goodwin, Ewing Mitchell, Burt Mustin, John War Eagle, Chief Yowlachie

**Credits:**                    **Paramount**

*Director* Lewis R. Foster; *Producers* William H. Pine, William C. Thomas; *Writers* David Lang, Daniel Mainwaring; *Cinematography* Loyal Griggs; *Music* Lucien Cailliet; *Editor* Howard A. Smith; *Art Direction* Lewis H. Creber; *Set Decoration* Alfred Kegerris; *Costumes* Edith Head; *Sound* Harold Lewis; *Assistant Director* Howard Pine; *Makeup* Kay Shea, Errol K. Silvera, Paul Stanhope; *Stunts* Chuck Roberson; *Wardrobe* Chuck Keehne; *Color Consultant* Robert Brower

## Synopsis:

Confederacy forces have been intercepting gold shipments bound for the North's Union forces. Jeb Britten (Bruce Bennett) is charged with seeing the next shipment gets through. Vance (Ronald Reagan) another Union Officer, wants to make sure the Apache don't get involved in the brewing conflict. He knows they would be a danger not only to his soldiers, but to the whole Arizona Territory. When an Apache chief is shot by a renegade white, the Confederate and Union forces have to band together when they are caught in a revenge attack.

Vance is intent on saving the life of his ex-fiance, Julie (Rhonda Fleming), who is in the surrounded fort with her husband (John Ridgely).

## Reviews:

"It's sometimes humorous and well photographed at Old Tucson, but it's contrived kid stuff." *Western Films: A Complete Guide* Brian Garfield (Da Capo Paperback, 1982); "Reagan and Bennett pair excellently as the opposing brothers." *Variety* (April 11, 1951); "(F)ilmed in Technicolor with blazing arrows flying through the air and the cavalry riding hell-for-leather, a pretty endeavor it is too.....This is elementary school stuff." *The New York Times* (June 22, 1951); " ...lacks the fast-moving quality that usually helps to make a William Pine-William Thomas production look twice as good as its budget....Reagan exhibits a great deal of riding form and skill as the leader of the marauding Southern cavalry troop and carries off his role as a boldly resourceful officer with romantic charm and agreeable humor....the sweeping, hard-riding cavalry in motion stirs up the blood." *The Los Angeles Examiner* (Lynn Bowers, June 13, 1951); "Reagan, very good as the hero..." *The Paramount Story.* John Douglas Eames (Crown; London, 1985)

## Notes:

Filmed on location in Old Tucson and at the San Xavier del Bac Mission near Tucson, Arizona in October 1950 on a budget of $620,000. It generated domestic rentals of nearly $1,200,000 for the studio and was the biggest hit for the production team of Pine and Thomas.

Reagan rode his own horse, Tarbaby.

In a career that spanned nearly forty years (1920-1959) Lewis R. Foster (1898-1974) worked as a writer, second unit director, director, composer and producer. He has 59 writing credits for the screen and has directed 36 features including *Men O'War* (1929), *Armored Car* (1937), *El Paso* (1949, also wrote the screenplay) and *The Eagle and the Hawk* (1950). Foster also directed Reagan in *Hong Kong* and *Tropic Zone* and in the late fifties, helmed episodes of the television series *The Adventures of Jim Bowie, Zorro* and *Swamp Fox*.

Popularly known as "the Queen of Technicolor" Rhonda Fleming (born Marilyn Louis, 1923- ) had a career that included over fifty motion pictures and starring roles opposite most of the leading men of the late 1940s and the 1950s including Gregory Peck, Charlton Heston, Kirk Douglas, Rock Hudson, Robert Mitchum, Bob Hope, Bing Crosby and Burt Lancaster. Some of the five-times married actress' most popular films included *Spellbound* (1945), *Out of the Past* (1947), *Little Egypt* (1951), *Pony Express* (1953), *Gunfight at the O.K. Corral* (1957) and *The Big Circus* (1959). She worked with Reagan in four features.

Second-male lead Bruce Bennett (born Herman Brix, 1906- ) appeared in over 120 films (first as Brix then Bennett) and was a shot-putter in the 1932 Olympics that were held in Los Angeles. When MGM auditioned athletes for the role of Tarzan, Bennett was one of the finalists but lost out to fellow Olympian Johnny Weissmuller. In 1935, after having bit-roles in a dozen films, Edgar Rice Burroughs personally selected Bennett for his own production of Tarzan, *The New Adventures of Tarzan*. Republic then signed the 6' 3" well-muscled actor for a number of their serial adventures including *Flying Fists* (1937), *The Lone Ranger* and *Fighting Devil Dogs* (both 1938) and *Daredevils of the Red Circle* (1939). Often appearing in up to 20 films a year, the actor moved up to A-features and was seen opposite Joan Crawford in *Mildred Pierce* (1945), Humphrey Bogart in both *Dark Passage* (1947) and *The Treasure of Sierra Madre* (1948), Gary Cooper in *Task Force* (1949) Jimmy Stewart in *Strategic Air Command* (1955) and Elvis Presley in *Love Me Tender* (1956) .

Hugh Beaumont (1909-1982) from Lawrence, Kansas made nearly 90 films over a 25 year span of time (1940-1965), yet is best remembered as Theodore "Beaver" Cleaver's wise, understanding father in the television series *Leave It to Beaver* (1957-1963). Some of his better remembered motion pictures included *Wake Island* (1942), *The Fallen Sparrow* (1943), *Objective Burma!* (1945), *The Blue Dahlia* (1946) and the science fiction flick *Lost Continent* (1951).

Both Bill Williams (born Herman Katt, 1916-1992) and Chief Yowlachie (born Daniel Simmons, 1891-1966) spent much of their careers typecast in Western films. Beginning with a role in the war flick *Thirty Seconds Over Tokyo* (1944) Williams worked in over 70 films until he retired from the screen in 1981. His better-known Westerns include *Fighting Man of the Plains* (1949), *Son of Paleface* (1952), *The Hallelujah Trail* (1965) and John Wayne's *Rio Lobo* (1970), which was also director Howard Hawks' last effort. Williams also played the lead role in the short-lived television series *The Adventures of Kit Carson* (1951). Yowlachie, born on the Yakima Reservation in the state of Washington, also made over 70 films including DeMille's *Northwest Mounted Police* (1940), Wayne's *Red River* (1948), Bob Hope's *Paleface* (1948), *Tulsa* (1949), *Winchester '73* (1950), *Lone Star* (1952) and *The FBI Story* (1959).

Competition at the nation's screens came from the comedy *Half Angel* (Fox) with Loretta Young and Joseph Cotton, the Ann Blyth toplined comedy *Katie Did It* (Universal), *The First Legion* (United Artists) a Charles Boyer dark drama and *He Ran All the Way* (United Artists) another drama starring John Garfield and Shelley Winters.

When shown in some parts of Los Angeles the Western was part of a double-bill with the Republic oater *Thunder in God's Country* starring Rex Allen.

Reissued in 1962, the film's title was changed to *Cavalry Charge.*

# Bedtime for Bonzo

**release date: April 5, 1951**                    **running time: 83 minutes**

**Cast:** Ronald Reagan, Diana Lynn, Walter Slezak, Lucille Barkley, Jesse White, Herbert Heyes, Herb Vigran, Harry Tyler, Edward Clark, Edward Gargan, Joel Friedkin, Brad Browne, Elizabeth Flournoy, Howard Banks, Perc Launders, Brad Johnson, Billy Mauch, Ann Tyrrell, Ginger Anderson, Leslie Banning, Tommy Bond, Bridget Carr, Larry Carr, Larry Crane, John Daheim, Irmgard Dawson, Johnny Duncan, Jack Gargan, Ed Jarga, Philo McCullough, Chip Perrin, Midge Ware, Steve Wayne, Larry Williams

**Credits: Universal**

*Director* Frederick De Cordova; *Producer* Michael Kraike; *Writers* Ted Berkman, Raphael Blau; *Cinematography* Carl E. Guthrie; *Music* Frank Skinner; *Editor* Ted J. Kent; *Art Direction* Bernard Herzbrun, Eric Orbom; *Sound* Leslie I. Carey, Joe Lapis; *Set Decorators* Russell A. Gausman, Ruby R. Levitt; *Costumes* Rosemary Odell; *Makeup* Joan St. Oegger, Bud Westmore;

## Synopsis:

Peter Boyd (Ronald Reagan) is a professor of psychology who has a thief for a father. Partly to defend himself from libelous remarks, but also to impress Dean Tillinghurst (Herbert Heyes), whose daughter, Valerie (Lucille Barkley) he wants to marry, he sets out to prove that environment is a more important factor in life than heredity.

He borrows a chimp called Bonzo from Professor Neumann (Walter Slezak), and intends to raise it as if it were human.

He hires a nurse, Jane (Diana Lynn) to play the role of mother. Their lives become fairly normal. Valerie becomes jealous. Bonzo begins to become unruly when he senses his home life is under threat.

Bonzo is fascinated with jewelry and he begins to steal. He is jailed and Peter is accused of training the chimp to steal.

Bonzo returns the jewels and clears Peter, who marries Jane and gives Bonzo a permanent home.

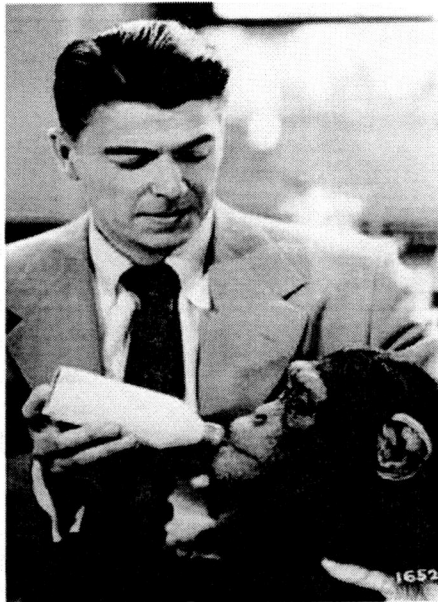

## Reviews:

"...will amuse the general audience.....beguiling nonsense with enough broad situations to gloss over plot." *Variety* (January 17, 1951); "The movie is merry, the acting energetic. Nobody proves anything and Bonzo earns all the laughs." *Motion Picture* (March 1951); "(I)t is a minor bit of fun yielding a respectable amount of laughs but nothing actually, over which to wax ecstatic." *The New York Times* (April 6, 1951); "Bonzo's antics are so thoroughly delightful that audiences take him to their hearts at once....a real threat in store." *The Los Angeles Examiner* (Shirle Duggan, March 17, 1951)

**Notes:**   *"I fought a losing battle against a scene-stealer with a built-in edge-he was a chimpanzee."*

Filmed in November 1950 on a budget of $800,000. It proved successful enough to spawn a sequel, *Bonzo Goes to College*

(1952) which starred Maureen O'Sullivan, Edmund Gwen and Charles Drake.

Reagan earned $75,000 for starring opposite the chimp in his second Universal project. The actor refused to do the third and fourth films, *Fine Day* (aka *Steel Town)* and *Just Across the Street,* due to poor, undeveloped scripts. He ended his contract with Universal after starring in *Law and Order.*

New York City-born director Frederick De Cordova (1910-2001) started as a dialogue director in several films including *Between Two Worlds, To Have and Have Not* (both 1944) and Errol Flynn's Western *San Antonio* (1945) before turning fulltime to direction of low budget entries. His films during this period included *Too Young to Know* (1945), *For the Love of Mary* (1948), *The Desert Hawk* (1950), *Little Egypt* (1951) and *Yankee Buccaneer* (1952). He is perhaps best remembered as director and sometimes on-stage screen presence, for over twenty years, on *The Tonight Show Starring Johnny Carson.*

Female-lead Diana Lynn (born Dolores Loehr, 1926-1971) was a child prodigy who performed at public piano recitals before the age of seven. She made her screen debut, aged thirteen, playing the piano, in *They Shall Have Music* (1939). Between 1942 and 1955 she appeared in 27 motion pictures including Ginger Rogers' *The Major and the Minor* (1942), *The Miracle at Morgan's Creek* and *Our Hearts Were Young and Gay* with Gail Russell (both 1944), the sequel *Our Hearts Were Growing Up* (1946), *My Friend Irma* (1949), *Track of the Cat* (1954) and *You're Never Too Young* (1955). She died at the age of 45, nine days after suffering a stroke.

Born in Vienna, Austria, Walter Slezak's (1902-1983) father was Metropolitan Opera star Leo Slezak. By the age of twenty the younger Slezak was already acting in German produced films. Coming to the United States in the thirties he found work on Broadway performing in an assortment of dramas and musical revues. With the onset of World War II Hollywood needed actors who could credibly portray any type of evil German official. Slezak fitted the bill with chilling roles in *Once Upon A Honeymoon* (1942), *This Land Is Mine* and *The Fallen Sparrow* (both 1943), and *Till We Meet Again* (1944). The now portly actor also had significant parts in Hitchcock's *Lifeboat* (1944), *The Spanish Main* (1945), *Sinbad the Sailor* and *Born to Kill* (both 1947), Danny Kaye's uproarious comedy *The Inspector General* (1949), *White Witch Doctor* (1953) and *Come September* (1961). From 1922 to 1972 he made nearly 50 motion pictures. Despondent over deteriorating health, Slezak took his own life in 1983.

Universal-International had previous successes with animal stars both real and imaginary including James Stewart playing a rabbit in *Harvey* and the *Francis, the Talking Mule* series of comedies. Before the film's release, the ape playing Bonzo died unexpectedly. World premiere was held in Indianapolis, Indiana.

Playing on the bottom-half of the double-bill in many areas was *Mask of the Dragon* (Lippert Pictures) starring Richard Travis and Sheila Ryan.

The film faced competition on the nation's screens from *Royal Wedding* starring Fred Astaire, *I Was A Communist for the FBI*, *Riptide* a French import starring Gerard Philipe and the lavish MGM musical *The Great Caruso* with Mario Lanza.

# Hong Kong

**release date: April 4, 1952**                  **running time: 92-94 minutes**

**Cast:**  Ronald Reagan, Rhonda Fleming, Nigel Bruce, Marvin Miller, Mary Somerville, Lowell Gilmore, Claude Allister, Danny Chang, Lee Marvin,

# Credits:        Paramount

*Director* Lewis R. Foster; *Producers* William H. Pine, William C. Thomas; *Writers* Lewis R. Foster, Winston Miller; *Music* Licien Cailliet; *Cinematography* Lionel Lindon; *Editor* Howard A. Smith; *Art Direction* Lewis H. Creber; *Set Decoration* Alfred Kegerris; *Sound* Harold Lewis, Walter Oberst; *Assistant Director* Howard Pine; *Makeup* Norman Pringle, Kay Shea; *Costumes* Edith Head; *Wardrobe Supervisor* Chuck Keehne; *Color Consultant* Robert Brower

## Synopsis:

Jeff (Ronald Reagan) is a down at heel ex-soldier. He is hard and selfish. He must escape the Communists in China. He comes across an innocent young boy, (Danny Chang) who is lost and alone. Jeff takes him with him and carries him to a mission run by an American Red Cross worker, Victoria (Rhonda Fleming). She has chartered a plane to escape to Hong Kong.

She takes them with her, but when they land they find it is impossible to get hotel accommodation. In desperation they take someone elses's booking.

Jeff, exposed to the charm of the boy and the generous nature of Victoria, begins to soften. He becomes less bitter toward life and people.

However, he also knows that the ancient Chinese idol that the boy carries is of value and he approaches an art dealer to sell it. The dealer is in league with a gang of crooks. They kidnap the child. Jeff makes a deal with them, but it all goes wrong and in the end they are all saved by the arrival of British police of Hong Kong.

Jeff decides to settle down. He marries Victoria and makes regular visits to the child in the orphanage.

## Reviews:

"Reagan gives an easy, likeable delivery to his adventure role." *Variety* (November 14, 1951); "The miracle of 'Hong Kong' .....is that the picture manages to keep going at all....another corn meal special...the stars meander around against some faked, pleasantly hued Chinese backgrounds...Foster's pedantic direction enshrouds the whole thing in deadly familiarity, harmless though it may be. Mr. Reagan plays an ex-G.I. drifter in his own solid citizen style...." *The New York Times* (April 5, 1952); "Reagan...worked hard to give a good performance in this unusual and imaginative adventure film....Danny Chang plain steals the film from his competent and attractive elders." *The Los Angeles Examiner* (Kay Proctor, March 13, 1952); "...a surefire action entry whose entertainment values, in all respects, live up to expectations....Ronald Reagan's persuasive playing of the hero contributes much toward making *Hong Kong* convincing....put together with fist rate technical resourcefulness." *The Hollywood Reporter* (November 13, 1951)

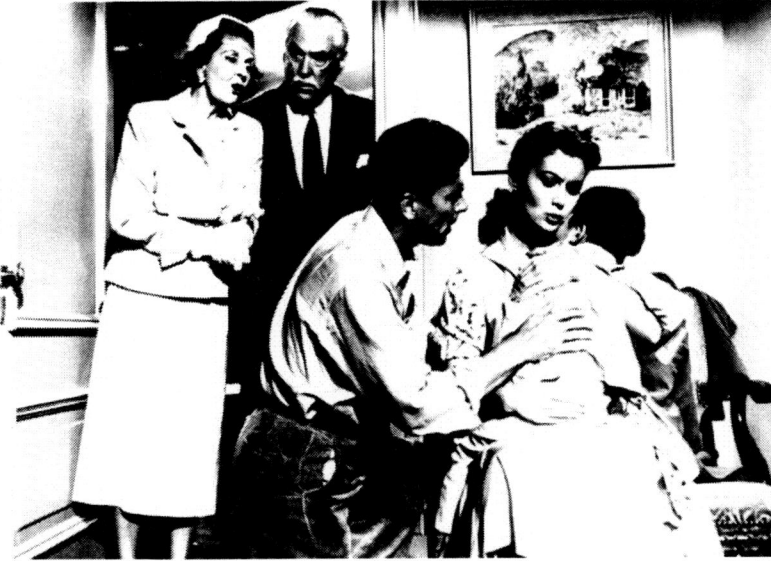

## Notes:

Reagan was paid $45,000 (at the rate of $4500 a week for 10 weeks) for this starring effort which was to have started production in late April 1951. Filmed entirely on the Paramount lot on a budget of $625,000. Rhonda Fleming was paid $30,000.

Third-billed Nigel Bruce (1895-1953) was born in Ensenada, Mexico of British parents. He worked on the London stage for a decade before journeying to Hollywood in 1929 and making the first of 77 screen appearances with his debut film *Birds of Prey* (1930). Some of his early screen work included *Stand Up and Cheer* (1934), *The Scarlet Pimpernel* (1934), *The Lonesome Pine* (1936) and *The Charge of the Light Brigade* (1936). In 1939 he played the character Dr. Watson, side-kick to Basil Rathbone's Sherlock Holmes in the first of fourteen mysteries. When Sherlock Holmes also appeared on radio as a weekly series, Bruce and his character also made the transition. In 1950 the actor worked at

RKO on Howard Hughes' *Vendetta* and in 1952 appeared in support of Charlie Chaplin in *Limelight*.

After college, character actor Marvin Miller (1913-1985) began working in the medium of radio on a local station in St. Louis. By 1945 he was in Hollywood and working on his first assignment for the James Cagney drama *Blood on the Sun*. Some of his catalogue of films include *Just Before Dawn* (1946), *Dead Reckoning* (1947), *Smuggler's Island* (1951), *The Golden Horde* (1951), *The Story of Mankind* (1957) and *Swing Shift* (1984). He is best remembered for playing Michael Anthony and dispensing a check for $1,000,000 each week for five weeks, in the television series *The Millionaire* (1955-60).

British-born Mary Somerville (1883-1972) appeared in only one other motion picture, *Mr. Peabody and the Mermaid* (1948). Her main claim to fame was that she is the mother of actor Peter Lawford.

Child-actor Danny Chang (1947- ) was born in China and came to the United States when the Communists drove the Nationalists off the mainland to the island of Formosa. He appeared in only four other films: *Battle Circus* (1953), *South Sea Woman* (1953), in support of Clark Gable and Susan Hayward in *Soldier of Fortune* (1955) and *China Doll* (1958).

When reissued in 1962 the title was changed to, *Bombs Over China*.

In the Los Angeles market this film was double billed with the Paramount Western *Flaming Feather* that starred Sterling Hayden and Forrest Tucker.

The film faced competition at the nation's screens from: *Red Mountain* (Paramount) with Alan Ladd and Lisabeth Scott; the comedy western, *Callaway Went Thataway* (MGM) starring Fred MacMurray and Dorothy McGuire, the western, *Man In the Saddle* (Columbia) with Randolph Scott, and the latest Abbott and Costello comedy *Jack and the Beanstalk* (Warners). On Broadway at the Shubert Theater, the new Lerner and Lowe musical *Paint Your Wagon* opened to near unanimous positive reviews.

# The Winning Team

release date: June 20, 1952          running time: 98-100 minutes

**Cast:**  Doris Day, Ronald Reagan, Frank Lovejoy, Eve Miller, James
Millican, Russ Tamblyn, Gordon Jones, Hugh Sanders, Frank
Ferguson, Walter Baldwin, Dorothy Adams,      Charles Horvath,
Frank McFarland, Henry Blair, Larry J. Blake, Gordon Clark, Russ
Clark, Jimmie Dodd, Tom Dugan, Bonnie Kay Eddy, Pat Flaherty,
Alan Foster, Art Gilmore, Tom Greenway, John Hedloe, Thomas
Browne Henry, William Kalvino, John Kennedy, Donald Kerr,
Frank Marlowe, Fred Millican, Robert Orrell, Arthur Page, Paul
Panzer, Kenneth Patterson, Alex Sharp, Glen Turnbull, Billy
Wayne, Allan Wood, George Sherwood, Morgan Brown, Herb
Lytten, Ralph Volkie, Harry Lauter, Tom Daley, Alay Ray, Bill
Slack, Rodney Bell, Jack Wilson, Les O'Pace, Clarence Straight,
Dick Bartell, Steve Darrell, Dick Ryan, Kay Marlowe, Frank
Scannell, Lou Manley, Jack Carr, Ralph P. Gamble, Dayton
Lummis, Billy Vernon, Jack Lemmon, Jack Kenny, Ward Brant,
Joel Ray, Joe McGuinn, Brick Sullivan, Charles Sullivan
Major Leaguers in cameo and bit roles: Bob Lemon, John
Baradino, Jerry Priddy, Peanuts Lowrey, George Metkovich, Irving
Noren, Hank Sauer, Al Zarilla, Gene Mauch

**Credits:**                    **Warner Bros.**

*Director* Lewis Seiler; *Producer* Bryan Foy; *Writers* Merwin Gerard,
Seeleg Lester, Ted Sherderman; *Cinematography* Sidney Hickox;
*Music* David Buttolph; *Editor* Alan Crosland Jr.; *Art Direction*
Douglas Bacon; *Set Decorations* William Kuehl; *Costumes* Leah
Rhodes; *Special Effects* Hans F. Koenekamp; *Makeup* Gordon Bau

**Synopsis:**

The film begins with Grover Cleveland Alexander's (Ronald
Reagan) early days as a telephone lineman in Nebraska and his first
successes in Midwest bush-league baseball in 1908. Within three
years his incredible skill as a pitcher lifts him to stardom with the
Philadelphia Phillies. During his first year with them he helps them
achieve twenty eight victories.
His luck turns when he is hit on the head and he begins suffering
dizzy spells.
During his service with the artillery in the First World War he is
exposed to thunderous noise, worsening his condition.
He begins to suffer periods of double vision, and he drinks to help
the pain. The drinking increases as his baseball career declines.
He is dismissed from the major leagues. He takes whatever jobs he

can find with semi-pro teams, but his seizures are mistaken for drunkenness. He eventualy leaves baseball and works as a sideshow attraction in a sleazy circus. His wife, Aimee (Doris Day) stands by him, and with the aid of his faithful friend, pitcher Bill Killifer (James Millican), she persuades renowned baseball manager Rogers Hornsby (Frank Lovejoy) to give Alexander another chance.

As the film of this true story reveals, Alexander did have more success when, in 1926, he became the toast of baseball when he pitched for the St Louis Cardinals against the New York Yankees at Yankee Stadium. He saved the World Series and made history, pitching against names such as Babe Ruth, Lou Gehrig and Lou Lazzeri.

## Reviews:

"(A) fair to average biopic... (with an) indifferent screenplay" *The Warner Bros. Story* Clive Hirschhorn (New York; Crown, 1979); "Seiler's direction is splendid...the tempo is absorbing and he (Seiler) draws wonderful performances from Ronald Reagan...and Doris Day...Reagan is excellent as Alex, turning in a moving characterization that reflects all the triumphs and tragedies of the hurler. Miss Day gives her finest dramatic performance to date." *The Hollywood Reporter* (May 22, 1952); "Reagan is fine as the Hall of Fame hurler, and the film boasts good reenactments...." *Leonard Maltin's Movie & Video Guide 2000* (Penguin Putnam, 1999)

## Notes:

*"Making this picture was as happy a chore as I'd had since playing 'The Gipper.' "*

In production from December 10, 1951 to January 28, 1952 under the title *The Big League* and *Alexander, The Big Leaguer.* The negative cost of the film was $1,003,000. It earned domestic rentals of $1,440,000 and a further $168,000 from the overseas markets.

Reagan was again paid $6,250 a week for twelve weeks or $75,000. Doris Day, climbing the charts of America's box-office favorites, received top billing but earned less than Reagan for this film.

In November Reagan spent three weeks with major leaguers Bob Lemon (Cleveland Indians) and Jerry Priddy (Detroit Tigers) learning the finer points of pitching in the pros.

Character actor Frank Lovejoy (1914-1962) made a career of playing military men or police officials. Nearly half of his 32 films had him cast in either role. Although his motion picture career spanned barely more than a decade (1948-1958), he did appear in some memorable films including *Breakthrough* (1950), *I Was A Communist for the FBI* (1951), *Retreat, Hell!* (1952), *House of Wax* (1953), *The Charge at Feather River* (1953), *Men of the Fighting Lady* (1954), *Strategic Air Command* (1955), and in the title role of *Cole Younger, Gunfighter* (1958), his last film.

Los Angeles-born Eve Miller (1923-1973) had a film career which consisted of only 20 motion pictures. Between 1947 and 1959, she appeared in dozens of television series and had screen roles in *I Wonder Who's Kissing Her Now* (1947), *Inner Sanctum* (1948) and *Arctic Fury* (1949). Professionally her biggest year was 1952 when, besides appearing in the Reagan picture, she also featured in *The Big Trees,* Reagan's *She's Working Her Way Through College, The Story of Will Rogers* and *April In Paris.* Her film and television career ended in the late 1950s and in 1973 after several personal losses, at the age of fifty, she committed suicide.

Bit-player Jack Lemmon (1925-2001) in one of his earliest roles, would go on to become one of the top-ten box-office stars during the late 1960s. His brand of sophisticated comedy and dramatic roles endeared him to a significant sector of the movie-going public of that time. His biggest hits of that era included *Some Like It Hot, The Apartment, The Days of Wine and Roses, Irma La Douce, Under the Yum Yum Tree, The Odd Couple* and *Save the Tiger.*

On March 4, 1952, Reagan married actress Nancy Davis.

This was Reagan's last film for Warner Bros. Prior to his departure he was to have appeared in two other studio projects: the comedies *Sally* and *Miss America.*

Competition for audiences at the nation's screens included: *African Treasure* (Monogram) the latest Bomba the Jungle Boy adventure starring Johnny Sheffield, Gary Cooper in the Oscar winning Western *High Noon* and the medieval knights tale *Ivanhoe* starring Robert Taylor and Elizabeth Taylor

# She's Working Her Way Through College

**release date: July 9, 1952**                    **running time: 104 minutes**

**Cast:**   Virginia Mayo, Ronald Reagan, Gene Nelson, Don DeFore, Phyllis Thaxter, Patrice Wymore, Roland Winters, Raymond Greenleaf, Ginger Crowley, Norman Bartold, Jimmy Ames, Betty Arlen, Jessie Arnold, Larry Craig, Jack Gargan, Patricia Hawks, Chuck Hicks, Donald Kerr, Ray Linn Jr., Mark Lowell, Charles Marsh, Paul Maxey, George Meader, Malcolm Mealey, Eve Miller, Roland Morris, Jimmy Ogg, John Perri, Amanda Randolph, Richard Reeves, Donna Ring, Barbara Ritchi, Hope Sansburry, Frank J. Scannell, Hazel Shaw, Henrietta Taylor, Glen Turnbull, Valerie Vernon, Charles Vernon, Charles Watts, Jack Wise, Frances Zucco, Edward Clark, Charles Williams, Charles Cutelli, Lonnie Pierce, Danny Jackson, Lucille Vance, Peggy Leon, Felice Richmond, Fay Lively, Peggy Wynne

## Credits:             Warner Bros.

*Director* H. Bruce Humberstone; *Producers* William Jacobs, Herman Shumlin; *Writer* James Nugent, Elliott Nugent; *Cinematography* Wilfred M. Cline; *Music* Vernon Duke; *Editor* Clarence Kolster; *Art Direction* Charles H. Clarke; *Set Decoration* G.W. Bernsten; *Sound* Charles David Forrest, Leslie G. Hewitt; *Costumes* Marjorie Best Travilla; *Makeup* Gordon Bau; *Musical Director* Ray Heindorf; *Lyricist* Sammy Cahn; *Music Arranger* Norman Luboff; *Choreographer* LeRoy Prinz; *Color Consultant* Mitchell Kovaleski; *Transportation Coordinator* Hal Derwin; *Virginia Mayo's singing voice* Bonnie Lou Williams

## Synopsis:

Burlesque queen Angela Gardner (Virginia mayo) decides to become a writer. Ronald Reagan is her mild mannered professor.

## Reviews:

"...a likeable standard mixture of songs, dance, comedy, with about average chances at the general boxoffice." *Variety* (June 11, 1952); "(I)t starred a rather ineffectual Ronald Reagan as the Professor..." *The Warner Bros. Story.* Clive Hirschhorn (New York; Crown, 1979): "..the stubborn endeavor to weave a musical story into the stoic fabric of 'The Male Animal'-and such a silly musical story line at that-has resulted in a combination that does credit to neither one." *The New York Times* (July 8, 1952); ".....spirited direction of Bruce

'Lucky' Humberstone....Offsetting Miss Mayo's high-jinks in fine style is co-star Ronald Reagan." *The Los Angeles Examiner* (Dorothy Manners, July 12, 1952)

## Notes:

In production from mid-October to November 26, 1951.

Working title, *We're Working Our Way Through College.*

The film had a negative cost of $1,360,000 and returned domestic rentals of $2,320,000 to the studio and an additional $673,000 from overseas markets. The worldwide box-office gross was $6,100,000.

Reagan paid $75,000 at the rate of $6250 a week with a twelve-week guarantee. Virginia Mayo was paid at the rate of $3000 a week.

A loose adaptation of the play, *The Male Animal* by James Thurber and Elliott Nugent.

Director H. Bruce Humberstone (1901-1984) started out in the industry as a juvenile actor then became a script clerk, assistant director and in 1924 he directed the first of 47 features. During the 1920s he learned his craft from the likes of Allan Dwan, King Vidor and Edmund Goulding but was rarely afforded the opportunity to work on major productions. His films included *If I Had A Million* (1932), *King of the Jungle* (1933), four Charlie Chan features between 1936 and 1938, *Sun Valley Serenade* (1941), *Wonder Man* (1945), and three low-budget Tarzan epics, *Tarzan and the Lost Safari, Tarzan's Fight for Life* and *Tarzan and the Trappers* (1957-58).

Third-billed Gene Nelson's (born Eugene Leander Berg, 1920-1996) specialty before the cameras was dancing. He tried to follow in the footsteps of his idol, Fred Astaire. For several years in the late 1930s he performed on ice skates as part of Sonia Henie's ice show. After service with the army during World War II he danced his way through a dozen films including *This Is the Army* (1943) in bit roles. During the 1950s he secured better parts in bigger-budgeted productions including *Tea for Two* (1950), *The West Point Story* (1950), *Three Sailors and a Girl* (1953) and *Oklahoma* (1955). With over 20 films in his resume, Nelson retired from the screen after a role in the Blake Edwards comedy *S.O.B.* (1981).

During a career that spanned 34 years, actress Phyllis Thaxter (1921-) also appeared in just over 20 films. She started with a small role in the war classic *Thirty Seconds Over Tokyo* (1944) and had parts in *Weekend at the Waldorf* (1944), *Blood on the Moon* (1948), *The Breaking Point* (1950), *Springfield Rifle* (1952), *The World of Henry Orient* (1964) and *Superman* (1978) as Martha Kent the mother of Clark Kent.

Character actor Roland Winters (born Roland Winternitz, 1904-1989) started in films as the screen's third Charlie Chan. Between 1947 and 1949 he starred as the astute sleuth in six episodes of the low-budget series. In the late 1940s and early 1950s the actor plied his trade in a number of gritty crime genre motion pictures. He also appeared in *So Big* (1953), *Jet Pilot* (1957), *Blue Hawaii* (1961) and *Follow That Dream* (1962).

In the Los Angeles area this film played on a double-bill with the French-made, Lippert released *Pirate Submarine* (aka *Casabianca*).

Competition at the nations theaters included: John Ford's romantic adventure *The Quiet Man* starring John Wayne and Maureen O'Hara, *Carrie* (Paramount) with Laurence Olivier and Jennifer Jones; the spy thriller, *Diplomatic Courier* (Fox) with Tyrone Power and Patricia Neal and the pale comedy *We're Not Married* with Ginger Rogers, Fred Allen and Marilyn Monroe.

# Tropic Zone

**release date: December 1952**          **running time: 94 minutes**

**Cast:**   Ronald Reagan, Rhonda Fleming, Rico Alanez, Noah Beery, Jr.,
Argentina Brunetti, Pilar Del Rey, Maurice Jara, Estelita
Rodriguez, John Wengraf, Grant Withers,

**Credits:**          **Paramount- Pine-Thomas Productions**

*Director* Lewis R. Foster; *Producers* William H. Pine, William C.
Thomas; *Writers* Lewis R. Foster, Tom Gill; *Cinematography*
Lionel Lindo; *Music* Lucien Cailliet; *Editor* Howard A. Smith; *Art
Direction* A. Earl Hedrick, Hal Pereira; *Costumes* Edith Head;
*Choreographer* Jack Baker

## Synopsis:

Rougish Dan McCloud (Ronald Reagan), on the run from a
neighboring republic following his involvement with a deposed
political group, arrives in town. He is an expert fruit farmer and is
given a job by local banana baron Lukats (John Wengraf). He

controls much of the state of Puerto Barrancas. Lukats wants to take control of all the plantations in the area. Flanders White (Rhonda Fleming) refuses to sell.

## Reviews:

"Blah actioner set in South America with Reagan fighting the good cause to save a banana plantation." *Leonard Maltin's 2000 Movie & Video Guide* Penguin Puntnam 1999); "Reagan and Miss Fleming, the latter very attractive in Technicolor and several brief outfits....make a pleasing hero-heroine team." *Variety* (December 17, 1952); "Until I saw this picture, I never realized that raising bananas could involve so much intrigue and colorful photography...Ronald Reagan is a fascinating hero..." *The Los Angeles Examiner* (Shirel Duggan, January 15, 1953); "....has all the color, intriguing backgrounds and fine production that one always expects from Pine-Thomas....the customary sustained action associated with the

two Bills is missing in this tale...Performances are good, particularly that of Ronald Reagan, who jaunts through his role with engaging, half-bantering nonchalance and handles his brawling scenes with a gay, convincing vigor." *The Hollywood Reporter* (December 12, 1952)

Filmed on the Paramount lot and the Arboretum in Pasadena on a budget of slightly under $600,000. Reagan was paid $45,000 and Rhonda Fleming received $30,000. The film reported domestic rentals of under $700,000.

Based on the book, *Gentleman of the Jungle* by Tom Gill. British-born Gill (1916-1971) was also an actor who appeared in nearly 50 films between 1935 and 1971.

New York City-born character-actor Noah Beery, Jr. (1913-1994) was the son of actor Noah Beery and the nephew of Wallace Beery. In a career that spanned 63 years (1920-1983) he appeared in over 110 films and 5 television series. Beery had roles in the *Mark of Zorro* (1920) and *Penrod* (1922) and throughout the 1930s was in constant demand working in B-films and serials including *Heroes of the West* (1932), John Wayne's serial *The Three Musketeers* (1933), *Fighting with Kit Carson* (1933) and two *Tailspin Tommy* chapterplays in 1934 and 1935. By the end of the decade he began to appear in larger-budgeted productions including *Only Angels Have Wings* and *Of Mice and Men* (both 1939), *Sergeant York* (1941), *Gung Ho!* (1943), *Red River* (1948), *The Story of Will Rogers* (1952), *Inherit the Wind* (1960) and *Walking Tall* (1973). He will best be remembered as the irascible Rocky Rockford the father of Jim Rockford (James Gardner) in the television detective series *The Rockford Files* (1974-1980).

Former newspaperman Grant Withers (1904-1959) of Pueblo, Colorado, started acting in films in the mid-1920s. His short marriage to an underage Loretta Young was annulled in 1931. A veteran of over 200 films, Withers was in four episodes of the *Mr. Wong* detective series, always in the role of a police captain. Several of his more popular screen entries include *Billy the Kid* (1941), *Tennessee Johnson* and *In Old Oklahoma* (both 1943), *Dakota* (1945), *Fort Apache* (1948), *Rock Island Trail* (1950) and *Fair Wind to Java* (1953). A close friend of John Wayne, Withers was a long-time alcoholic who lost many a screen role because of his disease. Wayne spent thousands of dollars seeking medical help and rehabilitation for his friend. In 1959, unable to deal with his problems, Withers committed suicide.

In the Los Angeles market this film ended up on the bottom half of a Paramount double-bill which headlined *The Turning Point* an absorbing drama starring William Holden and Alexis Smith.

At the nation's theaters the film was up against competition from

Danny Kaye's *Hans Christian Andersen,* the 3-D adventure *Bwana Devil,* John Huston's *Moulin Rouge,* Allied Artists' *Torpedo Alley* starring Mark Stevens and Dorothy Malone and the drama *The Bad and the Beautiful* with an all-star cast headed by Kirk Douglas and Lana Turner.

# Law and Order

release date: May 1953          running time: 80 minutes

**Cast:** Ronald Reagan, Dorothy Malone, Preston Foster, Alex Nichol, Ruth Hampton, Russell Johnson, Barry Kelley, Chubby Johnson, Jack Kelly, Dennis Weaver, Wally Cassell, Richard Garrick, Holly Bane, Gregg Barton, Stanley Blystone, Lane Bradford, Johnny Carpenter, Wheaton Chambers, Tristram Coffin, Harry Cording, Richard H. Cutting, Jack Daly, Watson Downs, Sam Flint, Don Garner, Martin Garralaga, Don Gordon, William Gould, Jimmy Gray, Harry Harvey, Al Haskell, Thomas Browne Henry, Thor Holmes, Jack Ingram, Valerie Jackson, Ethan Laidlaw, Kenneth MacDonald, Kermit Maynard, William O'Neal, Eddie Parker, Victor Homito, Buddy Roosevelt, Tom Steele, James Stone, William Tannen, Jack Tornek, Dale Van Sickel, Britt Wood, Mike Ragan, Helen Noyes, Ted Jordan, Lorin Raker, Phil Chambers, Watson Downs, Roy Butler, Tom Hubbard, Harte Wayne, Chuck Hamilton, Jack Harden, Philo McCullough, Frank Cordell, Jack Stoney, Carl Anore, Boyd "Red" Morgan, Gary Epper

**Credits:**                                    **Universal**

*Director* Nathan Juran; *Producer* John W. Rogers; *Cinematography*
Clifford Stine; *Writers* W.R. Burnett, Inez Cocke; *Music* Henry
Mancini, Milton Rosen, Frank Skinner, Hans J. Salter; *Editor* Ted
J. Kent; *Art Direction* Robert Clatworthy  Alexander Golitzen; *Set
Decoration* John P. Austin,  Russell A. Gausman; *Costumes*
Rosemary Odell; *Assistant Director* Fred Frank; *Sound* Leslie I.
Carey,  Robert Pritchard; *Stunts* Johnny Carpenter; *Makeup* Joan
St. Oegger,  Bud Westmore; *Musical Director* Joseph Gershenson;
*Color Consultant* William Fritzsche

## Synopsis:

Frame Johnson (Ronald Reagan) is a gunslinging lawman, solid
and conventional. But he wants to hang up his guns to retire to his
ranch in Cottonwood.

The old town residents beg him to reconsider. They need help
getting rid of the evil Kurt Durning.

Eventually, after his brother is killed by one of Durning's sons, he
agrees.

## Reviews:

"Reagan is all right in this remake, but it's a tired echo." *Western
Films: A Complete Guide* Brian Garfield (Da Capo Paperback,
1982); "Neither film (the original and the Reagan remake) had
anything much to offer. The psychological context had vanished."
*The Filming of the West* Jon Tuska (Doubleday, 1976); "...a good
western...should prove a satisfactory grosser...plenty of action to
keep the plot moving satisfactorily....Reagan handles himself
easily in the top role...." *Variety* (April 8, 1953); "...goes about its
familiar business at an ambling pace...Ronald Reagan looks at
ease...(He) has no chance at an Oscar." *Photoplay* (June, 1953); "A
top-ranking Western......will satisfy the most exacting fans. It is
done on a large scale, has a good plot and cast." *The Exhibitor*
(April 1953)

**Notes:** *"A picture that I can only excuse because it was a Western."*

Filmed in January 1953 at Red Rock Canyon, California, a location
used by Hollywood since the mid-1920's. Reagan earned $75,000
for his role in this western which was budgeted at $530,000.

This was, at least, the fourth remake with the same title. Previously filmed in 1917 (with Chet Ryan and Francis Parker), 1932 (with Walter Huston and Harry Carey), and 1940 (with Johnny Mack Brown and Fuzzy Knight). Leading-lady Dorothy Malone (1925- ) started out in films as a brunette and was changed to a blonde for her role in *Young at Heart* (1954). Between 1942 and 1992 she is credited with appearances in 66 films. Starting out as a bit player in the early 1940s, she had minor roles in several *Falcon* series entries, worked noteworthy assignments in the two 1946 releases *Night and Day* and opposite Bogart in *The Big Sleep,* alternated between B-Westerns and low-budget dramas for the rest of the decade and into the 1950s, and started getting more substantial parts by 1955. The actress had one of her rare sympathetic roles in the war story *Battle Cry* (1955), played opposite Martin & Lewis in *Artists and Models* (1955), was seen in *Tension at Table Rock* (1956), and had the best dramatic roles of her career in the years between 1956 and 1958. She won an Oscar in 1956 for playing the rich, spoiled, emotionally disturbed sister of Robert Stack in *Written on the Wind.* She also starred in *Man of a Thousand Faces* and in 1958 played Robert Stack's wife in *Tarnished Angels, Too Much, Too Soon, Warlock* (1959) and *The Last Sunset* (1961), her third pairing with Rock Hudson). She appeared sporadically in films into the nineties but was seen more frequently on television in series such as *Peyton Place* (1964-69). Third-billed Preston Foster (1900-1970) worked primarily as a stage performer for nearly a decade before signing a contract with Warner Bros. to star in a series of well-received dramas such as *Doctor X, The Last Mile* and *I Am A Fugitive From a Chain Gang* (all 1932). In the mid-1930s he signed with RKO and was seen in John Ford's *The Informer, Last Days of Pompeii* and *Annie Oakley* (all 1935), *The Outcasts of Poker Flats* and *You Can't Beat Love* (both 1937). In the 1940s and 1950s he either starred or had

character roles in several notable films including *Northwest Mounted Police* (1940), *Guadalcanal Diary* (1943), *The Harvey Girls* (1946), *Kansas City Confidential* (1952), *I, the Jury* (1953) and *Destination 60,000* (1957). Besides appearing in nearly 100 motion pictures over 39 years, Foster was also a talented composer and song writer as well as guitarist and writer of novels.

Supporting cast members Russell Johnson achieved cult status as "The Professor" on television's *Gilligan's Island* while Jack Kelly had a recurring role alongside James Garner in the tremendously popular *Maverick* television Western series and Dennis Weaver became a star on the small screen with his role as Chester in *Gunsmoke* and as detective *McCloud*.

W.R. Burnett (1899-1982), a prolific writer who wrote novels and is credited with the screenplays for over 45 films, broke into Hollywood with his riveting work on *Little Caesar* (1931). He wrote or added dialogue to *Law and Order* and *Scarface* (1932), *The Whole Towns Talking* (1935), *King of the Underworld* (1939), John Wayne's *Dark Command* (1940), Bogart's *High Sierra*

(1941), *Wake Island* (1942), *Crash Dive* (1943), *The Asphalt Jungle* (1950) and *The Great Escape* (1963).

This western was populated with familiar faces of character actors and stuntmen from the 1930's and 1940's including, Kermit Maynard, Eddie Parker, Sam Flint, Lane Bradford, Ethan Laidlaw, Jack Ingram, Buddy Roosevelt, Tom Steele, and Dale Van Sicklel.

As part of a double-bill with Universal's *Abbott and Costello Go to Mars, Law and Order* opened in Los Angeles on May 13, 1953.

Throughout the country the film faced competition on the nation's screens from: *Julius Caesar* with Marlon Brando, Otto Preminger's controversial *The Moon Is Blue,* the musical-comedy *Gentlemen Prefer Blondes* with Marilyn Monroe and Jane Russell, *Man on a Tightrope* (Fox) a suspense melodrama with Frederic March and Terry Moore, the 3-D science-fiction flick *It Came From Outer Space* and *Never Let Me Go* (MGM) starring Clark Gable and Gene Tierney.

# Prisoner of War

**release date: May 4, 1954**　　　　**running time: 80-82 minutes**

**Cast:** Ronald Reagan, Steve Forrest, Dewey Martin, Oskar Homolka, Robert Horton, Paul Stewart, Harry Morgan, Stephen Bekassy, Leonard Strong, Darryl Hickman, Weaver Levy, Rollin Moriyama, Ike Jones, Clarence Lung, Jerry Paris, John Lupton, Ralph Ahn, Robert Nichols, Alan Orrie, Mike Berry, Ray Boyle, Lester C. Hoyle, Byron Keith, Harry Landers, William Yip, Rye Butler, Leo Needham, Strother Martin, Robert Ellis, Otis Greene, Peter Hansen, Lewis Martin, Edo Mita, Gordon Mitchell, Gene Reynolds, Lalo Rios, Leon Tyler, Stuart Whitman, Owen Song, Harold Fong, Tommy Walker, Wilson Wood, Jerry Singer, Harry Harvey Jr., Richard Garland, Dick Sargent,

**Credits:**　　　　　　　　**MGM**

*Director* Andrew Marton; *Producer* Henry Berman; *Cinematography* Robert H. Planck; *Writer* Allen Rivkin; *Music* Jeff Alexander; *Editor* James E. Newcome; *Art Direction* Malcolm Brown, Cedric Gibbons; *Set Decorations* Jack D. Moore, Edwin B. Willis; *Makeup* William Tuttle; *Sound* Douglas Shearer; *Assistant Director* Joel Freeman; *Special Effects* A. Arnold Gillespie, Warren Newcombe; *Technical Advisor* Robert H. Wise

## Synopsis:

Web Sloane (Ronald Reagan) is an army officer who volunteers to find out about the rumors of brutality in Korean prisoner of war camps. He parachutes behind the lines and sneaks into a group of Americans being marched to such a camp. There he sees evey kind of torture and undergoes savage treatment himself. He is forced to attend lectures of indoctrination.

Russian colonel (Oscar Homolka) directs viscious brainwashing sessions. Among the prisoners are soldier (Steve Forrest) who defies his captors at every turn, and another (Dewy Martin), who appears to give in in order to obtain drugs for a suffering fellow prisoner. The story, scripted by Riukin, was based on ex-prisoner's stories

## Reviews

"...the presentation here is uninspired so there's little shock value...production and direction handling gives it a 'quickie' look and routine treatment will not grip and hold an audience." *Variety* (March 24, 1954); "...routine and grim dramatization...largely uninspired fare, whose shocks appear superficial and hastily contrived.....Mr. Reagan's portrayal...(is) altruistic but no better than standard." *The New York Times* (May 10, 1954); "..this effort to convey the nature of the Communist in war is hardly a convincing one. The characters ...are deliberately constructed stereotypes rather than individuals....Reagan's acting is as good as can be expected" *The Exhibitor* (May 1954); "The picture is one of those it is almost obligatory to see, considering the fact that thousands of young American men have been subjected to the tortures of the death march, the brutality of the sadistic prison camp officials, the inhumane conditions under which the prisoners live and the attempts of the Communists to indoctrinate these Americans in the enemy ideology." *The Los Angeles Examiner* (Lynn Bowers, May 13, 1954)

**Notes:** *"At the lowest point of all, just prior to Christmas, a script came from MGM...."*

Filmed in twenty-eight days on the MGM lot and outdoor locations in Agoura, on a threadbare budget of $675,000. Reagan paid $30,000.

Director Andrew Marton (1904-1992) was born in Budapest, Hungary, worked in the film industry of Germany and Eastern Europe in the 1920s, emigrated to the United States in the 1930s and worked as an editor and second-unit director (*Dragon Seed* and *The Seventh Cross*, both 1944). In the mid-1930s he took assignments involving second unit work and directing features. The better known of his 27 American features include *Gallant Bess* (1947), *King Solomon's Mines* (1950), *Men of the Fighting Lady* and *Green Ice* (both 1954), *The Longest Day* (1962, American sequences only), *The Thin Red Line* (1964) and his last work, *Africa-Texas Style* (1967).

Second-billed Steve Forrest (1924- ) a big-Texan whose older brother was Dana Andrews, worked his way up from bit-roles during World War II to decent parts in nearly 40 films of the late 1940s through the 1960s. His better known motion pictures included the multi-Oscar winner, *The Bad and the Beautiful* (1952), *Battle Circus* (1953), *So Big* (1953), *Phantom of the Rue Morgue* (1954), *It Happened to Jane* (1959), *Flaming Star* (1960), and as part of the international cast of *The Longest Day* (1962). He will best be remembered for his starring television role as Lt. Dan

"Hondo" Harrelson, head of the Los Angeles elite police unit known as *SWAT* (1975-76).

Dewey Martin (1923- ) was another Texan who came to Hollywood after a stint on the stage. After minor roles in *Battleground* and *Kansas Raiders* director Howard Hawks signed him for a lead role in his science-fiction yarn *The Thing, From Another World* (1951), *The Big Sky* (1952). In the 1950s and early 1960s Martin could be seen in *Men of the Fighting Lady* (1954), *Land of the Pharaohs* and *Desperate Hours* (1955), *The Proud and the Profane* (1956) and the all-star war film *The Longest Day* (1962). From 1956 to 1958 Martin was married to popular singer Peggy Lee. By the mid-1970s his film and television career had ground to a halt.

The portly Vienna, Austrian-born Oscar Homolka (1898-1978) appeared in German films for over a decade before leaving for the United States in the mid-1930s. His career extended to the mid-1970s and number over 30 American films including *Sabotage* (1936), *Seven Sinners* and *Comrade X, Ball of Fire* with Gary Cooper and Barbara Stanwyck *(1941), I Remember Mama* (1948), *The Seven Year Itch* (1955) with Marilyn Monroe at her best, *War and Peace* (1956), *A Farewell to Arms* (1957) and *The Madwoman of Chaillot* (1969).

Other cast members went on to greater fame in the medium of television: John Lupton (1928-1993) played Indian agent Tom Jeffords in the adult western *Broken Arrow (1956-60);* Stuart Whitman (1926- ) starred as Marshal Jim Crown in *Cimarron Strip* (1967-1971) *;* Robert Horton (1924- ) was part of the ensemble cast of *Wagon Train (1957*-60); Dick Sargent (1930-1994) became the second Darrin Stephens, husband to a witch for three seasons, in the hit comedy, *Bewitched;* and Harry Morgan (1915- ) from 1954 to 1986, co-starred in a near-record ten television series (*December Bride, Pete & Gladys, The Richard Boone Show, Kentucky Jones, Dragnet, The D.A., Hec Ramsey, M\*A\*S\*H, After M\*A\*S\*H* and *Black's Magic*).

Competition at the nation's screens included: the unusual Joan Crawford Western *Johnny Guitar,* John Wayne in *The High and the Mighty,* Hitchcock's *Dial M for Murder* with Ray Milland and Grace Kelly, *The Iron Glove* (Columbia) with Robert Stack, *Elephant Walk* (Paramount) starring Elizabeth Taylor and Dana Andrews and the Korean war film *Men of the Fighting Lady* (MGM) starring Van Johnson.

# Cattle Queen of Montana

**release date: November 1954**         **running time: 88 minutes**

**Cast:**  Barbara Stanwyck, Ronald Reagan, Gene Evans, Lance Fuller, Anthony Caruso, Jack Elam, Yvette Duguay, Morris Ankrum, Chubby Johnson, Myron Healy, Rodd Redwing, Jonathan Hale, Hugh Sanders, Dorothy Andre, Bob Burrows, Wayne Burson, John L. Cason, Danny Fisher, Byron Foulger, Roy Gordon, Betty Hanna, Burt Mustin, Riza Royce, Ralph Sanford, Tom Steele, Bob Woodward

**Credits:**               **RKO-Filmcrest Productions**

*Director* Allan Dwan; *Producer* Benedict Bogeaus; *Writers* Thomas W. Blackburn, Robert Blees, Howard Estabrook; *Cinematography* John Alton; *Music* Louis Forbes;  *Editor* James Leicester, Carlo Lodato; *Production Supervisor* Lee Lukather; *Production Design & Art Direction* Van Nest Polglase; *Set Decoration* John Stutevant; *Costumes* Gwen Wakeling; *Assistant Director* Nathan Barranger; *Sound* Francis M. Sarver

## Synopsis:

Sierra Nevada Jones (Barbara Stanwyck), who despite her name is from Texas, and her father, Pop Jones (Morris Ankrum) arrive in Montana with a vast herd of cattle that they have driven up from Texas in order to settle in the lush mountain meadows.

Their plans are shattered when they are raided by Indians who steal the cattle and kill Pop.

The Indians are in the employ of local outlaw Tom McCord (Gene Evans), who plans to build his own cattle empire.

Farell (Ronald Reagan) is an undercover army officer sent by Washington to investigate the Indian disturbances and reports on rustling.

Farrell puts a stop to McCord's plans and soothes the restless Indians. He also falls in love with Sierra Nevada Jones and marries her. They get the cattle back and run the ranch together.

## Reviews:

".....beautifully lit by cinematographer Alton....Reagan is the mysterious gunman (and Government undercover agent) who comes to Stanwyck's rescue." *The Overlook Film Encyclopedia: The Western* Phil Hardy (Overlook Press, 1983); "Stanwyck gives a far better performance than the movie deserves, but she usually does that." *Western Films: A Complete Guide*  Brian Garfield (Da Capo Publication, 1983); "The above-average production values, exciting action elements and solid performances by the two principals helped overcome...trite screenplay." *The RKO Story* Richard B. Jewell with Vernon Harbin (Arlington House, 1982);

"...a listless and ordinary western.....screenplay is short on imagination and long on cliché...The performances are professionally competent." *Variety* (November 17, 1954); "Highly improbable Technicolor adventure....Mr. Reagan is stalwart and obvious." *The New York Times* (January 26, 1955); "...is a lush, expensive looking production in Technicolor....has enough action to satisfy the most frenetic western fan." *The Los Angeles Examiner* (Lynn Bowers, December 9, 1954)

**Notes:**   *"Gives us a chance to play tourists on company time."*

Back in December 1949 Hal Wallis announced that he would produce a bid-budgeted "A" western with Barbara Stanwyck entitled, *Cattle Kate*. The basic premise for the story did not go into production for another 4 fi years.

Filmed from June to July 1954 at Glacier National Park in Montana, and at the Iverson Ranch in Chatsworth.

Stanwyck, in her seventy-first feature, performed most of her own stunts. Her previous western films included *Union Pacific* (Paramount, 1939), *The Great Man's Lady* (Paramount, 1942), and *The Maverick Queen* (Republic, 1956). Prior to working in this low-budget entry she had co-starred in the $1,250,000 budgeted drama *Executive Suite*.

Director Dwan (1885-1981) helmed over 150 motion pictures of which 70 were done in the sound era. Dwan, trained as an electrical engineer, initially worked in films as a writer then scenario director. Learning about filmmaking from the legendary D.W. Griffith in the late teens and 1920s he directed heavyweight Douglas Fairbanks and Gloria Swanson in some of their biggest hits. In constant demand, Dwan directed *While Paris Sleeps* (1932), *Heidi* (1937), *Rebecca of Sunnybrook Farm* (1938), *The Three Musketeers* (1939), *Brewster's Millions* (1945), and John Wayne in the quintessential war film, *Sand of Iwo Jima* (1949). He retired in 1961.

World War II veteran Gene Evans (1922-1998) made his major film debut in *Under Colorado Skies* (1947). The overwhelming majority of his films were in the Western, war, and science fiction genres. He played the role of an army sergeant in half a dozen features including *Steel Helmet* and *Fixed Bayonets* (both 1951), *Thunderbirds* (1952) and *The Sad Sack* (1957). Some of his other notable films include *The Asphalt Jungle* (1950), *Wyoming Renegades* (1954), *The Bravados* (1958), *Operation Petticoat* (1959), *The War Wagon* (1967) a big John Wayne-Kirk Douglas Western and the unconventional

Western, *Pat Garrett and Billy the Kid* (1973). After a minor role in the B-film *Splint* (1989) as an evangelist, he retired from acting.

Kentucky native Lance Fuller (1928-2001) of English, French and Cherokee lineage began in films at Universal during World War II. He had bit roles in *Frankenstein Meets the Wolfman* (1943) and the Warner Bros. Bogart detective film *To Have and Have Not* (1944). Other titles in his 33 film resume include *Taza, Son of Cochise* (1954), *This Island Earth* (1955), *The She Creature* (1956), *Voodoo Woman* (1957), *God's Little Acre* (1958) and *The Love Machine* (1971).

Character actor Morris Ankrum (1896-1964), a USC law school graduate, practicing lawyer and economics professor, entered films in 1933 and worked continuously to the time of his death in 1964. Often appearing in up to 15 features a year, he had roles in nearly 200 motion pictures.

Extras came from the local Blackfoot Indian tribe.

After film was completed, Reagan's agent began negotiations with the General Electric Company for him to appear in a weekly, half-hour television anthology series. *The General Electric Theater* made it's debut on September 26, 1954 over the CBS Television network. Reagan received $125,000 for his hosting and occasional guest appearances in the program.

General nationwide release delayed until January 1955.

Competition at the nation's screens came from *The Violent Men* (Columbia) with Glenn Ford, Barbara Stanwyck and Edward G. Robinson; Paramount's Korean War epic *The Bridges at Toki Ri* with William Holden and Grace Kelly; Spencer Tracy in the modern Western *Bad Day at Black Rock; Blackboard Jungle* with Glenn Ford and Sidney Poitier and *The Intruder* (Associated Artists) starring Jack Hawkins.

# Tennessee's Partner

**release date: September 21, 1955**　　　　　**running time: 87 minutes**

**Cast:**　John Payne, Ronald Reagan, Rhonda Fleming, Coleen Gray, Anthony Caruso, Morris Ankrum, Leo Gordon, Chubby Johnson, Joe Devlin, Myron Healy, John Mansfield, Angie Dickinson, Frank Jenks, Pierce Lyden, Jack Mulhall

**Credits:**　　　　　**RKO-Filmcrest Productions**

*Director* Allan Dwan; *Producer* Benedict Bogeaus; *Writers* C. Graham Baker, D.D. Beauchamp, Allan Dwan, Bret Harte, Milton Krims, Teddi Sherman; *Cinematography* John Alton; *Music* Louis Forbes, Dave Franklin; *Editor* James Leicester; *Art Direction* Van

Nest Polglase; *Set Decoration* Alfred E, Spencer; *Production Supervisor* George Moskov; *Assistant Director* Nate Watt; *Sound* Terry Kellum, Bert Schoenfeld, Jean L. Speak; *Makeup* Mel Berns, Shirley Madden; *Costumes* Gwen Wakeling

### Synopsis:

Slick gambler, Tennessee (John Payne), makes a good living at the gaming tables in the raucous mining town of Sandy Barr. His lady friend, Elizabeth Farnham (Rhonda Fleming) runs a saloon called "The Marriage Market". Any gambler who questions his luck risks getting killed as Tennessee is also good with a gun.

When Tennesse is up against one disgruntled customer, the hard-hitting Cowpoke (Ronald Reagan) arrives and saves Tennessee. They are soon friends.

Cowpoke has come to Sandy Bar to marry his girlfriend, Goldie (Coleen Gray), a gold digger in the worst sense. Tennessee doesn't like her and feels she is a scheming trollop, not good enough for his new friend. In order to save him from Goldie, Tennessee woos her himself, causing conflict between the two men. Cowpoke comes to Tennessee's rescue once again when he is in danger of being killed by claim jumper Turner, (Anthony Caruso), who is trying to frame Tennessee for the murder of prospector, Grubstake McNiven (Chubby Johnson). Saving Tennessee's life costs Cowpoke his own, when he is gunned down in the fight.

Tennessee gives his friend a good send off and marries Elizabeth, who understood what Tennessee was trying to do.

## Reviews:

"Alton's cinematography is simply lustrous and Dwan's direction has that melodramatic serenity that characterizes his handling of *Cattle Queen of Montana.*" *The Overlook Film Encyclopedia: The Western* Phil Hardy *(The Overlook Press, 1983);* Tame but amiable film reduces the Harte classic to a "B" yarn." *Western Films: A Complete Guide* Brian Garfield (Da Capo Paperback, 1982); Allan Dwan's heady direction extracted plenty of guts and gutso...narrative...smooth and exciting throughout." *The RKO Story* Richard B. Jewell with Vernon Harbin (Arlington House, 1982); "a generous mixture of sex, suspense and six guns...director Allan Dwan moves things along at a brisk pace..." *Variety* (September 28, 1955); "It should be hitting the B trail before long, pardners....this tale of the Gold Rush days is no bonanza." *The New York Times* (November 5, 1955)

## Notes:

Filmed between January and February 1955 on the RKO lot in Culver City and at the Iverson Ranch in Chatsworth on a budget of $625,000.

Loosely based on a Brete Harte story that had been filmed twice before as the silents, T*ennesse's Pardner* (Paramount, 1918) produced by Jesse L. Lasky and *Flaming Forties* (PDC, 1924) with Harry Carey in the lead.

Virginia-born John Payne (1912-1989) attended Columbia University, the Julliard School, was a singer on the stage, and made his film debut in the drama *Dodsworth (1936)*. In the early 1940s he signed with Fox and was placed in several of the studio's musicals (*Tin Pan Alley, Sun Valley Serenade, Springtime in the Rockies* and *The Dolly Sisters*) opposite their biggest leading ladies: Betty Grable, Alice Faye and Sonia Henie. Payne also did well in their dramatic and western entries: *The Razor's Edge* (1946), *Miracle on 34<sup>th</sup>. Street* (1947), *El Paso* (1949), *Tripoli* (1950), *Kansas City Confidential* (1952), *Hell's Island* (1955) and *The Boss* (1956). The actor made his greatest impact on the public when he starred as Vint Bonner in *The Restless Gun* television series from 1957 to 1959. His motion picture career consisted of 58 features.

Second-female lead Coleen Gray (1922 ) was born Doris Jensen in Nebraska, graduated from a local college, and upon a visit to Hollywood, was signed to a contract by Fox. Between 1944 and 1985 she appeared in 40 mostly forgotten films. Her most active period was from the end of the 1940s to the early 1960s when she was featured in *Kiss of Death* (1947), *Nightmare Alley* (1947), *Red River* (1948) as John Wayne's love interest, *Apache Drums* (1951), *Kansas City Confidential* (1952), *Arrow in the Dust* (1954), *The Killing* (1956), *Johnny Rocco* (1958), *The Leech Woman* (1960) and *Town Tamer* (1965).

Cinematographer John Alton (1901-96), born in the Austria-Hungary empire, came to the United States in the early 1920s and worked at MGM as a lab technician. By the 1930s he was directing films in Argentina and Mexico and gaining an international reputation for his innovative camera techniques. Alton returned to the United States in late 1937 and began work on the first of his over 80 American- directorial efforts, *The Courageous Dr. Christian*. Stuck in the world of low-budget B-films throughout the decade of the 1940s he entered the 1950s with a new contract at MGM and worked on segments of *An American In Paris* (1951) for which he would win an Oscar. His other big films in the decade included *Father's Little Dividend* and *It's A Big Country* (both 1951), *Battle Circus* (1953), *The Steel Cage* (1954), *Tea and Sympathy* and *Teahouse of the August Moon* (both 1956). Alton retired from the big screen after working on *Elmer Gantry* (1960), but in 1966 came out of retirement and photographed the pilot episode for the highly popular television series *Mission Impossible*.

Menacing and intimidating heavy, Leo Gordon (1922-2000), was memorable as a scoundrel in the John Wayne Westerns *Hondo* (1953) and *McLintock* (1963). Between 1953 and 1994, he is credited with having appeared in over 80 films and writing screenplays for more than a dozen features and episodes of television programs including Rock Hudson's World War II adventure film, *Tobruk* (1967).

Competition for the movie audience came from: *The Tall Men* (Fox) a Western with Clark Gable, Jane Russell and Robert Ryan; *Count Three and Pray* (Columbia) a low-budget post-civil war western with Van Heflin and Joanne Woodward in the leads, Hitchcock's *To Catch A Thief* with Cary Grant and Grace Kelly, Audie Murphy's biography *To Hell and Back* and the Broadway musical adaptation *Guys and Dolls* starring Frank Sinatra and Marlon Brando.

# Hellcats of the Navy

**release date: May 1957**          **running time: 81-82 minutes**

**Cast:**    Ronald Reagan, Nancy Davis, Arthur Franz, Robert Arthur, William Leslie, William 'Bill' Phillips, Harry Lauter, Michael Garth, Joe Turkel, Don Keefer, Thomas Browne Henry, Selmer Jackson, Maurice Manson, Robert Nichols, Admiral Chester W. Nimitz

**Credits:**                **Columbia**

*Director* Nathan Juran; *Producer* Charles H. Schneer; *Cinematography* Irving Lippman; *Writers* Charles A. Lockwood, Hans Christian, David Lang, Bernard Gordon; *Music* Mischa Bakaleinikoff; *Editor* Jerome Thoms; *Art Direction* Rudi Field

## Synopsis:

Fleet Admiral Chester W Nimitz (who was the supervisor of the 1944 campaign in the Tsushima Strait and the Sea of Japan) introduces the picture. In the film he is played by Selmer Jackson. The "Hellcats" of the title are a branch of the submarine service charged with unusual operations. They are to bring back sample Japanes mines from enemy waters so US navy experts can learn why they are resistant to sonar detection.

The man assigned to the mission is Commander Casey Abbott (Ronald Reagan), who succeeds in penetrating the mine fields with a submarine, The Starfish. He is forced to abandon frogman Barton (Harry Lauter) when they are attacked by an enemy warship.

His action incurs the resentment of second in command, Landon (Arthur Frantz).

Landon's resentment builds up when Abbott lists him as a good junior officer, but unsuitable for command. Back at base, Helen (Nany Davis) assures Abbott that her friendship with the diver had not been serious.

The starfish is sent back to the Tsushima Strait. The navy has solved the sonar problem, and an attack can now be launched. Abbott devises a way to map a course through minefields. He loses his submarine when it is damaged in an encounter. He and a handful of men survive and are picked up by a navy flying boat.

He is given a new submarine and wreaks havoc on his enemy. En route home, the rudder developes problems and Landon is sent out to fix it. Landon is still in the water as a Japanes destroyer approaches. He orders the submarine to submerge. Landon survives the attack and begins searching the water for his commanding officer, he finds him wounded. On his recovery Abbott submits another report, commending Landon for bravery and recommending him for command.

# Reviews:

"(It is) laced with a formula plot which at times gets awfully trite…Reagan plays it sternly, without being the typical film version of a martinet." *Variety* (May 1, 1957); "…solid excitement of the factual exploit…makes for first-rate drama." *The Los Angeles Examiner* (Kay Proctor, April 18, 1957) "Satisfactory actioner of WW2 exploits of U.S. submarine and its crew." *Leonard Maltin's 2000 Movie & Video Guide* (Penguin Putnam, 1999); "…routine production…" *The Columbia Story.* Clive Hirschhorn (Hamlyn; London, 1999) "Might have qualified as a comedy…..Derives a sense of authenticity from the appearance of….Admiral Chester Nimitz, who delivers a foreword…" *Sailing on the Silver Screen: Hollywood and the U.S. Navy* Lawrence Suid (Naval Institute Press, Annapolis Md., 1996); "…lackluster, uninspired World War II battle drama…..the direction is as dry as a military briefing on CNN. Production values are typical of Columbia's bargain-basement mentality in the 1950s….It's tough to get involved…because the cast seems so detached." *DVD Review* (July 2, 2003)

# Notes:      *"Truth and the Navy went down to defeat before the production office string-savers."*

Filmed on location in San Diego on a budget of $525,000.
First and only teaming of Ronald Reagan and his second wife, Nancy Davis.
Film based on the book, *Hellcats of the Sea.*
Austrian-born director Nathan Juran (1907-2002) started in Hollywood in the mid-1930's as an art director. In this capacity, working for legendary John Ford, he won the Academy Award for Best Art Direction for his assignment in the 1941 film, *How Green Was My Valley.* Among the features he helmed through the fifties were, *The Black Castle* (1952), *Gunsmoke* (1953), *Law and Order* (1953) with Reagan, *20 Million Miles to Earth* (1957), *Attack of the Fifty Foot Woman* (1958), and *Good Day For A Hanging* (1959). While he continued directing films into the seventies, he increasingly worked in the medium of television on such series as, *Men Into Space* (1959), *World of Giants* (1959), *Voyage to the Bottom of the Sea* (1964), *Daniel Boone* (1964) *A Man Called Shenandoah* (1965), and *Lost In Space* (1965). He retired from filmmaking in 1973 after directing *The Boy Who Cried Werewolf.*

Female-lead Nancy Davis (1921- ), wife of Reagan, was nearing the end of her film career when she made *Hellcats of the Navy*. *Crash Landing*, released in 1958, was the last of her twelve motion pictures. The actress started in 1948 with an uncredited role in *Portrait of Jenny* then had featured parts in *East Side, West Side* (1949) and *Shadow on the Wall* (1950). She was also in *The Next Voice You Here* (1950), *It's A Big Country* (1951) and the low-budget science fiction thriller *Donovan's Brain* (1953). Davis continued working in television until 1962 with guest appearances in *Wagon Train, 87th Precinct, The Dick Powell Show* and *General Electric Theater.*

New Jersey-born Arthur Franz's (1920- ) film career consisted of supporting roles in 50 features over a thirty-five year period (1948-1982). Some of his better known films include *Sand of Iwo Jima* (1949) starring John Wayne, *Flight to Mars* (1951), *Sniper* (1952), *Invaders from Mars* (1953), *The Caine Mutiny* and *Steel Cage* (1954), *Battle Taxi* (1955), *The Young Lions* (1958), *The Carpetbaggers* (1964) with George Peppard, *Alvarez Kelly* (1965) and *That Championship Season* (1982).

Irving Lippman (1906- ) started in films as a still photographer in 1931. In 1953, after shooting photographs for more then seventy features, he was assigned to be the cinematographer for the television series' *Tales of the Texas Rangers* and *Jungle Jim*. He jumped to films and in the year leading up to his first feature-length production, *Hellcats of the Navy,* shot a number of Three Stooges-Columbia shorts. Lippman lensed the sci-fi film *20 Million Miles to Earth* (1957), *The Three Stooges Go Around the World in a Daze* (1963), *The Great Sioux Massacre* (1965), *Tarzan and the Valley of Gold* (1967) and *Tarzan and the Great River* (1968). During his lengthy career Lippman worked on over 17 television series including *The Wild, Wild West, Route 66, I Dream of Jeannie, The Monkees, The Partridge Family, Columbo* and Fantasy Island.

World premiere held in San Diego on April 9, 1957. The east coast premiere was held at the New London, Connecticut U.S. Navy submarine base, also in April.

In the Los Angeles market the film was part of an action double-bill with the Randolph Scott Western *The Tall T,* co-starring Richard Boone and Maureen O'Sullivan.

Competition for the movie audience came from: the sophisticated comedy *Desk Set* starring Spencer Tracy and Katharine Hepburn, Jerry Lewis' first solo film without Dean Martin, *The Delicate Delinquent,* the low budget Westerns *The Oklahoman* (Allied

Artist) with Joel McCrea and *Gun Duel in Durango* (United Artists) starring George Montgomery and *Something of Value* (MGM) Rock Hudson and Dana Wynter.

# The Young Doctors

**release date: August 23, 1961**     **running time: 100-103 minutes**

**Cast:**   Frederic March, Ben Gazzara, Dick Clark, Ina Balin, Eddie Albert, Phyllis Love, Edward Andrews, Aline MacMahon, Arthur Hill, Rosemary Murphy, Barnard Hughes, Joseph Bova, George Segal, Matt Crowley, Dick Button, Dolph Sweet, Robert Dahdah, Gloria Vanderbilt, James Broderick, Ronald Reagan, William Hansen, Addison Powell, Ella Smith, Nora Helen Spens

**Credits:**          **Drexel Films-Millar Turman Productions**
**United Artists**

*Director* Phil Karlson; *Producers* Stuart Miller, Lawrence Turman; *Writer* Joseph Hayes; *Cinematography* Arthur J. Ornitz; *Editor* Robert Swink; *Music* Elmer Bernstein; *Production Design* Richard Sylbert; *Art Direction* Jim Di Gangi Angelo Laiacona; *Costumes* Ruth Morley; *Production Manager* George Justin; *Assistant Director* Angelo Laiacona; *Sound* Jim Shields; *Technical Advisor* Dr. Charles F. Begg of St. Lukes Hospital; Filmed with the assistance of The American Medical Association.

## Synopsis:

Highlights the work done by pathologists.

**Reviews:**

**Notes:**

Reagan's sole role in this production was to serve as the narrator.

Filmed in New York City at the Women's Hospital, Manhattan General, and St. Luke's Hospital and Vassar Brothers Hospital in Poughkeepsie, New York.

Based on the novel, *The Final Diagnosis* by Arthur Hailey, who also wrote *Hotel* (1965), *Airport* (1968), *Wheels* (1971), and *The Moneychangers* (1975).

In the early 1930s, Phil Karlson (born Phil Karlstein, 1908-1985) worked at Universal Studios as a propman while attending Loyola University Law School. Deciding to stay in the motion picture business he worked his way up to 2nd. assistant director, cutter, editor, second-unit director and finally, after working on over 40 films, a full-fledged director in 1944. The majority of his 50 features were of the B-variety, yet he managed to make them absorbing, dramatic and on budget. Some of his better known films include *Lorna Doone* and *The Texas Rangers* (both 1951), *Kansas City Confidential* (1952), the cult favorite *The Phenix City Story* (1955), *Kid Galahad* (1962) with Elvis Presley, Dean Martin as Matt Helm in *The Silencers* (1966), *Ben* (1972), and his most successful work *Walking Tall* (1973).

Frederic March (born Ernest Frederick McIntyre Bickel, 1897-1975) spent much of his career alternating between performing on the stage and working in films. His body of work in both mediums was acknowledged by his peers with numerous awards. A graduate of the University of Wisconsin, an officer during World War I and a banker, in the early 1920s he turned to stage acting in New York. During this period March also appeared as an extra or bit-player in numerous films shot in the metropolitan area. While touring with a repertoire company on the west coast he decided to concentrate on acting for the screen and stayed in Hollywood for the next decade. In the role of Dr. Henry Jekyll, March won his first Oscar for best actor (*Dr. Jekyll and Mr. Hyde*, 1931). He appeared as Robert Browning in *The Barretts of Wimpole Street* (1934), was in *Anna Karenina* (1935), played Norman Maine in *A Star is Born* (1937) and won his second Oscar for his riveting performance in *The Best Years of Our Lives* (1946). As he alternated between working on the stage and screen March also delivered impressive performances in Arthur Miller's *Death of a Salesman* (1951), *The Bridges at Toko-Ri* (1955), *The Man in the Gray Flannel Suit* (1956), as Matthew Harrison Brady in *Inherit the Wind* (1960), playing the President of the United States in *Seven Days in May* (1964) and *Hombre* (1967). In a career that spanned over fifty years March was seen in at least 76 films.

Ben Gazzara (1930- ) appeared in over 40 American films a like number of foreign features, but is most famous for his dramatic work on television. The New York City-born actor started out in the theater having substantial roles in the original versions of *Cat on a Hot Tin Roof* and *A Hatful of Rain*. He made his film debut in 1957 as cadet Jocko DeParis in *The Strange One* then was cast by Otto Preminger for an integral role opposite James Stewart in *Anatomy of A Murder* (1959). Some of his other memorable films include *The Bridge at Remagen* (1969), *Capone* (1975), *Voyage of the Damned* (1976), *Saint Jack* (1979), Peter Bogdanovich's *They All Laughed* (1981) and *The Big Lebowski* (1998). For several seasons, beginning in 1965, he played Paul Bryan in the television series *Run For Your Life*.

Dick Clark (1929- ), popularly known as "The world's oldest teenager," parlayed his fame as host of the long-running *American Bandstand* television program (started in 1955 in Philadelphia) into a vast entertainment empire which has spawned numerous game shows, specials, and made-for-television movies. His first film role was in the movie *Because They're Young* (1960).

Although she appeared in 17 films and dozens of television shows, Ina Balin (born Ina Rosenberg, 1937-1990) was never comfortable in front of the cameras. Through professional help she regained her confidence and searched for a new meaning to life. Balin took up the cause of Vietnamese orphans during the Vietnam War. She repeatedly flew to Saigon to rescue hundreds of children and find home for them throughout the world. She also adopted three waifs in 1976. Her better known films include *From the Terrace* (1960) with Paul Newman, *The Comancheros* (1961) starring John Wayne, the Jerry Lewis comedy *The Patsy* (1964) and *The Greatest Story Ever Told* (1965).

Phyllis Love (1925- ), a graduate of the Actor's Studio (1948) appeared in only two other motion pictures: *So Young, So Bad* (1950) and Gary Cooper's *Friendly Persuasion* (1956). Appearing in at least eight major hits, she did have an extended career on Broadway.

# The Killers

**release date: July 7, 1964**                    **running time: 93-95 minutes**

**Cast:**   Lee Marvin, Angie Dickinson, John Cassavetes, Clu Galager, Claude Akins, Norman Fell, Ronald Reagan, Virginia Christine, Don Haggerty, Robert Phillips, Kathleen O'Malley, Ted Jacques, Irvin Mosley, Jimmy Joyce, Davis Roberts, Hal Brock, Burt Mustin, Peter Hobbs, John Copage, Tyler McVey, Seymour Cassel, Scott Hale, Richard Lane, Don Siegel

**Credits:**                    **Universal-Revue Studios**

*Produced and Directed by* Don Siegel; *Cinematography* Richard L. Rawlings; *Writer* Gene L. Coon; *Based on a story by* Ernest Hemingway; *Editor* Richard Belding; *Art Direction* Frank Arrigo, George B. Chan; *Set Decoration* John McCarthy Jr., James Redd; *Costumes* Helen Colvig; *Makeup* Larry Germain, Bud Westmore; *Assistant Director* Milton Feldman; *Sound* David H. Moriarty; *Music Supervisor* Stanley Wilson; *Music Score* Johnny Williams; *Singer* Nancy Wilson; *Dialogue Coach* Scott Hale; *Editorial*

*Department* David J. O'Connell; *Technical Advisor* Hall Brock; *Song* "Too Little Too Late," by Henry Mancini and Don Raye

## Synopsis:

The two killers, Charlie Strom (Lee Marvin) and Lee (Clu Gulager), are commissioned to end the life of Johnny North (John Cassavetes), an ex-racing driver who now teaches in a school for the blind. After he is murdered, the thugs wonder why their victim had shown no resistence and why anyone would pay $25,000 to have him killed.

They learn that he had been involved in a million dollar robbery several years ago. They want to know what happened to the money. They piece the story together, talking to several people who had known their victim.

North had been a successful racer until he met and fell in love with the beautiful Sheila Farr (Angie Dickinson), the mistress of powerful underworld figure Browning (Ronald Reagan).

North had been persuaded by Sheila to take part in a major robbery as the getaway driver. Knowing that Browning will cheat them, North and Sheila plan to take off together with all the money.

What North doesn't know until it is too late is that Sheila is already married to Browning, and is part of the crook's elaborate double cross. None of the plans work out satisfactorily and all the main particpants are killed.

## Reviews:

"Uninspired remake of the old yarn...emerges as a throwback to the period of crime and violence that monopolized the screen in the late '30s and early '40s....Reagan fails to crash convincingly through his good guy image." *Variety* (May 27, 1964); "What the studio neglected to supply was a script...It is all close-ups and broad cutting effects, with the subtle character development and the more cinematic sequences neatly omitted...Reagan ill at ease as the criminal mastermind...Hemingway is the victim of all of this. All that remains of the original story is the author's name...giving discredit where it is far from due." *The New York Times* (July 18, 1964); "...it was actually as good a picture as the original version." *Dark Victory: Ronald Reagan, MCA and the Mob* Dan E. Moldea (Viking, New York, 1986); "Owed more to Producer-Director Don Siegel's taste for brutality than to Ernest Hemingway's short story." *The Universal Story.* Clive Hirschhorn (Octopus Books. London, 1983)

# Notes:

Filmed at Riverside International Speedway, California and on the Universal lot at a cost of $600,000.

Originally produced as a made for television movie, it was deemed to violent for the small screen. While being filmed for television the title of the project was *Johnny North.*

While he was making this production, Reagan, as a spokesman for General Electric, was earning $150,000 a year.

By 1964 Angie Dickinson (born Angeline Brown, 1931- ), having appeared in over 25 features, was a much sought after actress in Hollywood. The North Dakota native, between her motion picture debut in 1954 and 1957, was cast in a dozen B-westerns including Reagan's *Tennessee's Partner.* She made a major impact when cast opposite John Wayne in the Howard Hawks classic Western *Rio Bravo.* Other roles quickly followed including *Ocean's Eleven* (1960), *The Sins of Rachel Cade* (1961), *The Chase* (1966), *Cast A Giant Shadow* (1966), *Point Blank* (1967), *Big Bad Mama* (1974) and Brian DePalma's *Dressed To Kill* (1980). From 1974 to 1978 Dickinson headlined her own highly successful television series *Police Woman.*

New York City-born John Cassavetes (1929-1989) was not only an actor but also a renowned writer and director of unorthodox motion pictures. A graduate of The Academy of Dramatic Arts in New York, he worked frequently in the days of live television before making his motion picture debut in 1951. Although he had substantial roles in less than 20 films, the intensity of his portrayals made it hard to forget him. As an actor he worked in *Edge of the City* (1957), *The Dirty Dozen* (1967) for which he received an Oscar nomination, *Rosemary's Baby* (1968), *Capone* (1975), *The Fury* (1978) and *Love Streams* (1984). He directed and wrote the seminal films *Husbands* (1970), *Minnie and Moskowitz* (1971), *A Woman Under the Influence* (1974) for which he was nominated as Best Director and *Gloria* (1980).

Virginia Christine (1920-1996) also appeared in the original *The Killers* in 1946 that starred Burt Lancaster. After signing a contract with Warner Bros. her over twenty-five year film career began in 1942. In the 1960's she began a twenty-one year run as the television spokesperson, in commercials, for Folgers Coffee.

Director Siegel did a Hitchcock by having a cameo role as a cook in a diner sequence.

Lee Marvin (1924-87) won the 1966 BAFTA award for Best Foreign Actor. He was also nominated for a Golden Laurel as Best

Action Performer of 1965. Within 2 years he was one of the top-ten box-office stars in the United States.

Opened in New York on September 12, 1964.

The film faced summer competition at the nation's theaters from the Richard Burton-Ava Gardner steamy drama *Night of the Iguana,* the screen version of Harold Robbins epic fictionalized account of the life of Howard Hughes, *The Carpetbaggers, A Distant Trumpet* (Warners), a low-budget Western starring Troy Donahue and Suzanne Pleshette, Alfred Hitchcock's *Marnie* with Tippi Hedren and Sean Connery in the leads and the Beatles debut film the frenzied, *A Hard Days Night.*

Throughout Ronald Reagan's Hollywood years he was involved in a number of other pictures where he either did not get a credit or his scenes were deleted and during the war years he also made a number of training films; *For God and Country* (1943), *Cadet Classification* (1943), *Target Tokyo* (1943) and *Rear Gunner* (1944).

In 1951 he worked in a Government propoganda film, *The Big Truth.*

In 1954 he made the political short *Jungle Trap..*

# Cast and Credits

| Name | Film | Title |
|---|---|---|
| Acuff, Eddie | Love Is On the Air | actor |
| Albert, Eddie | Brother Rat | actor |
| Albright, Lola | Girl from Jones Beach | actor |
| Alton, John | Tennessee's Partner | cinematography |
| Anderson, Eddie | Going Places | actor |
| Ankrum, Morris | Cattle Queen of Montana | actor |
| Arden, Eve | Voice of the Turtle | actor |
| Averill, Anthony | Girls on Probation | actor |
| Bacon, Lloyd | Cowboy from Brooklyn | director |
| Bailey, Raymond | Girl from Jones Beach | actor |
| Baker, Art | Night Unto Night | actor |
| Balin, Ina | Young Doctors | actor |
| Bassermann, Albert | Knute Rocke | actor |
| Beaumont, Hugh | Last Outpost | actor |
| Beery, Noah, Jr. | Tropic Zone | actor |
| Bellamy, Ralph | Boy Meets Girl | actor |
| Bennett, Bruce | Last Outpost | actor |
| Berkeley, Busby | Hollywood Hotel | director |
| Berlin, Irving | This Is the Army | music |
| Bernhardt, Curtis | Million Dollar Baby | director |
| Bishop, Julie | International Squadron | actor |
| Bogart, Humphrey | Swing Your Lady | actor |
| Borg, Veda Ann | Submarine D1 | actor |
| Bracken, Eddie | Girl from Jones Beach | actor |
| Bradna, Olympe | International Squadron | actor |
| Brent, George | Submarine D1 | actor |
| Brewer, Betty | Juke Girl | actor |
| Broderick, Helen | Naughty but Nice | actor |
| Bromley, Sheila | Accidents Will Happen | actor |
| Bruce, Nigel | Hong Kong | actor |
| Bryan, Jane | Girls on Probation | actor |
| Buckner, Robert | Knute Rocke | writer |
| Burnett, W.R. | Law and Order | writer |
| Busch, Niven | Angels Wash their Faces | writer |
| Byington, Spring | Louisa | actor |
| Calhoun, Rory | That Hagen Girl | actor |
| Carson, Jack | John Loves Mary | actor |
| Cassavetes, John | Killers | actor |
| Chandler, Lane | Murder In the Air | actor |
| Chang, Danny | Hong Kong | actor |
| Christine, Virginia | Killers | actor |

| Name | Film | Title |
|---|---|---|
| Clark, Dick | Young Doctors | actor |
| Clemens, William | Accidents Will Happen | director |
| Coburn, Charles | Louisa | actor |
| Cochran, Steve | Storm Warning | actor |
| Coleman, Nancy | Desperate Journey | actor |
| Colonna, Jerry | Naughty but Nice | actor |
| Corrigan, Lloyd | Girl from Jones Beach | actor |
| Crawford, Broderick | Night Unto Night | actor |
| Crisp, Donald | Sergeant Murphy | actor |
| Cummings, Robert | King's Row | actor |
| Davis, Nancy | Hellcats of the Navy | actor |
| Day, Doris | Storm Warning | actor |
| Day, Larraine | Bad Man | actor |
| De Cordova, Frederick | Bedtime for Bonzo | director |
| Dickinson, Angie | Killers | actor |
| Downing, Joe | Smashing the Money Ring | actor |
| Drake, Dona | Girl from Jones Beach | actor |
| Dwan, Alan | Cattle Queen of Montana | director |
| Eason, B. Reeves | Sergeant Murphy | director |
| Emerson, Faye | Nine Lives Are Not Enough | actor |
| Enright, Ray | Swing Your Lady | director |
| Evans, Gene | Cattle Queen of Montana | actor |
| Fazenda, Louise | Swing Your Lady | actor |
| Fehr, Rudi | Desperate Journey | editor |
| Fellows, Robert | Angel from Texas | producer |
| Field, Betty | King's Row | actor |
| Field, Virginia | John Loves Mary | actor |
| Fitzgerald, Geraldine | Dark Victory | actor |
| Fleming, Rhonda | Last Outpost | actor |
| Foran, Dick | Cowboy from Brooklyn | actor |
| Forrest, Steve | Prisoner of War | actor |
| Forrest, William | Girl from Jones Beach | actor |
| Foster, Lewis R. | Last Outpost | director |
| Foster, Preston | Law and Order | actor |
| Foy, Bryan | Love Is On the Air | producer |
| Franklin, Dean | Code of the Secret Service | writer |
| Franz, Arthur | Hellcats of the Navy | actor |
| Fuller, Lance | Cattle Queen of Montana | actor |
| Gazzara, Ben | Young Doctors | actor |
| Gill, Tom | Tropic Zone | writer |
| Glennon, Bert | Juke Girl | cinematography |
| Godfrey, Peter | That Hagen Girl | director |
| Goodman, Benny | Hollywood Hotel | actor |
| Gorcey, Leo | Hell's Kitchen | actor |

| Name | Film | Title |
|---|---|---|
| Gordon, Leo | Tennessee's Partner | actor |
| Gottlieb, Alex | It's A Great Feeling | producer |
| Goulding, Edmund | Dark Victory | director |
| Graham, Fred | Smashing the Money Ring | actor |
| Granville, Bonita | Angels Wash their Faces | actor |
| Gray, Coleen | Tennessee's Partner | actor |
| Grinde, Nick | Love Is On the Air | director |
| Gwen, Edmund | Louisa | actor |
| Hale, Alan | Desperate Journey | actor |
| Hall, Alexander | Louisa | director |
| Haller, Ernest | Brother Rat | cinematography |
| Halop, Billy | Hell's Kitchen | actor |
| Hamilton, John | Smashing the Money Ring | actor |
| Harvey, Paul | Brother Rat and Baby | actor |
| Hayes, Peter Lind | Naughty but Nice | actor |
| Hayward, Susan | Amazing Dr. Clitterhouse | actor |
| Heisler, Stuart | Storm Warning | director |
| Homolka, Oscar | Prisoner of War | actor |
| Howe, James Wong | King's Row | cinematography |
| Humberstone, H. Bruce | She's Working Her Way Through College | director |
| Hussey, Ruth | Louisa | actor |
| Jenkins, Allen | Going Places | actor |
| Juran, Nathan | Hellcats of the Navy | director |
| Karlson, Phil | Young Doctors | director |
| Keighley, William | Brother Rat | director |
| Kennedy, Arthur | Desperate Journey | actor |
| Kern, James V. | Stallion Road | director |
| Lane, Rosemary | Hollywood Hotel | actor |
| Lansing, Joi | Girl from Jones Beach | actor |
| Laurie, Piper | Louisa | actor |
| Lemmon, Jack | Winning Team | actor |
| Leslie, Joan | This Is the Army | actor |
| Lindfors, Viveca | Night Unto Night | actor |
| Lindsay, Margaret | Hell's Kitchen | actor |
| Lippman, Irving | Hellcats of the Navy | cinematography |
| Litel, John | Secret Service of the Air | actor |
| Litvak, Anatole | Amazing Dr. Clitterhouse | director |
| Lord, Robert | Brother Rat and Baby | producer |
| Louis, Anita | Going Places | actor |
| Love Phyllis | Young Doctors | actor |
| Lovejoy, Frank | Winning Team | actor |
| Lundigan, William | Santa Fe Trail | actor |
| Lupton, John | Prisoner of War | actor |

| Name | Film | Title |
|---|---|---|
| Lynn, Diana | Bedtime for Bonzo | actor |
| Lynn, Jeffrey | Million Dollar Baby | actor |
| Lys, Lya | Murder In the Air | actor |
| Maguire. Mary | Sergeant Murphy | actor |
| Malone, Dorothy | Law and Order | actor |
| March, Frederic | Young Doctors | actor |
| Marley, J. Peverell | John Loves Mary | cinematography |
| Martin, Chris-Pin | Bad Man | actor |
| Martin, Dewey | Prisoner of War | actor |
| Marton, Andrew | Prisoner of War | director |
| Marvin, Lee | Killers | actor |
| Massey, Raymond | Santa Fe Trail | actor |
| Maxwell, Lois | That Hagen Girl | actor |
| Mayo, Virginia | Girl from Jones Beach | actor |
| McCord, Ted | Secret Service of the Air | cinematography |
| McGann, William C. | Girls on Probation | director |
| Mendes, Lothar | International Squadron | director |
| Miller, Eve | Winning Team | actor |
| Miller, Marvin | Hong Kong | actor |
| Mix, Art | Sergeant Murphy | actor |
| Moore, Clayton | Cowboy from Brooklyn | actor |
| Morgan, Dennis | It's A Great Feeling | actor |
| Morgan, Harry | Prisoner of War | actor |
| Morris, Wayne | Submarine D1 | actor |
| Morse, Terry O. | Smashing the Money Ring | director |
| Murphy, George | This Is the Army | actor |
| Nelson, Gene | She's Working Her Way Through College | actor |
| Nicholls, Anthony | Hasty Heart | actor |
| O'Connell, L. William | Accidents Will Happen | cinematography |
| Olsen, Moroni | Code of the Secret Service | actor |
| Page, Gale | Naughty but Nice | actor |
| Parker, Eleanor | Voice of the Turtle | actor |
| Payne, John | Tennessee's Partner | actor |
| Perry, Joan | Nine Lives Are Not Enough | actor |
| Peters, Susan | Santa Fe Trail | actor |
| Punsly, Bernard | Hell's Kitchen | actor |
| Purcell, Dick | Accidents Will Happen | actor |
| Raine, Norman Reilly | Tugboat Annie Sails Again | writer |
| Rambeaur, Marjorie | Tugboat Annie Sails Again | actor |
| Rapper, Irving | Voice of the Turtle | director |
| Rhodes. Ila | Secret Service of the Air | actor |
| Richmond, Kane | Knute Rocke | actor |
| Risdon, Elisabeth | Girls on Probation | actor |

| Name | Film | Title |
|---|---|---|
| Robertson, Dale | Girl from Jones Beach | actor |
| Robinson, Casey | Dark Victory | writer |
| Robinson, Edward G. | Amazing Dr. Clitterhouse | actor |
| Robson, May | Million Dollar Baby | actor |
| Roosevelt, Buddy | Girl from Jones Beach | actor |
| Sargent, Dick | Prisoner of War | actor |
| Scott, Zachary | Stallion Road | actor |
| Sheffield, Johnny | Knute Rocke | actor |
| Sheridan, Ann | Cowboy from Brooklyn | actor |
| Sherman, Vincent | Hasty Heart | director |
| Siegel, Don | Night Unto Night | director |
| Slezak, Walter | Bedtime for Bonzo | actor |
| Smith, Alexis | Stallion Road | actor |
| Smith, Noel | Secret Service of the Air | director |
| Somerville, Mary | Hong Kong | actor |
| Stanwyck, Barbara | Cattle Queen of Montana | actor |
| Stephenson, James | International Squadron | actor |
| Stevenson, Margot | Smashing the Money Ring | actor |
| Stone, Milburn | Angel from Texas | actor |
| Sutherland, A. Edward | Nine Lives Are Not Enough | director |
| Temple, Shirley | That Hagen Girl | actor |
| Terry, Ruth | Angel from Texas | actor |
| Thaxter, Phyllis | She's Working Her Way Through College | actor |
| Thomas, Frankie | Angels Wash their Faces | actor |
| Thorpe, Richard | Bad Man | director |
| Tobias, George | Juke Girl | actor |
| Todd, Richard | Hasty Heart | actor |
| Towne, Rosella | Code of the Secret Service | actor |
| Travis, June | Love Is On the Air | actor |
| Treacher, Arthur | Brother Rat and Baby | actor |
| Trevor, Claire | Amazing Dr. Clitterhouse | actor |
| Van Sickle, Dale | Storm Warning | actor |
| Warwick, Robert | Murder In the Air | actor |
| Wead, Frank | Submarine D1 | writer |
| Weston, Doris | Submarine D1 | actor |
| Whiterspoon, Cora | Dark Victory | actor |
| Whitman, Stuart | Prisoner of War | actor |
| Whorf, Richard | Juke Girl | actor |
| Williams, Bill | Last Outpost | actor |
| Wills, Chill | Tugboat Annie Sails Again | actor |
| Wilson, Marie | Boy Meets Girl | actor |
| Winters, Roland | She's Working Her Way Through College | actor |

| Name | Film | Title |
|---|---|---|
| Withers, Grant | Tropic Zone | actor |
| Wood, Sam | King's Row | director |
| Wylie, Philip | Night Unto Night | writer |
| Wyman, Jane | Brother Rat | actor |

# Bibliography

*An American Life Ronald Reagan*
*The Autobiography* (Simon and Schuster 1990)

*The Overlook Film Encyclopedia The Western*
(Overlook Press 1983)

*Early Reagan The Rise to Power*
Anne Edwards  (William Morris 1987)

*Ronald Reagan His Life and Rise to the Presidency*
Bill Boyarsky (Random House 1981)

*Where's The Rest of Me?*
Reagan, with Richard G Hubler (Duell, Sloane and Pearce 1969)

*The Hollywood Professionals Don Siegel*
Tod Browning  (Tantivy Press 1975)

*Don Siegel* (Faber and Faber 1993)

*The Films of Ronald Reagan*  Tony Thomas

*"B" Actor "A" President? Reagan*
Edward Scofield (American Progress 1983)

*Ronald Reagan Hollywood, Movies and Politics*
Stephen Vaughn. (NY 1994)

*Dark Victory, Ronald Reagan, MCA and the Mob*
Dan Moldea (Viking 1986)

*Hollywood on Ronald Reagan*
Doug McClelland (Winchester 1983)

*The Wind at My Back, The Life and Times of Pat O'Brien by himself.*
(Doubleday 1964)

*Errol Flynn, The Untold Story*
Charles Higham

*Stanwyck*
Axel Madse

*Jane Wyman, A Biography*
Morella and Epstein (Delcorte Press 1985)

*Ronald Reagan*
George Sullivan (Julian Messner 1985)

*Reagan, The Man and his Presidency*
Deborah Hart Strober and Gerlad S Strob (Houghton Miffun 1998)

*Dutch, A Memoir of Ronald Reagan*
Edmund Morris (Harper Collins 1999)

I Love You, Ronnie The Letters of Ronald Reagan to Nancy Reagan
(Random House 2000)

Warner Brothers Story    Clive Hirschorn
The following papers and articles, held at the BFI were also used:

*TV Times,* 31 Oct 1981, "A potted history of Reagan's life and career" by
    Ken Roche
*Picture Show,* 31 Jan 1953, Article
*Classic Images,* Feb 1986, "A look at some of Reagan's B Movies"
*Radio Times,* 1 Dec 1990, "What's Ronnie's Secret" Clive James'
    impressions of Reagan.
*Listener,* 31 July 1986, Article on Reagan's presidential TV image
*Photoplay,* Nov 1980, The Life of Ronald Reagan
*Take One,* August 1976, Interview with Reagan about his film career.
*Journal of the Producers Guild of America,* March 1974, comments by
    Reagan about the problems of the film industry.
*Photoplay*, May 1981, Reagan's separation from Jane Wyman.
*Classic Images*, May 1993, "A Life-filled Legacy", Frank Dolven.
*Sight and Sound*, July 1994, Review of "Ronald Reagan in Hollywood"-
    Vaughn.
*Film Comment*, Jly/Aug 1980, Reagan's film career.
*Empire*, May 1994, Review of "Ronald Reagan in Hollywood"
*Favorite Westerns*, 1990, "The Cowboy who became President, Robert
    Nareau.
*Films in Review*, April 1981, Reagan's TV Work.
*Film Comment*, May/June 1987, "No method to his Madness"
*Picturegoer*, 19 July 1947, "Postwar Reagan" – WH Mooring.
*Film Review*, May 2001, Reagan in Nazi Uniform.
*Films in Review*, April 1967, Career of Reagan. Jack F Hunter.

# Also from Sammon Publishing

**The Lost Films of John Wayne**
**John Wayne a Giant Shadow**

## And coming soon

**Where Have all the Cowboys Gone?**

**For further details go to www.sammonpublishing.com**